Women's Voices across Musical Worlds

03.19.04

To Jim —
On the occasion of
the 2nd Women in
Music Festival.
Congratulations,

With love,

Women's Voices across Musical Worlds

EDITED BY JANE A. BERNSTEIN

Northeastern University Press

BOSTON

NORTHEASTERN UNIVERSITY PRESS

Library of Congress Cataloging-in-Publication Data

Women's voices across musical worlds / edited by Jane A. Bernstein.
p.   cm.
Includes bibliographical references (p.   ) and index.
ISBN 1–55553–589–5 (alk. paper) — ISBN 1–55553–588–7 (pbk. : alk. paper)
1. Feminism and music.   2. Gender identity in music.   3. Women musicians.   4. Music—Social aspects.   I. Bernstein, Jane A.
ML82.W697   2003
780′.82—dc21   2003008327

Designed by Janis Owens

Composed in Minion by Coghill Composition Company in Richmond, Virginia.
Printed and bound by Edwards Brothers, Inc., in Ann Arbor, Michigan.
The paper is EB Natural, an acid-free sheet.

MANUFACTURED IN THE UNITED STATES OF AMERICA
08   07   06   05   04   5   4   3   2   1

For Judith Tick on her sixtieth birthday

Contents

ILLUSTRATIONS xi

ACKNOWLEDGMENTS xv

INTRODUCTION: ON WOMEN AND MUSIC 3
Jane A. Bernstein

PART ONE

Public Voices, Private Voices

Introduction 13

CHAPTER ONE
The Power of Class:
Fanny Hensel and the Mendelssohn Family 18
Nancy B. Reich

CHAPTER TWO
The Illusion of India's "Public" Dancers 36
Carol M. Babiracki

CHAPTER THREE
"Fighting in Frills":
Women and the Prix de Rome in French Cultural Politics 60
Annegret Fauser

PART TWO

Cloistered Voices

Introduction 87

CHAPTER FOUR
Music for the Love Feast:
Hildegard of Bingen and the Song of Songs 92
Margot Fassler

CHAPTER FIVE
Putting Bolognese Nun Musicians in their Place   118
Craig A. Monson

PART THREE
Empowered Voices

Introduction   143

CHAPTER SIX
Voices of the People:
Umm Kulthūm   147
Virginia Danielson

CHAPTER SEVEN
"Thanks for My Weapons in Battle—
My Voice and the Desire to Use It":
Women and Protest Music in the Americas   166
Jane A. Bernstein

CHAPTER EIGHT
Tori Amos's Inner Voices   187
Bonnie Gordon

PART FOUR
Lamenting Voices

Introduction   209

CHAPTER NINE
Having Her Say:
The Blues as the Black Woman's Lament   213
Tammy L. Kernodle

CHAPTER TEN
Abandoned Heroines:
Women's Voices in Handel's Cantatas   232
Ellen T. Harris

PART FIVE
Gendered Voices and Performance

Introduction   257

CHAPTER ELEVEN
The Nightingale and the Partridge:
Singing and Gender among Prespa Albanians   261
Jane C. Sugarman

CHAPTER TWELVE
Women Playing Men in Italian Opera, 1810–1835   285
Heather Hadlock

CHAPTER THIRTEEN
Shifting Selves:
Embodied Metaphors in *Nihon Buyo*   308
Tomie Hahn

SELECTED BIBLIOGRAPHY   327
LIST OF CONTRIBUTORS   341
INDEX   345

Illustrations

Figures

1.1 Portrait of Fanny Mendelssohn Hensel by Wilhelm Hensel   21

2.1 Kistomani (*nacnī*) dancing Nagpuri *mardana jhumar* with men   38

3.1 Portrait of Juliette Toutain, by V. Michel   69

3.2 Portrait of the six candidates for the *Prix de Rome* in 1904   72

3.3 Portrait of the six candidates for the *Prix de Rome* in 1908   76

3.4 Portrait of Lili Boulanger   80

5.1 Plan of the Convent of Santa Cristina della Fondazza in Bologna   121

5.2 Convent of Santa Cristina della Fondazza in Bologna. Windows of the nuns' choir, facing the former public courtyard   123

5.3 Convent of Santi Domenico e Sisto in Rome. Grilled windows extending around the public, outer church, up near the vaults   124

6.1 Umm Kulthūm in Abu Dhabi, ca. 1969   156

6.2 Umm Kulthūm in 1939   157

7.1 Mercedes Sosa in 1980   172

7.2 Joan Baez in 1971   179

8.1 Tori Amos singing and playing piano   191

10.1 *Ariadne Abandoned by Theseus on Naxos* (1774) by Angelica Kauffmann   241

11.1 Prespa women singing at an evening gathering (Toronto, 1985)   276

12.1 Portrait of Giuditta Pasta as Tancredi   290

12.2 Portrait of Rosmunda Pisaroni   295

13.1 Portrayal of the male traveler in "Ame no shiki"   315

13.2 Portrayal of a mother with her child in "Ame no shiki"   316

13.3 Iemoto Tachibana Yoshie with the author. Tachibana School, Tokyo, Japan   322

Tables

4.1   General dating of Hildegard's works   94

4.2   Text of "O Ecclesia": Hildegard's sequence for St. Ursula   103

11.1 Comparison of the wedding singing of Prespa Albanian women and men   279

Music Examples

2.1   *Mardānā jhumar* song   49

2.2   *Janānī jhumar song*   50

4.1   Hildegard of Bingen, "O Ecclesia": sequence for St. Ursula   106

5.1   Giovanni Battista Biondi, *Cantabant sancti canticum*   126

5.2   Lucrezia Orsina Vizzana, *O invictissima Christi martir*   129

6.1   Maqām rast   150

6.2   Opening of "Salū Qalbī"   150

6.3   Excerpt from "Salū Qalbī"   151

6.4   Excerpt from "Huwwa Ṣaḥiḥ il-Haw'a Ghalāb"   153

6.5   Maqām ṣabā   153

6.6   Maqām rāḥit al-arwāh   154

6.7   Excerpt from "al-Aṭlāl"   154

7.1   Rhythmic pattern of the *milonga* and tango   175

7.2   Closing refrain of the song "Los hermanos"   175

8.1   Amos, "Me and a Gun," mm. 1–4 and 8–11   197

8.2   Amos, "Me and a Gun," mm. 12–16   197

8.3   Amos, "Silent all these Years," mm. 27–33   201

8.4   Amos, "Silent all these Years," mm. 1–4   205

10.1 Handel, *Lucrezia*, second recitative (ending)   238

10.2 Handel, *Abdolonymus*, opening recitative   238

10.3 Handel, *Lucrezia*, "Il suol che preme"   239

10.4 Handel, *Abdolonymus*, first aria, opening ritornello   240

10.5 Handel, *Abdolonymus*, first aria, B section, mm. 41–44   240

10.6 Handel, *E partirai, mia vita?*, opening recitative 244

10.7 Handel, *E partirai, mia vita?*, second recitative 245

10.8 Handel, *E partirai, mia vita?*, second aria 246

10.9 Handel, "Dunque se il tanto piangere" and "If guiltless blood be your intent" 251

10.10 Handel, "Come, o Dio" and "Who calls my parting soul" 251

11.1 "Po kyo anë e lumit" 270

11.2 "Në plepat Bilishtit" 272

11.3 "Vjeshtë e tretë më të dalë" 274

Acknowledgments

THIS PROJECT GREW out of the course on women in music I have taught at Tufts University over the past seven years. I am indebted to all the undergraduate and graduate students—at both Tufts and Brandeis University—who participated in these seminars. Their enthusiasm for the subject and the freshness of their ideas both challenged and greatly stimulated me. This course, like the field itself, has continued to evolve and change; it remains for me a rewarding experience.

When I asked the authors in the present volume to contribute to this project, I was overwhelmed by their positive response. I am grateful to them, not only for their superb essays, but also for their patience and keen interest in the book.

I would also like to acknowledge the Boston Area Gender and Music Seminar and its many participants for six years of enlightening papers and discussions. In addition, several of my colleagues at Tufts University have contributed in diverse ways to this enterprise. Michael Ullman graciously provided me with his photograph of Joan Baez. Laurence Senelick generously lent me the portrait of Giuditta Pasta from his private collection. My graduate student Samuel Dorf assisted me with bibliographical matters. Gabriela Cruz patiently listened to what I had to say about the book over countless lunches.

I also wish to express my gratitude to my friends and colleagues in the "gang of five": to Jessie Ann Owens, for starting the Boston Area Gender and Music Seminar; to Kay Kaufman Shelemay, for her generosity and encouragement; to Ellen T. Harris, for her essay and her friendship; and to Judith Tick, whose substantive comments and criticisms, as one of the readers for the press, helped me to recognize how I might improve the book.

I wish to acknowledge a number of people who facilitated turning the manuscript into a book. I am indebted to the staff at Northeastern University Press, in particular to Elizabeth Swayze, for advice and support, and to Ann Twombly and Emily McKeigue for being so flexible and responsive in the production of this book. Special thanks goes to Hyunjung Choi for her patience and resourcefulness in creating the complex musical examples. And to my dear colleague, Bonnie Blackburn, who served as copyeditor of this book, I am particularly grateful. All the contributors to this project have benefited from her keen eye for detail as well as her deep understanding of music and language. Her astute comments and suggestions have greatly enhanced this book.

As always, the greatest debt I owe is to my wonderful family. I want to thank my husband, James Ladewig, and my daughter, Lily, for their endless patience and fortitude throughout the process.

At a time when the musicological establishment did not take this field seriously, Judith Tick persevered in her scholarly commitment to women's studies. Each step in her career has served as a touchstone for others to follow. Her dissertation on nineteenth-century American women composers was a first of its kind. She helped organize the first session on women in music held at the joint national meeting of the American Musicological Society and College Music Society in 1976. The book she co-edited with Jane Bowers, *Women Making Music: The Western Art Tradition, 1150–1950,* has become a classic in the field. And her award-winning biography of Ruth Crawford Seeger serves as an inspiration to us all. It seems only fitting that I dedicate this book to her in celebration of her sixtieth birthday.

Women's Voices across Musical Worlds

Introduction

ON WOMEN AND MUSIC

What has all this to do with the history of art?

JACQUES BARZUN

It has to do with the relation of women to music, which
is quite enough for one book.

SOPHIE DRINKER

IN 1948 SOPHIE DRINKER published the first large-scale feminist study
devoted to women in music.[1] Hers was an ambitious undertaking: to make
known the role of women in music throughout the world and throughout
time. Completely alien to the academic establishment, her project avoided a
traditional historical narrative. Instead it functioned as a compendium or
"story," as Drinker herself called it, culled from anthropological, iconograph-
ical, mythological, and historical sources.[2] Drinker's book was prophetic in
its topical and multicultural approach. Though an eccentric work, it did
contain an important message: only by acknowledging a variety of cultures
could one gain a better understanding of women's place in music.

Like Drinker's visionary opus, this book seeks to expand the horizons
of musical studies by exploring issues concerning women from a thematic
perspective. Comprising an unusual constellation of essays, it explores music
making and the roles women have played as creators and performers in various spheres. It also considers representations of women and what they reveal
about the cultures from which they emerge. The book encompasses a wide
selection of subjects, ranging in time from the twelfth century to the present.
Geographically, it spans the globe from Asia, Europe, and the Middle East to
the Americas. More significantly, it embraces the diverse musics of popular,
world, and Western art traditions.

Women's Voices across Musical Worlds is the first book to take as its point
of departure specific musical activities and expressions of women from both

3

a cross-cultural and cross-historical perspective. Unlike earlier texts,[3] this volume is not ordered chronologically into historical periods or laid out according to geographical areas. Neither is it organized according to specific theoretical approaches.[4] Instead, it centers on significant issues and themes that emerge when women and music come together. It thus encourages inter-disciplinary speculation with gender as its main focus of inquiry.

The prominence of the word "voice" in the title remains particularly relevant because of its broad range of meanings that runs throughout the book. The space between the term's literal definition as the musical sound produced by singers and its metaphorical significance as the representation of female vocality includes an extensive variety of musical and social connotations. Female voices can embody the multiple personae of traditional Japanese dance or they can masquerade as men in early nineteenth-century Italian opera. They can be disembodied, as in the case of the Bolognese nuns, whose performances could be heard but not seen.

Singers' voices can empower other women, as seen in early twentieth-century rural and classic blues women and the pop star Tori Amos. They can also "speak" for whole communities, whether it be for political, social, national, or universal causes, as in the case of Umm Kulthūm, Joan Baez, and Mercedes Sosa. Conversely, voices can be disempowered through segregation and/or subjugation, as observed in the chapters dealing with public and private voices and the cloistered voice.

Voices not only signify gender, but also ethnic, national, and religious identities around the world. Wedding rituals of Albanian rural life, the singing of a thousand-year-old form of Arabic poetry, or the stylized movements of traditional Japanese dance—these performance genres act as media of expression for their cultures. Finally, Western societies of the past and present can communicate to us through voices reflecting their own time. They can be rallying cries for national unity and/or peace throughout the Americas, persistent clamors for professional equality in nineteenth- and early twentieth-century Europe, or spiritual utterances from the medieval and early modern Catholic Church.

"Voice" has also been used as a metaphor in feminist discourse. Such catchphrases as "having a voice" and "in a different voice," as Leslie Dunn and Nancy Jones have pointed out, express autonomy, authority, and agency that have been denied to women.[5] More apropos to this volume, the term reflects the many methodologies encountered in feminist music scholarship over the last few decades. In order to understand the eclectic nature of the contributions in this book, it might be useful to recount the history of this young field.[6]

Young women . . . you are, in my opinion, disgracefully ignorant. You have never made a discovery of any importance. You have never shaken an empire or led an army into battle. The plays of Shakespeare are not by you, and you have never introduced a barbarous race to the blessings of civilization. What is your excuse?

VIRGINIA WOOLF,
A Room of One's Own

It was not until the 1970s that scholars from different humanistic disciplines began to come to grips with Woolf's question in a significant way. Historians examined the lives of notable women, literary critics explored the novels and poetry of women authors, and in the field of art history, women painters and sculptors were rediscovered. In the world of music scholarship, historical musicologists began by investigating the lives of women musicians and recovering their music. Ethnomusicologists, in turn, focused on the roles women played in living musics throughout the world.

Music scholars utilized the conventional tools of their trade. For the ethnomusicologist, it meant employing traditional fieldwork methods; they conducted interviews with performers and audiences, recorded and transcribed music, produced video recordings, and, in some cases, actively participated in performances by women. The historical musicologist, in turn, delved into primary source materials (archival documents, letters, journals, newspapers, and magazines) in libraries and archives, uncovered contemporary paintings, photographs, and engravings for images of women and music making (iconography), and compiled bibliographies of secondary literature; they also located the sources and created modern editions of musical works by women.

This research endeavored to expand the scope of traditional musical studies, but in the 1980s it became apparent to feminist scholars that the data they had unearthed flew in the face of conventional discourses in their fields. They concluded that the absence of women from traditional accounts of music history and their marginalization in studies dealing with the culture of music had more to do with class, status, and power than with art and culture. Historical musicologists began to query the validity of the musical canon—that is, the musical works and composers found in textbook histories of Western art music.[7] They also raised questions about the phenomenon of the individual genius and the standards of aesthetic values set by a male-dominated Western society.[8]

Ethnographers likewise realized the male bias inherent in their fieldwork, both in the collection of data primarily from male informants as well as the inhibition of female informants.[9] Influenced by feminist anthropologists, they began to explore the larger issues of sexuality and gender, concentrating on the effect that gender had on music making, and conversely, the role that music played in defining the cultural constructs of gender and power. By turning their attention to gender ideologies, these ethnomusicologists not only had a profound impact on their own field, but on the study of music as a whole.[10]

By the end of the 1980s, the construction of gender and sexuality also became a focal point of music criticism. The confluence of poststructural thought and feminist music scholarship proffered entirely new ways to interpret the very musical works that had been canonized by mainstream musicology.[11] In opera and other texted genres, music historians centered on the representation of gender and sexuality in both plot and music. Non-narrative instrumental works also received gender-encoded readings. Scholars even addressed issues relating to gendered rhetoric used by earlier theorists.[12]

Gender issues, however, do not stand alone, but connect with other social structures and power dynamics. Indeed, other modes of analysis found in postcolonial studies, psychoanalytical studies, literary and film criticism, and queer studies also focused on power relationships in culture. Influenced by these fields, feminist music scholars broadened and refined their concepts of gender theory. The binary construction of male/female found in earlier scholarship soon transformed into what Suzanne Cusick calls an "eclectic multiplicity," where ideologies concerning sexuality, race, ethnicity, and class intersect with feminist scholarship.[13]

Over the past decade, a paradigm shift has taken place as an explosion of studies concerning gender and sexuality has entered the mainstream of music scholarship. Moving away from traditional readings of the music text, scholars have increasingly paid attention to performance and performance theory. Musicologists, indebted to French poststructuralist theory, have looked at the representation of the audible voice in various musical and literary spheres. In opera studies, for example, ideas about the voice and the transference of authority of a musical work from composer to singer have eclipsed conventional modes of musical analysis.[14] Some opera specialists have gone further in identifying the body as a site of gender, sexuality, and power. Drawing on Peter Brooks's work on French melodrama, they have discovered the importance of physical gesture on stage.[15] Scholars of popular music have also focused on the body in performance. Using the influential work of Judith Butler on sex and gender as performative, a new wave of musical studies has concentrated on gendered performance as perceived through costume and movement.[16]

All of these discourses in feminist studies have brought about an exciting transformation of the study of music as a whole. Reflecting this diversity of expression, the present book stresses pluralism in the assortment of theoretical approaches utilized in the essays. Because gender cuts across all categories of thinking, these scholarly voices run the gamut from traditional scholarship in historical musicology and ethnomusicology to some of the more recent intellectual trends in cultural studies.

My aim is to cross the artificial boundaries of our subdisciplines by juxtaposing studies in world music with those in popular and Western art music. In organizing the contributions around five broadly defined subjects relating to women and music, I hope to interweave the various skeins of this diverse discipline. Each of the five parts of the book opens with an introduction that presents a broad overview of the topic. Setting the stage for the essays that follow, this prefatory matter helps clarify the subject and suggests further areas of inquiry. Within each section, two or three essays on completely different musical areas serve as case studies for comparative study. Selected bibliographies, listing important books, articles, and websites, as well as audio and video performances, appear at the end of the volume. Grouped according to the five themes of the book, they provide useful information for further reading and study. This book, then, can be perceived as a unified text or as a versatile sourcebook. The approach offered here affords unlimited flexibility, in which topics can be read in any order or specific sections can be extracted from the book.

The five parts of the book represent traditional spheres of musical activities as well as genres intimately linked to women. "Public Voices, Private Voices," for example, considers issues of boundaries concerning gender and status and their effect on musical activities across various cultures. The topos of the lament and its strong association with women can be observed in "Lamenting Voices." "Gendered Voices and Performance" explores gender identity and construction through performance and the body. The sequestration of women's music making serves as a point of departure for "Cloistered Voices." At the other end of the continuum, "Empowered Voices" considers the woman's voice as a force for political and social change.

The essays located within these frameworks have been carefully chosen to provide significant, often unusual exemplars of their respective topics. The studies situated in the lament chapter, for example, do not investigate the traditionally prescribed roles women play in mourning rituals throughout the world. Instead, Tammy Kernodle proposes the blues as a metaphor for the black woman's lament, by tracing women's connection with the genre from its African beginnings to its rural and urban forms. She also describes how the rural and classic blues singers acted as mediators in communicating the private experiences of black women to a public audience. Ellen Harris, in turn, distinguishes between men and women's voices in the cantatas of George Frideric Handel. She concentrates on the persona of the abandoned woman as Handel's primary representation of female vocality. From there she wonders whether the impassioned and unrestrained voices heard in these early cantatas had any personal resonance for Handel, both as a young composer developing his own musical voice and as a German expatriate in a foreign land.

The two studies in "Cloistered Voices" transcend traditional musical description of female conventual life. Craig Monson contextualizes musical activities in the convents of seventeenth-century Bologna. He does this by exposing the sexual politics that occurred between the Church hierarchy and the nuns, who fought against the suppression of their music and their voices. He also deglamorizes musical life in female monastic orders in his discussion of discounted dowries and music making as employment for nuns. Margot Fassler, in her essay on Hildegard of Bingen, offers major insights into the work of this great medieval woman. Here in the world of a twelfth-century convent, Fassler uncovers the significance of the Song of Songs by tracing the theme of a sacramental love feast in Hildegard's theological treatise *Scivias*, her chants for the virgin martyr St. Ursula, and her musico-liturgical drama *Ordo virtutem*. Through a close reading of the sequence "O Ecclesia," she reveals how Hildegard crafted an important statement about singing by the nuns, and how the diverse creations of this remarkable theologian, artist, poet, and composer come together to form a powerful, complete artwork by a female voice in the service of God.

The "Public Voices, Private Voices" essays go beyond the dichotomous notion of women as amateur and professional musicians by raising complex questions concerning class and sexual politics. In her classic study, Nancy Reich explains the power relationship between Fanny Mendelssohn Hensel and her family and the conflicting worlds of the domestic and professional musician in nineteenth-century German culture. She demonstrates how religion, family tradition, and prevailing societal beliefs contributed to the stifling of Hensel's creativity. Carol Babiracki, in turn, explicates the subtlety and ambiguity of the private and public persona of the *nacnīs*, female professional dancers in northeast India. She introduces a set of paradoxes about the art and life of these dancers that blur traditional social boundaries. Here, caste, religion, and the commerce of sex play an intrinsic role in the discussion. Annegret Fauser presents the fascinating story of women's efforts to win the coveted *Prix de Rome* in music composition within the changing cultural and political climate of fin-de-siècle France. She relates how four women composers constructed very different personae in their quest for the prize, from the *bourgeoise* socialite who performed at *salons* and the *femme nouvelle* with professional ambitions, to the unthreatening image of the *femme fragile.*

In "Empowered Voices," women rise above their roles as professional divas by touching the social consciousness of their listeners. More powerful than political leaders, they achieve mythical status and become legendary figures of their time. Virginia Danielson, in her study of the Egyptian singer Umm Kulthūm, grapples with the concept of "voice of the people." She considers the process by which a woman musician in Muslim society becomes this voice, what value the exceptional individual has for society, and what implications these issues have in the writing of biography. In my own essay, I address empowered female voices from the standpoint of heroic identity. Turning to the protest song movements of mid-twentieth-century Latin America and the United States, I look at how the public personae of such political singers as the Argentine Mercedes Sosa and the American Joan Baez have been transformed into the idealized female figures of protective mother and virgin warrior. Bonnie Gordon, in turn, tackles the topic of rape through a close reading of Tori Amos's video performance of "Me and a Gun." She demonstrates how Amos articulates with her voice and body her experience as a rape victim. By making public a deeply hidden trauma, Amos gains empowerment both for herself and for her listeners.

"Gendered Voices and Performance" covers a broad spectrum of cross-cultural subjects that explore musical performance and the body as vehicles for conveying gender identity. The topics range from the construction of traditional male/female gender roles to cross-dressed and multi-role performance. In her award-winning study, Sugarman examines the binary opposition of gender in the celebratory musical performances of a rural community. She discloses how the singing styles of Prespa Albanians serve not only as a metaphor for gender, but also as a means to act out the community's ideals of femininity and masculinity. The two other studies deal with performances that transcend gender. Heather Hadlock traces the phenomenon of the *musico*s, the so-called "trouser" roles in early nineteenth-century Italian opera. She considers the different ways travesty performances by women were perceived by examining the careers of three famous singers in conjunction with the specific operatic roles they sang. Tomie Hahn takes a more personal approach in her discussion of *nihon buyo,* traditional Japanese dance. Here, she delves into the embodiment of multiple roles—both gendered and cross-gendered—by a single performer. She traces the concept of codeswitching in all-female dance performance and what its relationship is to daily life in Japan.

Suzanne Cusick has recently suggested that by "opening all the doors" to the multiple visions of feminist music scholarship we will make tangible those things about musical culture that were heretofore invisible.[17] The essays brought together in *Women's Voices across Musical Worlds* champion this idea by offering a heterogeneous discussion of women and gender issues in music. In celebrating the global diversity of women's voices, this book proposes a holistic view of women in all kinds of musical endeavors. Like Sophie Drinker's path-breaking study, it stands as a broad scheme that serves as a point of departure for further insights and thoughts in this vibrant field.

NOTES

~

1. *Music and Women: The Story of Women in their Relation to Music* (New York: Coward-McCann, 1948; Washington, D.C.: Zenger Publishing, 1977; repr. with preface by Elizabeth Wood and afterword by Ruth A. Solie, New York: Feminist Press at the City University of New York, 1995).

2. Ruth A. Solie, "Sophie Drinker's History," in *Disciplining Music: Musicology and Its Canons*, ed. Katherine Bergeron and Philip V. Bohlman (Chicago: University of Chicago Press, 1992), 26.

3. Christine Ammer, *Unsung: A History of Women in American Music* (Westport, Conn: Greenwood Press, 1980); Sally Placksin, *American Women in Jazz: 1900 to the Present: Their Words, Lives, and Music* (New York: Wideview Books, 1982); *Women Making Music: The Western Art Tradition, 1150–1950*, ed. Jane Bowers and Judith Tick (Urbana: University of Illinois Press, 1986); *Women and Music: A History*, ed. Karin Pendle (Bloomington: Indiana University Press, 1991; 2d ed., 2001); *Rediscovering the Muses: Women's Musical Traditions*, ed. Kimberly Marshall (Boston: Northeastern University Press, 1993); *Women and Music in Cross-Cultural Perspective*, ed. Ellen Koskoff (Urbana: University of Illinois Press, 1989); and *Music, Gender, and Culture*, ed. Marcia Herndon and Susanne Ziegler, International Council for Traditional Music Study Group on Music and Gender, Intercultural Music Studies, no. 1 (Wilhelmshaven: Florian Noetzel, 1990).

4. *Cecilia Reclaimed: Feminist Perspectives on Gender and Music*, ed. Susan C. Cook and Judy S. Tsou (Urbana: University of Illinois Press, 1994); and *Music and Gender*, ed. Pirkko Moisala and Beverley Diamond (Urbana: University of Illinois Press, 2000).

5. *Embodied Voices: Representing Female Vocality in Western Culture*, ed. Leslie Dunn and Nancy Jones (Cambridge: Cambridge University Press, 1994), 1.

6. I am indebted to several recent historiographical essays on this subject, most particularly Judith Tick, "Women in Music," in *The New Grove Dictionary of Music and Musicians*, ed. Stanley Sadie and John Tyrrell, 2d ed. (London: Macmillan, 2001) (hereafter *New Grove II*), 27:519–21; Ruth Solie, "Defining Feminism: Conundrums, Contexts, Communities," *Women & Music* 1 (1997): 1–11; Suzanne Cusick, "Gender, Musicology and Feminism," in *Rethinking Music*, ed. Nicholas Cook and Mark Everist (Oxford: Oxford University Press, 1999), 471–98; ead., "'Eve . . . Blowing in Our Ears?' Toward a History of Music Scholarship on Women in the Twentieth Century," *Women & Music* 5 (2001): 125–39; Ingrid Monson, "Music and the Anthropology of Gender and Cultural Identity," *Women & Music* 1 (1997): 24–32; Susan C. Cook,

"'R-E-S-P-E-C-T (Find Out What It Means to Me)': Feminist Musicology and the Abject Popular," *Women & Music* 5 (2001): 140–45; Margaret Sarkissian, "Gender and Music," in *Ethnomusicology. I: An Introduction,* The New Grove Handbooks in Music, ed. Helen Myers (New York and London: W. W. Norton, 1992), 337–48; and ead., "Thoughts on the Study of Gender in Ethnomusicology: A Pedagogical Perspective," *Women & Music,* 3 (1999): 17–27.

7. See in particular Marcia J. Citron, *Gender and the Musical Canon* (Cambridge and New York: Cambridge University Press, 1993).

8. Ruth Solie, "Feminism," *New Grove II,* 8:664. On genius in general see Christine Battersby, *Gender and Genius: Towards a Feminist Aesthetics* (Bloomington: Indiana University Press, 1989).

9. Bruno Nettl, *The Study of Ethnomusicology: Twenty-Nine Issues and Concepts* (Urbana: University of Illinois Press, 1983), 334–35.

10. See the introduction to *Women and Music in Cross-Cultural Perspective,* ed. Koskoff; Carol E. Robertson, "Power and Gender in the Music Experiences of Women," in *Women and Music in Cross-Cultural Perspective,* 225–44; and Koskoff, "Gender Power and Music," *The Musical Woman: An International Perspective* 3 (1986–90): 769–88.

11. Susan McClary was the first to interpret canonic musical works from the standpoint of gender and sexuality in *Music and Society: The Politics of Composition, Performance, and Reception,* ed. Richard Leppert and Susan McClary (Cambridge and New York: Cambridge University Press, 1987) and then *Feminine Endings: Music, Gender, and Sexuality* (Minneapolis: University of Minnesota Press, 1991).

12. The pioneering work in opera studies is Catherine Clément, *Opera, or, The Undoing of Women,* trans. Betsy Wing (Minneapolis: University of Minnesota Press, 1988), originally published as *L'Opéra, ou, la défaite des femmes* (Paris: Bernard Grasset, 1979); Clément, a French feminist theorist, deals only with opera plots. Susan Mc-Clary's brilliant monograph on *Georges Bizet, Carmen* (Cambridge and New York: Cambridge University Press, 1992) has become a touchstone for later work in gender and sexuality in opera. On a gendered interpretation of a texted non-operatic work, see Ruth A. Solie, "Whose Life? The Gendered Self in Schumann's *Frauenliebe und Leben,*" in *Music and Text: Critical Inquiries,* ed. Steven Scher (Cambridge and New York: Cambridge University Press, 1992), 219–40. In instrumental music, see Jeffrey Kallberg, "Harmony of the Tea Table: Gender and Ideology in the Piano Nocturne" and other essays in *Chopin at the Boundaries: Sex, History, and Musical Genre* (Cambridge, Mass.: Harvard University Press, 1996). On theoretical rhetoric see, for example, Suzanne G. Cusick, "Gendering Modern Music: Thoughts on the Monteverdi-Artusi Controversy," *Journal of the American Musicological Society* 46 (1993): 1–25; David Lewin, "Women's Voices and the Fundamental Bass," *Journal of Musicology* 10 (1992): 464–82; and Gretchen A. Wheelock, "'Schwartze Gredel' and the Engendered Minor Mode in Mozart's Operas," in *Musicology and Difference: Gender and Sexuality in Music Scholarship,* ed. Ruth A. Solie (Berkeley: University of California Press, 1993), 201–21.

13. The term was coined by Suzanne Cusick in "'Eve . . . Blowing in Our Ears?,'" 138. Feminist studies in queer theory and music appear in *Musicology and Difference,* ed. Solie; *Queering the Pitch: The New Gay and Lesbian Musicology,* ed. Philip Brett, Elizabeth Wood, and Gary C. Thomas (New York: Routledge, 1994); *Audible Traces: Gender, Identity, and Music,* ed. Elaine Barkin and Lydia Hamessley (Zurich and Los Angeles: Carciofoli Verlagshaus, 1999); and *Queer Episodes in Music and Modern*

Identity, ed. Sophie Fuller and Lloyd Whitesell (Urbana: University of Illinois Press, 2002). In opera studies see also *En Travesti: Women, Gender Subversion, Opera,* ed. Corinne E. Blackmer Smith and Patricia Juliana (New York: Columbia University Press, 1995) and *The Work of Opera: Genre, Nationhood, and Sexual Difference,* ed. Richard Dellamora and Daniel Fischlin (New York: Columbia University Press, 1997). Race and gender issues are the focus of Hazel Carby's influential article, "'It Jus Be's Dat Way Sometime': The Sexual Politics of Women's Blues," in *Feminisms: An Anthology of Literary Theory and Criticism,* ed. Robyn R. Warhol and Diane Price Herndl (New Brunswick, N.J.: Rutgers University Press, 1991), 746–58; Venise T. Berry, "Feminine or Masculine: The Conflicting Nature of Female Images in Rap Music," in *Cecilia Reclaimed: Feminist Perspectives on Gender and Music,* ed. Susan C. Cook and Judy S. Tsou (Urbana: University of Illinois Press, 1994), 183–201; and Ellie M. Hisama, "Voice, Race, and Sexuality in the Music of Joan Armatrading," in *Audible Traces,* ed. Barkin and Hamessley, 115–30.

14. On representation of the audible voice see Dunn and Jones, *Embodied Voices.* The idea of vocal authority occurs in the writings of Carolyn Abbate, with its feminist implications most particularly expressed in "Opera or the Envoicing of Women," in *Musicology and Difference,* ed. Solie, 225–59, and more recently in her book *In Search of Opera* (Princeton: Princeton University Press, 2001). The subject of singers and vocal authority also appears in Heather Hadlock, *Mad Loves: Women and Music in Offenbach's Les Contes d'Hoffmann* (Princeton: Princeton University Press, 2000) as well as the work of Mary Ann Smart: "The Silencing of Lucia," *Cambridge Opera Journal* 4 (1992): 119–41; "The Lost Voice of Rosine Stoltz," *Cambridge Opera Journal* 6 (1994): 31–50; and "Verdi Sings Erminia Frezzolini," *Women & Music* 1 (1997): 33–45.

15. Brooks's *Melodramatic Imagination: Balzac, Henry James, Melodrama, and the Mode of Excess* (New Haven: Yale University Press, 1976) is featured prominently in several essays in *Siren Songs: Representations of Gender and Sexuality in Opera,* ed. Mary Ann Smart (Princeton: Princeton University Press, 2000).

16. On performance and the body in pop culture see, for example, *Sexing the Groove: Popular Music and Gender,* ed. Sheila Whiteley (London and New York: Routledge, 1997) and Lori Burns and Mélisse Lafrance, *Disruptive Divas: Feminism, Identity and Popular Music* (New York and London: Routledge, 2002). An explanation of sex and gender as performative appears, among other places, in Judith Butler's *Gender Trouble: Feminism and the Subversion of Identity* (New York: Routledge, 1990). On the application of Butler's ideas to music see Suzanne G. Cusick, "On Musical Performances of Gender and Sex," in *Audible Traces,* 25–43 and Ingrid Monson, "Music and the Anthropology of Gender," 27–28.

17. "Gender, Musicology, and Feminism," 496–98.

PART ONE

Public Voices, Private Voices

My lord of Hunsdon drew me up to a quiet gallery, . . .
where I might [hear] the Queen [Elizabeth I] play upon
the virginals . . . I entered within the chamber, and stood
a pretty space hearing her play excellently well. She appeared to be surprised to see me, and came forward, seem-
ing to strike me with her hand; alleging she used not to
play before men, but when she was solitary to shun melancholy.

SIR JAMES MELVILLE OF HALHILL,
Memoirs

THE CONCEPT OF musical role divisions along gender lines
has been widely discussed in all fields of music research. During the
1970s and 1980s, ethnomusicologists focusing on the study of music
and social structure applied binary oppositions—female/male, private/
public, domestic/professional, and "inside/outside" of society—to designate
prevalent musical domains in various cultures.[1] This binary theoretical
frame, as we have already noted, was soon subsumed in a broader approach
that included a continuum of domains, reflecting the great diversity of contexts in which women have musically involved themselves.

In mapping female performance traditions, both historians of Western
music and ethnographers have considered the status of women in the larger
cultural context of a predominantly androcentric society. A distinction has
been drawn between music as a feminine accomplishment, that is music
performed by women amateurs for consumption within the secure confines
of their domestic domain, and performance by professional female musicians, who, having achieved a measure of independence in the public sphere,
have been consigned mainly to the status of outsiders in their society.

Music performed in private environments by amateur women can be
traced throughout the history of Western Europe. Noblewomen from the late
Middle Ages, for example, were taught to perform music not only for the

amusement of themselves, but also as an element of courtly life.[2] During the Renaissance, members of the rising merchant class emulated their noble counterparts by educating their daughters to sing and play such instruments as the lute and the virginals, a keyboard instrument presumably so named for its association with female performers.[3] Beginning in the seventeenth century, salons and concerts established by wealthy upper-class women in their private homes were used as means of social as well as political advancement. The notion that music was the highest of feminine accomplishments continued to dominate European (and by default American) society in the nineteenth and early twentieth centuries, where the piano, harp, and guitar became the musical instruments of choice for the lady dilettante.[4]

The restriction of women's musical performances to private environments is also found in other parts of the world. In traditional Japanese performing arts, for example, middle-class women, prohibited from performing publicly in kabuki theater, continued to study dance, known as *nihon buyo*, as part of their etiquette training.[5] Musical instruments such as the koto (a type of zither with movable bridges) and shamisen (a three-stringed lute) were favored for domestic entertainment. In contrast, the shakuhachi (end-blown flute), with its phallic shape and historical association with ex-samurai warriors posing as spies, was considered unsuitable for musical performance by the wives and daughters of the mercantile class, not to mention how indecorous women would appear while playing such an instrument.

In contrast to the safe yet restrictive haven afforded amateur musicians, professional female performers inhabited a world outside societal boundaries. They served as courtesans or entertainers in various court traditions of Asia, the Middle East, Europe, and North Africa.[6] In ancient China, they performed at the palaces and mansions of wealthy families. Slave girls known as *qiyān* were highly prized in early Arabic cultures for their refined musical performances,[7] and in the Ottoman Empire there was a long tradition of entertainment by female musician/dancers known as *çengi*, dating from the fifteenth century until the mid-nineteenth century.[8]

Courtesans also worked as professional singers and dancers outside of the patronage of the court. In ancient Greece, they held drinking parties or symposia, and in the Indian cities of Delhi and Lucknow, *tawā'ifs* presided over their own salons, where they offered erudite conversation and refined musical performances.[9] Japanese geishas entertained wealthy clients in tea houses. Residing in all-female abodes, they spent their lives perfecting their art as singers, instrumentalists, dancers, and conversationalists.[10] Of all the cities of sixteenth-century Europe, Venice was the most renowned for her *cortigiane oneste* or "honest courtesans." Some of them, such as Veronica Franco, Barbara Strozzi, and Tullia d'Aragona, were not just well versed in the arts, they were also celebrated poets and composers of their time.[11]

Throughout the world, courtesans were looked upon in contradictory terms. While admired as highly refined musicians and dancers, these unmarried women were also denigrated for their independent lifestyle and sexual freedom. By transgressing the boundary from their prescribed role in domestic music making to public performance, they became outcasts, forced to live outside the conventional structure of their society.

The division between public and private appropriated by past scholars has served as a useful paradigm in identifying the cultural contexts of women and music. Yet it must not be regarded as a fixed entity. In the changing world of post-colonial India, for example, conflicts can be observed in the careers of musician-dancers (*tawā'ifs* and *nacnīs*), who have left the patronage of private courts and salons for public performance. No longer marked as outsiders, some have married and/or adapted themselves as solo singers on the concert stage. While they have, in the process of moving "inside" caste society, gained respectability, at the same time, their voice and art as courtesans have been erased.[12]

As early as the sixteenth century, the illusion of propriety became a crucial factor in the persona of professional female musicians, who wished to divorce themselves from anything that smacked of the courtesan tradition. When in 1580, Duke Alfonso II of Ferrara founded a trio of professional women singers known as the *concerto delle donne*, he made sure that they would have an honorable place at court. He provided them with dowries, husbands, and respectable positions as ladies-in-waiting to the duchess.[13]

Propriety for professional women who appeared in public also meant proper chaperoning. The fathers, brothers, or husbands of these women assumed the role of protector, often serving as business managers. The great nineteenth-century pianist Clara Wieck Schumann, for example, performed as a child prodigy under the guidance of her father; when she married the composer Robert Schumann, she toured with him or with a female chaperone. Only after her husband's death did she continue her international concert career, manage her affairs, and support a large family on her own.[14]

What female performers wore on stage also played an important part in the creation of a modest image. Clara Schumann dressed in black not only in remembrance of her husband, but also to remind audiences of her status as a respectable widow. The nineteenth-century Swedish singer Jenny Lind, who did not marry until her thirties, always appeared in white to denote her purity and innocence. And in the twentieth century, the renowned Egyptian singer Umm Kulthūm projected an image of propriety by emulating Cairo's wealthy Muslim women in the long-sleeved, conservative European-style outfits she wore onstage.[15]

The essays presented here offer three case studies that illuminate issues concerning the status of women as public and private musicians. Nancy Reich deals with domestic music, where she looks at the conflicting world of Fanny Mendelssohn Hensel, who, though the equal of her brother Felix as an exceptional composer and pianist, was forced to remain an amateur musician. Carol Babiracki elucidates the courtesan tradition in northeast India as seen through the art and life of Kistomani, a *nacnī* or professional singer-dancer. In her essay, she raises significant questions about female agency within the patriarchal system of a quasi-feudal world. Annegret Fauser describes the changing status of female composers that occurred in fin-de-siècle France by focusing on the *Prix de Rome* competition during the years in which women were first allowed to participate. All three studies illustrate the binarisms discussed above, but more importantly they also reveal the complex issues surrounding the notion of public versus private.

NOTES

1. For a general discussion on these binarisms see Ellen Koskoff, "Gender, Power, and Music," in *The Musical Woman: An International Perspective*, ed. Judith Zaimont, 3 (1986–90), 769–88, and Jennifer C. Post, "Erasing the Boundaries between Public and Private in Women's Performance Traditions," in *Cecilia Reclaimed: Feminist Perspectives on Gender and Music*, ed. Susan C. Cook and Judy S. Tsou (Urbana: University of Illinois Press, 1994), 35–51.

2. See Howard M. Brown, "Women Singers and Women's Songs in Fifteenth-Century Italy," in *Women Making Music*, ed. Bowers and Tick, 62–89; Kimberly Marshall, "Symbols, Performers, and Sponsors: Female Musical Creators in the Late Middle Ages," and Paula Higgins, "The 'Other Minervas': Creative Women at the Court of Margaret of Scotland," in *Rediscovering the Muses: Women's Musical Traditions*, ed. Marshall, 140–68 and 169–85.

3. Kristine Forney describes the musical education of a Renaissance women in "'Nymphes gayes en abry du laurier': Music Instruction for the Bourgeois Woman," *Musica Disciplina* 49 (1995): 151–87.

4. See Judith Tick, "Passed Away Is the Piano Girl: Changes in American Musical Life, 1870–1900," in *Women Making Music*, ed. Bowers and Tick, 325–48.

5. See Tomie Hahn's essay in this book, chap. 13.

6. For a cross-cultural overview of courtesans see Veronica Doubleday, "Courtesan," *New Grove II*, 6:609–11.

7. L. JaFran Jones, "A Sociohistorical Perspective on Tunisian Women as Professional Musicians," in *Women and Music in Cross-Cultural Perspective*, ed. Ellen Koskoff (Urbana: University of Illinois Press, 1989), 70–71.

8. Walter Zev Feldman, "Ottoman music," *New Grove II*, 18:813.

9. Veena Talwar Oldenburg, "Lifestyle as Resistance: The Case of the Courtesans of Lucknow, India," *Feminist Studies* 16 (1990): 259–87.

10. Liza Dalby, *Geisha* (New York: University of California Press, 1985).

11. See Margaret F. Rosenthal, *The Honest Courtesan: Veronica Franco, Citizen and Writer in Sixteenth-Century Venice* (Chicago: University of Chicago Press, 1992), and Ellen Rosand, "The Voice of Barbara Strozzi," in *Women Making Music,* ed. Bowers and Tick, 168–90.

12. Regula Burckhardt Qureshi, "In Search of Begum Akhtar: Patriarchy, Poetry, and Twentieth-Century Indian Music," *The World of Music* 43 (2001): 97–137.

13. Anthony Newcomb, "Courtesans, Muses, or Musicians? Professional Women Musicians in Sixteenth-Century Italy," in *Women Making Music,* ed. Bowers and Ticks, 90–115.

14. Nancy Reich, *Clara Schumann: The Artist and the Woman* (Ithaca: Cornell University Press, 1985).

15. See Virginia Danielson's essay in this book, chap. 6.

CHAPTER ONE

The Power of Class

FANNY HENSEL AND THE MENDELSSOHN FAMILY

Nancy B. Reich

> Had Madame Hensel been a poor man's daughter, she
> must have become known to the world by the side of Ma-
> dame Schumann and Madame Pleyel, as a female pianist
> of the very highest class. Like her brother, she had in her
> composition a touch of that southern vivacity which is so
> rare among the Germans. More feminine than his, her
> playing bore a strong family resemblance to her brother's
> in its fire, neatness, and solidity. Like himself, too, she was
> as generally accomplished as she was specially gifted.
>
> HENRY F. CHORLEY,
> "Mendelssohn's Sister and Mother"

THE BRITISH MUSIC CRITIC is speaking, of course, of Fanny Hensel *née*
Mendelssohn Bartholdy, the older sister of Felix Mendelssohn Bartholdy.[1]
The "accomplished" pianist gave only one public performance: a benefit
concert in 1836; the "gifted" composer lived to see publication of only forty-
two out of some 400 works. Unlike her brother's music, hers was known
only to a small circle and heard only at home musicales. When Fanny Hensel
finally summoned up the courage to publish her work, defying the brother
who disapproved of professional music making by a woman, sudden death
cheated her of the satisfaction and triumph she surely would have had.

The constraints placed on Fanny Hensel were many: her gender, religion,
family tradition, and prevailing intellectual beliefs all contributed to her position as a dilettante. Above all, as we learn from Chorley, the power of class
was a potent force in keeping her work in the private realm.

The myths and legends about the Mendelssohns are gradually dispersing;

access to heretofore unpublished letters have changed our perceptions of the family; new information about Fanny Hensel's creative output has led to examination, performances, and recordings of her works; and the recent publication of her diaries has revealed much about the inner life and soul of the woman.[2] For over one hundred years, the major source of information about the Mendelssohns had been the family biography, written by Fanny Hensel's devoted son, Sebastian Hensel, and first published in 1879.[3] His book offers a portrait based on letters, diaries, and memories: through Sebastian's eyes, we see the entire family, proudly beginning with the grand forebear, Moses Mendelssohn, the great German-Jewish philosopher. But it is precisely because Hensel gives what he refers to as a picture of a "good German middle-class family"[4] that we must look further for the whole story. And that is what we are beginning to uncover.[5] We begin with a look at the Mendelssohn family.

Fanny Caecilie Hensel, the eldest child of Abraham and Lea Mendelssohn and a granddaughter of Moses Mendelssohn, was given the same education as her brother Felix, three and a half years her junior. The two studied first with their mother, and, for a short time, with Marie Bigot, while on a family trip to Paris in 1816. They were then sent to Ludwig Berger for piano lessons and eventually to Carl Friedrich Zelter for theory and composition lessons. Zelter, a composer and conductor of the Singakademie, the Berlin choral society that Fanny and Felix joined in 1820, was the most influential Berlin musician of the time. The general education the Mendelssohn children received was thorough and intense: Fanny (1805–47), Felix (1809–47), Rebecka (1811–58), and Paul (1812–74) all had private tutoring from the finest scholars in Berlin. Besides music, they studied modern and classical languages, mathematics, history, geography, as well as drawing (in which Felix was particularly gifted), and dancing. The schedule drawn up for the young Mendelssohns—which also included physical exercise—left no idle time: beginning at five in the morning, every moment in the day was accounted for. In addition to the rigorous working schedule and the intellectual stimulation from distinguished friends, relatives, and guests, Fanny attended lectures on a wide variety of subjects given by Berlin's leading scholars.

The paths of the sister and brother diverged as they reached adolescence. All were musical—Fanny and Felix exceptionally so, as Rebecka jokingly explained many years later: "My older siblings stole my artistic fame. In any other family, I would have been much praised as a musician and perhaps even have directed a small circle. But next to Felix and Fanny, I could not have succeeded in attaining any such recognition."[6]

Although it was clear to the family that Fanny had talents equal to those of her brother Felix, she was reminded by her father of the feminine duties and responsibilities that would not permit the professional activity open to Felix. In July 1820, Abraham Mendelssohn wrote to her: "Music will perhaps become his profession while for you it can and must always be only an ornament, never the root of your being and doing. We may therefore pardon him some ambition and desire to be acknowledged in a pursuit which appears very important to him, because he feels a vocation for it. . . . your very joy at the praise he earns proves that you might, in his place, have merited equal approval. Remain true to these sentiments and to this line of conduct; they are feminine, and only the truly feminine graces the woman."[7] On her twenty-third birthday, her father reminded her again: "You must prepare yourself more seriously and diligently for your real calling, the *only* calling for a young woman—to be a housewife."[8]

When Abraham spoke of her future as a housewife, he envisioned, of course, a future as the mistress of a Berlin establishment befitting a member of the Berlin Jewish bourgeois aristocracy.[9] (The Mendelssohn children were converted to Christianity in 1816 and their parents later, in 1822. Nevertheless, they were referred to as a Jewish family long after they left that faith and were subjected to anti-Semitic comments during and after their lifetimes.)

The prescribed role of the cultivated Berlin lady was familiar to Fanny Hensel. All her female relatives were educated and cultured women: grandmother, mother, aunts, and great-aunts on the maternal side were members of the very wealthy Itzig family, who used their talents to establish salons, to build libraries, to support musicians, artists, and composers. It was expected that Fanny would marry and follow the tradition of her Itzig relatives—and she did so in almost every way. We learn from her diary that she was not only interested in Mendelssohn family matters, and involved with music, literature, and art, but that she was also concerned with events in Berlin, in Germany, and the world. After a lengthy engagement, Fanny married Wilhelm Hensel (1794–1861), the Prussian court painter and professor of art, in October 1829,[10] and remained for most of her life a devoted and obedient daughter, wife, mother—and frustrated composer. (See Fig. 1.1.)

Two aunts on her father's side, Dorothea Veit Schlegel (1764–1839) and Henriette Mendelssohn (1775–1831), daughters of Moses Mendelssohn, however, were not well-to-do. Both were involved in the Berlin literary salons in their youth, and both turned to intellectual pursuits and supported themselves by teaching and writing.[11]

Their father, Moses Mendelssohn, had arrived in Berlin in 1743 and, as a Jew, barely gained entrance into that city. Recognized as one of the great thinkers of the Enlightenment, he carried on his intellectual labors only during the part of the day in which he was not engaged in his regular job, first as a bookkeeper in a textile factory, later as a partner in that enterprise. He

Figure 1.1. Portrait of Fanny Mendelssohn Hensel by Wilhelm Hensel.
From S. Hensel, *Die Familie Mendelssohn (1880)*.

was greatly concerned about the education of his children and took as much
pride in the intellectual achievements of his eldest child, Dorothea, as in his
sons. (Henrietta was only ten when he died.) But when Dorothea was eighteen, a husband was chosen for her without regard for her feelings or
wishes.[12] Dorothea remained in a loveless marriage for sixteen years and
ultimately divorced her husband to live with and later marry Friedrich
Schlegel (1772–1829), the writer and critic. Yet, even before her marriage to
her second husband, Dorothea worked as his copyist, editor, and writer, and,

it seems, gladly took a subordinate position. In her journal is an entry: "[One goal for me] would be to be able to earn so much by writing that Friedrich need not write for money anymore."[13] To a mutual friend, the Berlin theologian Friedrich Schleiermacher, she wrote on 14 February 1800:

> I feel myself so rich in many talents and gifts that it would be wrong of me and a sin if I permitted my lack of money to depress me too much. If only good fortune would favor me so that I could continue supporting my friend for several more years, then I would certainly be secure! . . . He is also working honestly and tirelessly, but how can one expect an artist to deliver a work of art each year just to be able to exist? He *cannot* create more. . . . To bring pressure on the artist to become a mere craftsman—that I cannot do. And it would not succeed anyway. What I can do lies within these limits: to create peace for him and to earn bread humbly as a craftswoman until he is able to do so. And I am honestly determined to do just that.[14]

Her novel, *Florentin,* does not carry her name on the title page. Schlegel is listed as the "editor."

Henriette, the younger Mendelssohn sister, never married. She founded a renowned boarding school for girls in Paris and then worked as the governess and companion to the daughter of the wealthy French General (later Marshall) Sebastiani. After many years of teaching in Paris, she returned to Berlin in 1824, lived with the family of Lea and Abraham Mendelssohn, and died there.

Although Abraham and his family were fond, perhaps even proud, of the achievements of Dorothea and Henriette Mendelssohn, and offered them financial support when necessary, the sisters were not Fanny's role models. The Itzig connection—her mother, grandmother, and great-aunts—served that function. Lea Mendelssohn *née* Salomon (1777–1842) was a granddaughter of Isaac Daniel Itzig (1723–99), the court banker and probably the wealthiest man in Berlin. Powerful and privileged, his palace was opposite the king's own. He was a "protected Jew," and unique in that his children and grandchildren were permitted to inherit land and houses in the Prussian capital, a privilege that for other Jewish families extended only to one son, if at all. Itzig was the first of a small number of Jews to receive the rights of citizenship.[15] Of his eleven daughters (he also had five sons), we are particularly interested in four: Bella Salomon (1749–1824), the grandmother of Fanny, and three of her sisters: Sara Levy (1761–1854), Fanny von Arnstein (1758–1818), and Caecilie von Eskeles (1760–1836)—the great-aunts after whom Fanny Caecilie Mendelssohn was named. All the Itzig daughters were talented musicians and all appeared to be content with their roles as *salonières*, dilettantes, or patronesses. There is some controversy as to whether it was the grandmother Bella Salomon or the great-aunt Sara Levy who gave Felix Mendelssohn the handwritten score of the *St. Matthew Passion* in 1823, which led to the famous revival he conducted in 1829, but it could very well have been either because all the sisters were well acquainted with the music of Johann Sebastian Bach at a time when little of it was published and still less performed publicly. Sara Levy studied with Wilhelm Friedemann Bach and was a friend and patron of Carl Phillip Emanuel Bach. Married to a banker chosen by her father, Madame Levy had amassed a large collection of Bach manuscripts, which she donated to the Singakademie library. "Tante Levy" was not only an early member of the chorus but was reported to have performed as harpsichord soloist (unpaid, of course) with the Singakademie instrumental ensemble.[16]

The Baronesses Fanny von Arnstein and Caecilie von Eskeles married Viennese court bankers and settled in that city. Fanny von Arnstein, a charming, witty woman over whom duels were fought, brought the intellectual tradition of the Berlin salon to the Habsburg capital. She was a pianist and befriended Beethoven and other Viennese composers. The musical *soirées* she gave during the Congress of Vienna were renowned, and benefit concerts she organized led to the founding of the Gesellschaft der Musikfreunde.[17] Her daughter, Henrietta Pereira-Arnstein (1780–1859), also a fine pianist, aided Haydn in his last years and continued the musical traditions of the Arnstein family.[18] Lea Mendelssohn particularly admired her aunt Fanny and there was close contact with the Viennese relatives, who visited and corresponded regularly.

For most of her life, Fanny Hensel followed the pattern set by the Itzig women. She married, supervised a large home and the education of her one child, entertained family, friends, and her husband's colleagues and students, and maintained a large and lively correspondence and the private musical traditions of the Mendelssohns. Like many of the Mendelssohn family women, her intimates were her sister and other relatives, some converted Jews, others who remained Jewish. Almost all were musicians or music-lovers; many, with Fanny, participated in the choral activities of the Singakademie until 1833. In January of that year, however, Felix was rejected for the post of conductor of the Singakademie and the family left that organization.

The musical activity that engaged her energies and talents and that proved to be most rewarding was the Mendelssohn family *Sonntagsmusik*, the Sunday musicales, held first in her parent's mansion on Leipzigerstrasse 3 and then later in the garden house on their property, where she lived with her husband and son. These private musicales became brilliant Berlin musical affairs attended by aristocracy and bourgeois music-lovers alike.[19]

Her Sunday musicales have often been described as musical salons similar to the Berlin literary and intellectual salons presided over by such women as Rahel Levin Varnhagen von Ense, Henriette Herz, and Sara Levy, Fanny's great-aunt.[20] These women were educated, charming hostesses who stimulated discussions among writers, philosophers, statesmen, intellectually curious aristocrats, and well-to-do businessmen. But the Hensel musicales were of a different order. Assuming the responsibilities of music director, Madame Hensel planned the music programs, performed as a soloist and accompanist, played her own compositions, and conducted the choir made up of skilled amateurs and an orchestra of professional musicians hired from the Königstadt Theater. Her Sunday musicales introduced to Berlin audiences the music of the Bach family and Gluck. Her musicians performed scenes from Beethoven's opera *Fidelio,* and sections from Handel oratorios. Fanny also premiered many of her brother's works as well as her own. That she composed and conducted was perfectly acceptable as far as the family (and Berlin society) was concerned, since it was an amateur activity carried on in her own home and for which she was not paid.

The *Sonntagsmusik* provided an opportunity for this multi-talented woman to meet with and perform for the leading European musicians of her time. Clara Wieck Schumann (1819–96), a professional pianist and composer, a working woman from the artist-musician class,[21] and universally acknowledged to be one of the top-ranking pianists of her time, was especially impressed by Fanny Hensel's musicianship. In February and March 1847, Clara and Robert Schumann were in Berlin for performances of Robert Schumann's oratorio *Das Paradies und die Peri* and for several concerts in which Clara Schumann was the soloist. The Schumanns saw the Hensels frequently and Clara sat for a portrait by Wilhelm Hensel, Fanny's husband. On 8 March 1847, Clara Schumann gave a concert in their lodgings for invited guests. The program included a song by Fanny Hensel and Clara Schumann's own Trio, Op. 17.[22] Soon afterwards Clara wrote in her diary, "I had a great affection for Madame Hensel and felt especially drawn to her in regard to music. We were always in harmony with each other and her conversation was always interesting."[23] The Schumanns gave serious consideration to resettling in Berlin, and Fanny Hensel's presence in that city played a large part in their discussions.

When Fanny Hensel died suddenly and unexpectedly in May, a few months later, Clara wrote to her old friend, Emilie List: "The situation in regard to Mendelssohn's sister is very sad! I had just learned to know her better in Berlin and esteemed her highly. We saw each other daily and had already arranged between us that when we would come to Berlin we would see each other often and play music together. She was undoubtedly the most distinguished musician [*Musikerin*] of her time and an important person for the entire Berlin musical life—one heard only the best at her place. I had dedicated my Trio, which I am awaiting from the printer daily, to her and now she is dead! This catastrophe has deeply shaken my husband and me!"[24]

Clara Schumann programmed Hensel songs at a number of her public concerts but they were songs that had appeared under Felix Mendelssohn's name or were unpublished. Strong objections would have been raised by Fanny's father, and later her brother Felix, if her songs had been published under her name. Moses Mendelssohn, the great Enlightenment philosopher, is often referred to as an emancipator. But the liberalism of the man who led the German Jews out of the ghetto and into German secular society did not extend to women. Like the *philosophes* and other Enlightenment thinkers whose influence was felt long after the French Revolution, Mendelssohn saw the roles of women primarily as those of mothers and wives. In their history of documents concerning women, Bell and Offen point out that "after the French Revolution, discussion of female education took a distinctly conservative turn. . . . The secular political goals . . . were challenged by a resurgent moral conservatism that recast and reformulated female education in terms of traditional religious piety, chastity, and obedience."[25] This viewpoint coincided with the traditional Jewish position on women.[26] For Moses, for his son Abraham, and for his grandson Felix, men for whom children and family life were of great importance, these sentiments made sense. They chose wives who willingly accepted this familiar pattern.

Why did Fanny Hensel remain a "dilettante" despite her skills? And why did her father and brother feel so strongly about public appearances and publication? Although there were a number of professional women pianists and composers active at this time (Clara Schumann and Marie Pleyel, for example, cited by Chorley above), they were not women from the bourgeois aristocratic class: they worked because of need.[27] To the Mendelssohn men, a career as a musician placed a woman of Fanny's class in an untenable position: money would be exchanged, her name would be in print, and she would appear on stage. All the traditions of the family (Jewish, Christian, Enlightenment philosophy) united in prescribing "modesty" and "obedience" for females, qualities that could not be preserved while appearing in public and pursuing a career. In addition, it is difficult not to suspect that the social position of this Jewish-Christian family in Berlin also influenced their attitude.

Consequently, when six of Fanny's songs were published in early collections of Felix, they came out under his name—not to deceive the public or because he could not compose songs—but because her "modesty" would have been at stake. Felix's objections to separate publication of his sister's works have been variously described as stemming from jealousy of his sister's talent; as "inherited" from his father; as a male chauvinist position intended to keep women in their place; as guilt at having succeeded in an arena in which she, equally gifted, was prevented from competing; and as a desire to protect his sister against the barbs of the critics. I believe there is some truth in all of these statements.

The musical kinship between sister and brother was very close; the two had studied together and the competition was a stimulus to each. Fanny reminded him of this in June 1837: "think back to the time when we were constantly together, when I immediately discovered every thought that went through your mind, and knew your new things by heart even before they were notated, and . . . remember that our relationship was a particularly rare one among siblings, in part because of our common musical pursuits."[28]

For many years, Fanny and Felix were musical confidantes: they discussed musical problems, and criticized and trusted each other. At his request, she wrote detailed critiques of his works and took his place at Berlin rehearsals of his oratorio *St. Paul* to assure a correct performance. He wrote comments on her work, and repeated to her praise of her playing and compositions from Kalkbrenner, Moscheles, and Goethe. Occasionally, he was caught between his prejudices and his musical judgments. While he was concerned about Fanny's "femininity" (to be "unfeminine" or "*unweiblich*" was anathema to the Mendelssohns), he could not help complimenting her on the fact that there was no trace of the feminine in her *Lobgesang,* a cantata she composed in 1831.

The Mendelssohn men had a horror of *femmes savantes* like Rahel Levin Varnhagen and Bettina von Arnim, and Fanny shared their feeling. In a letter to the mother of Madame Bigot, their childhood piano teacher, Felix praises his sister's musicianship but takes pains to deny that she is an intellectual or "unfeminine": "It makes me sad, that since her marriage she can no longer compose as diligently as earlier, for she has composed several things, especially German Lieder, which belong to the very best which we possess of Lieder; still it is good on the other hand, that she finds much joy in her domestic concerns, for a woman who neglects them be it for oil colors, or for rhyme, or for double counterpoint always calls to mind instinctively, the Greek [language] from the *femmes savantes,* and I am afraid of that. This is then, thank God, not the case with my sister, and yet she has, as said, continued her piano playing still with much love and besides has made much progress in it recently."[29]

Although Felix could praise Fanny to others, he was not always so generous to her. One must suspect a certain amount of sibling rivalry when, responding to her complaint that she had lost all inspiration after her child was born, he wrote: "You can hardly expect a man like me to wish you some musical ideas; it is just greediness for you to complain of a scarcity of them; . . . if you wanted to, you would already be composing with might and main and if you do not want to, why do you fret so dreadfully? If I had my child to nurse, then I would not want to write scores. . . . But seriously, the child is not even a half year old, and you already want to think of ideas other than Sebastian? (not Bach) Be happy that you have him, music fails to appear only when it has no place."[30] Fanny Hensel was unable to ignore Felix's arguments and did not protest. Instead, she threw herself into the *Sonntagsmusik* with more energy than ever. The home musicales became her primary musical outlet.

THE MUSIC OF FANNY HENSEL

Only in the past two decades have we had the privilege of seeing and hearing a number of works by Fanny Hensel, recently described as "without doubt, the most significant woman composer of the nineteenth century."[31] Unlike her brother, Fanny was not given the opportunity to study string instruments (which would have facilitated her string and orchestral writing), to travel in order to hear new music and make contacts with foreign composers, to try out works for large audiences and make the necessary revisions after rehearsals, to hear painful criticism that would enable her to grow and develop as a composer. For most of her creative life, except for her brother's comments, she heard only praise from the home musical circles around her, not necessarily a healthy situation.

The extent of her oeuvre has still to be determined, but it is known that she wrote keyboard music that includes sonatas, studies, contrapuntal works, and character pieces; works for organ; vocal music that encompasses solo songs, duets, trios, and choral works; works for chorus and orchestra including an oratorio and several cantatas; an orchestral overture; and chamber music including a piano quartet, string quartet, a piano trio, and instrumental duos.[32] Although the bulk of her work remained in manuscript, there is no doubt that Fanny Hensel thought of herself as a composer. Except for an enormous need for her brother's approval, we find few traces of the self-derogation and lack of confidence about her creative efforts from which many women composers, including Clara Schumann, suffered.[33] The question remains: why did Fanny Hensel wait so long to accept publishing offers?

She herself explains in a letter from July 1846 to her brother why she withheld her work:

> Actually, I wouldn't expect you to read this rubbish now, busy as you are, if I didn't have to tell you something. But since I know from the start you won't like it, it's a bit awkward to get underway. So laugh at me or not, as you wish: I'm afraid of my brothers at age 40, as I was of Father at age 14—or more aptly expressed, desirous of pleasing you and everyone I've loved throughout my life. And when I now know in advance that it won't be the case, I thus feel *rather* uncomfortable. In a word, I'm beginning to publish. I have Herr Bock's[34] sincere offer for my Lieder and have finally turned a receptive ear to his favorable terms. . . . I hope I won't disgrace all of you through my publishing, as I'm no femme libre[35] . . . I trust *you* will in no way be bothered by it, since, as you can see, I've proceeded completely on my own in order to spare you any possible unpleasant moment, and I hope you won't think badly of me. If it succeeds—that is, if the pieces are well liked and I receive additional offers—I know it will be a great stimulus to me, something I've always needed in order to create.[36]

This revealing letter confirms what Fanny had often hinted at: that the very special bond with her brother had been a burden as well as a joy throughout her life, and that his approval was essential to her creativity.

Excerpts from Fanny's letters to her brother offer further support for this interpretation:

> 8 APRIL 1835
> For I'm so unreasonably afraid of you anyway (and of no other person, except slightly of Father), that I actually never play particularly well in front of you, and I wouldn't even attempt to accompany in front of you, although I know I'm very good at it.[37]

> 12 JANUARY 1836
> it's necessary for you to know everything in my life and approve of it. Therefore I'm also very sad, truly not out of vanity, that I haven't been able to be grateful to you in such a long time for liking my music. Did I really do it better in the old days, or were you merely easier to satisfy?[38]

> 30 JULY 1836
> I don't know exactly what Goethe means by the demonic influence . . . but this much is clear: if it does exist, you exert it over me.[39]

I have to admit honestly that I'm rather neutral about it [publishing], and Hensel, on the one hand, is for it, and you, on the other hand, are against it. I would of course comply totally with the wishes of my husband in any other matter, yet on this issue alone it's crucial to have your consent, for without it I might not undertake anything of the kind.[40]

With this history, Fanny Hensel's decision to accept offers from publishers seems astonishing. The support of friends and her artist-husband, Wilhelm Hensel, certainly figured in her decision, but three other events in her life enabled her to overcome the "demonic influence" of her brother and the loyalty to family and class: her Italian trip of 1839–40, her mother's death in December 1842, and her friendship with Robert von Keudell.

Fanny Hensel's first Italian trip was an ecstatic experience that awakened her to a full realization of her musical powers. Her letters and diary give a detailed description of the sights and sounds and the liberating effect of the Mediterranean culture on her northern soul. Furthermore, she found herself—for the first time in her life—away from Berlin and its associations, from her mother, from her brother's influence, and—perhaps more importantly—freed from the heavy weight of prescriptive family conventions and expectations. She, her ten-year-old son Sebastian, and her husband Wilhelm spent much of their time with artists from the French Academy (the *Prix de Rome* winners) and three young Frenchmen, the composers Charles Gounod and Georges Bousquet, and the painter Charles Dugasseau, all of whom evidently adored Madame Hensel. In his memoirs, Gounod described those glorious Roman days:

Madame Hensel was a musician beyond comparison, a remarkable pianist, and a woman of superior mind; small and thin in person but with an energy that showed itself in her deep eyes and in her fiery glance. She was gifted with rare ability as a composer. . . . M. and Madame Hensel came to the Academy on Sunday evenings. She used to place herself at the piano with the good grace and simplicity of those who make music because they love it, and thanks to her fine talent and prodigious memory, I was brought to the knowledge of a mass of the chefs-d'oeuvres of German music of which I was completely ignorant at that time, among others, a number of pieces by Johann Sebastian Bach—sonatas, concertos, fugues, and preludes—and several Mendelssohn compositions which were, also, a revelation to me from an unknown world.[41]

Fanny had never been so much appreciated before, and her self-confidence as a musician blossomed. Her letters, diary, and the creation of *Das Jahr*, a cycle of twelve piano works each depicting a month (plus a postlude), reveal a new and joyous woman.

DAS JAHR

Das Jahr, composed between August and December 1841, after her return to Berlin, is a musical diary of the trip to and from Rome and the months spent in the Eternal City. The Hensels left Berlin on 4 September 1839 and returned one year later. Why the work was not printed until 1989 remains a mystery, but as soon as it became available, *Das Jahr* was performed and recorded by leading pianists in Europe and the United States. The first publication was based on a manuscript in the Mendelssohn Archive of the Berlin Staatsbiblio-thek.[42] In 2001, a facsimile edition based on the *Reinschrift* (fair copy), which had been in the possession of a family member for over one hundred years, was finally made public.[43] Each of the twelve pieces is written in the fair copy on a different color paper. A short poem (whether by the composer or by her husband is not certain) and an appropriate illustration by Wilhelm Hensel appear at the beginning of each piece. Though Fanny Hensel did not choose to publish *Das Jahr*, there is no doubt that she valued—perhaps even treasured—this musical diary of the happiest year of her life.[44]

The first piece in the cycle, "January," subtitled "Ein Traum" (A Dream) is prefaced with the verse:

Ahnest du, o Seele wieder   Oh my soul, do you sense once more
Sanfte, süsse Frühlingslieder?   The gentle, sweet songs of spring?
Sieh umher die falben Bäume,   See the pale yellow trees around us,
Ach! es waren holde Träume.   Ah! they were but sweet dreams.

Opening with a dream-like sequence marked "Adagio, quasi una Fantasia," "January" proceeds like an overture as we hear motives from forthcoming months. We hear fragments of "February," "March," "May," and "August" before the pianist plunges into the second piece, "February," subtitled "Scherzo." This Presto movement goes beyond the fairy-like scherzos of Felix Mendelssohn to invoke the wild excitement of Carnival time in Rome. The verse inscribed at the head of "February" reads:

Denkt nicht ihr seid in deutschen	Think not that you are in German
Gränzen,	borders,
Von Teufels-Narren-und Todtentänzen	With dances of devils, fools, and death
Ein heiter Fest erwartet Euch.	A merry celebration awaits you.

Das Jahr is breathtaking in its virtuosic, poetic representation of the Italian journey; moreover, these twelve movements tell us much about the composer's special gifts. From the demands placed upon the performer, it is clear that Fanny Hensel was a pianist of the first order, on a par with contemporary keyboard artists like Sigismund Thalberg, Clara Schumann, and Franz Liszt. The inclusion and working out of the Protestant chorales "Christ ist erstanden" in "March"; "Von Himmel hoch, da komm ich her" in "December"; and "Das alte Jahr vergangen ist" in the "Postlude" remind us not only of Fanny Hensel's religious affiliation, but her total familiarity with chorales and variations in the baroque style as well as Bach and his musical world. Hensel's bold harmonies and intricate rhythmic patterns confirm her confidence and craftsmanship. The depiction of a dream in "January," the Roman carnival in "February," the flowing of the river in "September," the elation expressed in "May" (subtitled "Spring Song"), for example, attest to her mastery of the imaginative romantic "character piece," a genre generally associated with Robert Schumann, Frederic Chopin, and Felix Mendelssohn, and in which she excelled.

The death of her mother, Lea Mendelssohn, in December 1842, broke another tie with the traditions of the wealthy cultivated Berlin *salonières* and the Itzig family. Although Lea had encouraged Fanny's composing and even urged Felix to give his approval, the change in the family constellation undoubtedly had an effect on the eldest daughter.

In May 1846, Fanny Hensel was beginning to consider publishing her works but hesitated because she had not yet received approval from her brother. It was about this time that she became very friendly with Robert von Keudell,[45] whose critical judgment and encouragement of the kind she had not experienced since she left Rome helped free her from her dependence on Felix. By the end of July she recorded: "Keudell looks at everything new that I write with the greatest interest and points out to me if there is something wanting and in the main, he is correct. So, I have now decided to publish my things."[46]

In 1846, at the age of forty, Fanny Hensel chose for publication a number of piano pieces and songs from the many hundreds of her works. These were published by two Berlin publishers, Bote & Bock and Schlesinger. Favorable reviews appeared in the leading music journals of Berlin and Leipzig. Heartened, Fanny continued to compose both for publication and for her Sunday musicales. During the summer of 1846, she wrote in her diary that she was always busy and felt gratified and successful. She added that perhaps never in her life—except for a short period during her first trip to Rome—had she felt so content and blessed.[47]

On the afternoon of Friday, 14 May 1847, Fanny Hensel was rehearsing her chorus for a Sunday performance of Felix's *Walpurgisnacht,* and suddenly felt ill. She quickly lost consciousness and died that evening. Obituaries appearing in the Berlin newspapers lauded the musician: "Fanny Hensel was an artist in the most exalted sense of the word; in her, the happiest gifts of nature always went hand in hand with the most careful cultivation of rare talents. Just as she shone as a gifted and accomplished pianist, so do the works only recently published under her own name testify to that heartfelt depth of feeling, which, precisely in this sphere, is fundamental to a lofty and nobler creation."[48]

Soon after her sudden and unexpected death, Felix (who died six months later) arranged to have a number of her compositions, including her Trio for Piano, Violin, and Cello, published posthumously.

Her class was no longer a barrier.

NOTES

~

An earlier version of this essay appeared as "The Power of Class: Fanny Hensel," in *Mendelssohn and his World,* ed. R. Larry Todd (Princeton: Princeton University Press, 1991), 86–99. It has been revised and appears here with permission of Princeton University Press.

1. In W. A. Lampadius, *Life of Felix Mendelssohn Bartholdy,* trans. W. L. Gage (Boston: Oliver Ditson, 1865), 210–11. The name Bartholdy was added to Mendelssohn (without a hyphen) when Abraham had his children converted to Christianity, but it was not used consistently by his children. In this essay, the name will be given as Mendelssohn.

2. *Fanny Hensel Tagebücher,* ed. Hans-Günter Klein and Rudolf Elvers (Wiesbaden: Breitkopf & Härtel, 2002).

3. Sebastian Hensel, *Die Familie Mendelssohn 1729–1847: Nach Briefen und Tagebüchern,* 2d rev. ed., 2 vols. (Berlin: B. Behr's Buchhandlung, 1880). An English translation, *The Mendelssohn Family (1729–1847): From Letters and Journals,* trans. Carl Klingemann and an American Collaborator (New York: Harper & Brothers, 1881), followed almost immediately. (Carl Klingemann, of the Hanoverian legation in London, was a lifelong friend of the Mendelssohn family.) References in this essay will be to the 1880 German edition. All translations are mine unless otherwise indicated.

4. Hensel, *Die Familie Mendelssohn,* 1:5.

5. See, for example, the path-breaking dissertation by Victoria Ressmeyer Sirota, "The Life and Works of Fanny Mendelssohn Hensel" (Boston University, 1981) and *The*

Letters of Fanny Hensel to Felix Mendelssohn, collected, edited, and translated with introductory essays and notes by Marcia J. Citron (Stuyvesant, N.Y.: Pendragon Press, 1987), cited hereafter as Citron, *Letters.* Most useful, but unfortunately not translated into English, is the volume by the historian Felix Gilbert, who was himself a Mendelssohn descendant, *Bankiers, Künstler und Gelehrte: Unveröffentlichte Briefe der Familie Mendelssohn aus dem 19. Jahrhundert* (Tübingen: J. C. B. Mohr, 1975). See Selected Bibliography for additional sources.

6. Quoted from Johanna Kinkel's *Memoiren,* in Konrad Feilchenfeldt, "Karl August Varnhagen von Ense: Sieben Briefe an Rebecka Dirichlet," *Mendelssohn Studien* 3 (1979): 56–57.

7. Hensel, *Die Familie Mendelssohn,* 1:97.

8. Ibid., 1:99.

9. The term "bourgeois aristocracy," from William Weber, *Music and the Middle Class: The Social Structure of Concert Life in London, Paris and Vienna* (New York: Holmes & Meier, 1975), 8, is a more appropriate classification for the family of Abraham and Lea Mendelssohn than Hensel's "good German middle-class family."

10. Fanny met Wilhelm Hensel, the son of a poor Protestant pastor, at an exhibition of his work in Berlin in 1822. Although they fell in love, her parents would not permit an engagement nor even a correspondence between them until he was well established. Hensel, who had received a travel stipendium from the king, went to Rome, where he studied, painted, and was successful enough to be appointed a court painter on his return to Berlin five years later.

11. For an insightful discussion of the Berlin salons, see Deborah Hertz, *Jewish High Society in Old Regime Berlin* (New Haven: Yale University Press, 1988).

12. The great-grandson of Moses Mendelssohn, Sebastian Hensel, referred indignantly to this arrangement as an "oriental view of a woman as an object." Hensel, *Die Familie Mendelssohn,* 1:44. It is interesting to note that "Oriental" and "Asiatic" were terms used by many, including Hensel and his great-aunt Dorothea Schlegel, as substitutions for "Jewish."

13. Quoted in *Florentin: A Novel,* translated, annotated, and introduced by Edwina Lawler and Ruth Richardson (Lewiston, N.Y.: Edwin Mellen Press, 1988), xxviii.

14. Ibid., cxv–cxvi. My translation.

15. Gilbert, *Bankiers, Künstler und Gelehrte,* xvii–xviii.

16. See Peter Wollny, "Sara Levy and the Making of Musical Taste in Berlin," *Musical Quarterly* 77 (1993): 651–88.

17. See Hilde Spiel, "Jewish Women in Austrian Culture," in *The Jews of Austria,* ed. Josef Fraenkel (London: Vallentine, Mitchell 1967), 97–102.

18. The musical salons of all three women are described by Johann Friedrich Reichardt in his *Vertraute Briefe geschrieben auf einer Reise nach Wien und den österreichischer Staaten zu Ende des Jahres 1808 und zu Anfang 1809,* ed. Gustav Gugitz, 2 vols. (Munich: Georg Müller, 1915), 1:104–5 et passim. Excerpts in English about the Viennese great-aunts and cousin can be found in Nancy B. Reich, "A Commentary on and a Translation of Selected Portions of *Vertraute Briefe geschrieben auf einer Reise nach Wien und den österreichischer Staaten zu Ende des Jahres 1808 und zu Anfang 1809,* by Johann Friedrich Reichardt, 1752–1814" (Ph.D. diss., New York University, 1972), 258–61, 269–71.

19. In March 1844, Fanny wrote to her sister Rebecka, "Last Sunday, we had the most brilliant *Sonntagsmusik* ever. . . . There were twenty-two carriages in the courtyard and Liszt and eight princesses in the room." Hensel, *Die Familie Mendelssohn,* 2:293.

20. See Marcia Citron, *Gender and the Musical Canon* (Cambridge: Cambridge University Press, 1993), 104–6. For a discussion of the Jewish *salonières* in Berlin, see Hertz, *Jewish High Society*.

21. See Nancy B. Reich, "Women as Musicians: A Question of Class," in *Musicology and Difference: Gender and Sexuality in Music Scholarship*, ed. Ruth A. Solie (Berkeley: University of California Press, 1993), 125–26, for a discussion of the "artist-musician" class.

22. "Lied" by Fanny Hensel and Clara Schumann's Trio, Op. 17 are listed in Program 247a in Clara Schumann's program collection, Robert-Schumann-Haus, Zwickau. The Trio, composed in 1846 but not published until September 1847, must have been played from manuscript at the Berlin concert.

23. Berthold Litzmann, *Clara Schumann: Ein Künstlerleben nach Tagebüchern und Briefen*, 3 vols. (Leipzig: Breitkopf & Härtel, 1907), 2:161. My translation. Litzmann is also available in English translation: *Clara Schumann: An Artist's Life Based on Material Found in Diaries and Letters*, trans. and abridged by Grace E. Hadow, 2 vols. (New York: Da Capo, 1979), 2:429. See also pp. 430 and 440.

24. *"Das Band der Ewigen Liebe": Clara Schumanns Briefwechsel mit Emilie und Elise List*, ed. Eugen Wendler (Stuttgart: Metzler, 1996), 148–49. The Trio was published without any dedication. Before the publication of Wendler's book, it had not been known that Clara Schumann intended to dedicate her Trio to Fanny Hensel.

25. *Women, the Family, and Freedom: The Debate in Documents*, ed. Susan Groag Bell and Karen M. Offen, 2 vols. (Stanford: Stanford University Press, 1983), 1:83.

26. Sebastian Hensel, *Die Familie Mendelssohn*, 1:88, refers to Abraham's parenting as having a trait of "Jewish despotism" within it. ("Die Erziehungsweise Abraham's war streng, es herrschte noch etwas jüdischer Despotismus darin.")

27. Camilla Pleyel, née Marie Moke (1811–75), a professional French pianist, continued performing after her marriage to piano builder Camille Pleyel.

28. Citron, *Letters*, 234. This was part of a letter in which Fanny was berating her brother because he had not brought his wife to meet the family.

29. Quoted by Sirota, "Life and Works," 85, from a letter of 1 June 1835. It is interesting to note that "Tante Schlegel" was exempted from Felix's hostility toward women intellectuals. By the time Felix and Fanny knew her, Friedrich Schlegel had died and Dorothea was devoting herself to children and grandchildren. Moreover, Dorothea herself had always taken the Enlightenment position that her role was to nurture the creative (male) genius.

30. Letter of 16 November 1830, quoted in Sirota, "Life and Works," 59. I have modified her translation.

31. Franz Krautwurst, "Fanny Hensel," in *Die Musik in Geschichte und Gegenwart*, ed. Friedrich Blume, vol. 16 (Kassel, 1979), 662.

32. For an extended discussion of her compositions, see Sirota, "Life and Works," chaps. 4, 5, and 6. For recent work-lists, see Marcia Citron's article in *The New Grove Dictionary of Music and Musicians*, ed. Stanley Sadie and John Tyrrell, 2d ed. (London: Macmillan, 2001), 16:388–89, and Camilla Cai, "Fanny Mendelssohn Hensel," in *Women Composers: Music through the Ages*, vol. 6: *Composers Born 1800–1898: Keyboard Music*, ed. Sylvia Glickman and Martha Schleifer (New York: G. K. Hall, 1999), 21–43. See also Selected Bibliography.

33. See chap. 11, "Clara Schumann as Composer and Editor," in Nancy B. Reich, *Clara Schumann: The Artist and the Woman* (rev. ed., Ithaca, N.Y.: Cornell University Press, 2001), esp. 211, 215–18.

34. Gustav Bock (1813–63) founded the music publishing house of Bote & Bock with Eduard Bote in 1838 and became sole proprietor in 1847.

35. Fanny is referring to women like the *femmes savantes* who so distressed her brother.

36. Citron, *Letters,* 349–50.

37. Ibid., 182.

38. Ibid., 195.

39. Ibid., 209.

40. Ibid., 222.

41. Charles Gounod, *Memoirs of an Artist: An Autobiography,* trans. Annette E. Crocker (Chicago: Rand McNally, 1895), 125. Note: Gounod's well-known "Ave Maria," based on the C Major Prelude from Bach's Well-Tempered Clavier, Book 1, was undoubtedly inspired by Fanny Hensel's mentorship.

42. Fanny Hensel, *Das Jahr: 12 Charakterstücke für das Forte-Piano,* ed. Liana Gavrila Serbescu and Barbara Heller, 2 vols. (Kassel: Furore Edition 138, 1989).

43. Fanny Hensel, *Das Jahr: 12 Charakterstücke (1841) für das Forte-Piano. Illustrierte Reinschrift mit Zeichnungen von Wilhelm Hensel; Faksimile nach dem Autograph aus dem Besitz des Mendelssohn-Archivs der Staatsbibliothek zu Berlin* (*The Year: Twelve Character Pieces [1841] for Fortepiano*; illustrated fair copy with illustrations by Wilhelm Hensel; facsimile of the autograph owned by the Mendelssohn Archives at the National Library in Berlin); epilogues by Beatrix Borchard, Ayako Suga-Maack, and Christian Thorau (Kassel: Furore Edition 892, 2000).

44. "September" is the exception; it appeared as "Andante con moto" in her *Vier Lieder für das Pianoforte,* Op. 2, No. 2, published by Bote & Bock in 1846.

45. Baron Robert von Keudell (1824–1903), a diplomat who served as Prussian envoy to Constantinople and Rome, was also an exceptionally talented amateur composer and editor.

46. *Tagebücher,* 265.

47. Ibid., 266. This entry was made on 24 July, before she received Felix's blessing. Hensel, *Die Familie Mendelssohn,* 2:375, gives the date, incorrectly, as 14 August.

48. Reprinted from *Die Preussische Zeitung* in the *Signale für die musikalische Welt* (May 1847): 190–91.

CHAPTER TWO

The Illusion of India's "Public" Dancers

Carol M. Babiracki

SHE WAS A TINY, frail old woman with thin gray hair, but when she began to dance, she seemed twenty years old again. Kistomani, the "Jewel of Krishna," was once among the most famous "public dancers," or *nacnī*s (lit., female dancer) of Jharkhand, an area of hills, forests, and plateaus, now a new state nestled between the Indian states of Bihar, Bengal, Orissa, and Madhya Pradesh. On this night, in the pre-dawn hours of 14 June 1993, she was dancing outdoors in a village, a lone woman in front of a line of young and old male dancers and drummers. She smiled invitingly at them, all *rasi-kā*s, men able to appreciate the *ras* (lit., juice, essence; aesthetic quality, senti-ment) of the *nacnī* and her art. As they danced counter-clockwise around the courtyard *akhāṛā* (arena, dancing ground), the group sang the following song in the Nagpuri language, composed in the voice of the cowherd woman Radha, about her attraction to the Hindu god Krishna and their love-play (*līlā*):[1]

REFRAIN:

e daiyā, dadhī bike hama paguḍhārī	Oh friend, whenever I step out to sell curds
dik karaē banwārī	The Forest-Dweller [Krishna] disturbs me.

VERSE, REFRAIN:

sakal śriṅgāra kair	Fixing my ornaments,
kalsī ke siredhair	Holding the decorated pot on my head,
e daiyā, umaṅge calalī baṛ bhārī	Oh friend, I set out with much anticipation,
dik karaē banwārī	The Forest-Dweller disturbs me.

VERSE, REFRAIN:

kiye prabhu bala jora	God [Krishna] used too much force
gorasa kuṇḍan phoṛī	And broke the pot of curds.
e daiyā, cholī band delaē chaṭakārī	Oh friend, he untied my blouse-cloth,
dik karaē banwārī	The Forest-Dweller disturbs me.
[unclear verse]	

REFRAIN:

hae daiyā ānand ke kar upakārī	Oh friend, help Anand [the poet],
dik karaē banwārī	The Forest-Dweller disturbs me.

Though Kistomani did not join the forceful singing, shouts, and whoops of the men, her very presence could still capture the *ras* of the song text in a way that the men's voices could not, and not simply because she was a woman. She might not have looked the part of Radha, dressed in such a simple sari and sparse ornaments, but by virtue of being a *nacnī*, she *was* Radha, not only in the dancing ground but in her daily life as well.

This performance was the culmination of a night-long musical gathering that Kistomani called a *mahfil* (assembly, dance party). It was held in the village courtyard of an elderly former landlord (*zamīndār*) and *rasikā*, famed for sponsoring and performing in dance parties with Kistomani in their youth. The group of thirty performers was seated on a large platform made of wooden beds, illuminated by a few kerosene lanterns. All were men, except for Kistomani, myself, and a *launda* (female impersonator, a man who dressed and danced as a *nacnī*). I had performed a couple of tunes on bamboo flute, but otherwise I spent the evening documenting the performance, hidden behind a video camera. Kistomani and the *launda* were the only professionals, that is, people who made their living through performance. Surrounding the "stage," an audience of villagers, mostly men, sat in the shadows, silent except for quiet titters when the old *nacnī* danced. This performance wasn't for them. It was for the *rasikās*, as a court or landlord's *mahfil* might have been fifty years earlier. This is only one of many venues for *nacnī* performances. They also perform for audiences of mixed gender at more public events, such as marriages, birth celebrations, the many spring festivals associated with the god Krishna, and other all-night village entertainments.

Missing from this *mahfil* was Kistomani's "keeper" (*rakhnewālā*), who had died five or six years earlier.[2] Kistomani referred to him as her "husband" or as "Krishna," as many *nacnī*s do. His name, Ganesh Ram Dube, was tattooed on her forearm. Since his death, Dube's "social" (*samājik*) wife and his sons' families had allowed Kistomani to continue to live in a tiny room apart from the rest of the household, thus outside "general" society, where she had

Figure 2.1. Kistomani *(nacnī)* dancing Nagpuri
mardānā jhumar with men at a musical gathering in
Sanga village, 14 June 1993. Photograph by Carol
Babiracki.

languished and fallen ill.[3] But this night she had come alive, reliving the
glories of her past, traveling outside her village, performing outdoors all
night. "If you stay for the whole night," she said, "you'll be praising it your
whole life. If it's not for the whole night, there'll be no *mazā* [relish, delight,
pleasure]."[4] She danced, played drums, smoked strong, home-grown ciga-
rettes (*biṛi*), and drank heavily, all in the company of men, without shame,
shyness, or deference to anyone, as a *nacnī* would (see Fig. 2.1).[5]

The old *rasikā*s assembled that night were reliving their youths as well.
One of them, Jaimangal Singh, recalled, "I was going [to programs] on a
bicycle with a *nacnī* on the back, singing and singing, driving with one hand
and showing the melody with the other."[6] He spoke about Kistomani with
admiration and anticipation before the *mahfil*: "She had the beauty and form
of a goddess."[7] "When someone like Kistomani dances, the *real* Lord Krishna
will *have* to come, because it is the *real ras* . . . Her *bhāv* [quality, disposition,
feeling] was such that when she sang, I got tears in my eyes and my throat
closed. Even now, when I remember, my eyes fill with tears."[8] Watching the
video after the *mahfil*, he commented, "The *nacnī* is our mother goddess.
She dances and blesses us with her inner and outer qualities. We need her
blessing. The man who dances with her is her favored son. That's why she

has no children."[9] This recalls a passage from the ancient Sanskrit text, the Brahamavaivatar Purana: "You [Radha] are the Mother of the world, Hari is the Father. The guru of the Father is the Mother, to be worshipped and honored as supreme."[10]

A PUBLIC WOMAN

To *rasikās*, *nacnīs* like Kistomani and the many younger ones performing today may be embodiments of a "mother goddess" or of Krishna's divine consort, but to many people of the "general" public, including those who attend their public performances, they are simply prostitutes. They are disdainfully called "public" dancers, not only because they perform in public but because their sexuality is public and on public display. By definition and practice, a *nacnī* is a sexually active woman whose sexuality is not controlled by society (father, brothers, husband, in-laws). One of the *rasikās* she dances with is her sexual partner, unsanctioned by any social agreement between families, in violation of caste endogamy, and not for the purpose of having children or perpetuating a lineage.[11] Her allure is that she is sexually free; she can be enticed away from her keeper at any time, even if his name *is* tattooed on her forearm. She is bound to him simply by love and art. The song and dance performance of a *nacnī* celebrates her sexual abandon as an aspect of the romantic love between Radha and Krishna. Even Kistomani, long past her prime, flirted shamelessly, but selectively, with the male *rasikās* on stage with her, strategically parceling out her favors as the old men competed for her attention. Her free sexuality was essential for all participants to create and savor the *ras* of romantic love and passionate devotion. This understanding of a "public" woman—publicly on display, publicly sexual and available—has also been used to characterize other courtesan communities in India, particularly that of the *devadāsī* ("servant of the god"),[12] and it is often the rationale for practices of veiling in Muslim societies.[13] *Nacnīs* are also "public" in the sense that they participate in public music making that is otherwise male. Scholars have noted a conventional alignment of public with male musical activities and private or domestic with female in diverse places in the world, including Greece, Afghanistan, and Egypt,[14] and in early Christian and Judaic communities.[15] In Jharkhand, too, Hindus segregate their musical activities by gender, with the exception, of course, of "public" dancers and female impersonators, who cross the gender line. Men's music making is more public, whether they are dancing at a festival or singing on the stage, where men dominate. Men are also the instrumentalists, playing wind and stringed instruments and drumming at dances, entertainments, temples, and village ceremonies. Women's singing (with or without a male drummer) takes place in the house or courtyard. Dancing in public is considered an immoral and degrading activity for women, especially those of higher status. It is only "lower" caste women who regularly take part in gender-segregated group dancing at weddings and household rituals. In Jharkhand's tribal (*ādivāsī*, aboriginal) communities men and women dance together publicly, but they, like *nacnī*s, live outside of caste society.

The *nacnī* performs in public, for the public, but she is not part of the public. For this reason, the term that *nacnī*s themselves use to describe their social position seems more appropriate. As Janki Devi, a former *nacnī*, put it, *nacnī*s are "outside" and general women are "inside." When Janki was recruited into the profession, by force and trickery, her family held the requisite *jāti-bāhar* (out-caste) ceremony, much like a death ceremony. By definition, then, *nacnī*s are free of caste affiliation and so are not permanently connected to family and place, be it birth home or marriage home. Each lives with her "keeper's" family, which may include a "social" wife, brothers and their wives, parents, and even other *nacnī*s. But they live outside the usual obligations of wives, such as cooking and bearing children. In fact, since the *nacnī* is usually from a "low," or rather "small" (*choṭa*, Janki's term) caste and her keeper from a higher caste (primarily Rajputs and some Brahmans), she is forbidden from cooking for the family or the ancestors. As Janki said, "I spent twenty years with men [Rajputs] who would not take food from my hand."[16] Just a month before this conversation, Janki had become the first, and perhaps still the only, *nacnī* to have moved back "inside" society by negotiating a "social" marriage for herself with a man of her own caste. From this secure position, she spoke more frankly to me about her life as a *nacnī* than she had when we first met ten years earlier.

When we consider the *nacnī* through the frame of outside and inside, it is clear that the question of whether she is a "mother goddess" or a prostitute is not the only paradox at work. There are many that wrap her in mystery. She is literally "out-caste," publicly sexual and unchaste, but her performances are considered auspicious and central to life-cycle events associated with fertility and to festivals involving Krishna, which attract large crowds from surrounding towns and villages. Her profession socially degrades her, yet a man enhances his own wealth and social status by keeping her. A keeper like Dube, a Brahman, could have sexual relations with a lower-caste *nacnī* like Kistomani, but he could not take cooked food from her. She said that she tattooed his name on her forearm at his request, as a mark of Krishna's touch, so that she could at least give water to him and his guests.[17] The *nacnī* is "super female," in the words of *rasikā* Mukund Nayak, my research assistant. She is a woman of heightened female sexuality, but in the dancing ground she is a master of musical activities that are considered male, such as drumming. Even the songs she sings—songs in the voice of Radha—are composed by male poets in genres that are marked as male. For example, the song at Kistomani's *mahfil* quoted above is a *mardānā jhumar*, or men's *jhumar* song.

BAHĀNĀ: A CURTAIN OF PRETENSE

After seven months of close contact at performances and interviews with seven *nacnī*s and the constellations of keepers and *rasikā*s around them, for me the most salient paradox about them—and the most frustrating—was that little about these "public" women was of public knowledge. So I envisioned my research in the terms of other researchers' moves "inside" the private worlds of female performers.[18] I wanted to go backstage, behind the curtain, to understand the private *nacnī* (metaphorically, of course, since the outdoor arenas of their performances are circular and uncurtained). Instead, my research assistant and I found layers of *bahānā* (pretense, feigning, masquerade). Every *nacnī* we got to know, including those who became close friends and confidantes, fooled and misled us or left us swimming in ambiguity at one time or another. We would move behind the "curtain" only to find another and another. *Nacnī*s were especially vague about their pasts, about who their *rasikā*s had been, and especially about whether or not they had had children. As Radhas, living free of domestic obligations, they should ideally remain childless, and it is widely believed by *nacnī*s and *rasikā*s that having children saps the strength needed to dance. Women with children are also not free to travel as *nacnī*s must, since they rarely perform in their villages of residence. Each of the seven *nacnī*s we interviewed was said by others to have had children, but several denied it to us or simply ignored the question.

Uncovering the mysteries of *nacnī*s was a favorite pastime of their patrons and *rasikā*s. They were proud of their "insider" knowledge and reveled in the glimpses behind the curtain that a *nacnī* might allow. Knowledge was clearly a sign of familiarity. Unlike *nacnī*s, they were eager to share their "truths" with me, to tell me "the reality," though they could never be certain of it. This discourse about *bahānā* is as important as is the *nacnī*'s manipulation of it in performance and conversation in constituting the *nacnī*'s art and life.

It isn't surprising that *nacnī*s might conceal uncomfortable or incongruent aspects of their lives. Nearly all have come to the profession by virtue of being disenfranchised and marginalized somehow. All are recruited from the "lowest" castes, since these are the castes in which girls learn to sing and dance together early. Some find their way to the profession because they have been sold by impoverished parents, or beaten and abused, or abandoned by a husband. Others choose the profession to escape unhappy marriages or out of love for a *rasikā*. Fewer choose to become *nacnī*s purely out of a love of performance. As *nacnī*s, they succeed by their wits and talents, always competing with others for a good position. For many, then, secrecy may mean survival.

But the *nacnī*'s *bahānā* is more than this. Her performance on stage (and in informal musical gatherings offstage) reconciles the distinctions of human and divine, mother goddess and sex goddess, and male and female into a singular essence of sentiment. In her daily life and among *rasikā*s, her play with realities and "truths" engages and challenges the meaning of cultural symbols, gender norms, and social conventions and values. *Bahānā*, playing with illusion, is the essence of the *nacnī*'s life as theater.

I have come to appreciate *nacnī*s' *bahānā* as a kind of performative *pardah* (curtain, veiling, or seclusion). *Pardah* is a practice common among the social wives of Brahmans and Rajputs in Jharkhand, as it is elsewhere in India. The seclusion of women in the home, away from the glances of outside men and even certain relatives, protects the purity, honor, and prestige of the family, preventing any confusion between them and "public" women. I know that to associate *nacnī*s with *pardah* is a rather paradoxical notion; perhaps it is the result of hanging out with them. As "public" women, *nacnī*s represent the antithesis of *pardah*. Braj Kishore Dube, the son of Ganesh Ram, explained that landlords kept *nacnī*s because of the *pardah* system; unlike their social wives, *nacnī*s could leave the house and freely socialize with men.[19] *Nacnī*s are a kind of public surrogate for all women and for their female, sexual energy.

But onstage and off, *nacnī*s manipulate *bahānā* like an unseen curtain, controlling how much they conceal and reveal, partially cloaking themselves in plain view, inviting all to try to see inside. This recalls to me a popular *gat* (short composition) in North Indian *kathak* dance, once the dance of *tawā'if*s, the "classical" courtesans of large courts and urban centers. The dancer mimes a veil, pulling aside just enough of it to entice her patron or client (now audience) into believing that he may see what's inside. Ann Grodzins Gold, writing about women's stories of *pardah* in Rajasthan, has observed that "women may think of *purdah* [*sic*] as a cover behind which they gain freedom to follow their own lights."[20] Veena Oldenburg found that even courtesans in the urban center of Lucknow chose to wear the *burqa*, a head-to-toe covering, outside their salons because it gave them similar freedom, in effect appropriating "the power of the gaze."[21]

Cloaking hidden mysteries and secrets of the trade is common in most courtesan cultures, and the captivating theatricality and evanescence of music and dance performance serves that objective well. In many courtesan traditions—particularly those of *tawā'if*s in India and geishas in Japan—courtesans live together in a separate, exclusive inner community dominated by women and out of the reach of the male clientele.[22] In these communities, courtesans are experts, not only in the arts of music and dance, but also in the arts of pretense, feigning love and affection, shyness, or injury to charm clients out of their money. *Nacnī*s are somewhat different in that they have no separate, cohesive, female-dominated community. There is no inner place where they gather, no pleasure quarters, no salon. And there is no transient client to be parted from his money.

Though a social "outsider," a *nacnī* physically lives within her keepers' household, or in some cases with her keeper in a separate household. She may stay with him for six months or for most of her adult life, as Kistomani stayed with Dube, but if she is lucky, she won't be without a keeper for long. Her keeper, her "husband," serves as her performance partner, her manager, and her protector. He is what distinguishes her from the common prostitute (*randī*, "pro"). She may be symbolically, or essentially, married to the god Krishna, but as a *rasikāin* (female *rasikā*) she requires a male *rasikā* as a partner. The *nacnī* performance tradition is fundamentally about couples. In this sense, *nacnī*s are more integrated into the patriarchal world than either *tawā'if*s or geishas.

In my experience, *nacnī*s do not consider their keepers to be clients, but "husbands" and partners. These days, with landlord patronage disappearing fast, both *nacnī* and *rasikā* struggle equally as a team to scrape together a subsistence living from their performances as long as they are together. Typically, what breaks them apart is infidelity, or his desire to keep an additional *nacnī* or to marry socially, or her move to a more accomplished performer or manager. While *nacnī*s and *rasikā*s certainly manipulate their relationships to their best advantage, none of the *nacnī*s I interviewed spoke of the kind of feigned routines of manipulation documented by others who have studied courtesan cultures, not even about former, abusive keepers, not even in secluded women-only conversations.

KNOWING THE INSIDE

*Nacnī*s' performative *bahānā* is also different from the fantasy theater of the geishas, who by all accounts see their performance persona, their "business face," as distinct from "the real me."[23] For *nacnī*s there is no aesthetic distance between themselves and Radha. I believe this is why miming story lines, which is so central to classical Indian dances, is nearly absent from *nacnī* performance. For the same reason, they don't feign love, or perhaps they are reticent to represent themselves as someone who would. Their own experience of Radha's *bhāv*, her single-minded devotion, love, abandon, and transcendent joy, is central to their identity and power. Communicating that experience, creating it in *rasikā*s and in the audience, is the artistic objective of their performance. All *rasikā*s and *bakht*s (devotees) aspire to experience what the *nacnī*-Radha does. By composing and singing songs in Radha's voice, the *rasikā* seeks to become the ideal devotee himself, a task considered more difficult for men, especially those of high caste, than for women, children, or the low caste.[24]

This experience, aesthetically coded as *ras*, is the "essential," inner truth or understanding that is the privilege of Radha and the *nacnī*. Janki Devi explained it to me this way:

CAROL: Is there any special place for Krishna in the heart of *kalākār* [artist]?[25]

JANKI: There is! That's why we have no shame. We show our art with an open heart. . . . What will happen? We won't open our clothing! . . . As much joy as we will take, that much we will give. Our hearts will be overjoyed.

*Nacnī*s and *rasikā*s believe, as do professional musicians in general in Jharkhand, that only they have access to a true understanding of this hidden, inner essence by virtue of their god-given *kismat* (good fortune, fate), *śaktī* (power, specifically female in nature), and *diwāṅs* (grace).[26] Janki continued:

JANKI: We people make a different type of love or of talking. Other women are women, but we are not like that type of woman.

CAROL: *Kalākār*s? You're talking about *kalākār*s?

JANKI: I don't know about others, but I know the matter of my heart. Just as we decorate a song, as we bring *ras*, like that our heart . . .

MUKUND: . . . like that, we make *śriṅgār*-love [erotic, romantic, aesthetic]. *You* know [looking at Janki and laughing].

JANKI: Yes [looking back at him and laughing], *you* know.

A *rasikā*, Umacharan Mahto, said of his *nacnī*, Mangala Devi, "No woman has a *man* [heart-mind] like this. [Even if] you neither talk to her nor love her, the meaning of all is still known to her."[27] And here is an even more cryptic observation from Kistomani: "Whoever really understands *nacnī* dance, that person will *know!*"[28]

Finally, here is a lesson about illusion and seeing beyond it—knowing—from a *rasikā* and fine singer, Bhondo Ram Patar, then the "husband" of the *nacnī* Somwari Devi. Patar told his story in Hindi for my benefit, but sang the song in the Pancpargania language:[29]

> The poet Ram Krishna Ganguli, the composer of songs, you must have heard his name. He was a Brahman of a good family, whom people considered high caste. We licked the sand of his feet [i.e., showed him deference]. He was a big fan of *jhumar* [one of the *nacnī* genres]. He had a *nacnī*, too. Kings, emperors, and all the landlords [i.e., Rajputs] had begun to say [to him], "You are a great Brahman of a good family, from whom we take the sand. Being such a man, you [nevertheless] are moving around and dancing with a simple *nacnī*. If you do such vulgar work, we won't accept you as a *guru* [i.e., as a teacher, spiritual leader]. [He replied,] "The people respected me at the *rāj darbār* [king's court]. If it's bad, then I shouldn't have been respected." One day he invited all the kings and emperors, landlords, and literate people to his home. After inviting them all, he said, "All right, I will obey your word. [But] I want to sing. I want to sing one thing." At that very moment, he quickly composed a song. Bhuneshwar Babu [Patar turns to Bhuneshwar Mahto, who was present], you must have heard this from others:

bhramarā jānye kamal mādurī	The Black Bee knows the sweetness of the lotus.
se to tāhāre cāe go	Like that, he wants you.
sai raso biraso moṇḍūko tāe	The frog is near that very *ras*,
nikaṭe ṭhākī nā pāe go	But he doesn't perceive (experience) it.
āī chūnna prem kī gūṛha maram	Oh, choose the secret of love, the inner meaning.
sakhī sakale ki jāne tāe go	Oh friend, how will (can) everyone know that?

> *Maṇḍūk* means the frog who lives under the lotus plant. That frog is nearby, but he doesn't get the taste [of the lotus]. The Black Bee comes from the jungle [far away] and takes the juice of that [lotus] and goes back. They [the Brahman's visitors] said, "This is something we didn't know. Now we shall not object to you." . . . Superior musical training is a weightier thing than anything, and bigger than all. But only if the people will know, only then. Only if they will have the capacity to know, only then.

In this parable, the poet Ganguli, although a Brahman, has the insight of a *rasikā* (a connoisseur), an insight that he shares with the narrator, who also happens to be the keeper of a *nacnī*.[30] Both are able to see through layers of illusion to taste the hidden meaning. As our friend Bhuneshwar Mahto later explained, the frog in this song represents the "general" Brahman (an analogy also found in the ancient Vedic texts) and all others who are trapped inside society. True understanding, the secret of love, the inner sweetness of the lotus (Radha, the *nacnī*) are concealed from him by a curtain of illusion, the water. The Black Bee (Krishna), however, flies freely outside the constraints of society, and so he is better able to reach the sweet essence hidden inside the lotus. In *bhakti* thought, that freedom is associated with being literally "outside" the village, in the forest, in nature. There are also some typical *bhakti* reversals at play here. Nature's simple bee, responding to the sweetness of the lotus, has greater access to its esoteric knowledge than does the learned frog trapped under the water. In the imagery of the song, what others might call the "outside" world (out of society, out of the village) is clear, expansive, and lofty, while the society's "inside" world is obscured below in the shadows of illusion.

The sexual allusions and imagery of water in Patar's parable are also significant for other reasons. Sexual activity, especially outside of marriage, has strong associations with water. As my research assistant Mukund Nayak liked to say (in English), "Radha and Krishna were soluble. Krishna was like water, and Radha was like sugar."[31] In rural India, water, in the form of the monsoon rains, is associated with the fertility of nature and crops. So, sexual union, when it is defined as "outside," may be unchaste and antisocial, but it is also powerfully auspicious in bringing good fortune and fertility. From the perspective of *bhakti*'s "inside" understanding, there is no real contradiction. The auspiciousness of the *nacnī* is simply independent of, or outside of, her social status, and necessarily so. Hence the association of *nacnī* performances (and her public sexuality) with occasions of fertility: weddings, births, and spring festivals that precede and coincide with planting. And perhaps this explains the "juiciness" of the *ras* of her performances, especially those that take place during the dry, hot months preceding the June monsoon. For this reason, too, *devadāsīs* are dedicated to temples in neighboring Orissa, and the *outside* walls of those temples are decorated with erotic sculptures.[32]

In the sections that follow, I will explore two sides of the *nacnī*'s discursive, performative play with illusion, with turning the "outside" inside out: her dance around and between male and female genres, and her discursive stretching of the curtain of performance to reveal her own voice.

DANCING BETWEEN THE LINES
〜

I became familiar with Jharkhand's segregated male and female village community dancing during my earlier research projects in 1981 and 1983–84, long
before I began my research with the *nacnī*s. In that earlier research, I observed and participated in gendered dance events of both of the two major,
regional linguistic-musical traditions in Jharkhand: Nagpuri in the west and
central regions and Pancpargania in the east. What they had in common was
the segregated gendering of dance and therefore of musical genres. In my
mind, these male and female songs and dances existed in separate, discrete
universes, each associated with different rituals, contexts, places in the village,
drums and drumming patterns, and movements. During my research on the
*nacnī*s in 1993, I slowly began to see men's and women's dance as interconnected by the *nacnī* herself in some interesting ways. In the course of her life,
she moves from one to the other, spending her childhood performing wom-
en's songs and dances and her adulthood, beginning around puberty, performing with men as a *nacnī*. She is like a line of communication between
the two, in effect constructing the men's genre in relation to the women's. In
her own performance, she subtly blends the two, fixing herself performatively
somewhere in between, or perhaps reducing the two to a single *ras.*

In both Nagpuri and Pancpargania stylistic regions, the "general" population marks its song/dance genres for gender, though in different ways. In the
Pancpargania and adjacent areas of Bengal, men and *nacnī*s perform *jhumar*
songs and dances, though they are not specifically marked as male. Women
sing a particular kind of *jhumar*, called *bhādoria jhumar*, in effect marking
these songs as non-male.[33] In Nagpuri villages, both gendered genres are
marked as such: *mardānā jhumar* (men's *jhumar*) and *janānī jhumar* (wom-
en's *jhumar*). In both regions, women's collective performance by "low-
caste" women in the courtyards of their homes is associated with rituals of
fertility, especially tree worship, in which women ensure the good fortunes of
their crops, households, and male relatives. Men's song/dance performance,
which is solo or in small, loose groups in Pancpargania communities and
collective in Nagpuri, is properly accompanied by a *nacnī* and so takes place
at weddings, births, festivals associated with Krishna, and night-long entertainments. I say "properly" because I have attended a *mardānā jhumar* dance
held in a Nagpuri village at the time of a tree worship ritual in which there
was no *nacnī*. However, as I moved around the men in the dancing ground,
tape recording and taking photos, I became uncomfortably aware that the

men were singing to and for me, as if I were the *nacnī* at the event. As one musician put it to me, "the *nacnī* completes men's *jhumar*."

Nagpuri dance events are the only ones in which *nacnī*s perform with a group of men, and Nagpuri genres are also the most clearly marked for gender linguistically and stylistically. Such a clear dichotomy raised questions in my mind: Are men's and women's *jhumar* songs and dances essentially gendered, apart from contextual associations? Does the presence of a *nacnī* confuse the gender identity of the dance and songs? How is her own, performed gender identity influenced by the gendering of dance and songs? Nagpuri men's and women's *jhumar* performances merited a closer look.

Nagpuri *jhumar* songs, regardless of their gender, are composed to flexible, conventional melody types that carry traditional or newly composed texts. In both cases, singers and poets adjust the melody types slightly to fit the words. Men's and women's *jhumar* each have their own, unique set of melody types. In the past, these melody types moved with the passage of time at a dance, with a type for each period of the night, but few singers today know the complete repertory of either genre. Still, most can readily recognize the gender identity of any given song, even when performed in solo stage performances, where either genre may be sung by men or women. The identification may be to some extent a matter of convention; these gendered repertories are not distinguished in any necessary way by their melodic materials. Both share scales and melodic contours and the conventions of verses that begin high and descend and refrains that undulate in a lower range.

What does more often shape their gendered musical identities in village performance, and even on the stage, is the distinct rhythmic character of each genre and its drum accompaniment. Men's (thus, *nacnī*s') songs and dances are accompanied by *dholak* and *nagāṛā* drums, the former a wooden, double-headed barrel-shaped drum played with the hands, and the latter a large kettledrum with buffalo-hide head, played with sticks. The *dholak*, with its clear, loud, sharp, rapping sound, leads the ensemble of drummers. Women's *jhumar* does not require a drum at all, but when a drummer is present, he plays a *māndar*, a large barrel-shaped drum made of clay, its heads held with a tight, close network of lacing. The sound of a *māndar* is softer, more diffuse, and more varied than that of the *dholak*; its high tones are ringing and "sweet," as drummers say. The drumming patterns associated with each genre, and therefore the metric character of the songs, are perhaps the most salient mark of their difference. The majority of men's *jhumar* songs march along with a duple subdivision of the beat, while the majority of women's songs have a lilting triple subdivision. There are exceptions in both cases, but every men's *jhumar* song I have heard in the dancing ground has conformed to the duple subdivision; it is the rhythm that best reflects the men's bouncing, jumping dance steps.

Recorded in dancing ground performances, Examples 2.1 and 2.2 provide us with characteristic exemplars of Nagpuri men's and women's *jhumar* songs. The men's *jhumar* song (Ex. 2.1) is the one that Kistomani and her old friends performed at the *mahfil*, the song I quoted at the beginning of this chapter. The composed text, "signed" Anand in the last stanza, identifies the poet with the voice of Radha. When the *nacnī* sings in Radha's voice on stage, the words are not of her own creation. I never found a stage song that was composed by a *nacnī*. Janki Devi, an ex-*nacnī* and now a stage singer, told me she had composed songs "in her mind" and hoped that her social husband would write them down for her. Like most *nacnīs*—and quite unlike classical courtesans like *tawā'ifs*—Janki does not read and write. Song composition today is increasingly a literate practice, effectively limiting it to *rasikās*. Most male singers keep handwritten "songbooks" of texts that they have collected, learned, or composed.

I have transcribed only the general outlines of these songs in the excerpts found in Examples 2.1 and 2.2, both at a common relative pitch. The small

EXAMPLE 2.1. *Mardānā jhumar* song, recorded in Sanga village, 14 June 1993

Refrain:

Verse:

Tāl (drumming pattern):

EXAMPLE 2.2. *Janānī jhumar* song, recorded in Pundag village, 18 September 1984

details, melodic turns, and elaborations vary considerably from verse to verse and singer to singer. The group of men who performed Example 2.1 that night in Sanga village exhibited more individual variation than did the larger group of women who sang Example 2.2 in penetrating unison. I recorded this women's *jhumar* song at a tree-worship ritual called *jitia* in Pundag village in September 1984. The men in Sanga had sung men's *jhumar* for only part of the night, and they varied their melody type from song to song. By contrast, the women of Pundag, myself among them, sang this same women's *jhumar* melody type all night long, recalling traditional texts and extemporizing new ones. Compare the following brief couplet of Example 2.2 with the text of Example 2.1 at the beginning of this chapter:

REFRAIN:

raūra lagīna ekādasī karalī re	I did the eleventh day [went through fasting] for you.
kā dose rājā māralī	For what fault, my king [husband] did you beat me?

VERSE, REFRAIN:

na me [ham] coranī, na hame [hama] caṭanī	I'm neither a thief nor a glutton,
kā dose rājā māralī	For what fault, my king, did you beat me?

The identities of the women singing are at one with the complaint of the couplet. Most of the texts they sang that night were similar, commentaries of their own creation in which women spoke to men and to themselves, about themselves, in their own voices. This is a song about confrontation, not coupled love. It is the song of "socially" married women, not of a courtesan free of society's bonds.

There were no drummers present for most of the Pundag women's night of singing, but the rhythmic character of the women's *jhumar* drumming pattern (*tāl*) is reflected in their song and especially their dance style.[34] The eight beats of the pattern (see Ex. 2.2), like the song's melody, skip along in gentle, triple subdivisions. We danced in a line, hip-to-hip, holding each other closely by the hand held at waist level. We moved along as one body, walking to our right, pausing, moving back to our left, hopping slightly, advancing again. Our hips swayed, and the whole line undulated forward and back, our clasped hands moving up and down with our bodies. Our feet stayed beneath our bodies, moving in unison like the legs of a centipede. I made good friends with these women by dawn.

The *tāl* and melodic rhythm of the men's *jhumar* song (Ex. 2.1) are in sharp contrast. In the dancing ground, the even, duple subdivisions of the beat were each marked by loosely coordinated bouncing, made possible because the men were holding each others' hands with arms hanging at their sides in the spaces between them. They advanced around the circle in large steps and jumps, stopping to raise their arms, pumping them gently from the shoulder, then advancing again without retreating in the other direction.

In my early attempts to understand what might be gendered about *jhumar*s, I questioned whether my objective observations about the rhythmic character of the music and dances were significant and whether these differences were really understood in terms of gender. When I asked musicians, male and female, what was male about one and female about the other, they invariably answered in terms of movement, even when I specifically (persistently and creatively, I thought) tried to direct their attention to sound. Even more interesting, their responses varied with their different, embodied experiences of the two dances. When speaking about their "own" gender's dance, both men and women spoke in rich, nuanced terms. Men called their *jhumar* thick, heavy, big, brave, heroic, jumping, running. Women referred to theirs as elastic, springy, bending, dance-like. But when they spoke only from observation about the "other's" *jhumar*, both men and women fell on simplistic, dualistic stereotypes. Men described women's *jhumar* as soft and sweet; women described the men's as hard. In this respect, their understandings of *jhumar*s were certainly gendered, based on their differently embodied—and disembodied—experiences of each. It seems that those who initially responded to my questions about gender differences with a dismissive "men do one, and women do the other" had gotten right to the heart of the matter.

The participation of the *nacnī* in men's *jhumar* might seem at first glance to muddy these neat gender codes, but her subtle accommodations to the men's style ultimately reconcile the differences. In crossing over from the women's dancing ground to the men's, a *nacnī* must refashion her vocal technique. "General" men and women all sing as high as possible in their vocal ranges, forcefully projecting their voices over the pounding drums. But *nacnī*s, like the great *tawā'if* singers, sing lower in their range, in unison with the *rasikā*s' high voices. In performances, it can be difficult to distinguish which is which. Her adjustment to the men's vocal range is ironic, given the "voice" of the song, but it effectively strips the performance of audible, timbral difference, replacing it with a singular identity and iconically underscoring the message, the *ras*. But the *nacnī* alone makes the accommodation, in effect capitulating to a man's timbral world, following his lead.

Her movements follow as well, though differently in Pancpargania and Nagpuri styles. In the Pancpargania dancing ground, a *rasikā* actually leads his *nacnī* around the arena, determining when she changes direction, when she spins, and how many times; he may link arms with her for long periods of time to enact their romantic union. She watches and responds. In Nagpuri style, a *nacnī* dances independently of any specific man, "free" and from her "own mind," as Kistomani put it.[35] Kistomani was once one of the most skilled Nagpuri *nacnī*s in "matching" the steps of the man leading the dance line and the style and pattern of the lead *dholak* player, but she pointedly said she did not "follow" anyone. In her prime, she boasted, she once matched the steps and styling of sixteen different men in one night who had come just to see how good she was. Even at the *mahfil*, in her old age and deaf in one ear, she articulated perfectly the accents of the drumming pattern with her body, subtly pumping her shoulders or sinking into her knees at just the right moment. But she moved her body more smoothly than the men, using smaller steps, bending forward and back, swaying her hips, moving her upper and lower torso in opposite directions, gracefully tracing her body movements with her hands. In other words, the style of her movements was distinctly *janānī*, female, though they rhythmically matched the men's movements. In this sense, her dance reconciled the two gendered styles, the "hard" and the "soft." Her women's *jhumar* dance styling "completed" the male genre, or rather helped construct it as male, just as her free and "public" sexuality surely did as well. In the context of our conversation about what was "male" or "female" about *jhumar*, Kistomani observed, in an obvious reference to her own style in relationship to the men's, "There is no need of strength in dance. One dances with the system. *Bhāv* [internal sensibility] will dance. Why shall I use strength?" The identity, crafted by the Nagpuri *nacnī* in performance, lies somewhere between the conventional, "general" male and female, blurring stereotypical distinctions. Her voice and dance rhythms are "harder," while her bodily movements are "softer." Or perhaps she simply transcends those distinctions, reducing all to the expression of herself as the embodiment of *ras* and *bhakti*.

Kistomani's old *zamīndārī* (landlord) style of performance is rapidly fading, and the numbers of *nacnī*s are decreasing as new performance opportunities are opening for them in solo stage performance as singers, without dance. In 1993, most women who performed on the stage were *nacnī*s, former *nacnī*s, daughters of *nacnī*s, or "kept" women who had chosen the stage over life as a public dancer. Without dance, however, even the *nacnī*s were not marked as such. Janki Devi was the first to exploit this new opportunity. Her identity as a singer rather than a *nacnī* made her move "inside" caste possible. Gradually, the old songs have lost their gendered identities as well. On stage, the gendered genres can be sung by everyone and in no particular order; they, too, have become unmarked for gender. Still, *rasikā*s have continued to regard women who know men's *jhumar* songs as closet *nacnī*s, so most women, *nacnī*s or not, have retreated to the safety and unambiguous identity of women's *jhumar*. The stage represents yet another opportunity for *nacnī*s to remake themselves, to remain performers without the social stigma, so it is not surprising that when trained, costumed troupes brought the gendered village dances to the urban stage, *nacnī*s declined to participate. Without them, the style and aesthetic of staged men's *jhumar* dance has become quite different from that of the Sanga dancing ground. On stage, young men have transformed it into a virile, heroic, martial dance, whose movements are larger, sharper, stronger, and "harder" than in the village dancing ground. The contrast between the men's *jhumar* of the stage, without the *nacnī*, and that of the Sanga dancing ground is testimony to the artistic power of the *nacnī* to draw all into her ambiguous, illusive, performative play with gender. In urban areas, the *launda*, the female impersonator, is rapidly replacing the *nacnī* with his theatrical, mimed parody of her dance. His illusion is only as deep as his costume; the aesthetic distance between him and his mimed character is obvious to all.

INTOXICATING PERFORMANCE

⁓

> See the two flowers in bloom.
> Oh Lotus, you will say later,
> Don't lose control of your emotions.

Oh Black Bee, think!
Or you'll break the green stems.[36]

The path to inner knowledge that *nacnīs* and *rasikās* seek opens to them only through exhilaration and abandon, through losing their bearings and "flying free, like a leaf," as Janki Devi put it. Boundless, uncontainable performance is the ideal vehicle. *Nacnīs* and their partners liken it to intoxication or madness, dangerous but enlightening. Their all-night performances recreate the boundless, dreamy love-play of Radha and Krishna that transcends time and society. After performing outdoors for my video camera and curious villagers in the middle of the day, the *nacnī* Mangala Devi explained to me why it hadn't pleased her: "During the day I felt ashamed to dance. Don't you, during the day? I can shake any part of my body, but in the daytime . . . shame. Night is better. In the day, also, shame doesn't come, but . . . just as intoxication comes from drink after some time, like that in music, too, when we start doing something, gradually the speed of the dance, the freeness develops, and *then* I feel no shame. It's easier to get at night."[37]

The curtain of night gives performers the illusion of being cloaked, out of view of society's "inside." In my experience, though, large public performances allow little space for the *nacnī* to play with the illusory, discursive power of performance, to manipulate its veil to conceal or reveal according to her own design. In the course of my research, such moments happened out of the arena, in informal gatherings that were as much conversations as song performances. Outside the performance arena, *nacnīs* and their partners were free to turn the voice of their songs to their own purposes, to say what they otherwise couldn't or wouldn't. For example, Kistomani answered my questions about Krishna with snatches of memories of her beloved Dube and songs that in retrospect seem to be more about him than the god:[38]

prem kare morile kālā	You were dying for love, Oh Dark One [Krishna],
āmāe preme dile dārūṇ jālā	You gave me great worries in love.
prem kare mañjile kālā	You trained me for love, Oh Dark One,
āmāe preme dile dārūṇ jālā	You gave me great worries in love.
āmi abalā jānī na cholā	Knowing I'm a powerless woman, don't cheat me
din mañjhāre go	In the middle of the day.
koto kāṅdibo, kāṅdibo koto	How much shall I weep, how much shall I weep?
tumār tole go,	Under your power,
koto kāṅdibo, koto kāṅdibo	How much shall I weep, how much shall I weep?

Another *nacnī* and her partner, under the pretext of explaining a song to me, carried on an animated conversation with each other in the voices of the divine couple. At some point, their own concerns took over as they argued about his decision to take a social wife, all of it still in the voices of Radha and Krishna.

One of the most memorable performative leaps out of convention and formality occurred during a party held at my research assistant's house in Ranchi city to mark the end of my research.[39] We had invited three *nacnīs* and two *rasikās* to join us: two younger women, one with her young *rasikā*, and Kistomani with her favorite *rasikā*, Jaimangal Singh. Some time around 1:30 A.M., when the younger performers were extremely drunk, the party began dancing in the Pancpargania style in the courtyard. As half the neighborhood peered around the walls of the compound, Jaimangal Singh launched into an only half-playful warning in a Pancpargania *jhumar* tune, obviously directing his words to the young *rasikā* Lakhicharan Mahto:

> *One bottle, neither this nor that [happens],*
> *Two bottles, you get drunk,*
> *Three bottles, just think what happens.*

Lakhicharan struggled to catch the song. His *nacnī*, Chaiti Devi, jumped in, picked up the song and launched her voice into a high, elaborate, improvisatory flourish of music and movement that carried her own commentary:

> *One bottle, neither this nor that,*
> *Two bottles, you forget all troubles,*
> *[she stopped and thought for a moment]*
> *Three bottles, I will put myself in my husband's [Krishna's] hands,*
> *And be conquered by him.*

The drummer, also quite drunk, favored her by joining in on the *dholak* drum, moving everybody to dance, and the other young *nacnī* to join the song. Chaiti repeated the above lines, both outsinging the elderly *rasikā* and cleverly outwitting and out-moralizing him by invoking her identity as Radha. She turned common drunkenness into Radha's rapture of abandon for Krishna: "Oh Swami [master teacher], you conquered me." Her young *rasikā* made another attempt to sing, but again didn't get far. After an awkward pause, Jaimangal responded:

> *One bottle, neither this nor that,*
> *Two bottles, you get pleasure,*
> *Three bottles, you are so drunk,*
> *What will you be able to do?*

Chaiti's response was musically and poetically definitive, with an improvisatory cascade that was higher and longer than the last:

> *Oh friend, one bottle, neither this nor that,*
> *Two bottles, you get drunk,*
> *Three bottles, you get pleasure,*
> *[she stopped again to think]*
> *I put myself in my husband's hands,*
> *Three bottles, I'm intoxicated.*

This illiterate, by birth "low-caste," by profession "out-caste" *nacnī* invoked the literate, male poet's transcendent "intoxication" to "defeat" him, though he was a much older, educated, and respected "upper-caste" gentleman. Only in this setting, under the cover of performance and the timeless night, could she challenge him so. Chaiti controlled this song and a couple more until the singers and drummer had exhausted the songs and themselves, and then she left the dancing ground to the old *rasikā* and Kistomani.

CONCLUSION

The *bahānā* of performance has the potential to empower *nacnī*s because it recognizes neither social boundaries nor the neat dichotomies of the societal "inside" that keep her out. Her performance both exposes her and covers her in mystery, and that play with illusion is her objective. For me, wading in the layers of illusion with *nacnī*s has been at times frustrating, but always fascinating, inviting me to look in the mirror of the lotus pond to consider my own, complexly gendered identities in Jharkhand and in the academy. I have explored this at length elsewhere,[40] so I will simply say here that I, too, was unexpectedly, perhaps inevitably, drawn into the *nacnī*s' play with the *bahānā*, the illusion of gender. In our desire to get close to *nacnī*s, Mukund and I often invoked my pseudo-*nacnī* identity: unmarried, traveling outside society, outside caste, a life devoted to music and dance, and playing bamboo flute, Krishna's (a man's) instrument. At the same time, he insisted that I not take up *nacnī* dancing myself, though the idea often tantalized me, since some might think he was my *rasikā*. *Nacnī*s are recruited from his caste, the Ghasi caste of professional drummers, often by force, and he had vowed never to exploit women in such a way. Mukund didn't want to be mistaken for a "high-caste" "keeper."

The limits of my imagined affinity with *nacnī*s became crystal clear in a private, "women's" conversation that a friend and I organized with three *nacnī*s in my hotel room, neutral ground, outside society, just before the farewell party. For the first time, these women spoke frankly about their personal lives with their partners. They told tragic tales of beatings, rape, and attempted suicides that left us all in tears. I finally gave up my naive illusions about our common bond, and rather helplessly observed, "This *nacnī* life is really very difficult, with much sorrow, isn't it?" At that point, one of the women turned the tables on me once again: "This isn't a matter of *nacnī*s, Carol, this is a matter of women. Look at your life; is it so good? Where's your husband, where are your children?" Just when I thought I was looking through clear water, a *nacnī* stirred the pond again.

NOTES
〜

This chapter is based on research I conducted for seven months in the spring of 1993, funded by a senior research fellowship from the American Institute of Indian Studies. I want to express my thanks to Bhuneshwar Mahto and Nandlal Nayak for transcription assistance and to Mukund Nayak for research assistance, transcription and translation assistance, and so much more.

1. Field trip collection, 1993; Video tape no. 11 (hereafter: V93[11]), 13 June 1993, Song #19, Sanga Village.
2. Kistomani herself died in early 1997.
3. Dube was of high caste, a Brahman, while Kistomani was by birth a Chirkuta, a cultivating caste of moderately low status. I use the word "general" as *nacnī*s do to refer to normative society and socially married women.
4. Field notes, 23 May 1993.
5. There is also another "courtesan" performance tradition in this area, called *bāī nāc* (or *bāī* dance), a solo entertainment by a woman to classicized songs and instruments. *Bāī* dance probably developed from *nacnī* dance and appears to have never been connected to the courts. It is also less integrated into ritual community life. Some women dance as both *nacnī*s and *bāī*s, though Kistomani never did.
6. Field notes, 17 June 1993. Jaimangal Singh is from a former landlord family that included many men who had kept *nacnī*s.
7. Field notes, 7 June 1993.
8. Field notes, 22 March 1993.
9. Field notes, 27 July 1993.
10. C. Mackenzie Brown, "The Theology of Radha in the Puranas," in *The Divine Consort: Radha and the Goddesses of India,* ed. John Stratton Hawley and Donna Marie Wulff (Boston: Beacon, 1982), 70.
11. For more information on normative gender relations in this region, see Lina Fruzzetti, *The Gift of a Virgin: Women, Marriage, and Ritual in a Bengali Society* (Delhi: Oxford University Press, 1990).
12. Frederique Apffel Marglin, *Wives of the God-King: The Rituals of the Devadasis of*

Puri (Delhi: Oxford University Press, 1985), 60, and Saskia C. Kersenboom-Story, *Nityasumangali: Devadasi Tradition in South India* (Delhi: Motilal Banarsidass, 1987).

13. Lila Abu-Lughod, *Veiled Sentiments: Honor and Poetry in a Bedouin Society* (Berkeley and Los Angeles: University of California Press, 1986), 159–67, and see Leila Ahmed, *Women and Gender in Islam* (New Haven: Yale University Press, 1992), 15.

14. Virginia Danielson, "Moving toward Public Space: Women and Musical Performance in Twentieth-Century Egypt," in *Hermeneutics and Honor: Negotiating Female "Public" Space in Islamic/ate Societies,* ed. Asma Afsaruddin (Cambridge, Mass: Center for Middle Eastern Studies, Harvard University, 1999), 116, 120–21; Susan Auerbach, "From Singing to Lamenting: Women's Musical Role in a Greek Village," in *Women and Music in Cross-Cultural Perspective,* ed. Ellen Koskoff (Urbana: University of Illinois Press, 1989), 25–44; and Hiromi Lorraine Sakata, "Hazara Women in Afghanistan: Innovators and Preservers of a Musical Tradition," in *Women and Music,* ed. Koskoff, 85–96.

15. See Karen Jo Torjesen, "Martyrs, Ascetics, and Gnostics," in *Gender Reversals and Gender Cultures* (London: Routledge, 1996), 79–91, and Ellen Koskoff, "The Sound of a Woman's Voice: Gender and Music in a New York Hasidic Community," in *Women and Music,* 213–24.

16. Field notes, 18 May 1993.

17. V93(6), 9 May 1993. Janki Devi told me the story of "Krishna's touch" in more detail. To paraphrase: Once Radha hid Krishna's flute in her clothing. To get it back, Krishna invented the *khodnī* (female tattooer) and took her form, as a pretense for moving close to Radha. In this way, he found the hidden flute and took it back and thus began the practice of tattooing (V93[9], 7 June 1993).

18. Liza Dalby, *Geisha* (Berkeley and Los Angeles: University of California Press, 1983); Abu-Lughod, *Veiled Sentiments*; and Veena Talwar Oldenburg, "Lifestyle as Resistance: The Case of the Courtesans of Lucknow, India," *Feminist Studies* 16 (1990): 259–87.

19. Field trip collection, 1993; Audio tape no. 23 (hereafter: T93[23]A), 22 March 1993.

20. Ann Grodzins Gold, "Purdah is as Purdah's Kept: A Storyteller's Story," in *Listen to the Heron's Words: Reimagining Gender and Kinship in North India* (Berkeley: University of California Press, 1994), 164–67.

21. Oldenburg, "Lifestyle as Resistance," 274.

22. See Oldenburg, "Lifestyle as Resistance"; Dalby, *Geisha*; and Jodi Cobb, *Geisha: The Life, the Voices, the Art* (New York: Alfred A. Knopf, 2000).

23. Cobb, *Geisha,* 57. I think this kind of theatrical distance of actor from character applies more to the *launda,* the female impersonator, though he aspires to the unity of identity that the *nacnī* embodies (Ganesh Ram Sahu, female impersonator, T93[58], 27 June 1993).

24. Ramanujan makes a case for the feminine nature of *bhakti.* His analysis of the stages of life of the female *bhakti* saint suggests many similarities with *nacnī* lives, and even includes "becoming a courtesan and getting her god as her lover" as one possible stage. A. K. Ramanujan, "On Women Saints," in *The Divine Consort,* ed. Hawley and Wulff, 316–24.

25. At this point in our relationship and within earshot of her birth family, both Janki and I were using the word *kalākār* as a euphemism for *nacnī.* Janki had recently left behind her profession and identity as a *nacnī.* Only later, in private, did she begin using the term *nacnī,* though always in the third person. Source: V93(9), 7 June 1993.

26. As it was put by Mukund Nayak and Janki Devi. Source: T93(49)B, 6 June 1993.
27. T93(25)B, 2 June 1993.
28. Field notes, 9–10 March 1993.
29. T93(38)A, 20 May 1993.
30. We can also note here that the song and its story serve to validate the keeping of a *nacnī* in terms that would be acceptable to a learned man of high caste.
31. V93(9), 7 June 1993.
32. Frederique Apffel Marglin, *Wives of the God-King: The Rituals of the Devadasis of Puri* (Delhi: Oxford University, 1985), 95–113. Despite remarkable similarities between Jharkhand's *nacnīs* and the *devadāsīs* of the Jagannath temple in Orissa, I have found no evidence of *devadāsīs* having served in temples in Jharkhand, not even in the Jagannath temple outside the city of Ranchi, though that temple continues to celebrate rituals (such as the cart festival) similar to those of the temple in Puri. Orissa's *devadāsīs* served not only in temples but in palaces whose rulers had political and marriage connections in Jharkhand. It is possible that those more southern courtesan traditions, which almost certainly antedate Jharkhand's *nacnī* tradition, migrated northward with regional rulers and landlords.
33. *Bhādoria* refers to the month of *bhādo,* when many of the important women's tree festivals are held. *Jhumar* derives from the verbal form "to *jhum,*" meaning to move to music, to groove.
34. My transcriptions of the *tāls* represent the rhythmic patterns and mnemonics that drummers use to "speak" drumming patterns. They are composites, including all the cardinal beats of the kettledrum and the *dholak*'s low, left head and some of the filler beats of its high, right head. The mnemonics represent the timbral qualities of strokes and stroke patterns.
35. Field notes, 13 June 1993.
36. V93(8), 3 June 1993, Umacharan Mahto and Mangala Devi.
37. Field notes, 2–3 June 1993.
38. Source: V93(6), 9 May 1993.
39. Source: V93(12), 27 July 1993.
40. Carol M. Babiracki, "What's the Difference? Reflections on Gender and Research in Village India," in *Shadows in The Field: New Perspectives for Fieldwork in Ethnomusicology,* ed. Gregory F. Barz and Timothy J. Cooley (Oxford and New York: Oxford University Press, 1997), 121–38.

CHAPTER THREE

"Fighting in Frills"

WOMEN AND THE *PRIX DE ROME* IN FRENCH CULTURAL POLITICS

Annegret Fauser

IN MARCH 1912, the influential music critic Emile Vuillermoz warned French men that women were on the point of taking over French public life, and that their achievements in the world of music would incite them to even bolder efforts: "The Conservatoire, where they already hold the majority, will end by becoming their personal property, and the classes that are called "mixed" will be those where the presence of two or three mustache-wearers will be tolerated. . . . In the director's office, Gabriel Fauré will be chased from his position by Hélène Fleury or Nadia Boulanger."[1] For music itself this would mean that "female" ways of behavior would determine the genesis of the artwork: fashion would replace creation. When, on 5 July 1913, Lili Boulanger became the first woman to win the French *Prix de Rome* in composition, Vuillermoz commented on this unsettling phenomenon in his article "La Guerre en dentelles" (Fighting in Frills): "A few months ago, in these columns, I warned musicians of the imminence of the 'pink peril': events have not been slow to prove me right. A young suffragette, Mademoiselle Lili Boulanger, has just triumphed in the latest competition of the *Prix de Rome* over all her male competitors and has won on her first attempt the *Premier Grand Prix,* with such authority, speed, and ease as to cause great anxiety to those candidates who have for long years sweated blood and tears striving for this goal."[2]

The awarding of the prize to Lili Boulanger in 1913 brought to fruition what journalists had announced in 1903 as a "great victory of feminism,"[3] the admission of women to the *Prix de Rome* competition. In the ensuing decade, four women played key roles in the process: Juliette Toutain,[4] who entered the competition in 1903 but could not participate; Hélène Fleury, who in 1904 became the first woman to receive a prize, the *Deuxième Second Grand Prix;* Nadia Boulanger, who failed to win the *Premier Grand Prix* in 1908 and 1909, even though on both occasions she was generally acknowledged to have written the best cantata; and her sister Lili Boulanger, who won first prize in 1913.[5] Telling the story of these four composers and their quest for the *Prix de Rome* sheds new light not only on strategies that women employed in order to succeed in the artistic world of fin-de-siècle Paris, but also on that era's dialectical interplay of male and female, its public and private spheres, its aesthetic and artistic conceptions, and the complex mechanisms of its cultural politics. The four women had to challenge the Académie des Beaux-Arts, an institution dedicated to defending the values of French culture, whose members now felt threatened in a new world of changing social, cultural, and political structures. Socialism was among the perceived threats, for it was intimately associated with the emancipation of women.[6] Moreover, the discussion about women and the *Prix de Rome* was inextricably linked with the highly polarized discourse on the antagonistic relationship of France and Germany following the French defeat in 1870. As Edward Berenson aptly puts it, the French concern with gender resulted in large part "from a perceived decline of French power that commentators related to moral decay and to changing relations between the sexes. If France was weak, writers commonly asserted, its weakness stemmed from a growing demographic deficit caused by the emancipation of women, the legalization of divorce, and the emasculation of men."[7] That the "pink peril" was regarded as a challenge not just to male privilege but to French culture itself is clear from the speech delivered by the painter and *académicien* Luc Olivier Merson (1846–1920), who denounced the admittance of women to the *Prix de Rome* in February 1903: "I protest at the innovation of Monsieur le Ministre, which I consider an attack on the moral dignity and, in consequence, the very existence of the Académie, wherein rest the strength and the honor of French Art. . . . The duty of the government should therefore be to consolidate the Académie de France by its powerful protection and to defend it against its many enemies."[8]

THE ACADÉMIE DES BEAUX-ARTS, WOMEN, AND THE *PRIX DE ROME*

~

The "many enemies" to which Merson alluded comprised not only the female interlopers in the competition but also the French government itself, which had forced the change upon the Académie des Beaux-Arts. In this respect, the conflict over the *Prix de Rome* reveals the delicate relationship between the Académie and its "patron," the government.

In 1903, the rapport between the Académie—a rather conservative institution—and the radical, left-wing government of Emile Combes's *Bloc* was strained at best. On 8 February, Joseph Chaumié (1849–1919), minister of Public Instruction, announced at the annual banquet of republican journalists his decision that henceforth women would be allowed to compete for the *Prix de Rome*.[9] Thus it was through the press that the members of the Académie des Beaux Arts first learned that the rules of "their" prize had changed. At first, they were incredulous. A week later tempers began to flare, and in the succeeding conflict over the admission of women to the *Prix de Rome,* two formerly separate questions became intertwined. On the one hand, there was the issue of the delicate balance of artistic independence and political control that defined the relationship between the government and the Académie, which depended upon it financially. On the other, we find the question of the right of women to have access to the Académie des Beaux-Arts and its prizes.

The history of women and the Académie dates back to the *ancien régime,* where female artists such as Elisabeth Vigée Lebrun and Adelaide Labille were full members of the Académie Royale.[10] With the French Revolution and the *Code Napoléon* (1804), French women lost the limited civic rights that at least aristocratic women had previously enjoyed.[11] After 1793, French women of all classes lived totally under the legal tutelage of their fathers, husbands, brothers, or other male relatives. "Republican motherhood" became the sole reason for their existence, and their education consequently had but one goal: to enable them to bring up future French soldiers, workers, and citizens in the best way possible.[12] The Republic gendered the public sphere as masculine after "the fall of the absolutist public sphere" in which "masculinity in and of itself carried some but not vast privileges," and this "structural change of public sphere" necessitated the creation of a counterpart in form of the feminine private sphere, demanding "women's domesticity and the silencing of 'public' women, of the artistocratic and popular classes."[13] The home emphatically developed into the "royaume de la femme,"[14] in which art, and especially music, served to educate children, entertain husbands and guests, and fill women's otherwise idle hours of leisure. Countless books on etiquette enumerated the benefits to women of dilettante musicianship, which if need be might even secure them socially acceptable employment as governesses or private piano teachers.[15] The Paris Conservatoire, founded in 1795, catered to such bourgeois girls by offering them a variety of programs: they could attend women's classes in solfège, harmony, piano, and piano accompaniment, duly chaperoned by their mothers or maidservants. But women musicians were not content with these restrictions: soon other Conservatoire classes opened for them, and they were allowed to join male students in classes such as counterpoint and fugue.[16]

Throughout the nineteenth century, women had to negotiate their space as creative artists within these gendered public and private spheres. In the official world of the arts, the *Prix de Rome* represented a supreme sign of public achievement for a young painter, sculptor, architect, engraver, or composer. The prize brought financial reward—funding for a period of residence at the Villa Medici in Rome—plus public attention and exposure, and artistic honor. Although a cynical attitude toward the prize was *de rigueur*—Debussy's comments are only the most famous—its importance and prestige should not be underestimated.[17] Women made repeated attempts to gain access to what was, throughout the nineteenth century, forbidden territory. The young composer Maria Isambert (*fl.* 1873–1905), for example, had sought admittance to the *Prix de Rome* competition in 1874, but in vain.[18]

Since the *Prix de Rome* was attached to the Académie and any changes in its constitution required governmental approval, the relationship between the government and the Académie was crucial. A strongly conservative institution such as the Académie might collude with a right-wing government to keep the *femme nouvelle* out of the sphere of official art: the more public space ceded to women, ran the argument, the greater the likelihood that they would renounce their assigned role of "republican motherhood" and become sterile *hommesses*.[19] Yet in 1902, the rise to power of Combes's radical party changed the political climate. Three young women, the painter Mademoiselle Rondenay, the sculptor Mademoiselle Rozet, and the composer Juliette Toutain, sought to participate in the 1903 *Prix de Rome.* Each played her cards carefully, writing to the minister in charge of the Académie, the radical politician Joseph Chaumié.[20] In pitting the radical minister against the conservative administration, the three women exploited the new political climate for their own ends. They succeeded for three reasons: the diverging political directions of the radical party and the Académie; the dependence of the Académie on the government; and the personal ambition of the then Directeur des Beaux-Arts, Henri Roujon (1853–1914).

In nineteenth-century France, all artistic matters fell under the aegis of the Direction des Beaux-Arts, headed by the Directeur, an administrative rather than a political figure, who could hold office indefinitely. This system encouraged stagnation and conservative cultural politics, since all ministerial directives were filtered through the office of the Directeur. The relationship between the Académie and the Direction des Beaux-Arts was, then, not just excellent but virtually symbiotic; at the time of the *Prix de Rome* affair, the Directeur des Beaux-Arts, Henri Roujon, was also a member of the Académie. Nevertheless, in the matter of women's enrollment in the *Prix de Rome*, Roujon was not entirely straightforward with the Académie: indeed, he failed to consult the Académie before announcing his decision to admit women to the competition. His justifications for his actions reflect his delicate maneuvering between the left-wing minister Chaumié and the Académie where his loyalty lay. Roujon tried to prevent an open clash between the Académie and the Chambre des Députés, which would have been unavoidable had the former been consulted beforehand. But his actions should also be interpreted in light of the Académie's internal politics. Secrétaire perpétuel Louis Laroumet was close to death, and Roujon would be a serious candidate for his post, especially if he could be seen to help the Académie through an awkward situation. Despite his urging to accept the situation as a *fait accompli,* the *académiciens* dispatched a delegation to the minister to protest "the painful surprise" sprung upon them. The minister's response made it clear, however, that any further resistance was useless and would incur financial retaliation.[21] At this point, the Académie backed down, and the registration of women candidates for the *Prix de Rome* went forward. As for Henri Roujon, he was elected the next permanent secretary on 24 October 1903.

JULIETTE TOUTAIN:
A *BOURGEOISE,* THE CONSERVATOIRE, AND THE WORLD
OF MUSICAL PROFESSIONALISM

~

Whereas the *Prix de Rome* conflict remained an internal affair between the Académie and the government, the story of Juliette Toutain became a public scandal. Her case brings into sharp focus the question of the public appearance of women—the perception of them as well as their self-representation— and its importance for the official recognition of women musicians. Toutain, a *bourgeoise* from a good Parisian family, sought public success as a composer. This was a contradiction in itself, and one that would be a recurring theme in the history of women and the *Prix de Rome.* The social and cultural framework of bourgeois femininity provided a powerful and complex semiotic system of imaginary and legislative structures that created horizons of expectation regarding women's appearance in public. Strict rules of decorum governed the behavior of a woman of good reputation, especially a virtuous young lady of the *bourgeoisie.* These issues certainly played a central role in the scandal surrounding Juliette Toutain; indeed, they made that scandal possible.

The *Prix de Rome* in the early twentieth century consisted of two rounds. In the first, preliminary part, the candidates had to compose a vocal fugue and a chorus accompanied by orchestra set to a poem chosen by the jury.[22] The competitors wrote these pieces while locked away in the Château de Compiègne, thereby precluding external help. Competitors had their own rooms—their *loges*—in which to work and sleep, and they shared their meals and recreation. A jury of specialists, consisting of the six musician members of the Académie at that time and three adjunct jurors, usually well-known composers, selected a maximum of six finalists after hearing their pieces performed. "Those six [or fewer] finalists selected by the music jury in the preliminary round were then given the opportunity to write a cantata on an original text that was chosen in another competition just before its poetry was dictated to the contestants. In the succeeding twenty-five days, each of the composers had to write and orchestrate a prelude and several vocal numbers that normally included airs for soprano, tenor, and bass soloists, as well as a duet and a trio."[23] After these twenty-five days of sequestration and the official deposition of their completed cantatas, the candidates had several weeks to prepare the last stage of the competition: the semi-public presentation of the works at the Académie des Beaux-Arts. Each finalist was responsible for choosing the singers and pianist for his or her cantata, rehearsing them, and conducting the final performance. Thus women candidates in the music competition of the *Prix de Rome* were highly visible, much more so than those in any other branch of the contest. They were seen to conduct, which added to the general problem of judging women candidates in the visual aspect of yet another artistic activity, which was—and still is—a male domain.[24] The self-representation of the women during these performances therefore became an essential ingredient of their success.

On 2 May 1903, the candidates for the *concours d'essai*, the first round of the *Prix de Rome*, were sequestered *en loge* in the Palais de Compiègne. Two women had enrolled: Juliette Toutain, a pupil of Fauré who, after finishing her studies at the Conservatoire in 1902, had campaigned for the admission of women to the *Prix de Rome* in composition; and Hélène Fleury, a student of Charles-Marie Widor. But when Toutain failed to appear for the *entrée en loge*, the competition started without her. The following week, Toutain publicly accused Théodore Dubois, the director of the Conservatoire, of having forced her to withdraw, because he neglected to ensure her good reputation by accommodating her demands. She denounced Dubois's behavior as a deliberate act of exclusion. What, then, had really happened?

The accounts of the participants in the affair differ in some salient details. After Toutain's enrollment, her father, a highly ranked civil servant in the Ministère de la Marine, went to see Théodore Dubois, the director of the

Conservatoire. He sought three provisions that would ensure his daughter could preserve her respectability while locked in a building together with nine young men: only a chambermaid should enter Toutain's *loge* for cleaning; a chaperone should be present at all times; and the women's meals and recreation should be separate from the young men's. In the context of women's status in this period, it is perhaps only logical that Toutain's father should have taken such precautions. Dubois, however, was in Italy, so Jules Toutain met Emile Bourgeat, Dubois's deputy. Here, the stories vary. Dubois and Bourgeat claimed that the first request had already been granted, but that Bourgeat had asked Monsieur Toutain to put his other two requests in writing. According to Bourgeat, Toutain failed to do so.[25]

There is no evidence to confirm whether Toutain's father actually wrote the letter or not. He did maintain, however, that Bourgeat had told him that he would send Toutain's written request to the Direction des Beaux-Arts, together with a recommendation for refusal.[26] Jules Toutain then went to meet Dubois a second time on 28 April. Surprised to hear his story, Dubois asked Toutain why he had not come earlier, and claimed that Bourgeat had neglected to inform him of the earlier visit. In the subsequent discussion, Dubois appeared reluctant to grant Toutain's request for a chaperone, and here Roujon seems to have interfered: "Monsieur Bourgeat added [to his report] that Monsieur Roujon had instructed him not to accept, on the account of the women, any modification of the practices followed in previous years."[27] The spirit of Minister Chaumié's original decision, in which he instructed the Académie to enroll women in the *Prix de Rome,* was deliberately misunderstood by the administration in order to inhibit women's involvement in the competition. In the end, Dubois refused in principle to give any special treatment to women, but agreed to grant the requests if the other competitors would accept a change of practice. Again, we find two differing accounts of the meeting on 28 April: Dubois states that he was cautious only during the discussion, but that he spent the next days arranging the matter; Toutain's father understood that Dubois had refused his request categorically.

On 1 May, Toutain's father wrote a letter in which he announced his daughter's withdrawal.[28] On the morning of 2 May 1903, all the requests were granted, but because Toutain did not appear at the *entrée en loge* (which began that day), it was too late. Clearly, Roujon and Dubois manipulated matters, whether because of their general antipathy to women or as a deliberate attempt to keep Toutain out of the competition: they knew, and could have anticipated, her scruples as a lady with social pretensions.[29] After all, not only had she actively campaigned for the admission of women to the *Prix de Rome* in the first place; she had also garnered a succession of first prizes at the Conservatoire, including that in fugue (the prize for composition) in 1902.

But there might be another reading of how the affair was handled: Toutain was at the point of transgressing the boundary between a *bourgeoise* and a professional composer. It is possible either that her father forbade her participation or that he exploited this conflict and misinformed her unconsciously—or even consciously—so as to keep her within both the limits of good behavior and the space of the salon, which was only semi-public. This space was already occupied by Toutain's mother, who organized one of the lesser-known salons attended by a number of musicians, including Massenet. Here, Juliette could show herself off in a safe social environment without exposure to the public sphere: "At Madame Toutain's, presentation of works by Massenet. . . . Mademoiselle Toutain, whose serious talent is already well known, executed with dexterity the *Improvisations,* fragments of the delicious ballet from *Thaïs,* and the famous *Toccata,* which was a triumph for this very young artist."[30]

Toutain also performed in concerts of the Société Nationale de Musique, another semi-public musical space whose programs were by invitation only. Even the final "public" competitions of the Conservatoire were located in a respected and controlled environment with restricted public access. Toutain's activities prior to her enrollment in the *Prix de Rome* competition were still—if only just—appropriate for a "jeune fille rangée." But by 1903, twenty-five-year-old Toutain was no longer a young girl; if she had continued to compete for the *Prix de Rome,* she would have had to remain unmarried, since the rules demanded that the candidates—male or female—be single. But candidates very rarely won the *Premier Grand Prix de Rome* on their first attempt. Had Toutain chosen to continue the pursuit of the prize, marriage might have been delayed until she was twenty-eight or twenty-nine years old. Her class and upbringing made such a deferral difficult to negotiate, since marriage and motherhood still defined the success story of a *bourgeoise.*[31]

Whatever the reasons, Toutain's exclusion from the first round of the 1903 *Prix de Rome* competition turned into a public scandal when the Toutains received a letter from Théodore Dubois—*after* she had already withdrawn from the competition—in which her requests were granted. Toutain immediately wrote to the Minister of Public Instruction, Joseph Chaumié, and asked for an annulment of the competition, which was already under way.[32] But Joseph Chaumié was away, and his deputy did not wish to take the decision upon himself. By the time the minister returned to Paris, the first round of the competition was over, and an annulment was ruled out. Outraged by this "abuse of power" by both the Conservatoire and the Académie, the Toutain family brought the incident to the attention of the Conseil d'Etat, and after the summer break, on 28 November 1903, it was even discussed in the Chambre des Députés. Such an affront to a highly placed state employee and his family provided moral grounds for their complaint and a guaranteed hearing. Both the Conservatoire and the Direction des Beaux-Arts were construed as guilty in the parliamentary debate.[33] The incident had other consequences as well: at the end of June 1903, Dubois asked the Académie to relieve the Conservatoire administration of organizing the *Prix de Rome*; there had been too much trouble recently, "especially since the admittance of women."[34] As for Toutain, she never did participate in the *Prix de Rome*. She married in March 1904, and apart from occasional appearances as pianist, her reputation was based mainly on her salon, where she received composers such as Saint-Saëns, Massenet, and her former teacher, Fauré.[35]

The official attention that this incident received was mirrored in its press coverage. For one week, such newspapers as *Le Temps, Le Figaro, Le Matin, Le Petit Journal,* and *Le Petit Parisien* published articles on the scandal and interviews with the parties involved. Now, for the first time, Toutain's own voice was heard in interviews and articles.

In her public appearances, Toutain sought to conform to the ideal image of a well-bred young lady. Journalists to whom she granted interviews described her as "amiable, elegant, with a svelte physiognomy and gestures full of grace."[36] A photograph (Fig. 3.1) in the fashionable music periodical *Musica* shows her surrounded by flowers, in a sumptuous evening dress, graciously leaning toward the piano in a self-consciously feminine pose, more the muse that she would eventually become than the composer she sought to be. In his study of the murder trial of Henriette Caillaux, Edward Berenson has analyzed how crucial the outward appearance of a woman was in determining public perception of her character.[37] Physical descriptions of a woman played a key role in newspaper reports, and the iconography of these portrayals was as accessible as that of pictures of saints, due to their relentless repetition in both press and popular novels.[38] These images were also a determining factor in the definition of a woman's public place. Toutain clearly set herself in the sphere of the elegant bourgeois salon through both her demeanor and her appearance, and the journalists translated this into code words that their readers would decipher without difficulty. Svelte grace, amiability, and elegance described the *bourgeoise* "grande dame" of aristocratic aspirations, thus presenting Toutain's class, manners, and social role as that of a "lady of the leisure class."[39]

Toutain's own words echoed these images. In her article for *Musica* from that period, her rhetoric avoids all reference to women's professionalism in the guise of the *femme nouvelle*. Her reasoning presented her as "true woman" of deep emotion. Being a "woman-artist," she claimed, corresponds

Figure 3.1. Portrait of Juliette Toutain, by V. Michel. From *Musica* 1
(1903), 141. Bibliothèque Nationale de France, Cliché 94 B 138 804.

to female nature in a much more essential way than any other—already
practiced—form of study such as medicine because it takes advantage of the
feminine leaning toward sentiment instead of favoring masculine intellect:[40]
"I love these two hyphenated words [women-artists]. The receptive nature
of the woman, her capacity to feel very deeply and very quickly the slightest
things, her gifts of assimilation prove the woman as a being particularly able
to seize and render the beauty of forms and sounds." Women could not be
a threat to men for whom music is a public profession, because "in music as
in anything else, woman maintains such a different personality from man."[41]
Toutain here taps into a well-established concept of "equality in difference,"
which tried to reconcile true republican womanhood with the emancipatory
aspirations of women.[42] Her explicit statement that any competition between

the sexes is but illusion reflects a discourse consciously employed by women to mitigate the perceived danger to the male establishment.[43] Self-deprecation and the denial of a desire to win the prize were principal elements of women's rhetorical repertory. It was a strategy that would be used by the next female *Prix de Rome* competitors as well.[44]

HÉLÈNE FLEURY: PROFESSIONALISM, *CAMARADERIE,* AND UNOBTRUSIVENESS

Juliette Toutain was not the only female participant in the 1903 competition. As noted in *Le Ménestrel,* the very first woman to enroll for the *Prix de Rome* in composition was Hélène Fleury, a student of Charles-Marie Widor: These two contestants provided bemused male journalists with an ideal opportunity to stage their participation as a cat-fight: on the one hand the "mondaine" and "redoutable" Mademoiselle Toutain, on the other Mademoiselle Fleury, "a very kind young woman, tall, with a most intelligent manner and a simplicity that does not exclude distinction."[45] Again, code words place the subject in a specific social context. Fleury emerges as a specimen of a relatively new female breed: the *femme nouvelle,* that is, the young, professional, middle-class woman who strives for social, economic, and political power. Her "intelligent manner" demonstrates her professional aspirations, and her "simplicity" her republican middle-class background.

Indeed, Hélène Fleury came from such a middle-class family. Her father's profession is given as "licencié en droit" in the transcription of her birth certificate, and he is later referred to as a provincial "fonctionnaire."[46] At the time of the 1903 *Prix de Rome,* twenty-six-year-old Hélène Fleury had begun to establish herself as an independent music teacher of middle- and upper-class girls.[47] She had published an organ composition and several piano pieces, among them her "valse de salon" *Espérance* (1897), and according to *Le Monde musical,* she had several pieces performed in concerts of the Société des Compositeurs de Musique and the Société de Musique Nouvelle.[48] Her training at the Conservatoire had only recently begun: she joined Charles-Marie Widor's composition class in 1899. Unlike Toutain—and later Nadia Boulanger—Fleury did not collect the Conservatoire's end-of-year prizes. Instead she had made her name in the Parisian musical world through participating in the more avant-garde Parisian concert life. Nevertheless, the *Prix de Rome* could provide her with both official artistic recognition and, finally, a legitimizing prize.

Although the musical press considered Fleury a serious candidate when she entered the competition in 1903, the general public became aware of her only after the Toutain scandal.[49] Through her professional and unobtrusive demeanor, Fleury proved herself as the ideal female candidate who could be held up as model by those critical of Toutain. Théodore Dubois, for example, pointed out that by presenting herself at Compiègne and thus implicitly trusting the patriarchal authority of the Conservatoire and the Académie, Fleury benefited from all the precautions taken to preserve the good reputation of women candidates. Indeed, correct behavior here consisted in placing faith in the state institutions to care for their "dependents" in the best possible way, rather than in challenging their sense of responsibility as had Toutain and her family. That Toutain might have been right not to rely on Roujon and Dubois was never acknowledged, and Fleury served as living proof of their unimpeachable behavior.

Once the Toutain scandal hit the newspapers, Fleury was trapped. She could either criticize the institutions and go down with Toutain, or she would have to show herself loyal to the Conservatoire and Académie by actively participating in the cat-fight that both the press and the Conservatoire had staged. Although Fleury carefully avoided any direct reference to Toutain, she chose to align herself with the two institutions. It was the only strategy she could adopt if she wished to retain any chance of success in future competitions. In an interview with *Le Petit Journal,* she described her sojourn in Compiègne: "I can only be delighted with everyone. The service of my *loge* was provided by a woman, and she also served my lonely meals. . . . During the first three days, I ate alone in this manner. Then my nine competitors of the stronger sex insisted that I dine at their table, and, what can I say, I capitulated."[50] The interview is interesting not only for its implicit criticism of Toutain—who insisted on taking meals and recreation apart from the men in obedience to good manners—but also for its rhetoric. In order to present herself as unthreatening and feminine, Fleury (or the journal's editor) used the traditional language of courtship in which a woman finally submits to the insistence of a man.

Fleury's unobtrusiveness and professionalism became apparent again when she participated in the competition the following year. Although she seemed intent on keeping a low profile, her picture appeared in several papers after she was admitted to the final round. As in the case of Toutain, these images reflected the persona she tried to convey. In a photograph that shows her with the other competitors in front of the Château de Compiègne, Fleury demurely poses at the edge of the group (see Fig. 3.2). She looks confidently into the camera lens, her sober appearance congruent with countless pictures of other professional women, although the richness of her fur collar and hat identifies her as a lady of some means as opposed to a

Figure 3.2. Portrait of the six candidates for the *Prix de Rome* in 1904, with Hélène Fleury seated on the right. Front page of *Le Monde musical* 16 (1904). Bibliothèque Nationale de France, Cliché 94 B 139 181.

woman of lesser status such as a primary school teacher.[51] Nor would anyone mistake Fleury for a dilettante society lady here. She creates an impression of well-calculated strictness; neither feathers nor other frills draw the observer's attention to her femininity.

Such exemplary behavior merited reward, and in 1904 Fleury found herself with a *Deuxième Second Grand Prix* for a cantata with "expressive declamation" and "skillful instrumentation."[52] She became the first woman in any discipline to be awarded a prize in the *Prix de Rome* competition. But she achieved her success, hailed as the "official triumph of feminism in musical art,"[53] through not only her musical skill but also through her self-representation as a good "republican" woman professional obedient to the Académie and Conservatoire in both the 1903 and the 1904 competitions.

Hélène Fleury had indeed conquered a portion of art's public arena. But it would be seven more years before the first woman—sculptor Lucienne Heuvelmans—would win a *Premier Grand Prix*. Up to this point, Fleury's participation in the *Prix de Rome* followed the usual pattern of successful candidates, in which the crown of the first prize was approached gradually. Contestants would generally participate at least twice if not three to four times, working their way up from admission to the final round, then to winning second prizes and—possibly—the *Grand Prix de Rome* itself. Fleury's next step might lead, for example, to the *Premier Second Grand Prix*.

Whereas in the seven years prior to her prize (1897–1904) Fleury had published only one piece for organ and six for piano, she now brought out seven compositions for various scorings within one year, most of them with Enoch & Cie. Her success encouraged women composers to participate in the *Prix de Rome,* and in the following year she was joined by Marthe Grumbach, a student of Fauré, and Marguerite Audan, like Fleury a student of Widor. None of them, however, moved to the final round. They were in good company: one of the male candidates who failed to reach the next stage was Maurice Ravel, who had won the *Deuxième Second Grand Prix* in 1901. Thus, two former prizewinners were excluded from the competition after the first round. This was unheard of, and suddenly Fleury found herself at the center of the next *Prix de Rome* scandal. As the press reported, "Since the foundation of the *Prix de Rome,* we have never seen permission to compete for the first prize withheld from the second *grands prix* of the previous years."[54]

The party responsible for this astounding breach of tradition is easily identified as Charles Lenepveu, one of the three composition teachers at the Conservatoire and the only Conservatoire teacher involved in the 1905 *Prix de Rome* jury because of his seat in the Académie. All six candidates admitted to the final round were in fact his students. Not a single student of either Widor or Fauré proceeded further in the competition. The focus of the scandal, however, soon shifted from the biased treatment of two candidates—Fleury and Ravel—to concentrate merely on Ravel, the hope of the young male avant-garde. The jury cited faults in his fugue technique as the reason for his exclusion from the final round. Ravel's supporters kept him in the spotlight; they did not bother to extend their outrage to include Fleury's case.[55] Yet one element of Lenepveu's plot to eliminate all but his own students might have been his desire to ensure that no woman candidate would proceed to the final round, and all three women were students of either Fauré or Widor. It would be ironic indeed if Ravel's exclusion was due—at least in part—to Lenepveu's well-known opposition to official recognition of women as composers. In fact, from the moment he stopped teaching the women's harmony class at the Conservatoire because of his accession to the late Ernest Guiraud's composition class in 1894, Lenepveu did not admit a single woman to his course. All his other colleagues (Massenet, Dubois, Fauré, and Widor) regularly had women composition students attending their classes. It appears almost as if Lenepveu wished to purge himself of having taught a female class for several years during the 1880s and 1890s. Preventing women from succeeding in the *Prix de Rome* would certainly have been one way of achieving that aim.

Hélène Fleury did not participate in the *Prix de Rome* competition again. The reasons are not clear, given that she had one more year in which she could compete before turning thirty on 21 June 1906. She did marry, but publications suggest that she did so after 1910. Most probably she lost confidence in the competition and recognized her second prize as the glass ceiling for female contestants. Fleury received at least some official acknowledgement after the scandal, though, when she was asked to compose the official end-of-year competition piece for the viola class of the Conservatoire, possibly a public gesture of support from the new director, Gabriel Fauré.[56]

NADIA BOULANGER:
ARISTOCRATIC BEHAVIOR AND THE RULES
OF THE COMPETITION
~

While Hélène Fleury continued her career as a piano teacher and composer after 1905, receiving less and less public attention, a new female star entered the arena of the *Prix de Rome* in the person of Nadia Boulanger. Already in 1904, Arthur Pougin had mentioned her name in the context of Fleury's success, asking, "Who knows if she will not triumph in the *Grand Prix de Rome* as once did her father?"[57] Sixteen-year-old Nadia had just won three important first prizes at the Conservatoire in a single year: fugue, organ, and piano accompaniment. And, indeed, her next goal was the *Prix de Rome.* After a year of intensive preparation, she entered the competition in 1906, but both women participants of that year—Marthe Grumbach tried her luck again—failed to proceed to the final round. In the next year, 1907, Boulanger was the only female participant among the fourteen candidates, and although she was one of the six to continue to the next stage, she did not receive a prize for her cantata. So far, she was following the usual path of candidates eventually successful in winning the *Prix de Rome.*

In 1908, Boulanger, now twenty years old, entered the next competition. Once again, she was the only woman to participate, together with nine male candidates, and this time she chose to distinguish herself by challenging the Académie. As already mentioned, candidates had to compose a four-part vocal fugue and a short chorus with orchestral accompaniment. Boulanger's setting of the given text—Sully Prud'homme's poem *L'Hirondelle*—conformed with these demands. Her fugue did not.

Each year, the fugue subject was invented by one of the composers of the Académie. Traditionally, the theme would have a rather sedate character. But from time to time, it would be more lively. The subject dictated by Camille Saint-Saëns in 1908, which Nadia Boulanger had to develop in her fugue, fell into the latter category, and its instrumental character inspired her to compose a string quartet instead of a vocal piece. At least, this is what she claimed. According to Léonie Rosenstiel, however, Boulanger's inherent "rebelliousness" partly accounted for this breach of practice.[58] Whatever the reasons, her action precipitated the next *Prix de Rome* scandal.

When on 9 May 1908 Nadia Boulanger arrived with her musicians in the room in which her pieces were to be judged, one member of the jury—probably Camille Saint-Saëns—objected that her fugue should not be allowed to be performed, since it did not adhere to the rules of the competition. The jury decided, however, to listen to Boulanger's pieces first and to settle the problematic issue of the string quartet later. The outstanding musical quality of Boulanger's submissions finally outweighed her transgression of the rules. The jury allowed her to continue with the competition as one of the six finalists, given that the work of the remaining four was not of sufficiently high standard to admit them to the *concours définitif* anyway.

The judgment of the jury was certainly informed by Nadia Boulanger's musicianship and family background, for most of them were friends of the Boulanger family. Other issues may have played some role, however, not least the recent scandal over Ravel's supposedly faulty fugue. Echoes of the public accusations of 1905—that the jury failed to acknowledge the most important (male) avant-garde composer of the time—are found in the wording of their statement regarding Boulanger's string quartet: "While regretting that this contestant had not conformed strictly to the rules, the jury felt that exclusion might perhaps show excessive rigor toward an artist who had just given more than enough proof, as much by this otherwise satisfactory work as by her chorus with orchestra, of her compositional abilities."[59]

Another scandal so soon after the last two in 1903 and 1905 was certainly undesirable, but the jury's hope of preventing one was nevertheless destroyed, presumably by the insulted Saint-Saëns whose fugue subject was implicitly criticized, through Boulanger's composition, as inadequate to its

Figure 3.3. Portrait of the six candidates for the *Prix de Rome* in 1908. Nadia Boulanger is surrounded by Marc Delmas, Edouard Flament, André Gailhard, Jules Mazellier, and Marcel Tournier. Photograph preserved in the Fondation Internationale Nadia et Lili Boulanger, Paris.

purpose. The story of the instrumental fugue was skillfully leaked to the journalists, and the "affaire fugue" made the front pages. Five years after the Toutain scandal, pictures of yet another woman candidate appeared in the press. Even worse, when Gaston Doumergue, the minister of Public Instruction in 1908, received an anonymous complaint—probably from Saint-Saëns—about the jury's decision, he postponed the beginning of the final round for a week in order to give the Académie enough time to sort things out.[60] The Académie defended its decision, and Nadia Boulanger entered the second part of the contest with her co-competitors on 19 May 1908. In a portrait of the six candidates for the *Prix de Rome* in 1908 (Fig. 3.3), Nadia Boulanger appears completely at ease with her comrades, in contrast to Fleury (Fig. 3.2), who appears isolated at the edge of the group. Beforehand, she had tried to set matters right with Saint-Saëns, but in a bitter response he accused her of an ethically questionable act, saying that she had wanted only to "dazzle" the jury with her unusual fugue and was now laughing at their gullibility.[61]

Under the eyes of a curious public, the six settings of the cantata *La Sirène* were judged on 14 July 1908. Henry Roujon, still the Secrétaire perpétuel, presided over both the specialist jury and the general assembly of the Acadé-mie. In the first round of voting by the specialist jury, the *Grand Prix de Rome* went to André Gailhard and thus once again to a student of Lenepveu. For the *Premier Second Grand Prix,* four judges voted in favor of Boulanger's cantata and one for that of Edouard Flamant. Four abstained. In the second round, however, Boulanger retained only two votes, with seven judges ab-staining. Their message was clear: only Boulanger's was considered worthy of second place after Gailhard's, but under no circumstances would the daring contestant receive such reward after the *faux pas* with her fugue. The prize was therefore not awarded. Next came the vote for the *Deuxième Second Grand Prix,* which Fleury had won in 1904. Again four judges—presumably the same as before—voted in Boulanger's favor; the other votes were split. Unusually, five more rounds of voting followed before a fifth judge joined the faithful four in their decision to award this prize to Nadia Boulanger.

Whatever the quality of Boulanger's cantata, it was highly unlikely that she, a student of both Fauré and Widor, could have won the *Prix de Rome* when Lenepveu had two of his favorite students—André Gailhard and Jules Mazellier—in the competition. But that she did not receive the next lower prize probably had to do with both the "affaire fugue" and her sex. As a rule, the awarding of the *Premier Second Grand Prix* hailed the crown-prince(ss) of the following year, whereas the *Deuxième Second Grand Prix* merely ac-knowledged achievement without committing the Académie to further rec-ognition. The lower second prize could thus be awarded to a woman since it did not represent a strong endorsement, particularly in such a high-profile case.

Nadia Boulanger's victory became the center of attention during the sum-mer of 1908; celebrated as a *femme nouvelle* with the abilities necessary to achieve her goals in the male world of official art, she was tipped to win the 1909 *Prix de Rome.*[62] Even more than Fleury, Boulanger embodied the *femme nouvelle* of the musical world. So far, she had proven herself a very successful young professional woman, recognized by her peers and earning enough money to keep the family afloat. Not yet twenty years old, she held the piano accompaniment class at the private Conservatoire Femina-Musica, and she had an ever-growing circle of private pupils to whom she taught various theoretical and practical skills. Her career as a concert pianist and organist was taking off, and her talent as composer began to be recognized. Boulan-ger's background lay at the basis of her career, with her father and his family being well-known musicians, and her mother a musical dilettante and Rus-sian princess.[63] This combination of artistic and aristocratic lineage created a different context from the bourgeois surroundings in which Juliette Toutain and Hélène Fleury grew up. Self-expression that flouted convention was so-cially accepted, if not expected, in aristocratic circles,[64] and children, both male and female, in musical families traditionally had a better chance of a musical career.[65] Instead of interpreting Boulanger's gesture to compose an instrumental fugue as "rebellious," as Rosenstiel did, one might call it "aris-tocratic," an attitude that did not care for the opinion of the lesser—even if they were members of the Académie.

The public persona that Boulanger developed in these years expressed and emphasized the feminine success story of her recent career. Photographs of that time show an elegantly dressed young woman radiating self-confidence. Journalists who covered the story of her *Deuxième Second Grand Prix* com-mented upon her appearance, praising her beauty and modesty. Boulanger, in gaining public acknowledgment of her musical achievements, had become a symbol of the *femme nouvelle.* Yet her self-confident and compelling em-bodiment of the new woman might have been one reason why the still con-servative Académie refused to go along with the scenario that had been developed in the press during that summer of 1908. Nadia Boulanger did not become the first woman to win the *Prix de Rome:* in fact, in the 1909 competi-tion she received no prize at all.

It is interesting to see how the jury came to this conclusion. A *Prix de Rome* candidate could receive only a higher prize in successive competitions, never an equal or lower one. Thus Nadia Boulanger could only be awarded the *Premier Grand Prix* or the *Premier Second Grand Prix* in 1909. When the jury of specialists cast their ballots for the first prize, Boulanger's cantata *Roussalka* received not a single vote. This can only have been a political decision, since no other candidate was judged to be sufficiently competent to receive the *Premier Grand Prix* in 1909. Consequently, the judges proposed that no first prize be awarded in that year: perhaps the time was not ripe for a female triumph in the competition. The next prize down developed into a "duel" between two candidates: Lenepveu's student Jules Mazellier and Fauré's and Widor's student Nadia Boulanger. The jury of eight composers (not nine, for Jules Massenet, a declared Boulanger supporter, was not pres-ent) was equally divided for three rounds of voting, but decided in the end to give the prize to Mazellier.[66] This decision—a slap in the face for Bou-langer—was political on two grounds: the sex of the candidates and the rela-tive power of their teachers. Even more pronounced in its bias was the subsequent general decision by the Académie des Beaux-Arts as a whole, which decisively overthrew the recommendation of the jury of specialists. Mazellier was awarded the *Grand Prix de Rome,* and two other Lenepveu students—Jean Gallon and Marcel Tournier—received the second prizes. Whereas the specialist jury had demonstrated at least some artistic responsibility by not awarding the first prize at all, given that it could not go to the woman contestant who had deserved it, the Académie's vote was blatantly gender-biased and as misogynous as the opinions voiced in the Académie debates of 1903. Many musicians perceived Boulanger's well-performed cantata to be "the most expert and original composition,"[67] and "would have preferred to have seen the prize awarded to Mademoiselle Nadia Boulanger."[68] The *Deuxième Second Grand Prix,* it appears, continued to be the glass ceiling for a woman composer. In spite of public support in both the general and the musical press, Nadia Boulanger did not compete again for the *Prix de Rome.* Like Fleury, she had doubtless learned her lesson, as had the other female students of the Conservatoire. No woman competed for the prize in 1910 and 1911.

LILI BOULANGER:
GENIUS, CREATIVITY, AND THE ICON OF
THE *FEMME FRAGILE*
~

Only in 1912 did a woman again enter the competition for the *Prix de Rome* in composition. Lili Boulanger may have felt encouraged to take that step because a *Grand Prix de Rome* had at last been awarded to a woman, the sculptor Lucienne Heuvelmans, the previous year. Things had changed in the Académie with the death of Charles Lenepveu in August 1910. In the 1912 competition, Lili Boulanger was not promoted to the final round. One year later, however, she and four male candidates set Eugène Adenis's cantata *Faust et Hélène* to music, and she became the first female musican to win the *Premier Grand Prix de Rome.* From the specialist jury, she received five votes out of eight in the first round, and she obtained an overwhelming majority in the general Académie election with thirty-one votes to five. It was sensational by any standards that a nineteen-year-old candidate had won the *Prix de Rome* both with her first cantata and with an unusual majority. Moreover, she was a young woman.[69]

Like Fleury, Lili Boulanger had enrolled in the Conservatoire for a brief period in order to study composition in an environment closer to the Académie and its *Prix de Rome.* But she did not compete for the Conservatoire's end-of-year prizes that her sister had collected so successfully. Because of constant illness,[70] the young and frail composer spent much time at home with private tutors, concentrating her limited energy on her priorities. Indeed, winning the *Prix de Rome* for the honor of the Boulanger family had become almost an obsession for her, especially after following closely her sister Nadia's vigorous but fruitless attempts to achieve this goal. Lili

Figure 3.4. Portrait of Lili Boulanger, May 1913. Photograph preserved in the Fondation Internationale Nadia et Lili Boulanger, Paris.

Boulanger recorded the "affaire fugue" of 1908 in detail in her diary. She was very much aware of every move her sister made to win the *Prix de Rome,* and she saw the professional and highly competent Nadia fail because of a misogynous jury. Accordingly she developed—probably consciously—a different strategy to deal with the public sphere of professional musicianship. Portraits and descriptions of her reveal a public persona carefully chosen and cultivated, which her physical frailty undoubtedly enhanced: the divinely chosen genius in the fragile body of a beautiful child—the literary icon of the *femme fragile.*[71] In a series of photographs released at the time of the 1913 competition she seems androgynous, her pose and her clothes evoking the familiar image, replicated a thousandfold in family portraits, of a young adolescent boy in a sailor suit (see Fig. 3.4). By using this androgynous imagery of the frail child-genius to separate herself from the icon of the mature woman professional—the *femme nouvelle*—Lili Boulanger also disassociated herself from the "pink peril"—in the guise of Hélène Fleury and Nadia Boulanger—invading public male space. An interview with Lili Boulanger and her mother in the aftermath of winning the *Prix de Rome* is revealing in this context. When asked if she could sleep after her success, she replied:

> "Oh yes, indeed. I dreamed that—didn't I, Mother?"
> "That what?"

"Well, that I was a little child and was teaching my little doll to play the piano."

"You see," said her mother, smiling, "she is still only a child."[72]

But Lili Boulanger's embodiment of the *femme fragile* constituted a carefully constructed role, in which she took on the unthreatening aspect of the eternal female who needed the support and help of the strong masculine sex. This portrayal of her can be found in the press reports of her victory.[73] There is no doubt that she won her prize because of her musical achievement: her cantata is an outstanding contribution to the genre. But she also received the *Premier Grand Prix* because she succeeded in conforming to a popular image of femininity that appeared not only in "decadent" literature[74] but also—once more—in the widely distributed popular novels. Evoking images of family happiness, Emile Vuillermoz's description of the candidate could well be found in any such novel: "The frail grace of Mademoiselle Lili Boulanger [moved] the audience, softened by the sight of the touching group formed by the contestant and her sister united at the piano in an attentive and affectionate collaboration."[75] Throughout the performance of her cantata, Lili Boulanger behaved passively and submissively in the manner of the ideal woman, avoiding any gesture that could be interpreted as directing or conducting her musicians. She did nothing that could be construed as aggressive, assertive, or arrogant. Her performance here physically enacted the plot of a feminine vocation through Art itself, which Carolyn Heilbrun likened to the storyline of romantic love: the woman is conquered against all obstacles by the hero—or in a religious context—God or Christ.[76] Journalists could not resist the implicit parallel with Jeanne d'Arc, the national, and by then, the right-wing, Catholic symbol of France: "The suffragettes smash windows and burn houses. But a maiden of France has gained a better victory."[77]

The story of women and the *Prix de Rome* before the First World War was not just one of ongoing prejudice against women by the Académie. It was also the story of women's attempts to quell the anxieties of the *académiciens*. Although both Hélène Fleury and Nadia Boulanger were taken seriously, Juliette Toutain's self-representation as *salonnière* and *jeune fille rangée* supplied her adversaries with the weapons they needed to undermine her professional ambitions. Indeed, each of the four stories illustrates the precarious balance that women competitors had to achieve between the journalistic and literary images of the ideal Republican woman, loyal and submissive to the state and its institutions, and the self-confident and professional composer who must be taken seriously. Because it was necessary to conduct the performance of the cantata, the physical appearance of a female contestant assumed more importance in the musical competition than it did in other artistic areas, in which artists such as sculptors or painters remained invisible behind the physical presence of their artifacts. Thus the persona of a woman composer became an integral part of her application. Each of the four women tried to craft an image that could earn her a position in the public arena of French official art; the successful strategy, however, proved to be that which yoked an excessive and frail femininity with images both religious and androgynous. Neither an aggressive socialite nor a "dangerous" *femme nouvelle*, the winner of the first musical *Prix de Rome* was an artist who skillfully negotiated the concerns over women's emancipation pervading the cultural politics of pre-war French society through an unthreatening rendition of the child-genius.

NOTES

The present text represents an abbreviated version of an article first published in the *Journal of the American Musicological Society* 51 (1998): 83–129, "*La Guerre en dentelles:* Women and the *Prix de Rome* in French Cultural Politics." Copyright © 1998 by the American Musicological Society. All rights reserved. I am grateful to the American Musicological Society for granting permission to reproduce it here in revised form.

1. Emile Vuillermoz, "Le Péril rose," *Musica* 11 (1912): 45.
2. Emile Vuillermoz, "La Guerre en dentelles," *Musica* 12 (1913): 153.
3. *Le Ménestrel* 69 (1903): 55.
4. I wish to thank Lesley Wright for having drawn my attention to this composer at the beginning of my investigations about women and the *Prix de Rome.*
5. For biographical details of the four composers, see the appendix to my article, "*La Guerre en dentelles.*" The prizes distributed in the *Prix de Rome* competition were, in ascending order, *mention honorable, Deuxième Second Grand Prix, Premier Second Grand Prix,* and finally the *Premier Grand Prix.*
6. Karen Offen, "Depopulation, Nationalism and Feminism in Fin-de-Siècle France," *American Historical Review* 89 (1984): 648–76 at 660; Debora Silverman, "The 'New Woman,' Feminism, and the Decorative Arts in Fin-de-Siècle France," in *Eroticism and the Body Politic,* ed. Lynn Hunt (Baltimore and London: The Johns Hopkins University Press, 1991), 144–63 at 148–49.
7. Edward Berenson, *The Trial of Madame Caillaux* (Berkeley, Los Angeles, and Oxford: University of California Press, 1992), 11.
8. Minutes of the weekly session of the Académie des Beaux-Arts [*Procès verbaux*] from 28 February 1903, preserved in the Archives of the Académie des Beaux-Arts at the Institut de France, Paris (hereafter AABA), shelf mark 2E21, p. 24.
9. The news was reported in the daily press; in *Le Temps,* for instance, the account of the banquet is found under the column "News of the day" (10 February 1903, p. 2). A more detailed account was reproduced in the weekly music journal *Le Ménestrel* from 15 February 1903.
10. See Tamar Garb, *Sisters of the Brush: Women's Artistic Culture in Late Nineteenth-Century Paris* (New Haven and London: Yale University Press, 1994), 42–43.

11. For an excellent study of the development of the bourgeois concept of gendered spheres, see Joan B. Landes, *Women and the Public Sphere in the Age of the French Revolution* (Ithaca, N.Y., and London: Cornell University Press, 1988).

12. For a short but detailed account of women's rights in nineteenth-century France, see Berenson, *The Trial of Madame Caillaux*, 103–17.

13. Landes, *Women and the Public Sphere*, 170, 2. My use of "structural change of the public sphere" appropriates Jürgen Habermas's beautifully coined title, *Strukturwandel der Öffentlichkeit: Untersuchungen zu einer Kategorie der bürgerlichen Gesellschaft* (Frankfurt am Main: Suhrkamp, 1990).

14. Berenson, *The Trial of Madame Caillaux*, 126.

15. Katharine Ellis discusses issues of women's professional musicianship in her "Female Pianists and Their Male Critics in Nineteenth-Century Paris," *Journal of the American Musicological Society* 50 (1997): 353–85.

16. In 1861, the year in which the first woman, Julie Daubié, successfully passed her *baccalauréat*, Charlotte Jacques gained a *Deuxième Accessit* in counterpoint, and from 1874 on, women were regularly successful in the composition classes, beginning with Marie Renaud's (1852–1928) *Deuxième Accessit* in 1874, *Premier Accessit* in 1875, and finally, *Premier Prix* in 1876.

17. Claude Debussy, "Considérations sur le prix de Rome au point de vue musical," in Claude Debussy, *Monsieur Croche et autres écrits*, ed. François Lesure, 2d rev. ed. (Paris: Gallimard, 1987), 175–79. On the *Prix de Rome*, see Eugene Bozza, "The History of the 'Prix de Rome,'" *Hinrichsen's Musical Yearbook* 7 (1952): 487–94 (including a list of the winners of the first prizes in Music); and Lesley Wright, "Bias, Influence, and Bizet's *Prix de Rome*," *19th-Century Music* 15 (1992): 215–28. Lesley Wright is currently preparing a book on the *Prix de Rome* as a central institution of French musical life.

18. I wish to thank Lesley Wright for this information. See also *Procès verbaux* from 9 May 1874, AABA, shelf mark 2E15, pp. 259–60.

19. See Silverman, "The 'New Woman,'" 149–50.

20. *Procès verbaux* from 21 March 1903, AABA, shelf mark 2E21, p. 37.

21. Ibid., 37–38.

22. Wright, "Bias," 217.

23. Ibid.

24. See, for example, Jeanice Brooks's case study on Nadia Boulanger's conducting career and her complex negotiating with traditional expectations, in "*Noble et grande servante de la musique*: Telling the Story of Nadia Boulanger's Conducting Career," *Journal of Musicology* 14 (1996): 92–116.

25. See Théodore Dubois's report to the Académie des Beaux-Arts, recorded in *Procès verbaux* from 9 May 1903, AABA, shelf mark 2E21, pp. 54–55.

26. Maurice Leudet, "Le cas de Mlle Toutain," *Le Figaro*, 10 May 1903, p. 4.

27. *Le Petit Journal*, 7 May 1903, p. 3.

28. Paris, Archives Nationales, F²¹ 5351 (1E).

29. In the realm of the Conservatoire, the "grand-bourgeois" attitude of Juliette Toutain and her family was notorious, as a letter from 8 April 1901 by Maurice Ravel to their common classmate Florent Schmitt reveals. See Maurice Ravel, *Lettres, écrits, entretiens*, ed. Arbie Orenstein (Paris: Flammarion, 1989), 65.

30. *Le Ménestrel* 61 (1895): 215.

31. See Gabrielle Houbre, *La Discipline de l'amour: L'Education sentimentale des filles et*

des garçons à l'âge du Romantisme (Paris: Plon, 1997), 244–54; Anne-Marie Sohn, *Femmes dans la vie privée (XIXᵉ–XXᵉ siècles)*, 2 vols. (Paris: Publications de la Sorbonne, 1996), 69–73, 449–547; Anne Martin-Fugier, *La Bourgeoise* (Paris: Bernard Grasset, 1983), 43–76.

32. It was impossible for Toutain to join the competition belatedly on 3 May because the Catholic journal *La Croix* had prematurely made the poem public. This might be interpreted as further evidence that the incident was a willful attempt to keep specifically Toutain out of the competition.

33. "Séance du 28 Novembre 1903," in *Annales de la Chambre des Députés* (1904): 855. I wish to thank Jann Pasler for a copy of the pages that refer to the incident.

34. *Procès verbaux* from 20 June 1903, AABA, shelf mark 2E21, p. 82.

35. See the introduction of Jean Bureau to the exhibition catalogue *Rétrospective Jules Grün, 1868–1938*, Caen, Hôtel d'Escoville, 4–25 May 1975.

36. *Le Petit Journal*, 10 May 1903, p. 1.

37. In this context, see also Anne Higonnet, "Frauenbilder," trans. Sylvia M. Schomburg-Scherff, in *19. Jahrhundert*, ed. Geneviève Fraisse and Michelle Perrot, vol. 4 of *Geschichte der Frauen*, ed. Georges Duby and Michelle Perrot (Frankfurt and New York: Campus Verlag, 1994), 313–65; Silverman, "The 'New Woman'"; and Virginia M. Allen, *The Femme Fatale: Erotic Icon* (Troy, N.Y.: The Whitston Publishing Company, 1983).

38. See Anne-Marie Thiesse, *Le Roman du quotidien: Lecteurs et lectures populaires à la Belle Epoque* (Paris: Chemin vert, 1984), 144–45, 158–65.

39. Bonnie G. Smith, *Ladies of the Leisure Class: The Bourgeoise of Northern France in the Nineteenth Century* (Princeton: Princeton University Press, 1981). Code words in the press were used not only with regard to women but also to French society in general. See Eugen Weber, *France: Fin de Siècle* (Cambridge, Mass., and London: The Belknap Press of Harvard University Press, 1986), 44–45.

40. On the attribution of emotional and intellectual qualities to women in nineteenth-century France, see Christine Battersby, *Gender and Genius: Towards a Feminist Perspective* (Bloomington: Indiana University Press, 1989); Marcia J. Citron, *Gender and the Musical Canon* (Cambridge: Cambridge University Press, 1993), 44–54; and Berenson, *The Trial of Madame Caillaux*, 100–17. With respect to artistic creativity, see the arguments discussed in Garb, *Sisters of the Brush*, 105–17.

41. Both quotations are taken from "Mlle Juliette Toutain et le concours de Rome . . . ," *Musica* 1 (1903): 140.

42. See Karin Offen, "Ernest Legouvé and the Doctrine of 'Equality in Difference' for Women: A Case Study of Male Feminism in 19th-Century Thought," *Journal of Modern History* 58 (1986): 452–84 at 454.

43. In her article "*Noble et grande servante de la musique*," Jeanice Brooks shows how this form of discourse became an essential element in the strategy that Nadia Boulanger and her entourage used in order to make her career as female conductor possible.

44. Recent research in women's biography and autobiography has shown that this form of rhetorical negotiation persists today. See, for example, Carolyn Heilbrun, *Writing a Woman's Life* (New York and London: W. W. Norton, 1988); Linda Wagner-Martin, *Telling Women's Lives: The New Biography* (New Brunswick, N.J.: Rutgers University Press, 1994).

45. *Le Petit Journal*, 10 May 1903, p. 2.

46. *Registres d'inscription des élèves admis au Conservatoire*, Paris, Archives Nationales,

Série AJ³⁷ 395, p. 93; "La première candidate au prix de Rome," *L'Illustration*, 21 May 1904, p. 351.

47. Her advertisement in the *Annuaire des artistes et de l'enseignement musical* (Paris, 1903), 29, reads as follows: "Hélène Fleury / Compositeur-Pianiste / Professeur de Piano / Harmonie, Contrepoint / Cours d'Accompagnement / Leçons en Français, Allemand, Anglais / 43, Rue de Douai, 43 / Mercredi de 4 à 6 heures."

48. *Le Monde Musical* 15 (1903): 132.

49. See, for example, the comparison between Toutain and Fleury ibid.

50. *Le Petit Journal*, 10 May 1903, p. 2.

51. Published in *Le Monde Musical* 16 (1904), front page for the issue of 30 May.

52. *Procès verbaux* from 2 July 1904, AABA, shelf mark 2E21, p. 261.

53. *Musica* 3 (1904): 368.

54. *Le Matin*, 21 May 1905, quoted in Gail Hilson Woldu, "Au-delà du scandale de 1905," *Revue de Musicologie* 82 (1996): 245–67, at 248.

55. Neither Arbie Orenstein nor Marcel Marnat mention Hélène Fleury in their accounts of the 1905 scandal or in the annotations to Ravel's letters. This biased coverage of the event turns the scandal into a personal vendetta of the conservative jury against a young avant-garde composer instead of taking into account the wider ramifications of the incident. See Arbie Orenstein, *Ravel: Man and Musician* (New York and London: Columbia University Press, 1975); Marcel Marnat, *Maurice Ravel* (Paris: Fayard, 1986); and Ravel, *Lettres, écrits, entretiens*, ed. Orenstein.

56. *Fantaisie* for viola and piano, Op. 18, published in 1906 by Enoch & Cie with the note on the title page: "imposée au Concours du Conservatoire (Année 1906)."

57. *Le Ménestrel* 70 (1904): 251. Ernest Boulanger won the *Prix de Rome* in 1835. He became a successful composer of *opéras-comiques* and a teacher of singing at the Conservatoire.

58. *Nadia Boulanger: A Life in Music* (New York and London: W. W. Norton, 1982), 66. For accounts of the 1908 events, see pp. 65–73; Jérôme Spycket, *Nadia Boulanger* (Lausanne: Payot, 1987), 28–30; and Jeanice Brooks, "*Noble et grande servante de la musique*," 99.

59. *Procès verbaux* from 16 May 1908, AABA, shelf mark 2E22, pp. 151–2.

60. Ibid., 150.

61. The full letter and a facsimile of its first and last pages are reproduced in Spycket, *Nadia Boulanger*, 28–29.

62. Extracts of an article of Camille de Sainte-Croix (*La Petite République*, 22 July 1908) are given in English translation in Rosenstiel, *Nadia Boulanger*, 71–73.

63. Rosenstiel doubts that Madame Boulanger—née Raïssa Myschetsky Shuvaliv—had been a princess of the noble Tatar Myschtsky family and labels her an "adventuress" (Rosenstiel, *Nadia Boulanger*, 13–15). Whether or not she was of noble descent is of little consequence in this context, however, given that both her daughters believed firmly in their aristocratic lineage. See Spycket, *Nadia Boulanger*, 12.

64. See Weber, *France*, 27–40.

65. Nancy B. Reich, "Women as Musicians: A Question of Class," in *Musicology and Difference: Gender and Sexuality in Music Scholarship*, ed. Ruth A. Solie (Berkeley: University of California Press, 1993), 125–46.

66. *Procès verbaux* from 26 June 1909, AABA, shelf mark 2E22, p. 172.

67. Review in *Le Courrier musical*, given in Rosenstiel, *Nadia Boulanger*, 83.

68. Profile of Jules Mazellier in *Musica* (May 1909), given in Rosenstiel, *Nadia Boulanger*, 83.

69. For an exact protocol of the events, see *Procès verbaux* from 5 July 1913, AABA, shelf mark 2E23, pp. 64–69. Léonie Rosenstiel reconstructs much of the competition in her biography of Lili Boulanger; see Léonie Rosenstiel, *The Life and Works of Lili Boulanger* (London and Rutherford, N.J.: Fairleigh Dickinson University Press, 1978), 54–82. For a more analytical approach with respect to Boulanger's cantata *Faust et Hélène*, see Manuela Schwartz, "Mehr als ein Gesellenstück: 'Faust et Hélène' von Lili Boulanger," in *Vom Schweigen befreit (3. Internationales Komponistinnen-Festival Kassel)—Lili Boulanger, 1893–1918*, ed. Roswitha Aulenkamp-Moeller and Christel Nies (Kassel: Internationales Forum "Vom Schweigen befreit" e.V., 1993), 64–71; Melanie Unseld, "'alles, was man erwarten und wünschen kann'—Gedanken zu Lili Boulangers Kantate *Faust et Hélène*," *Vivavoce* 41 (April–June 1997): 8–17.

70. Lili Boulanger "contracted a severe case of bronchial pneumonia" at age two (Rosenstiel, *Life and Works of Lili Boulanger*, 33). Her health remained very fragile, and during the last ten years of her life, she suffered from intestinal tuberculosis.

71. On the *femme fragile*, see Ariane Thomalla, *Die "femme fragile": Ein literarischer Frauentypus der Jahrhundertwende* (Düsseldorf: Bertelsmann Universitätsverlag, 1972). On the perception of Lili Boulanger as *femme fragile*, see Annegret Fauser, "Lili Boulanger's *La Princesse Maleine*: A Composer and Her Heroine as Literary Icons," *Journal of the Royal Musical Association* 122 (1997): 68–108.

72. "Young French Women Winning Honors," *Musical Leader* 26 (1913).

73. Lili Boulanger's diaries disclose that she had an iron will as well as determination to get what she wanted, even at the cost of her own health. Like any cunning young Parisian artist, she knew how to manipulate juries and the press, as her scheming to obtain the *Prix Lepaulle* in 1912 reveals. See Annegret Fauser, "Lili Boulanger's *La Princesse Maleine*," 107.

74. On "decadence" in literature, see Erwin Koppen, *Dekadenter Wagnerismus: Studien zur europäischen Literatur des Fin de siècle* (Berlin and New York: Walter de Gruyter, 1973).

75. Vuillermoz, "La Guerre en dentelles," 153.

76. Heilbrun, *Writing a Woman's Life*, 21.

77. *Le Matin*, 6 July 1913, p. 2.

PART TWO

Cloistered Voices

What vexed me was the iron grate, which suffered nothing
to escape but sounds and concealed from me the angels
of which they were worthy.

JEAN-JACQUES ROUSSEAU,
Confessions

ONE OUTGROWTH in the division between public and
private spheres of female musical performance is the total con-
tainment of the woman's voice in a sequestered domain.
Restrictions take place mostly in androcentric cultures, where
gender ideologies emphasize the provocative power of the female voice. This
results in the prohibition against women performing with men in sacred and
secular spheres. In these societies, female involvement in public activities,
musically or otherwise, has been strictly controlled by cultural and religious
beliefs.

The phenomenon of segregating the sexes so that men cannot hear women
sing occurs in several religions around the world.[1] In strict Orthodox Judaism, for example, the female voice is considered to be a serious distraction
to men. Women must sit high up in balconies and/or behind screens during
religious services. They celebrate weddings and other joyous occasions in
separate venues where their musical performances cannot be seen or heard
by men.[2] Strict segregation of the sexes is also upheld in traditional Islamic
societies. Muslim women must keep themselves secluded at home. When
they venture out, particularly in urban centers, they wear the chador, or
body-covering veil. Like their Orthodox Jewish counterparts, traditional
Muslim women perform music only in separate all-female gatherings. And
in the Roman Catholic Church, St. Paul's dictum that women should remain
silent in church continues to the present day with the exclusion of females
from officiating at services as celebrants.

While women musicians have been prohibited from public expression,
they have not remained silent. They have instead developed their own musical voice within the confines of their "cloistered" domains. The two essays
presented below explore musical life in one of these domains: the Roman

Catholic convent during the Middle Ages and early modern period. For centuries, female monastic orders have afforded a place for women to sing, play, and compose music in the service of God. Margot Fassler centers on the rituals of a twelfth-century German convent, which strictly followed the rule of St. Benedict. Its abbess, Hildegard of Bingen, fashioned a theological program for her congregation of nuns to use in their devotional singing as brides of Christ. As Fassler emphasizes, Hildegard created a sonic landscape that was uniquely female. She composed chants in a high range, with soaring leaps and highly ornamented melodies that "only women could comfortably sing." Even though some of her chants were commissioned by male monastic orders, Hildegard's music was first and foremost intended for her nuns to sing in the seclusion of their monastic enclosure and not to be heard by the outside world.

In contrast, Craig Monson, in his study of conventual life in early seventeenth-century Bologna, explains how the music performed by the nuns seeped through the walls of their sequestered convents into the public arena. As Monson reveals, the female monastic church served as a link with the outside world, where townspeople and tourists alike would flock to hear the disembodied "angelic voices" of the nuns. The architecture of the convent church created this ethereal sound with its two chapels—an inner one for the nuns and an outer one for the public—separated by a solid wall. Singing behind grilled windows that pierced the wall above the high altar, the nuns could thus be heard but not be seen.

Public performance by all-female musicians hidden from sight also occurred at the concerts of the *ospedali grandi,* the welfare institutions of Venice.[3] The most famous of these schools was the Pio Ospedale della Pietà, where Antonio Vivaldi and several other important musicians worked. Here orphaned and illegitimate girls, trained to be musicians, would perform for the public, usually behind grills or in high galleries. For the eighteenth-century traveler, the "grand tour" was not complete without hearing these all-girl ensembles at what was considered one of the most important tourist sites of Venice.

The isolation of female from male performers has also occurred in other cultures. Women musicians throughout the Islamic world have performed in segregated contexts. All-female bands in the town of Herat, Afghanistan, for example, earn their living by participating at wedding parties and other celebrations restricted to women.[4] In Turkey and Tunisia, there has been a long tradition of professional and semi-professional ensembles playing for women-only audiences.[5] Even in cosmopolitan Cairo, the famous singer Umm Kulthūm, at the start of her career, sang for women at the private gatherings of well-to-do families, as Virginia Danielson has related: "The ladies were in one room and Umm Kulthūm was singing . . . She wore a yellow dress of the plainest sort and a black head covering. After she sang the ladies literally pushed her into the men's salon to sing for them."⁶ In China, women were prohibited from performing in traditional Beijing Opera. Instead *dan* or *tan* singers (men cross-dressed as women) performed the female roles. It was only with the establishment of the Chinese Republic in 1911 that all-female troupes began to appear. The same restrictions occurred in Japan, where female impersonators or *onnagata* were used in kabuki and noh plays. Forbidden to perform in these theatrical art forms, women responded by making traditional Japanese dance (*nihon buyo*) their own. *Nihon buyo*, therefore, became an all-female genre, where one woman can take on multiple roles, male and female, in a single performance.⁷

In European society, the separation of women and men in musical groups continued to prevail in the nineteenth century. Amateur choral societies, where the sexes could sing and socialize in a segregated atmosphere, proliferated throughout Europe and America. Indeed, the roots of the a cappella groups so popular on college campuses today can be traced back to this social pastime. Even opera reflected this tradition, where separate choruses for men or women became conventionalized in the dramatic works of Italian, French, and German composers.

While educational opportunities for women widened as music conservatories in Europe and later in America opened their doors to female students during the nineteenth century, participation in professional orchestras, bands, and chamber ensembles continued to remain elusive for the female instrumentalist up into the mid-twentieth century. Excluded from performing in mainstream musical groups, women got together to form their own ensembles. Thousands of female instrumentalists found employment in ladies' orchestras throughout Europe from 1840 until the 1940s.⁸ In the United States, some thirty women's symphony orchestras appeared in several major cities from the 1920s to the 1940s.⁹ The type of music they performed varied from the symphonic and "light classical" repertory to popular music. Their venues were equally diverse, ranging from restaurants, hotels, and cafés to concert halls.

At the turn of the century, ladies' jazz bands, vaudeville troupes, and dance orchestras also made an appearance in America. All but forgotten (except for Billy Wilder's film classic, *Some Like It Hot*), the "all-girl" bands were derided as "freaks, gimmicks, spectacles."¹⁰ Yet hundreds of these female jazz bands traveled the country in the thirties and forties playing swing music in dance ballrooms, hotels, theaters, and USO shows.

In addition to the all-girl bands, professional female vocal groups became the rage in the thirties, forties, and early fifties. The most well-known acts were the Boswell Sisters, Andrews Sisters, and McGuire Sisters, who entertained America with their close harmonies and upbeat singing styles.[11] These trios served as the prototype for the new girl sound in rock music of the early sixties. From the Shirelles to the Supremes, the "girl groups" changed the all-male image of rock and roll of the fifties with their "girlish vocals fraught with adolescent idealism and pain."[12]

On the whole, while exclusion from "mainstream" music was intended to put women in their place, it ironically did just the opposite, for enforced segregation helped facilitate the establishment of strong autonomous musical domains for women. Compelled to find alternate outlets for their musical creativity, women continued to express themselves both within the context of their cloistered realms as well as in the public arena. In doing so, they created a voice of their own.

NOTES

1. On the limitation of women's musical involvement in religious practices see Ellen Koskoff, "Both In and Between: Women's Musical Roles in Ritual Life," in *Music and the Experience of God*, ed. David Power, Mary Collins, and Mellonee Burnim (Edinburgh: T. & T. Clark Ltd., 1989), 82–93.

2. For a discussion of women's music making in Orthodox Judaism see Ellen Koskoff, "The Sound of a Woman's Voice: Gender and Music in a New York Hasidic Community," in *Women and Music in Cross-Cultural Perspective*, ed. Koskoff, 213–23, and "Miriam Sings Her Song: The Self and the Other in Anthropological Discourse," in *Musicology and Difference*, ed. Solie, 149–63.

3. Jane L. Baldauf-Berdes, *Women Musicians of Venice: Musical Foundations, 1524–1855* (Oxford: Oxford University Press, 1993).

4. Veronica Doubleday, *Three Women of Herat* (Austin: University of Texas Press, 1990), 157–213.

5. Ursula Reinhard, "The Veils are Lifted: Music of Turkish Women," in *Music, Gender, and Culture*, ed. Marcia Herndon and Susanne Ziegler (Wilhelmshaven: Florian Noetzel, 1990), 101–3; Susanne Ziegler, "Gender-Specific Traditional Wedding Music in Southwestern Turkey," ibid., 87–88; and L. Jafran Jones, "A Sociohistorical Perspective on Tunisian Women as Professional Musicians," in *Women and Music in Cross-Cultural Perspective*, ed. Koskoff, 73.

6. Medhat Assem, communication cited in Virginia Danielson, "Artists and Entrepreneurs: Female Singers in Cairo during the 1920s," in *Women in Middle Eastern History: Shifting Boundaries in Sex and Gender*, ed. Nikki R. Keddi and Beth Baron (New Haven: Yale University Press, 1991), 298.

7. See Tomie Hahn's essay in this book, chap. 13.

8. Margaret Myers, "Searching for Data about European Ladies' Orchestras, 1870–1950," in *Music and Gender*, ed. Pirkko Moisala and Beverley Diamond (Urbana and Chicago: University of Illinois Press, 2000), 189–213.

9. Carol Neuls-Bates, "Women's Orchestras in the United States, 1925–45," in *Women*

Making Music: The Western Art Tradition, 1150–1950, ed. Jane Bowers and Judith Tick (Urbana: University of Illinois Press, 1986), 350.

10. Sherrie Tucker, *Swing Shift: "All-Girl" Bands of the 1940s* (Durham, N.C.: Duke University Press, 2000), 6.

11. On the Boswell Sisters see Jane Hassinger, "Close Harmony: Early Jazz Styles in the Music of the New Orleans Boswell Sisters," in *Women and Music in Cross-Cultural Perspective,* ed. Koskoff, 195–201.

12. Lucy O'Brien, *She Bop: The Definitive History of Women in Rock, Pop and Soul* (New York: Penguin Books, 1996), 68.

CHAPTER FOUR

Music for the Love Feast

HILDEGARD OF BINGEN AND THE SONG OF SONGS

Margot Fassler

HILDEGARD OF BINGEN'S long and extraordinarily productive life began in 1098 and ended in 1179. Her *curriculum vitae* reads like that of no other woman from the Middle Ages, her innovations in several fields making a parallel with her musical achievements.[1] She has more securely attributable monophonic chants assigned to her name than any composer from the entire Middle Ages; she is the only composer in the history of Western music who was also a serious and highly respected theologian; she is the first composer who arranged for the ordering, copying, and preservation of her musical compositions; she was the first to have promoted, and perhaps even planned, visual commentary for a theological treatise that includes song texts;[2] and her morality play was not only the "first," but also the only one of its type to be fully set to music.

It is useful to place the music she wrote against the backdrop of her three major theological treatises, for her music, always interactive with her religious writings, is most profitably understood as a part of her concentrated program of expanding the canon of religious writings and music for the explicit use of communities of religious women. It is not difficult to see that Hildegard, the abbess, teacher, and maker of liturgies, was most interested in the concept found in the title of the present book: the idea of a unique "female voice," in her case for the rendering of praise to God.[3] In fact, her deliberate and complex attempts to fashion a "female voice" in which to sing, and her many works defining this voice in a multiplicity of ways, constitute yet another first. Her music, received under divine inspiration, could lay claim to such femininity because it flowed through a woman, and first and foremost was for women singers; and because it was from and of God, it was a direct representation of those aspects of the divine nature that are female. Hildegard composed as a self-styled "poor little woman" for others of her kind, creating a vision of the female as interactive with the divine through her compositions, but also making God "sound" in a woman's voice. Whereas all other medieval liturgical "voices" known to us are generically male, Hildegard's is decisively otherwise. This does not mean that she left the male of the species out; far from it. Communities of men requested music from her, and she produced it, both specific pieces and a planned collection of her compositions. Even though Hildegard's "voice" is essentially female, she is willing and ready for all to join in the lofty and high-pitched song.

Exploring Hildegard's female voicing is a hard task, not only because she is a difficult thinker, but also because she wrote so many liturgical song texts of varied natures. One must reach for precise themes, and then hold fast to the cord while being whirled through the cascading images that are typical of her writing in all genres. The difficulty is compounded by the fact that precise dating for many of Hildegard's works, including her songs, is not possible. What we have are a few solid pillars, provided by the time periods for her three major theological treatises (see Table 4.1). As can be seen, periods of work on these treatises appear to divide her mature life into three stages: early middle age, later middle age, and old age. Because she mentions them in *Scivias,* we can ascribe the largest single block of her compositions to the first period, demonstrating at least that she composed from the start, and that her musical creativity was an intimate part of the ways in which she worked as a theologian. We also can compare some songs, those found in *Scivias,* to two groups we know were written later: the songs for St. Ursula and those written in honor of St. Disibod.

The music she wrote and its probable context has occasioned much debate. The circumstances of its production are unique both in the attention given to its copying, and in its attribution to Hildegard through inclusion in a larger body of her works. Both major surviving collections of her music were produced in her own monastic house, the Rupertsberg, most probably during her own lifetime and under her immediate supervision. Thus, although Hildegard's music has not been recorded in any liturgical books known to us, it is gathered into a corpus, sometimes with attention to genre, and commonly with titles supplied for particular pieces. The greater part of Hildegard's compositions were written for the Divine Office, that is, for the hours of monastic prayers that her nuns sang on a daily basis. The most common genres of works in the Office are antiphons, usually fairly short chants sung with intoned psalms and canticles, and responsories, long chants sung at the close of intoned readings, especially at Matins. Hildegard usually

TABLE 4.1

~

General Dating of Hildegard's Works

TREATISE AND DATE	EVENTS PERTINENT TO DATING OF MUSIC	MUSICAL WORKS CONNECTED WITH TREATISE AND/OR EVENTS
I.		
Scivias: 1141–51	Establishment of Rupertsberg: 1150	Songs for St. Rupert: probably by 1150
	Departure of Richardis: 1151	*Scivias* songs: by 1151
	Death of Richardis: 1152	*Ordo virtutem:* by 1151
	Disibod Songs commissioned: 1155	
	Relics of Ursula discovered in Cologne: 1156	Ursula songs: after 1156
II.		
Liber vite meritorum (Book of Life's Merits): 1158–63		
Book of Simple Medicine: by 1158		
Causes and Cures: by 1158		
III.		
Book of Divine Works: 1163–73	Death of Volmar: 1173	

wrote these pieces in pairs, and thus they could be used in a variety of ways in a given feast, or throughout the octave, the seven days following the feast. As I have explained elsewhere, the majority of her pieces are written for "commons," that is for categories of saints, such as apostles or martyrs, or for the Blessed Virgin, and thus they could be sung for the Office repeatedly throughout the church year, whenever the occasion called for such a work, or pair of works.[4] In addition, it is important to note that Hildegard writes infrequently for feasts of the temporal cycle, that is for feasts commemorating the birth, life, passion, death, resurrection, and ascension of the Lord. She is far more interested in music for feasts venerating the lives and passions of the saints. The reasons for this selection of subjects are complicated, but very important for understanding the feminine voice, especially as it praises God.

In order to move expeditiously through Hildegard's free-verse chant texts, their theological meanings, and her compositional style, I have chosen to focus on her understanding and fusion of two core scenes from the Bible, both of which she encountered in the liturgy: the love feast of the Song of Songs and the song of the Lamb's high court from the Book of Revelation. These two passages of Scripture and their well-established liturgical meanings were a great source of inspiration for Hildegard the composer. Hildegard's genius was in taking scriptural readings she knew well from the liturgy, constructing images with liturgical and theological import from these materials, and then transforming these pregnant and powerful images into songs meant to resound within a community. This ongoing process is elemental, and operates in everything that she does. The songs she creates both powerfully represent the highest truths and embody the truths themselves in their very sounding and singing. They capture a particular stream of her divinely inspired visions, allowing her to create treatises that are prophetic and music that is sacramental in its powers.

To explore these ideas, I will first briefly explain Hildegard's view of the Song of Songs and of the Lamb's high court as found in *Scivias,* book 2, vision 6.[5] After this, I will turn first to the songs for St. Ursula as one of the groups of pieces that embodies Hildegard's understanding of the Eucharist (the taking of communion, commemorating the Last Supper and Christ's sacrifice in the Mass)[6] as a love feast, and then in closing will trace some of these same ideas in her musical morality play, the *Ordo virtutum.*

LOVE SONGS AND THE MAKING
OF THE CHURCH
∿

The Song of Songs was one of the most commented upon books of the Bible in the Middle Ages. The poetry explores sexual longings—both male and female—within pastoral settings that merge impressionistically, creating a dream-like parade of points of view and images of fertility. In the Middle Ages, the longings were most commonly discussed in terms of the Church as the fertile bride of Christ, both yearning for their final joining at the end of time. The Mariological cast of these commentaries is also well known, and the liturgical use of the texts for Marian feasts and for feasts of the Dedication of the Church has been much explored by scholars.

We should not be surprised to find that Hildegard's interpretation of the Song of Songs is strongly Mariological, with Mary becoming a multilayered image of *Ecclesia,* the Church, and Christ the bridegroom, lifting *Ecclesia/*

Mary out of worldly life and into his eternal and heavenly embrace.[7] All of these themes operate in Hildegard's exploration of the intertwined powers of song and love as she expands on these more common topoi in her writings and in her music, commenting upon the sacramental force of the Eucharist and the importance of her mode of life in the cloister as well as in the Church. Hildegard inherited a tradition of studying the Song of Songs in the context of the feast of the Assumption of the Virgin (the taking up of the Virgin Mary into heaven), where this book of Scripture predominates in the liturgy. Hildegard's theology and her Mariology focus mainly on the Incarnation (the union of divinity with humanity in Jesus Christ), especially as a moment of change, both in history and in the individual soul. In her Marian chants and chants for other female saints, she borrows the language of love as first developed in the liturgy for the Assumption, reshaping it in the process.

Hildegard uses the biblical language of embrace—leading to intercourse and extending to conception—adapted from the Song to refer to moments of change in body and soul, seen and unseen. Several kinds of intercourse, mingling, or exchange are put side by side: the disobedient action that led to sexual shame and the fall from grace in the Garden of Eden, the Annunciation that provoked conception without penetration, the transformation of the elements of the Eucharist at Mass, and the new bridehood of virgins found in the history of the Church and in her own cloister. She can work with such complex imagery because her mode of exploration is so carefully constructed. She takes her essential understanding of the Song out of the context of the Feast of the Assumption, but subsequently both builds upon and transforms the meaning she knew first into a larger and more dramatic picture of God's encounter with human beings through the sacraments, especially the sacrament of the Eucharist.

In her work she fuses her understanding of the sexual power of the Song with the music of the high altar of the Lamb, as found in the Book of Revelation. The text of the "Sanctus," one of the great genres of ordinary Mass chants of the medieval church, is taken from this book of the Bible, and is sung in praise just before the process of consecrating the elements.[8] In her commentary, Hildegard makes it yet another great love song, and one that celebrates the mingling of the human and the divine through and in the eucharistic elements and their taking by the faithful.[9] Her use of two passages from these central scriptural texts in immediate proximity can be found in *Scivias* 2.6. As will be seen, her theological interpretation of the sacrament superimposes the garden of love upon the altar table of the Lamb's high feast.

The Eucharist is procreative, and the song it inspired embodies Christ, just as the action of taking the host also offers "Christ within." Hildegard's view joins the Song of Songs to the song of the virgins who praise the Lamb in the Book of Revelation, offering a picture of the eucharistic sacrifice at the end of time, a joining of the two historic songs that had special appeal for her as an artist. Like all medieval exegetes, Hildegard was accustomed to lying between the breasts of scriptural and liturgical images, nurtured from the one verse, and then another, drinking from several spouts of words. To find her mixing metaphors is not to be wondered at, but rather expected— the liturgy was her food, just as the singing of the Office and regular partici- pation in the Eucharist sustained her life and her understanding of what life was about. The Song of Songs, as she came to expound it, relates Mass and Office through common imagery, making the Eucharist a love feast with an incarnational heart, while the Christ who feeds is shaped with both masculine and feminine attributes. Many passages in *Scivias* 2.6 speak of the bride and bridegroom on the altar of the church, joined in the eucharistic sacrifice, but none is so all-encompassing as that of section 34, in which Solomon, in the words of the lover of the Song of Songs, speaks for the Church, and the kiss of the beloved is taken in the act of eating and drinking the elements of the Mass:

> "Who shall give you to me for my brother, sucking the breasts of my mother, that I may find you out of doors and kiss you, and no one will despise me?" (Song of Songs 8:1) What does this mean? With groans and devotion and with sure faith the people of the Church say, "Who will be merciful and give me, a miserable human in tribulation, You, the Bridegroom of the Church?—You, Whom I name my brother be- cause of Your Incarnation, and Who sucks the mercy and truth that nourish humanity from the Divinity, which is my mother in my cre- ation, giving me life and growth?" What does this mean? "The nour- ishments of the Church too are full of Your grace, for You Who are the Living Bread and the fountain of living water makes her fully abound in the sacrament of Your body and blood. And this You do that I may surely find You out of doors, knowing that You are the Son of God in Heaven but seeing You as a man on earth, for my mortal eyes cannot perceive You in Divinity; and that I may find You in the bread and wine of the divine mystery, the sacrament without deception or artifice. And thus I may kiss You, for You were incarnate for my salvation . . ."[10]

The Garden of the Altar welcomes those who have suffered the Fall to a second chance; the garden of the monastery sustains the lives of nuns who have ventured into a special relationship with God, whose Son is their

Sponsus—their bridegroom—and their Lamb. In the songs she wrote for St. Ursula, Hildegard fuses all these images; she places a song with new meaning in the mouths of the nuns who sing the Office, and who regularly taste the body and blood of the Lord at the altar of their own church. They offer a special song of love in the sequences Hildegard wrote for them to sing at Mass, one of which will be analyzed in some detail below.[11]

ST. URSULA: ARCHETYPAL VIRGIN MARTYR AND BRIDE OF CHRIST

The love feast that Hildegard spreads before our eyes in the *Scivias* is a banquet for the daily needs of those who strive on earth. But it is also a spiritual banquet for the saints who feed and drink joyfully, and whose actions call those not yet saintly through the inspiration of their miraculous deeds. Quotations from the Song of Songs are prominent in several of Hildegard's song texts, but none is worked out on the grand scale found in the chants for St. Ursula and her Companions. Here are many parallels between Hildegard's use of the Song to describe the sacrament of the table and the lives of the martyred virgins. This, along with works for the Virgin Mary, is Hildegard's fullest complex of chants: responsories, an antiphon, a set of antiphons for Lauds that includes two extra pieces for other Hours, a sequence for the Mass, and an Office hymn. The entire set of chant texts is bound together by Song of Songs imagery, much of which recollects the themes encountered in *Scivias* as described above. In the chants there is both narrative progression and a harking back to pre-established imagery. In the narrative, Ursula moves from love and the wedding feast to the sacrifice of death, which provides a kind of sacramental consummation: her blood, not that of the hymen in intercourse but that of the slain virgin, mingles with her lover's liquid life. He is the Lamb who was slain, and their life forces mingle in his high court, at the sonorous apex of the Church. I will discuss the texts of individual chants and groups of chants briefly as the poems embody and expand on themes already encountered. At the end I will focus on the sequence, both its text and its music, as a sounding manifestation of Hildegard's themes produced through the action of praise itself, related to her understanding of what music is and how it works within the human person for the purpose of transformation. Hildegard's sequence for St. Ursula is, like all her works in this genre, an exercise in deconstruction of the familiar, a process used not only to destroy but also to create liturgical meaning. It is especially important here because it is an exercise in the only chant genre for the Mass liturgy that has a significant representation in works by Hildegard, who was far more interested in composing for the Office than for the Mass.[12]

According to the story, Ursula was a fourth-century queen of Britain, who renounced her betrothed to join with other virgins in a life consecrated to God. The virgins were commonly wont to sail and to swim near their boat, and one day a sudden gale blew the entire company off to the Continent. There the virgins became famous agents of religious conversion, but their triumphant progress was cut short by Attila the Hun and his soldiers who, when he encountered them near Cologne, slaughtered Ursula and her virgin companions (later counted as 11,000). They had been asked to submit or to die, and only the latter course was acceptable.

Hildegard's texts include references to male companions, defenders who died with the virgins they sought to care for and protect. When bodies assumed to be those of the virgins were uncovered near Cologne in the mid-twelfth century, men were found buried with them. Elizabeth of Schönau wrote to Hildegard about this finding, and Elizabeth's own life of Ursula and her companions emphasizes the mixed character of the company, thus explaining the situation of the newly uncovered relics.

Hildegard's hagiographical exercise defends this position, which suggests that the songs date from after 1156, when this particular group of relics was discovered. With so many virgins and companions, the discovery provided relics for many churches and monastic foundations. The eagerness for Office music for this group of saints was tied to the recently elevated cult, and it may be supposed that Hildegard's own church received one of the widely dispersed relics from the dig; her songs may have been composed for their reception, as well as in support of Elizabeth's hagiographic ideals.[13] Hildegard, as we have seen, wrote her compositions with practical needs in mind, clearly hoping the works would be of use to religious communities, and especially to her own. But the works are always more than discrete pieces or groups of pieces, and all are tied to a larger theological program. One reads and listens in two ways: to the particular piece and its details, and also with attention to the ways in which the work was known in the context of her larger purpose.

The set of pieces Hildegard wrote for St. Ursula, like all her music, is both functional and deliberately out of keeping with tradition. This is true for carefully conceived theological reasons far too complex to explain here in their entirety. The first responsory and antiphon are appropriate for First Vespers of the feast; the second responsory would then have been used at Matins; the five Lauds antiphons make an appropriate set for the psalms of Lauds, with "Et ideo puellelae istae" serving for the Benedictus of this hour;

"Deus enim rorem" might have been used for the Little Hours, including that of Terce, which preceded Mass; and the last of the eight psalter antiphons for Second Vespers. The hymn is a mighty work, which could have served at any of the Office hours, and the sequence would have graced the Mass, set in its traditional place before the reading of the Gospel.

The texts reveal that the plan—if such it can be called—was to offer both a narrative and a time for lofty reflection with steady repeating of the most important imagery, especially that of blood. This is a feast venerating martyrs of the church, but in this case the slaughtered subjects were also a group of virgins. In mentioning the pieces in quasi-liturgical order here, my goal is to emphasize allusions to the Song of Songs and to demonstrate ways in which these allusions in the poetry join the pieces to the liturgical commentary of *Scivias* 2, the images and their theological context forming a useful divining rod for a difficult group of song texts.[14]

Just one example of this glorious fusion must suffice, and that is the opening of "Favus distillans." In this responsory, Ursula is seen as a woman who has had a dream in which Christ becomes her lover, causing her to reject her human spouse for union with the Godhead. Both the opening of the poem and the subsequent verse locate the saint in the Song of Songs as the *sponsa*, the bride, but make her spouse the paschal victim, the Agnus Dei, or Lamb of God. From the grove of the sweet lover, Ursula moves to the court of the Lamb, and then, more locally, to the dawn of monastic song and the morning liturgy, taking Hildegard and her community of nuns into this kaleidoscope of the exalted and the intimate, the general and the particular.

> RESPONSE: A dripping honeycomb was Ursula the virgin, who yearned to embrace the Lamb of God, honey and milk beneath her tongue. For she gathered to herself a fruitful garden and the choicest flowers in a flock of virgins.
>
> VERSE: So rejoice, daughter of Zion, in the most noble dawn.

Hildegard also invokes the favored poetic structures of the Song of Songs in the sequence "O Ecclesia," where Ursula becomes the Church as she is the bride of the Lamb. It begins:

> Ecclesia, your eyes are like sapphires, your ears like Mount Bethel; your nose like a mountain of incense and myrrh, your voice like the sound of many waters.

In the final verses, Ursula and her companions discover a new Cana in their wedding feast, and their blood's wine is a drink of special savor. "O Ecclesia" carries through with the sexual imagery and the jewels described in the Song, as the virgins become a necklace of wounds, blood-gleaming pearls that strangle the throat of the Devil, whose neck and head are characteristically described through phallic imagery in Hildegard's play and other writings. That they "surround" his throat and choke out his life is a richly textured reversal of the Fall, with its introduction of carnal intercourse and the devil's triumphant seduction of Eve, a scene that is most skillfully exploited in the Anglo-Norman "Ordo Representationis Ade."[15] The virginal pearls represent the newness that is briefly tasted by all who approach the communion table rightly.[16] The devil's *symphonia* that mocked the virgins as they were slain becomes the new symphony of triumph played round the altar, the high throne of the Agnus Dei.

The reversal celebrated in the sequence text is also reflected in the music, which appears as a deconstructed and refashioned example of the genre with some features preserved and others not. Hildegard's music is generative, much of it coming out of stock motives that she employs constantly. Hildegard creates a sonic fabric in which she can include motives from well-known chants borrowed from the liturgy, as well as develop particular twists and motivic details that bind pieces together or that allow for tone painting on certain words. She is also deeply sensitive to liturgical genre, using formal considerations to make further theological points. When considering her music, any group of pieces has to be understood on several levels: as a part of a sonic whole, as part of the context of the smaller group of works to which it relates, and then, of course, as part of the well-defined genres of liturgical chant that she knew so well from a lifetime of singing, and bent and twisted to her will. So it is with the hymn and the sequence for St. Ursula, both of which are part of a set of pieces that relate musically as well as textually, the opening motive of a fifth (which, of course, she uses elsewhere) being exploited throughout, regardless of the tonal center of the piece.

All of Hildegard's sequences rely on double-versicle structure, with texts in the free art prose employed by Notker and later poets who take their inspiration from him.[17] As is well known, Hildegard's sequences are much more melismatic and formally far freer than any other surviving works in the genre.[18] She buried kernels of similar melodic phrases within paired versicles in torrents of notes, reinventing the form as she went. Yet, although it may be difficult to discern at first, even "O Ecclesia"—the freest of all Hildegard's works in this genre—is tightly controlled, and her departures from the form she established and the musical language she chose to employ allow for heightened proclamation of the text and underscore poetic meanings. The nature of Hildegard's liturgical songs, the powerful interdependence of word on song and formal structure, and of music upon textual sense, reveal that she conceived both dimensions of her work as parts of a single process, singing as she verbalized, verbalizing as she sang. We can, as is common in contemporary scholarship, comprehend Hildegard's texts apart from their music, and study her music apart from the texts, but this was neither the manner in which she wrote the works nor the way she intended them to be known. Song, as she defines it, is made of music and words, and the two create parts of a breathing sonic organism, which, in the mouths of the praising faithful, make church, make Divinity: "And so the words symbolize the body, and the jubilant music indicates the spirit; and the celestial harmony shows the Divinity, and the words the Humanity of the Son of God."[19]

In Table 4.2, the Latin text of "O Ecclesia," organized into the poetic units found in the original sources, appears next to a literal English translation based on Newman.[20] The musical units are indicated in the left column.

Sequence poetry, whether set in the style of Notker from the late ninth century or Adam of St. Victor from the twelfth century, is dependent on melodic repetition.[21] The sequence is a through-composed chant form, with different music for every poetic unit, and yet with each sense unit (stanza or strophe) falling into two—or sometimes more—parts, each of which is sung to the same melody. Thus, the most typical musical form of the sequence is AABBCCDDEE, etc., with each letter representing a melodic unit, and, as can be seen, with each of them rendered twice. Hildegard respects this feature of the sequence as a genre. The text of "O Ecclesia," adapted to use my style of indicating versicles according to a musical plan, is organized as follows:[22]

I.1, I.2, I.3; II.1, II.2; III, II.3; IV.1, IV.2; V.1, V.2; VI; VII.1, VII.2

Or, if each melodic unit is represented by a letter:

AAA, BB, CB, DD, EE, F, GG

As with "O Jerusalem," the sequence for St. Ursula needs to be interpreted as the music "cuts" the text into units, binding some sections together very strongly and giving independence to other stanzas, even casting them out of the established musical framework.[23] Hildegard has joined the opening stanzas—those dependent on the Song of Songs—together, folding three sense units one upon the other (see Ex. 4.1). In the singers' (or listeners') minds, the Church described as "the beloved" in the Song becomes Ursula as she sees her bridegroom in a vision of true faith, and then in the third statement, as she joins him in the love feast of heaven, the sapphire sky (the jewel of his belly in the Song, as well as that of Ezekiel 1:26). The opening is

TABLE 4.2

~

Text of "O Ecclesia": Hildegard's Sequence for St. Ursula

MUSIC	TEXT	TRANSLATION

I.1	*1. O Ecclesia,*
	oculi tui similes
	saphiro sunt,
	et aures tue monti Bethel,
	et nasus tuus est
	sicut mons mirre et thuris
	et os tuum quasi sonus aquarum
	  multarum
		1. O Church,
		your eyes are
		like sapphire,
		and your ears like Mount Bethel,
		your nose like
		a mountain of incense and myrrh,
		and your mouth like the sound of many
		  waters.

I.2	*2. In visione vere fidei* *Ursula Filium Dei amavit* *et virum cum hoc seculo reliquit* *et in solem aspexit* *atque pulcherrimum iuvenem* *vocavit, dicens:*	2. In a vision of true faith, Ursula fell in love with the Son of God and renounced a husband along with this world. She gazed upon the sun and called to the fairest youth, saying:
I.3	*3. In multo desiderio* *desideravi ad te venire* *et in celestibus* *nuptiis tecum sedere,* *per alienam viam ad te currens* *velut nubes que in purissimo aere* *currit similis saphiro.*	3. In great yearning I have yearned to come to you and at the heavenly wedding feast sit with you, racing to you by a strange path like a cloud that, in the purest sky, races like sapphire.
II.1	*4. Et postquam Ursula* *sic dixerat,* *rumor iste* *per omnes populos exiit.*	4. And after Ursula had spoken thus, this report went out among all peoples.
II.2	*Et dixerunt:* *Innocentia puellaris ignorantie* *nescit quid dicit.*	And they said: In the innocence of girlish ignorance, she knows not what she says.
III (I.3cc, ee)	*5. Et ceperunt ludere cum illa* *in magna symphonia,* *usque dum ignea sarcina* *super eam cecidit.*	5. And they began to sport with her in great harmony, until the fiery burden fell upon her.
(II.3)	*Unde omnes cognoscebant* *quia contemptus mundi est* *sicut mons Bethel.*	Then all people recognized that scorn for the world is like Mount Bethel.

MUSIC	TEXT	TRANSLATION
IV.1	6. *Et cognoverunt etiam* *suavissimum odorem* *mirre et thuris,*	6. And they recognized also the sweetest fragrance of incense and myrrh,
IV.2	*quoniam contemptus mundi* *super omnia ascendit.*	because scorn for the world mounts above all.
V.1	7. *Tunc diabolus* *membra sua invasit,* *que nobilissimos mores* *in corporibus istis* *occiderunt.*	7. Then the devil entered into his members, who, in those bodies, slaughtered the noblest way of life.
V.2	8. *Et hoc in alta voce* *omnia elementa audierunt* *et ante thronum Dei* *dixerunt:*	8. And in a high voice all the elements heard and before the throne of God said:
VI.	9. *Wach! rubicundus sanguis* *innocentis agni* *in desponsatione sua* *effusus est.*	9. Wach! The scarlet blood of an innocent lamb at her betrothal is spilled.
VII.1.	10. *Hoc audiant omnes celi* *et in summa symphonia* *laudent Agnum Dei,*	10. Let all the heavens hear this and in supreme harmony praise the Lamb of God:
VII.2	*quia guttur serpentis antiqui* *in istis margaritis* *materie Verbi Dei* *suffocatum est.*	for the throat of the ancient serpent in these pearls from the matter of the Word of God is strangled.

especially powerful, given that the sequence was understood in Hildegard's time as a commentary on the "Alleluia" of the Mass liturgy. Hildegard's reference to this form in the elaborate opening gestures toward a common understanding of this sequence as a human translation of angelic sound, the Church on earth resounding with the Church above, and Ursula joining the former to the latter through her vision of a mystical union with the Lamb. Barbara Newman has written about the association of the eagle with mystical experience, and here Ursula, like the eagle, can look straight into the sun.[24] The price she will pay for her joining is suggested only by the myrrh, whose precious perfume was used to anoint the dead, making it a symbol of Christ's passion, and here of Ursula's death as well. The melody soars to its loftiest point both at the mention of the mouth of the beloved, which has the sound of many waters (*os tuum quasi sonus aquarum*), and of the purest air of the blue heavens (*in purissimo aere*), which calls Ursula to the nuptial kiss, through music's ability to raise the words on high.

The female voice is naturally a higher voice than the male, and Hildegard wrote music for this sound, putting her notes in a range that only women could comfortably sing, especially young women. John of Salisbury and others were disgusted by the "feminization" of music, by lofty ranges and flexible melismas then prevalent in much new music of the period; Hildegard flies in the face of any assumption that the female is somehow silly, somehow less worthy. In her sonic landscape, the ideal *is* female, and yet, of course, men are welcome to join this world of song, if they play by the rules of its unique harmonies. There is one masculine voice, however, that cannot join in the game, and that voice is the Devil's. He cannot sing (as in *Ordo Virtutum*), and when his works are represented in song, the voice is often low and growling, a point made in "O Ecclesia" at a dramatic moment.

The lofty and bejeweled opening of "O Ecclesia" is followed by the challenge of the world and of the Devil; this comes in words that Hildegard crafted to inspire and defend her nuns, who clearly were often scorned for their love of a bridegroom they could not see. The world says "you do not know what you say" when Ursula claims her lover; but the virtue of contempt for the world itself inspires respect, as she takes the fiery burden of her martyrdom, with reference to the passion of the bloody joining to follow. As can be seen, Hildegard uses repetition to bind the next three stanzas together as well, beginning with "Et postquam" and continuing through the end of what I have labeled as musical unit III. Unit III is a melodic hybrid. The opening notes are like those of I.3cc. The music shifts to elaborated material from I.3ee as the mocking symphony described in the text leads to Ursula's fiery burden. The music makes the connection between this and the mouth that sounds like many waters and the sapphire heavens.[25] In order to establish the structure for the sound and the violation of that framework, Hildegard must work carefully with convention. After two blocks of musically interconnected texts, and a third musical unit that borrows from each, she makes a true shift away from the opening music, all the while keeping to the large framework of the arch that is found in every line, a steady rising from the opening *a*, up to the highest ranges of the tessitura, and then a return at the end to the lower *a*, motion that can be seen (and heard!). In almost every poetic stanza this rising and falling occurs, and with some regularity.

When the Devil's minions kill Ursula's companions in Unit V, the musical openings are invaded by his base propensity for rape. Unit V, as can be seen in the example, begins low but then descends even lower, the *a* to *g*, and then

EXAMPLE 4.1. Hildegard of Bingen, "O Ecclesia": sequence for St. Ursula

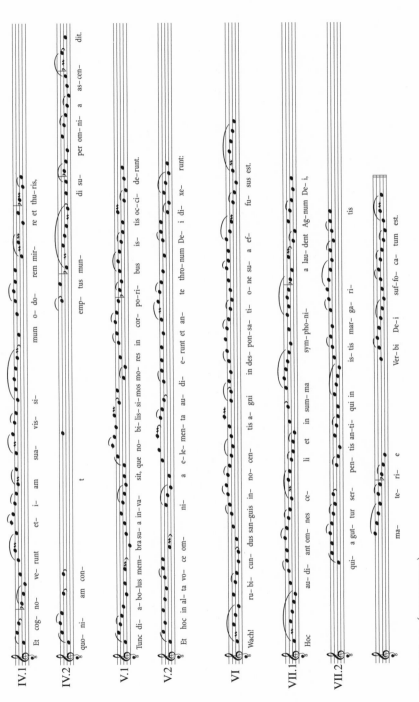

EXAMPLE 4.1. (CONTINUED)

D

I.1 et na- sus tu- us est si- cut mons mir- re et thu- ris et os tu- um qua- si so- nus a- qua-rum mul- ta- rum

E

d

I.2 et in so- lem a- spe- xit at- que pul- cher-ri-mum iu- ve- nem vo- ca- vit, di- cens:

e

dd

I.3 per a- li- e- nam vi- am ad te cur- rens ve- lut nu- bes que in pu-ris- si-mo a- e- re cur- rit si-mi- lis sa- phi- ro.

ee

(to II.1)

III Et ce- pe-runt lu- de- re cum il- la in ma- gna sym- pho- ni- a, us- que dum i- gne-a sar- ci- na su- per e- am ce- ci- dit.

(I.3ccee)

(to II.3)

EXAMPLE 4.1. (CONTINUED)

down to *e*, a note that could only be sung by the male voice (or very low female voices). The word here is "membra," a veiled reference to the male sex organ that has been filled with the Devil's sound, the sound of a fallen race. The high voices of the entire universe protest this action, beginning in the parallel stanza in the low range, but not as low as the notes on "membra," and then rising at the ends of the texts found in Unit V to the throne of the Lamb, who hears the universal cry of woe. We hear it too in Unit VI, on the dramatic "Wach!" that reaches to the high court where the blood streams into the chalice of the Church, making the food of the communion feast. Unit VI stands by itself, characteristically presenting a mingling of two martyrs' bloods in the heavenly bed of the Lamb's altar. Ursula is wed and her union consummated. The sorrowful "wach" turns to joy of understanding: suffering begets a new joy, and the wholeness of the virginal body kills the Devil himself. The point is made graphically through the device of repetition in Unit VII, and in two especially significant places. The "wach" of Unit VI becomes the "hoc" of Unit VII, joining these two musically different units with a rhyming pun, as the lament is introduced twice, the second time to do its work of salvation. The pitches, making a low arch from *a* to *c'* and back to the lower neighbor note of *g*, are transposed higher several times, both in Unit VI and then in Unit VII as the "wach" moves to "hoc" and then to the highest *symphonia*. This music joins with the Lamb and Ursula and her virgins become made of him, the matter of the Word of God. In this eucharistic action, they are fed and become food, joining his body to offer *Ecclesia* to those who take it into themselves. Their transformed bodies become pearls, a new necklace for the Devil's phallic throat, squeezing him with unblemished muscles that strangle him. The new sexuality is eucharistic; as discussed above, the host-like pearls are make of a new substance that transforms and saves. The notes for "materie" are the same as those for "guttur serpentis," and Hildegard uses the repetition to literally stuff the maw with substance (see Units VII.1 and VII.2).

Hildegard's music constantly interrelates and interprets her texts, and understanding and actually hearing the connections she makes would have required the years of practice that were possible within the monastic community. Knowing her subtle tricks depends on memory, and deep knowledge of the pieces. Once one grasps her tonal idioms, her music is not hard to sing, not at all, for it is highly formulaic and generative. But the inner sense of the texts and melodies takes as much deep reflection to appreciate as any sophisticated art music. Repetition is her favored device, and she uses it not only here in a sequence (as would be expected), but throughout her music—both on the largest of organizational levels as well as in the smallest details. Her musical devices depend on the texts, but the meanings of the

texts depend on the musical devices, large and small. The genres she explores
are all rooted in liturgical convention, as with "O Ecclesia" with its repeating
pairs or triples. But the genre does get altered, and the reasons for doing this
have to do with a theology of newness and transformation. The music became the nuns' food; their partaking of it was expected to change them, and
to prepare them for the reception of the bridegroom they encountered not
only in the prayer and praise of the Divine Office, but face to face in the
Mass. The sequence for Ursula served as preparation for this event, and so
too, I believe, did the *Ordo Virtutum*.

ORDO VIRTUTUM AS PREPARATION FOR THE SACRAMENTAL LOVE FEAST

The *Ordo Virtutum* is a complex work, drawing on traditions from the liturgical drama of the Prophets' plays and the battles of good and evil as found
in several classical and medieval texts.[26] The purposes and settings of the play
have been much discussed. Peter Dronke has suggested that the play was
designed for the dedication of Hildegard's new church at the Rupertsberg.[27]
Pamela Sheingorn has proposed that the play would have served to initiate
the nuns into the Benedictine way of life.[28] Gunilla Iversen has focused on
the play in the context of Hildegard's life, especially with reference to her
relationship with the nun Richardis von Stade.[29] I do not dispute the idea
that the play may have been performed on highly festive occasions such as
the Dedication of the Church or upon the occasion of the Consecration of
Nuns, but I think its use by Hildegard and the women in her convent was
probably far more common than the circumstances these once-in-a-lifetime
situations would have offered. The Virtues of the play appear in the costumes
of Hildegard's convent, with freely flowing hair and special attributes. The
illuminated *Scivias* shows them repeatedly, and both Madeline Caviness and
Sarah Bromberg have commented on the correspondences between the visu-
alized representations and the Virtues in the play.[30] The play also appears in
prose form in *Scivias* as the introduction to the final scene of joy and glory
that ends the treatise with a commentary on Psalms 148–50. The play's action
and featured characters—so central to Hildegard's theology—needed to be
encountered on a regular basis. The Song of Songs is a useful key to Hildegard's dramatic work, especially when her use of the text in the play is joined
with her exploration of it elsewhere. Anima, the Everywoman character
whose fall from grace and whose redemption after confession is the active
purpose of the work, is here engaged in a healing service with Christ as both

her doctor and her spouse. She prepares for a marriage that is the joining of his body in Eucharist as defined both in the *Scivias* and the Ursula songs. The play serves as a kind of group confession for the entire community, as they both forgive and embrace the fallen soul, who, once more, is given another chance to be redeemed.[31]

In his introduction to the play, Dronke refers to the importance of the Song and lists several places where the text is cited:

Royal Wedding Chamber: lines 75 and 104
The Kiss of the King: line 90
Burning in the King's embraces: line 105
The Flower in the Meadow: line 109
The Embraces of the Princess: lines 125 and 129
The Royal Nuptials: line 131
The Rocky Cavern (where the hiding dove becomes a warrior): line 154

The themes of love and joining also emerge at other crucial points in the play. The opening prologue, sung by the Patriarchs and Prophets, speaks of the beautiful body of the Word of God; both the men of old and the Virtues of the new order work to shine with him, "building up" the body (5). From the outset, this is a play encouraging the "joining" Hildegard describes in the eucharistic feast. The first chorus is of the embodied souls who wish to be "daughter of the King" (11). Anima is ready to have her love feast: "O let me come to you joyfully, that you may give me the kiss of your heart!" (24). The Virtues are ready to serve as handmaidens to this daughter of the king (25), but she wants to take off her garment, the new flesh of the consecrated virgin, the only robe worthy for this bridegroom's chamber. She cannot complete the mortification of flesh needed to "make the robe" of glory: "Woe is me, I cannot complete this dress I have put on. Indeed, I want to cast it off!" (39–40). This Song of Songs has a reluctant bride who ignores the song of longing issuing from the throne of the Lamb, the primal song of the Creator sung to all his flock: "Ah," the Virtues sing, "a certain wondrous victory already rose in that Soul, in her wondrous longing for God, in which a sensual delight was secretly hidden" (51–52).[32]

In the middle section of the play, the Virtues call the lost soul to the rightful love feast of the garden of bliss, to the royal *thalamus* (74–75). The flower of the garden is blasted, yet another flower calls it to join in radiant light. The mystical experience of Ursula, who like the eagle could stare into the sun, is invoked here as well, as the Virtues claim they can make the soul ready for the encounter with the Christ. Fear of God says: "I, Fear of God, can prepare you, blissful daughters, to gaze upon the living God and not die of it" (80–81). The gazing is part of joining and longing, a union that never will be severed. But, like the mockers in the Ursula songs, the Devil accuses the Virtues of a false theology. They have invented this mystical marriage with an unseen God. He croaks and mocks in words that are supremely challenging: "Bravo! Bravo! What is this great fear, and this great love? Where is the champion? Where the prize giver? You don't even know what you are worshipping" (84–85).

The Devil hits the nuns in the solar plexus of their beliefs in a mystical union. As with the transformation of the elements at Mass, their bridegroom cannot be seen and is a figment; their offspring are not real human beings. The altar is a barren stone table with no food, and with no actual host to serve the meal. But in their next lines, the Virtues extol the beauties of the love feast to the befuddled Anima, which the Devil cannot see. Obedience offers "the kiss of the king" (89–90); Faith promises the leaping fountain (95); and Chastity takes the company by the hand to the garden of the Song of Songs: "Maidenhood, you remain within the royal chamber. How sweetly you burn in the King's embraces, when the Sun blazes through you, never letting your noble flower fall. Gentle maiden, you will never know the shadow over the falling flower!" (104–8). The sexual imagery is reversed, for the blasted and impregnated human body will be wet with a new liquid, and also be freed from the curse of sin and death, as the Virtues promise, singing all together: "The flower in the meadow falls in the wind, the rain splashes it. But you, Maidenhood, remain in the symphonies of heavenly habitants: you are the tender flower that will never grow dry" (109–11). And further:

VIRTUES:	Royal daughter, you are held fast in the embraces the world shuns: how tender is your love in the highest God.
DISCIPLINE:	I am one who loves the innocent ways that know nothing ignoble: I always gaze upon the King of Kings, and, as my highest honour, I embrace him.
VIRTUES:	Angelic comrade, how comely you are in the royal nuptials (125–31).

Anima, who has fallen, and whose festering wounds stink of sin (170–71), crawls back; she has seen the royal virtues, graceful and beautiful, in the highest Sun (161–64). The Devil croaks again, this time in rage as his prey slips away: "You were in my embrace, I led you out. Yet now you are going back . . ." (210). One lover will be replaced by another.

Even as they bind him, the Devil rages against their unseen lover and his unseen offspring: "You don't know what you are nurturing, for your belly is devoid of the beautiful form that woman receives from man: in this you transgress the command that God enjoined in the sweet act of love; so you don't even know what you are!" (235–37).

The Devil's challenge, taken in the context of the love imagery of *Scivias,* especially as developed in the Ursula songs, strikes at the heart of the Christian mystery and belief in the power of the sacrament of the Eucharist. The answer to his challenge, as Chastity argues in her final retort, is belief in the presence of God's Son in human life: "I did bring forth a man, who gathers up mankind to himself, against you, through his nativity" (240–41).

The magnificent finale of the play includes a call from Christ to the Father to let the faithful come to him in order to bring the triumphant completion of the Holy Jerusalem that is the Church. Here Christ speaks for the lost souls, pleading as victim, and begging God that his suffering for their good be triumphant. When the Christ ceases speaking, the play closes with a plea for all to bend their knees. I believe the play to be a call to the altar, to the royal nuptials of the eucharistic feast. It makes great sense for such a work, filled as it is with the imagery Hildegard used in *Scivias* 2.6, and in her liturgical poetry, to be a community enactment of confession and forgiveness, the themes and rhythms of which are especially appropriate before the mystical union that the faithful soul could find regularly in the Mass liturgy.

In Hildegard's interpretation, the virgins offer the song of longing to their bridegroom, rather than the other way around. Yet, he is the song they sing, and he is present as the longed-for food that they take inside their bodies, making *Ecclesia* as they do so, making him who is *Ecclesia* as well. So he leads them on, beckoning to them—at the end of the play—when he calls them to the Cross and to the end of time. The *Ordo Virtutum* as a genre builds on the modes of praise exercised in the Office, and leads to and prepares for the sacrament as explored both through the *Scivias* and in the Office texts and the sequence discussed here.

The lush gardens of Hildegard's thought open most readily through a honeycombed multiplicity of interconnected passageways, and these different genres—liturgical commentary, Office texts, sequence text and music, and play—offer liturgical perspectives on the Mass, the Office, and the drama, this last a genre that, I would argue, serves to make a deliberate bridge from cloister, to choir, to altar. The texts define the singing of the nuns and help characterize the symphony of praise they offer, making a new love through the sacramental feast that was a climax to their lives of prayer and praise. In Hildegard's world of images, human/divine love is conditioned by a beautiful and efficient sexuality, a restored sense of longing and fulfillment that is both the means and the end of a salvific union with the divine. In order to achieve this sense in a practiced liturgy, Hildegard engages in a studied and serious "genre bending," making the familiar into the unfamiliar to craft a theological statement about singing and its importance, especially as the music is made by nuns.[33] In the *Ordo Virtutum,* the nuns had a transformed play of the prophets to sing, one in which the female Virtues replaced the old patriarchy and became the new agents leading the faithful to God, in a language that especially suits the love life of consecrated Virgins.

NOTES

1. For an overview of Hildegard's life and works, see Barbara Newman, " 'Sibyl of the Rhine': Hildegard's Life and Times," in *Voice of the Living Light: Hildegard of Bingen and Her World,* ed. Barbara Newman (Berkeley: University of California Press, 1998).

2. On the only known illuminated copy of Hildegard's *Scivias,* see Madeline Caviness, "Artist: 'To See, Hear, and Know All at Once,'" in *Voice of the Living Light,* ed. Newman, 110–24. This precious manuscript was lost during World War II, although black and white photographs survive.

3. On Hildegard's view of women and their importance in the history of salvation, see the pioneering study by Barbara Newman, *Sister of Wisdom: St. Hildegard's Theology of the Feminine* (Berkeley: University of California Press, 1987). Newman speaks of Hildegard's two strategies for coming to terms with the female: one is to develop the humility topos, especially with concentration on God's love for the Virgin Mary, who exemplifies this ideal; the other is to explore the feminine aspects of the Divinity itself.

4. See my discussion in "Composer and Dramatist: 'Melodious Singing and the Freshness of Remorse,'" in *Voice of the Living Light,* ed. Newman, 149–75.

5. See the English translation of *Scivias* by Mother Columba Hart and Jane Bishop, with an introduction by Barbara Newman, in the Classics of Western Civilization series (New York: Paulist Press, 1990), 237–89.

6. Readers who desire an introduction to standard liturgical structures and theological concepts, and further bibliography, may wish to consult *The Oxford Dictionary of the Christian Church,* ed. F. L. Cross and E. A. Livingstone, 3d ed. (Oxford: Oxford University Press, 1997).

7. For an introduction to Hildegard's Mariology, see Barbara Newman, *Sister of Wisdom;* Fassler, "Composer"; and Margot Schmidt, "Maria: 'materia aurea' in der Kirche nach Hildegard von Bingen," in *Hildegard von Bingen: Prophetin durch die Zeiten,* ed. Edeltraud Forster (Freiburg im Breisgau, 1997), 262–83.

8. On the "Sanctus," consult the second edition of the *New Grove Dictionary of Music and Musicians* (London: Macmillan, 2001), 22:228–29, and the appropriate sections in David Hiley, *Western Plainchant: A Handbook* (Oxford: Clarendon Press, 1993).

9. Before reading this discussion of *Scivias* 2.6, students are advised to read both the Song of Songs from the Old Testament and chapter 14 of Revelation (also known as the Apocalypse), the last book in the New Testament, which describes "the Lamb and the virgins that follow him."

10. See *Scivias,* 2.6 §35, pp. 259–60. Students are encouraged to read all of *Scivias* 2.6 for a fuller understanding of Hildegard's beautiful and unusual understanding of the sacrament. For ready comparison with other thinkers from the Middle Ages, see Gary

Macy, *The Theologies of the Eucharist in the Early Scholastic Period: A Study of the Salvific Function of the Sacrament According to the Theologians, c. 1080–c. 1220* (Oxford: Oxford University Press, 1984).

11. Scholars have explored Hildegard's views of love in interpersonal relationships in the context of her feelings for the nun Richardis. Some have seen Richardis as the model for the straying and subsequently recovered Anima in the *Ordo Virtutum*. Richardis left Hildegard's care to become an abbess herself, and shortly thereafter died, apparently claiming that she was sorry to have left the Rupertsberg. For an introduction to this topic, see Barbara Newman's essay on Hildegard's life in *Voice of the Living Light*, 12. The works Newman cites as essential reading are important in further situating Hildegard: Peter Dronke, "Hildegard of Bingen," in his *Women Writers of the Middle Ages* (Oxford: Oxford University Press, 1981), 144–201; Sabina Flanigan, *Hildegard of Bingen, 1098–1179: A Visionary Life* (rev. ed., London and New York: Routledge, 1998); and Edward Peter Nolan, *Cry Out and Write: A Feminine Poetics of Revelation* (New York: Continuum, 1994). In his provocative and elegant study, *Music, Body, and Desire in Medieval Culture: Hildegard of Bingen to Chaucer* (Stanford: Stanford University Press, 2001), Bruce Holsinger interrelates Hildegard's understanding of "musical pleasure" and "musical violence" (p. 101). I agree with Holsinger that music for Hildegard was "a sonorous vehicle of spiritual grace and moral clarity" (p. 101); I will look at other kinds of evidence to show that the sexuality described in Hildegard's song texts has scriptural and liturgical underpinnings, and depends primarily upon her view of the sacraments.

12. See Fassler, "Composer," 150–59.

13. In addition to the correspondence between Elizabeth of Schönau and Hildegard regarding St. Ursula, there is a letter to Hildegard from an abbess of the monastery at Cologne, a church dedicated to St. Ursula and near the supposed site of the martyrdom, which reveals great personal intimacy between these two figures. See *The Letters of Hildegard of Bingen*, vol. 2, trans. Joseph L. Baird and Radd K. Ehrman (New York: Oxford University Press, 1998), 104.

14. Before turning to a study of the sequence "O Ecclesia," readers are advised to read the entire set of poems for St. Ursula and the eleven thousand virgins, noting the several allusions to the Song of Songs and to the high court of the Lamb from Revelation. The Ursula poems are found in Barbara Newman's edition of Hildegard's *Symphonia: A Critical Edition of the Symphonia armonie celestium revelationum (Symphony of the Harmony of Celestial Revelation)* (2d ed., Ithaca, N.Y.: Cornell University Press, 1998), 230–47.

15. For discussion of the Mariology in this play, see Fassler, "Composer," and Schmidt, "Maria."

16. The importance of circumcision as a foreshadowing of the sacrament of baptism is developed at great length in Hildegard's *Scivias*. She sees the taming of lust beginning with circumcision, which points toward the salvific action of baptism. The Virgin Mary completed the task, and Christ and the Church perpetuate her action, extending it to all with the grace to accept it. See, for example, *Scivias*, 3.2, pp. 332–33. For the association of ring imagery with sexual intercourse, see Holsinger, *Music, Body, and Desire*, 142–52.

17. For discussion of the sequence in Hildegard's region during the early twelfth century, see Lori Kruckenberg, "The Sequence from 1050–1150: Study of a Genre in Change" (Ph.D. diss., University of Iowa, 1998). Analysis of the text–music relationship in the Notkerian sequence is provided in Richard Crocker, *The Early Medieval Sequence*

(Berkeley: University of California Press, 1977). Although the sequence texts by Notker are a securely attributable body of poems, the melodies are later, and the ways in which they were adapted to the texts are complex.

18. Several scholars have produced analyses of Hildegard's sequences, such as Michael Klaper in the commentary to Lorenz Welker, *Lieder: Faksimile Riesencodex (Hs. 2) der Hessischen Landesbibliothek Wiesbaden fol. 466–481v* (Wiesbaden, 1998), English translation by Lori Kruckenberg. Klaper compares his own analysis of the piece with that by Marianne Richert Pfau, "Hildegard von Bingen's 'Symphonia Armonie Celestium Revelationum': An Analysis of Music Process, Modality, and Text-Music Relations" (Ph.D. diss., State University of New York at Stony Brook, 1990), demonstrating how two capable scholars arrive at different understandings of its formal structure. For another view of several works in the genre, see Hildegard of Bingen, *Sequences and Hymns*, ed. Christopher Page (Lustleigh: Antico Edition, 1983).

19. *Scivias*, 3.13, §12, p. 533.

20. *Symphonia*, 238–43, with notes on 311–12. Newman provides two translations of all Hildegard's liturgical poetry, one free, the other literal and close to the structure of the original. I have provided the latter here, but encourage reference to both when studying Hildegard's poetry.

21. For comparison of the early sequence with the late sequence, see Margot Fassler, *Gothic Song: Victorine Sequences and Augustinian Reform in Twelfth Century Paris* (Cambridge: Cambridge University Press, 1993).

22. Study of the music can bring a completely different formal understanding of a piece such as this one, which, in comparison with Hildegard's other sequences, is even freer and more difficult to analyze. For another analysis of this work, see Janet Martin and Greta Mary Hair, "'O Ecclesia': The Text and Music of Hildegard of Bingen's Sequence for St. Ursula," *Tjurunga* 30 (1986): 3–62. The piece has been chosen for discussion here because so much work of varying kinds has been done on it. My own work is the first to place it in the larger theological context of the *Scivias*, using the lens of the Song of Songs for closer readings. Many of the details I do not have time to emphasize can be found in Martin and Hair's excellent study.

23. The sequence "O Ecclesia" (from Wiesbaden, Hessische Landesbibliothek, Hs. 2, fol. 477^{r-v}) is performed along with others of the Ursula set on Anonymous IV's recording "Eleven Thousand Virgins: Chants for the Feast of St. Ursula," 1997 (Harmonia Mundi 907200). The useful notes to the performance do not emphasize formal structures and their meaning. Readers are encouraged to listen with Example 4.1 in hand, exploring the ways in which the music is organized, and the way in which it orders the text. For a performance of "O Ecclesia" that mirrors the reading presented here more closely, see Gothic Voices, conducted by Christopher Page, "A Feather on the Breath of God: Sequences and Hymns by Hildegard of Bingen," 1984 (Hyperion CDA 66039).

24. See Newman, *Symphonia*, 311.

25. Hildegard's sophisticated uses of contrafacta technique are not surprising for a twelfth-century poet/composer. For an introduction to the technique and its central role in twelfth-century music, see Fassler, *Gothic Song*, especially chap. 8: "Contrafacta in the Parisian Sequence Repertories: An Introduction," 161–84.

26. See Fassler, "Composer," 168–75. A useful introduction to the play's meaning and its reliance on the Song is found on p. 169.

27. For summaries of his arguments and further bibliography, see his notes to the transla-

tion of the play in *Nine Medieval Latin Plays* (Cambridge: Cambridge University Press, 1994), especially pp. 152–53. He attacks the idea advanced by Eckehard Simon that Hildegard's play was not meant for performance; see Eckehard Simon, *The Theatre of Medieval Europe: New Research in Early Drama* (Cambridge: Cambridge University Press, 1991), xiii. All references to the play in this paper are from Dronke's edition and translation. The music for the play can be found in Hildegard of Bingen, *Lieder*, ed. Pudentiana Barth, M. Immaculata Ritscher, and Joseph Schmidt-Görg (Salzburg, 1969), and in a performance edition of the play by Audrey Ekdahl Davidson (Kalamazoo: Western Michigan University Press, 1985), which also has an English translation.

28. See her "The Virtues of Hildegard's *Ordo Virtutum*; or It *Was* a Woman's World," in *The* Ordo Virtutum *of Hildegard of Bingen: Critical Studies*, ed. Audrey Ekdahl Davidson (Kalamazoo: Western Michigan University Press, 1992), 43–62.

29. See "Réaliser une vision: La dernière vision de *Scivias* et le drame *Ordo virtutum* de Hildegarde de Bingen," *Revue de Musicologie* 86 (2000): 37–63. The idea was also proposed by Julia Holloway in "The Monastic Context of Hildegard's *Ordo Virtutum*," in *The* Ordo Virtutum, ed. Davidson, 63–77, and by Barbara Newman in *Sister of Wisdom*, 222–24.

30. See, for example, Caviness's discussion in her "Artist" (n. 2 above).

31. Dronke says in his introduction to the text, "At the opening, an image drawn from the parables of repentance (the lost sheep and the lost drachma) in Luke 15 offers a glimmer of hope that the errant Anima may be found again" (p. 149).

32. On the two kinds of songs Hildegard creates, of sorrow and of joy, see Fassler, "Composer," 168–75 and notes.

33. The phrase "genre bending" was used by my colleague Harold Attridge in his presidential address to the Society of Biblical Literature, 2001. His topic was the Gospel of John, the book of the Bible that, along with Revelation (which Hildegard also believed was by John the Evangelist), was Hildegard's favored text. Genre bending is characteristic of all she does as both theologian and as artist.

CHAPTER FIVE

Putting Bolognese Nun Musicians in their Place

Craig A. Monson

FIFTEEN YEARS AGO nun musicians were virtually unknown. Hildegard of Bingen's recent promotion to popular cult status, in venues as far from the cloister as MTV, did little to shed light on her many musical sisters behind convent walls. But concurrently, and less sensationally, scholars such as Robert Kendrick, Colleen Reardon, Kimberlyn Montford, and myself had begun to illuminate the unfamiliar realm of convent music in cities such as Milan, Siena, Rome, and Bologna.[1] As a result, the cloistered composer Lucrezia Orsina Vizzana from Bologna's most musical convent, Santa Cristina della Fondazza, recently found her way into the latest edition of Donald J. Grout and Claude V. Palisca's canonic *A History of Western Music*. A CD of Lucrezia Vizzana's complete motets became a "classical pick of the month" in a French chain of record stores, and was discussed on National Public Radio in 1999.[2] Lucrezia Vizzana is the heroine of Jeanne Marshall's stage play "Rapture," which opened in Montclair, New Jersey, in 2000 and was revived in Washington, D.C., late in 2001. Vizzana also turns up in a recent film documentary, "Looking for Lucretia," which premiered in 2001. Her rather eventful life has even been transformed into an even more eventful screenplay, which might end up at the neighborhood multiplex or on a TV movie channel some day.

TRIDENTINE CONVENT REFORM

Obviously, this was *not* what the Catholic Church hierarchy had in mind when it tried to put nuns in their place at the Council of Trent and repeatedly in its aftermath. The decrees from the final session of the Council in December 1563 had declared that nuns should, without exception, be confined within convent walls, and subsequent implementation of strict monastic enclosure forced the nuns of the Catholic world to retire within their cloisters. The former, relatively relaxed, comings and goings, the socializing with family, friends, and advocates were significantly curtailed, as walls rose higher and convent windows were bricked up or covered with metal grills and curtains. I have suggested, therefore, that in the emphatically altered monastic reality after Trent, music offered a mechanism for these women forced into seclusion to be heard beyond their convent walls, even if not seen. Gregory Martin's *Roma Sancta,* half guidebook and half propaganda for the glories of Rome after the Council of Trent, affirmed in 1581, for example: "being in the Churche [of a Roman convent] thou shalt only heare their voices singing their service most melodiously, and the Father himself, that is their Ghostly father heareth their confessions through a grate in the wall, where only voice and no sight goeth betwene. . . . And in Bononie [Bologna] and Rome having been many times at their service in their chappels and hearing their goodly singing, never did I see one of them."[3]

The convent's church thus became the primary nexus of the cloister and the world. The music that resounded there, which seems in fact to have burgeoned notably in the decades after the enforcement of enclosure, could "speak" to the world outside the walls in especially effective ways. This fact had not escaped the church hierarchy. But a preliminary attempt at Trent to banish all elaborate music except plainchant from convents was defeated, and the implementation of monastic reform was left to individual bishops and provincial synods at the local level. As a result, the reception of convent music varied widely from diocese to diocese throughout the early modern period. In "freer" cities such as Siena, nuns' music seems to have been highly valued as an important contribution to civic prestige, as Colleen Reardon has shown. And even in Rome, a Curia sensitive to the importance of providing an appropriate monastic paradigm was nevertheless quite ready to relax the rules so that convent musicians might enhance the splendor of the Holy Year 1675, as Kimberlyn Montford has demonstrated.[4]

In environments touched most intensely by the spirit of Tridentine reform, such as Bologna, church authorities developed and strove to enforce restrictive monastic policies. In Bolognese archbishop Gabriele Paleotti's program of monastic reform, music remained one of the hot-button issues, heading a list of convent abuses around 1580, for example, "because the greatest abuse results from music." Paleotti made this claim during a decisive campaign literally to put nun musicians in their place: "Since these excesses chiefly are hatched by the organ windows and galleries facing the public church, which were a new invention a few years ago, introduced solely so the sisters might be heard by outsiders, it seems essential to require that all music be performed down below, in the choir stalls, where the other nuns stand, and that the windows, galleries, and organs that face the public church be removed."[5]

These measures reinforced the most basic principle of female monastic architecture, designed to keep nuns separate, silent, and out of reach—visually and otherwise. The primary feature of convent ritual space, one that had a significant effect on the music there, involved the division of the church into the nuns' own, inner chapel (Fig. 5.1, B) and a public, outer chapel (Fig. 5.1, A). The inner and outer churches are separated by a solid wall, usually penetrated by a grilled window above the altar (also shown in Fig. 5.1), high enough so that outsiders could not see the nuns beyond the wall in their inner chapel. But the window was low enough for the nuns to witness the Elevation of the Host when the priest was officiating at Mass in the outer church. To reinforce the separation, the grate over the window was opened only at the Elevation of the Host in Bolognese convents, then closed immediately afterward, by contrast with the practice in other cities such as Milan, where the grates were kept open during the whole of Mass and sometimes even longer, as a traveling Bolognese priest Sebastiano Locatelli observed in 1664.[6] The separation can be so complete that one can wander into a convent outer church and not even realize that there is another, separate chapel at all—unless one learns to keep an eye out for the telltale grilled window. Thus, Cardinal Paleotti and other reformers managed to render the nuns invisible.

SINGING WITHIN (AND AROUND) CONVENT WALLS

∽

But nuns' voices were less easily controlled. Although the church hierarchy endeavored to keep nun musicians down in the choir stalls of their inner churches, convent divas nevertheless continued to find their way up to organ rooms, a convenient monastic alternative to the old, exposed organ and choir lofts. These organ rooms were technically inside the nuns' inner chapel, but had windows overlooking the outer chapel, windows that seem never to have stayed bricked up, as Paleotti had decreed. At Santa Cristina there were organ rooms on each side of the high altar (Fig. 5.1, C), with grilled windows facing the altar. These organ rooms also once had additional windows facing directly outward into the nave of the public church, toward the congregation,

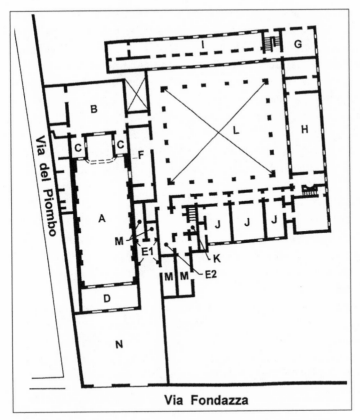

Figure 5.1. Plan of the Convent of Santa Cristina della Fondazza in Bologna. A = public, outer chapel; B = nuns' private, inner chapel; C = organ rooms; D = nuns' choir, above church portico; E1 = external reception room; E2 = interior porter's lodge; F = original, old chapel; G = small additional chapel; H = refectory; I = common rooms; J = infirmary; K = staircase; L = cloister; M = parlors; N = public courtyard. Reproduced from Craig A. Monson, *Disembodied Voices: Music and Culture in an Early Modern Italian Convent.* Copyright © 1995 The Regents of the University of California. Reproduced with permission of the University of California Press.

high up, probably between the capitals of the pilasters. In 1607 the organ repairman at Santa Cristina specifically pointed out that the two organs were intended to accompany double choir singing by the nuns, and much of the surviving music dedicated to them requires double choirs.

Santa Cristina also had another large nuns' choir room at the west end of the external church, above the church portico (Fig. 5.1, D)—a distinctive architectural feature of this institution, only occasionally encountered else-where, as at the convent of Santa Cecilia in Rome. At Santa Cristina, the three large grated windows in the east wall that joined this space to the adjacent public church would have permitted multiple choirs to perform, invisible from the external church, but in full view of each other within this large "coro." But this nuns' choir also had three large *west* windows, which faced directly into the public courtyard (see Fig. 5.2). This meant that at Santa Cristina the nuns' angelic voices resounded, not only into the pseudo-privacy of the *chiesa esteriore* within the convent, but also carried into the public space outside, literally over the convent walls to the world.

This arrangement of spaces thus constituted a particularly effective mu-sico-architectural ploy. They may have been hedged in by bricks and mortar, but, clearly, the nuns of Santa Cristina took every advantage of the dramatic/rhetorical possibilities of the architectural limitations imposed upon them. One can be quite certain that other musical nuns were comparably resource-ful in their individual situations. To take just one further example, the impos-ing Dominican convent of Santi Domenico e Sisto in Rome, known for its patronage by the Colonna, Aldobrandini, Borghese, and Chigi families, was likewise renowned for its unusually splendid architectural and decorative program, and also for music.[7] The lavish high altar at Santi Domenico e Sisto had the accustomed grated window above it, and also elevated windows to the right and left, facing the altar, similar to those at Santa Cristina. But, interestingly enough, there were several other small, grated windows situated all the way around the external church, high up near the vaults (Fig. 5.3). Nuns' voices, echoing amidst the heavenly hosts of the frescoed ceiling, would have sounded especially magical from there, even if they were simply singing plainchant.

The effect of the nuns' singing and the impact of their messages were thus reinforced by the nature of the architectural spaces imposed upon them. The so-called "angelic voices" of the convent singers, resounding from behind these grilled windows, where the nuns could be heard but not seen, also represented both effective illusion and allusion. For the mythological Echo, living in the seclusion of hidden, lonely caves after Narcissus had scorned her, likewise tossed back sounds to the world, just as the voices of singing nuns, constrained since Trent to live apart, behind convent walls, reechoed toward the world.[8]

Another aspect of musical nuns' enforced seclusion may have worked to their advantage. The cloister offers an intriguing analogue to the other hot-house, "secret" musical environment in which female virtuoso singing began to flourish in the secular world of the late Cinquecento—the so-called *con-certi delle donne* of north Italian courts. Post-Tridentine convent music had

Figure 5.2. Convent of Santa Cristina della Fondazza in Bologna. Windows of the nuns' choir, facing the former public courtyard. Photograph by Craig Monson, ca. 1988, prior to the restoration of the church.

truly become an alternative "musica segreta," hedged in behind cloister walls, performed by hidden voices for an exclusive audience (the nuns themselves and frequently patrician and noble ladies of the city), but whose echoes also reached the outside world through veiled and grilled windows penetrating the walls of convent churches. Just as Alfonso II d'Este of Ferrara jealousy guarded the private solo singing of the secular *concerto delle donne* that he was creating and patronizing in exactly the same years, the princes of the Catholic Church hierarchy fought a constant—and frequently a losing— battle to guard and control the music of their female monastic *musiche segrete*. Whereas many members of Italy's noble or patrician classes were

Figure 5.3. Convent of Santi Domenico e Sisto in Rome. Grilled windows extending around the public, outer church, up near the vaults. Photograph by Christina McOmber, reproduced with permission.

fascinated by reports of the alluring performances of the Singing Ladies of Ferrara, with no hope of ever hearing their closely guarded music, they could quite easily have the chance to hear outstanding female vocal ensembles at their own local *musiche segrete,* the convent churches of their cities.

There seems therefore to be something self-conscious—almost coy— about how frequently motets by nun composers and those dedicated to them call attention to singing and playing. Take the opening of Giovanni Battista Biondi's motet *Cantabant sancti canticum novum,* dedicated by the publisher to the nuns of Santa Cristina in Bologna in 1606, which begins: "The saints sang a new song, Alleluia, before the throne of God and the Lamb, Alleluia, and the earth resounded with their voices."[9] The text describes—and listeners would hear—the voices of the nuns, "saints," literally echoing and re-echoing: this is a piece for double choir, exploiting those hidden choir rooms at the convent of Santa Cristina. And if the original parts were transposed up a fourth, this motet could be presented by higher voices alone—no men need take part. At Santa Cristina it could thus be heard performed by the rare, still relatively novel combination of women's voices (see Ex. 5.1).

The words also echo the Book of Revelation, when John describes the 144,000 virgins who sing a new song and follow the Lamb ("These are they who are undefiled . . . who are without stain"). By an interesting process of inversion (John's original virgins had been male, and had resisted corruption by women), the nun-virgins not only sing, but sing about themselves, and pointedly reaffirm their singularity and virtue. Like the women of the courtly *concerti delle donne*, whose virtue and good names were closely guarded by their noble patrons, these angelic convent choirs pointedly set themselves apart from other female singers, paid to perform or parade themselves in more public venues. Even as late as 1740, for example, when the nuns of San Gugliemo in Bologna accepted a highly talented and resourceful singer, Anna Negri, going into retirement, they carefully made clear that she had never practiced her art in the public opera houses, but only in private, in the service of the king of Poland. Polite society's attitude toward women who sang in more public contexts is implicit between the lines of a remark passed by the Bolognese diarist Antonio Barilli on 15 October 1723: "The singer formerly under the protection of Signor Marchese Antonio Ghiselieri has taken the monastic habit of Saint Augustine among the sisters of San Giacomo." The sisters of San Giacomo were, of course, better known as the *convertite*, or reformed prostitutes.[10]

By contrast with Biondi's monastic musical publication, the motets of Bologna's only published nun composer, Lucrezia Orsina Vizzana, also from the convent of Santa Cristina, exploit the more contemporary medium of solo voices and basso continuo. This virtuosic, alluring solo style had been developing for fifty years in Bolognese convents by the time Vizzana's *Componimenti musicali de motetti a una e più voci* appeared in Venice in 1623. Ironically, this sort of attractive solo singing by nuns had unwittingly been encouraged by Bolognese church reformers as another means to control convent music. In 1580, Gabriele Paleotti had stipulated to nuns in his charge that "It is permitted . . . for a solo voice to sing to the organ at the times permitted." A dozen years later convent father confessor Don Ercole Tinelli likewise exclaimed to the Sacred Congregation of Bishops and Regulars in Rome, which oversaw and enforced monastic discipline, "it is enough for

EXAMPLE 5.1. Opening of motet *Cantabant sancti canticum* by Giovanni Battista Biondi (*fl.* 1605–30)

[the nuns of Bologna] to play their organs with a solo voice to the praise of God."[11]

These Bolognese churchmen, who must have had musical simplicity, austerity, and economy in mind, were once again misguided in their attempt to put convent performers in their place. For the style they demanded not only focused attention upon the individual rather than the community, helping to create convent divas, but also encouraged the nuns' participation in the novel, monodic style of the early Baroque—exactly the sort of ravishing music concurrently practiced by the virtuoso singing ladies of the secular *musiche segrete* at courts such as Ferrara and Florence, and also similar to the emerging dramatic solo style of opera. Interestingly enough, in 1597 in Florence, where both soloistic *musiche segrete* and monodic experiments were familiar, the Vicar General informed the Sacred Congregation of Bishops and Regulars, "In accordance with your command of last March 29, I prohibited in eight convents any unusual music, that is, with excessive voices and instruments in it. And also the solo voice, *which entices too much and attracts throngs of listeners.*"[12] This memorandum clearly articulates contemporary awareness of the powerful fascination of solo singing and its particular dangers in the monastic arena. But back in Bologna that possibility seems to have eluded Gabriele Paleotti.

O invictissima Christi martir, one of Vizzana's best motets, exploits the more overtly modern solo style, which had been the object of so much aesthetic interest and ecclesiastical concern (see Ex. 5.2).[13] Now double choirs have been replaced by a pair of solo sopranos, accompanied by keyboard, who call to one another and to the convent's matron saint, from the grilled windows up near the vaults. In this respect, Vizzana's motets were in step with general trends in convent music making, where such florid virtuosity by one or more soloists begins to eclipse *stile antico* liturgical settings from the 1620s onward.[14] Vizzana composed *O invictissima* to take full advantage of the performative circumstances in which she and her sisters found themselves. One soprano begins alone; shortly after she starts calling Saint Christina's name, the second soprano joins her, closely imitating the other soprano's musical line exactly. For a moment, it is unclear if this is one voice or two, or if it is an echo. But then, as one voice insistently echoes the other, it becomes clear that this is a play upon echo effects. Significantly, the voices first come together in concord at the mention of the "sweet spouse, Jesus Christ" (*dulce sponsum tuum Dominum, Jesus Christum*). Note also the bolder treatment of "spirit of fear" (*spiritum timoris*), whose terror is conveyed by the juxtaposition of G-minor and E-major chords, one of the bolder gestures of Vizzana's harmonic vocabulary. Then, of course, the concluding "that we may sing" focuses self-consciously on the virtuosic art for which

EXAMPLE 5.2. Motet *O invictissima Christi martir* by Lucrezia Orsina Vizzana (1590–1662)

EXAMPLE 5.2 (CONTINUED)

EXAMPLE 5.2 (CONTINUED)

the nuns of Santa Cristina were especially known. As if empowered by Saint Christina, on "cantare" the soloists spiral off into elaborate vocal pyrotechnics, first individually, then joining in mellifluous, concordant thirds, dissolving into the ecstasy of "alleluias."

CONVENT MUSIC MAKING, A CALLING OR JUST A JOB?

At wealthy, patrician convents such as Santa Cristina, where motets such as *Cantabant sancti canticum novum* and *O invictissima Christi martir* could serve as a powerful means of drawing the public to services, loosening its purse strings, establishing ties with noble families, and fostering their patronage, it should not be surprising that promising musicians who could perform such works were actively courted and, once accepted within the cloister, might enjoy what some perceived as a privileged lifestyle. Even taking into account its exaggerated tone, the following report from the time of Archbishop Paleotti's reforms gives some sense of the preferential treatment that outstanding sixteenth-century singing nuns in Bologna may have come to expect:

> Frequently [potential musicians] are accepted into the convents without a dowry, or with a meager one, only because they know how to sing and play, though in other respects they would be unworthy of acceptance, which is of greatest [financial] loss to the convents.
>
> They are so preoccupied with such music, because they must be heard by others [i.e., outsiders], that they spend all their time only in this activity, [and] they neglect everything else; and it seems to those who sing that by singing they have satisfied every obligation to such an extent that they need not take the trouble to attend any other sort of divine office.
>
> They desire exemptions and privileges to live in their own way, nor do they want to be required to perform any [other] jobs in the convent.[15]

The nun organist or *maestra del coro*, especially in aristocratic houses with important musical traditions such as Santa Cristina, could also garner a certain authority, particularly as an arbiter of taste. Although her personal performing skills had the most direct and obvious impact upon the convent and its musical reputation, the restrictions of the post-Tridentine church tended to concentrate many aspects of convent music making in her hands. The availability of her own disposable income for musical patronage, as much as personal musical talent, sometimes greatly enhanced her artistic effectiveness. The *maestra del coro* frequently paid for elaborate music by outsiders for particularly brilliant musical events, when the nuns could get permission to bring in such musicians. In 1644, for example, on the titular feast at the convent of San Guglielmo in Bologna, Suora Barbara Gioconda dal Medico, *maestra del coro,* underwrote at great expense First and Second Vespers and Mass by the musicians of San Petronio, "who performed concerti for the most beautiful instruments and very charming motets."[16] At San Guglielmo, in fact, the so-called *corista* commonly paid considerable sums for the annual feast of San Guglielmo and other musical festivities. After a pastoral visitation to San Guglielmo on 26 June 1735, the nuns were told that "because carrying out the offices in the monastery at their own expense causes considerable inconvenience to the nuns, it has been ordered that in future they obey the decrees of Pope Clement XI of blessed memory, paying the said expenses from the communal savings of the convent."[17] This requirement recurs like a refrain at various times and places throughout the convents of the Catholic world.

The Clarissan convent of Corpus Domini, which housed the shrine of the Blessed—and eventually Saint—Catherine Vigri, relied regularly on the musical services of outsiders to honor the saint (and her numerous patrician devotees) in an appropriately grand manner. Often this required overruling the objections of the local episcopal hierarchy, a task made easier by Saint Catherine's central importance to local prestige, in which several of the city's leading noble families were involved. In 1712, the year of Catherine's canonization, some sixteen such services with elaborate music took place at the convent. The one on 14 August was especially splendid, to judge by the following, especially breathless account, which provides some sense of the impressiveness of such occasions:

> 14 August 1712, in the church of Corpus Domini, nobly decorated with crimson damask and veils elegantly arranged, there was further demonstration of thanks to God in the highest for the canonization of our Holy Citizen [Catherine Vigri], sponsored by the generous piety of forty devout lay gentlemen, wishing to offer there a sign of their filial devotion . . . with Mass and a Te Deum performed by sixty virtuosi, both singers and instrumentalists, directed by Signor Antonio Frigeri, called "Il Ferrarese," which with harmony matched to his talent, ended amid a resounding concerto of trumpets and drums plus a barrage of 1,200 firecrackers, which extended from the city gate along a long stretch of road to the church of the great saint. Where with universal applause the solemn and sacred rite ended with a comparable Vespers Service, which offered after dinner a devout entertainment to the

ample concourse of the nobility, and a perfect end to the noble manifestation, which was accomplished through the generous liberality
practiced toward these Reverend Nuns, and was preceded on the previous evening by numerous volleys and fireworks, with illumination of
the facade of the church with torches and the echoing of trumpets and
drums to universal applause.[18]

Catherine Vigri, who died in 1456, in fact remains Bologna's best-known nun
musician. Her so-called "violetta," possibly the only member of the violin
family from the fifteenth century to survive intact,[19] is preserved as a relic in
a glass case at her shrine, near the musical saint herself, who is seated in a
chair, adorned in her nun's habit with crucifix in hand, and in a state of
preservation rivaling that of her violetta.

Lucrezia Orsina Vizzana and other publishing nun composers, who have
begun to find their way into recent music histories, clearly represent the most
illustrious among thousands of convent musicians. The musical collections
by such nun composers, the fulsome dedications of other publications that
the nuns patronized, and the praise of musical observers create a glamorous
view of convent music, which represents the side most likely to capture our
interest and imagination today, rather like the focus on "Great Men" in
traditional Rankean history. But these preeminent nun musicians represent
the reality of only the musically—and dynastically—most illustrious religious
houses. To put Bolognese nun musicians in their proper place, we must
remember that musical life experience for the majority of monastic performers and their audiences was considerably less elevated. Apart from the likes
of Lucrezia Vizzana, the 150 Bolognese nun musicians who have come to
light remained a rather faceless lot, filling the role of organist or *maestra del
coro* in unremarkable ways. Many found themselves in the position, less because of great talent or passion for music, than because musical training
rendered them eligible for dowry reductions of 50 percent available to potential convent organists, which greatly appealed to their parents.[20]

Reduced dowries for musical postulants particularly characterized female
monastic institutions of more modest musical resources, especially those
where primary responsibility for music fell to a single individual or two. At
Santa Cristina in Bologna, significantly, records of dowry reductions for nun
organists only become common in the eighteenth century, when the heyday
of music making by the nuns themselves had passed. Clearly, these dowry
reductions represented a kind of pay, in anticipation of services to be rendered in future, as is particularly apparent from the case of one Angela Venturoli. In 1781 the nuns of Santa Maria Nuova accepted Angela Venturoli,
twenty years old, "who sings Gregorian chant and plays the organ," with a

dowry of £1,000, saving her family no less than £3,000. But seven years later the convent doctor reported that Suor Angela could no longer fulfill her office due to heart ailments, and the nuns therefore kindly secured permission to relieve Suor Angela of her musical duties. The importance of that original dowry reduction is made clear, however, by the fact that Suor Angela's parents were gently reminded of the original terms under which their daughter had been accepted, "and of their own free will" presented a "gift" of an additional £1,000 to Santa Maria Nuova.[21]

The sense of music talent less as a gift than just another job qualification to compensate for a deeply discounted dowry occasionally emerges from the numerous petitions to the Sacred Congregation of Bishops and Regulars for the admission of potential nun musicians at a reduced dowry, or with no dowry at all. Music sometimes appears as merely one of many talents required of such potential postulants, as at Brescia in 1599, when the nuns of San Benedetto di Salò asserted their "very great need of someone who could teach the nuns, who must sing in choir, because the ones who sang are dead, and who could teach them to sew and do similar tasks for the good of the convent," or as in the diocese of Camerino in 1632, when the convent of San Luca in Fabbriano wished to admit gratis a possible teacher endowed with many talents, "among others, plainchant, polyphony, and various types of embroidery." In 1653, on the other hand, the convent of San Giovanni in Nocera requested permission to admit Catarina Nati, "gifted in organ playing, singing, . . . and arithmetic, which will prove exceedingly useful to the convent, there being none other who can do the accounts and keep the records of its interests."[22] Nati's accounting skills rather than her musical talents appear to have been the prime attraction.

The attitudes among some nun organists themselves toward dowry reductions and dowry payments suggest that they too recognized such positions as paid employment, from which they would sometimes retire if improved financial circumstances enabled them to do so. Thus, for twelve years Suor Maria Geltrude Nobili served as organist of Santa Maria Maddalena in Bologna. After the death of her father in 1733, however, her brothers generously paid the rest of the normal convent dowry, so that she need not continue to serve in that capacity. Similarly, when Maria Angela Soavi, who had professed as organist at Santi Naborre e Felice in 1760, inherited the estate of her late brother, she used her legacy to gain exemption from the burden of the organist's position.[23] Such examples more accurately color the romantic view of the cloister simply as an artistic haven for women musicians, free to exercise their creativity. For many of them, music making may have amounted to extra work, sometimes beneath their dignity in their own eyes or those of their sisters, which they would happily forgo. In the more patrician houses,

catering to women of the highest classes, the very idea of musical professionalism would have been unacceptable. As Robert Kendrick observed, "the
social status of musicians in Seicento Milan was so low that, even if questions
of gender had not been present, patrician nuns could never have considered
the option [of being professional musicians]."[24]

Apart from dowry discounts, further special financial arrangements and
concessions might be made to secure organists' services, and, once again,
create the impression of music as paid employment. In 1716, for instance,
Suor Angela Mariana Zavatieri entered the convent of San Lorenzo in Bologna not only with a reduced dowry of £1,200, but also with free room and
board "since she is organist."[25] In May 1695 the nuns of Santi Leonardo ed
Orsola in Bologna agreed to pay Anna Maria Bertolini £24 a year for life "in
recognition of her labors in filling the office of organist." About fifty years
later exactly the same stipend was established for Suor Maria Gesualda Orlandi by the Bolognese nuns of Santissima Concezione.[26]

Both Anna Maria Bertolini and Maria Gesualda Orlandi came from poor
families and went to convents not particularly known for music. Their cases
also illustrate how poor girls with musical backgrounds might take on musical jobs at musically unprepossessing convents with the help of public or
private philanthropy. Anna Maria Bertolini benefited from both types of
support when she entered Sant'Orsola. In December 1694 Signora Isabella
Franchini Paganelli had donated a piece of ground to the nuns of Sant'Orsola
"with the obligation to accept into their convent a girl who should know
how to play the organ, and to deduct the aforesaid piece of ground from her
dowry." Anna Maria Bertolini became the object of this generosity. But after
the deduction the girl's widowed mother was still left with an obligation of
£400, which was paid by the Opera Pia de' Vergognosi. Maria Gesualda Orlandi, on the other hand, had been reared, and had her dowry paid, by the
Ospedale degli Esposti.[27]

The intervention of such public service organizations in the training and
placement of nun musicians became a significant feature of Bolognese musical life in the eighteenth century. Carlo Vitali has traced some forty-eight girl
singers and organists placed in convents by the Ospedale between 1709 and
the end of the Settecento.[28] The 1740s marked the beginning of the heyday of
the Ospedale in this respect. Between 1742 and the end of the century more
than three times as many *zittelle degli Esposti* found positions as nun musicians than had entered convents in similar capacities during the preceding
thirty-five years. By then, the heyday of convent music in Bologna had
passed. The last known musical publication dedicated to a Bolognese nun
had appeared in 1672, for example.[29] Throughout the period, a majority of
the girls from the Ospedale were destined for convents outside Bologna,

where they were increasingly admitted gratis.[30] The third who entered Bolognese convents continued to pay some sort of dowry, often only £500 or so.[31]

Evidence rarely comes to light that documents, not only the legal and financial aspects, but also the more personal side of a nun musician's acceptance—convents' attempts to recruit promising musical prospects, families' efforts to obtain the most advantageous financial arrangements, or the roles of well-connected, influential sponsors as go-betweens in the process. Occasional singers seem even to have done a little self-promotion to gain advantageous admission. In 1646 the Sacred Congregation received a complaint that Giulia Albaracci of Ancona "passed through this city of Fano. . . . She sang in all these nuns' *parlatorios*, with not a little scandal because of the concourse of young people who flocked to hear her. Now some of these young people are trying by means of their nun relatives to get that singer accepted in the monastery of Sant'Arcangelo without any dowry at all, and a certain amount is even being assigned to each one [of these nuns] for her annual expenses."[32]

Every once in a while a potential musical "star" comes to light who provoked intense interest and widespread competition. One such apparent prodigy was the fifteen-year-old Francesca Giunta from Pesaro, who, the nuns of the Convent of the Purification claimed, was "by divine grace, gifted in plainchant and polyphony to such a degree that she composes most fluently. And her compositions have caused the leading professors of Rome to marvel. . . . And she has already been courted by the nuns of Ferrara, Jesi, and Cagli with their offers of her dowry." These assertions were seconded by her father, Bartolomeo Giunti, who requested that the Sacred Congregation agree to her acceptance in her hometown at a reduced dowry. The local bishop also confirmed the petition, with the justification that "this young lady can maintain the music in the monastery, and teach it to the others, and do some composition. This in fact will be the grounds for their not needing to have anything to do with musicians from outside." Since the Sacred Congregation left the final decision to the bishop, Francesca presumably remained near home, a satisfactory outcome for everyone.[33]

One further case offers a slightly fuller picture of the abilities and training of a moderately talented future nun musician from Bologna. In 1653, when the convent of Santa Chiara in Jesi sought an organist in Bologna, they discovered twenty-year-old Chiara Marchesini, daughter of a Venetian barber, long resident in Bologna, who had raised and educated her at home after the death of his wife ten years earlier. The nuns' petition to the Sacred Congregation for permission to admit Chiara gratis includes unusually detailed testimony to her good name and talents. Four witnesses testified, for example, that she was not only legitimate and of impeccable character, but also that she was "not deformed—on the contrary, rather eye-catching—nor defective in any part of her body."[34] Her music teacher, Giacomo Predieri, vice-*maestro di capella* of San Petronio, also commented in considerable detail on her musical abilities: "Chiara Marchesini, my student in the musical profession, is well trained, both on the organ and in accompanying, as well as in responding to the choir. She is highly knowledgeable about the modes, and skilled in counterpoint. She sings with a voice not overly full but pleasant, and is so accomplished that if she be given in advance some composition, either to play or sing, when she has looked it over once or twice, she will be sure of it, even if it is difficult. And consequently, she will be able to impart some of her talent to others."[35]

Chiara Marchesini's skills probably surpassed those of many nun musicians educated exclusively within the convents rather than at home, for she did not have to rely primarily or entirely upon the tutelage of other nuns, but could study with one of the more esteemed Bolognese musicians of her time. She in fact continued to study with Predieri for well over a year, for in November 1654 the Sacred Congregation granted her a license for further musical study in Bologna "to make her all the more capable for the service of the choir in that monastery."[36]

Such ploys to improve nuns' musical education in Bologna were not unusual because of the notably severe restrictions on outside music teachers there, which forced the nuns to find other ways to cope. The nuns of Santa Cristina simply hired Ottavio Vernizzi, organist of San Petronio, on the sly, until church authorities found out and put a stop to the practice in the early 1620s. San Lorenzo tried a less rebellious ploy. Around 1600 they accepted Dorothea Riviera as their future organist, but did not immediately admit her: "Because it is still necessary for the music teacher to see to her for a while longer, and since it is known that [music masters] cannot come to teach in the convents, therefore in this period of her acceptance she is being kept in her father's house, where she applies herself excellently to her studies."[37]

In 1602, finding themselves musically short-handed, the nuns requested permission to bring Dorothea Riviera in temporarily, promising to keep her just long enough to participate in the feasts of San Lorenzo, the Assumption, and the Nativity of the Virgin, then send her home again. The Sacred Congregation agreed to this request. But when the nuns of Santissima Trinità presumably got wind of San Lorenzo's success and tried a similar ploy four months later, promising to bring in a future singer only for a single day, their request was denied.[38]

Financial necessity probably required the barber Marchesini to look beyond the more desirable convents of Bologna to find a place for Chiara 125 miles from home. Ever since the late sixteenth century rising dowries and post-Tridentine restricted access to the convents of Bologna had forced less well-off residents such as the barber Marchesini to turn to convents in bordering towns and cities. A letter from the Bolognese senate to its ambassador in Rome, dated as early as 3 February 1582, makes this clear: "This is the reason that many Bolognese have found it necessary to make their daughters and relatives nuns outside the city in various places such as Ravenna, Rimini, Faenza, Imola, Carpi, Cento, Modena, Correggio, and in various other locations; because they cannot afford the dowries and excessive furnishings that these Bolognese convents require. It is really a great pity to send one's own flesh and blood outside one's homeland."[39] Perhaps this explains why two musically talented sisters from the Ferrabosco dynasty of Bolognese musicians ended up in two separate convents in Genoa in 1592 and 1593.[40] Almost 150 years later this continuing sad reality for less affluent Bolognese families is brought home by petitions to the Sacred Congregation, all dated 20 February 1730, when the convent of Santa Chiara in Jesi requested permission to admit two Bolognese musical sisters, Elena and Alessandra Raghetti, to their convent gratis. On that very same day another convent in that city, Santissima Annunziata, asked similar license for another young Bolognese musician, Maria Felicità "Ronchetti" of Bologna, presumably a third sister. All three young musicians were sent away from friends and family to live out their lives far from home, among strangers.[41]

Nuns would continue to sing from their choir and organ lofts until the Napoleonic suppression of the monasteries at the end of the eighteenth century. Then, these centers of intense female creative activity, and abiding objects of fascination in the world, would be quite forgotten. With their recent rediscovery the singing nuns are being put back in their place—their rightful place—in the rich and diverse musical culture of the early modern Catholic world.

NOTES

~

An abbreviated version of this paper was presented at the conference A Sense of Place: Seventy Years of Musicological Scholarship at Yale (Yale University, 7–9 December 2001). Some portions were also presented at the conference I monasteri femminili come centri di cultura fra rinascimento e barocco, convegno storico internazionale (Bologna, 8–10 December 2000), whose proceedings, edited by Gianna Pomata and Gabriella Zarri, will eventually be published by *Edizioni di storia e letteratura* (Rome).

1. Robert Kendrick, *Celestial Sirens: Nuns and Their Music in Early Modern Milan* (Oxford: Clarendon Press, 1996); Colleen Reardon, *Holy Concord within Sacred Walls: Nuns and Music in Siena, 1575–1700* (Oxford: Oxford University Press, 2002); Kimber-

lyn Montford, "Music in the Convents of Counter-Reformation Rome" (Ph.D. diss., Rutgers University, 1999); Craig Monson, *Disembodied Voices: Music and Culture in an Early Modern Italian Convent* (Berkeley: University of California Press, 1995).

2. Donald J. Grout and Claude V. Palisca, *A History of Western Music*, 6th ed. (New York: W. W. Norton, 2001), 290. Vizzana's motets appear on the compact disc *Songs of Ecstasy and Devotion from a 17th-Century Italian Convent: Lucrezia Vizzana Componimenti Musicali (1623)*, recorded by Musica Secreta (Linn Records, CKD 071).

3. Quoted in Montford, "Music in the Convents of Counter-Reformation Rome," iv.

4. On Sienese valorization of convent music, see Reardon, *Holy Concord*; Kimberlyn Montford discussed Roman accommodations for the Holy Year 1675 in "L'anno Santo and Female Monastic Churches: The Politics, Business, and Music of the Holy Year in Rome (1675)," read at the national meeting of the American Musicological Society, Boston (31 October 1998); see also her "Music in the Convents of Counter-Reformation Rome."

5. Bologna, Archivio Arcivescovile (hereafter AAB), Misc. Vecchie 808, fascicolo 6.

6. Excerpts from Locatelli's "Viaggio in Francia" appear in Kendrick, *Celestial Sirens*, 460–61.

7. On the noble patrons of SS. Domenico e Sisto, see Montford, "Music in the Convents of Counter-Reformation Rome," 43. The most detailed study of the convent's patronage and artistic program is Christina McOmber, "Recovering Female Agency: Roman Patronage and the Dominican Convent of SS. Domenico e Sisto" (Ph.D. diss., University of Iowa, 1997).

8. Robert Kendrick makes this point with reference to an echo piece by Giovanni Paolo Cima dedicated to Paola Ortensia Serbellona, a Milanese nun from the convent of San Vincenzo. See *Celestial Sirens*, 245. An alternative explanation was that Echo had been torn to pieces by shepherds driven mad by Pan, who had loved her in vain. Earth hid the pieces of Echo's body, which still reflect other sounds.

9. The piece is recorded on *Canti nel chiostro: Musica nei monasteri femminili dell '600 a Bologna*, Cappella Artemisia (Tactus TC 600001 [1994]). For a complete score, see *Three Motets for Eight Voices (1589–1606)*, ed. C. Smith and B. Dickey (Music from the Convents of Bologna; Sala Bolognese: Artemisia Editions, 1998).

10. Bologna, Archivio di Stato (hereafter ASB), Demaniale 80/814 (San Guglielmo), *Racordi p[er] il Monastero di S. Guglielmo*, "Adi 22 Ottobre 1740"; Bologna, Biblioteca Universitaria, MS 225 III, fol. 66ʳ.

11. Craig Monson, "Disembodied Voices: Music in the Nunneries of Bologna in the Midst of the Counter-Reformation," in *The Crannied Wall: Women, Religion, and the Arts in Early Modern Europe*, ed. Craig Monson (Ann Arbor: University of Michigan Press, 1992), 192, 202.

12. Archivio Segreto Vaticano (hereafter ASV), Sacra Congregazione dei Vescovi e Regolari, posizione 1597, lettere C–G. Italics added.

13. The piece is recorded on *Canti nel chiostro* and on *Songs of Ecstasy and Devotion*. The text translates: "O most invincible martyr and Christ's virgin, Saint Christina, our protectress, vehemently intercede with your sweet spouse, Lord Jesus Christ, for the sins of your handmaidens. And may it come to pass that you will deign to bestow the spirit of fear and of love upon us, and upon those committed to it. And make us steadfast, so we may sing, 'Alleluia.'"

14. Kendrick, *Celestial Sirens*, 188.

15. AAB, Misc. Vecchie 808, fascicolo 6.

16. ASB, Demaniale 80/814 (S. Guglielmo), *Racordi p[er] il Monastero di S. Guglielmo,* no. 840.

17. ASB, Demaniale 79/813 (S. Guglielmo).

18. The original Italian appears in Craig Monson, "La pratica della musica nei monasteri femminili bolognesi," in *La cappella musicale nell'Italia della Controriforma,* ed. Oscar Mischiati and Paolo Russo (Cento: Centro Studi Girolamo Baruffaldi, 1993), 150.

19. See Marco Tiella, "The Violeta of S. Caterina de' Vigri," *Galpin Society Journal* 28 (1975): 60–70.

20. As a minister of Archbishop Girolamo Boncompagni reported to the nuns of Santa Chiara in the village of Pieve di Cento in 1664, "the custom in other similar cases is that [organists] may be admitted for half the normal dowry at least, plus their furnishings, but always with special license of the Ordinary." ASB, Demaniale 3/7900 (S. Chiara della Pieve di Cento), fol. 202. The same percentage could also be applied in the case of supernumeraries, postulants who wished to enter convents whose populations already exceeded the maximum number set by the Apostolic Visitor to Bologna in 1574 and reconfirmed by the Sacred Congregation of Bishops and Regulars in 1588. The numbers set by the Vatican are listed in ASV, Sacra Congregazione dei Vescovi e Regolari, posizione 1588, lettere A–B (Bologna, 21 settembre 1588).

21. ASB, Demaniale 166/733 (S. Maria Nuova), 13 ottobre 1781.

22. ASV, Sacra Congregazione dei Vescovi e Regolari, posizione 1599 (A–B); ibid., sezione monache, l'anno 1632 (gen.–luglio) "Camerino . . . 23 Jan.rij 1632"; ibid., sezione monache, l'anno 1653 (agosto–settembre), "Nocera . . . 26 7bris 1653."

23. For Maria Geltrude Nobili, see Bologna, Biblioteca Comunale dell'Archiginnasio (hereafter BCB), MS B3283, *Raccolta di notizie del Monastero e Monache di S M[ari]a Maddalena;* for Maria Angela Soavi, see BCB, MS B919, 164.

24. Kendrick, *Celestial Sirens,* 185n.

25. ASB, Demaniale 112/3480 (San Lorenzo), *Vachetta delle Memorie,* 13 giugno 1715; 20 ottobre 1715; 21 novembre 1715; 26 novembre 1716.

26. On Anna Maria Bertolini, see ASB, Demaniale 102/5005, 29/3271, and 97/5000 (SS. Leonardo ed Orsola); on Maria Gesualda Orlandi, see ASB, Demaniale 32/5128 (Santissima Concezione), 242–43.

27. ASB, Demaniale 102/5005 (Santi Leonardo ed Orsola), *Inventario de tutte Le Scritture . . . nel Archivio del Monast[er]o . . . di S[an]ta Orsola: 1695,* under "li 4 di Maggio." For the agreement with Maria Gesualda Orlandi, see ASB, Demaniale 32/5128 (Santissima Concezione), *Sommario estratto dalle Scritture S. Orsola 1705,* 242–43. For the additional arrangements at Sant'Orsola, see ASB, Demaniale 29/3271 (Santi Leonardo ed Orsola), no. 13, *Sig[no]ra Isabella Franchini Paganelli.* See also ASB, Demaniale 97/5000 (Santi Leonardo ed Orsola), *Sommario,* 1003–105.

28. Carlo Vitali, "'La scuola della virtù delle Zitelle': Insegnamento e pratiche musicali fra Sei e Ottocento presso il Conservatorio degli Esposte di Bologna," in *I Bastardini: Patrimonio e memoria di un ospedale bolognese* (Bologna: Edizioni AGE, 1990), 126–27.

29. Giacinto Quintanilla, *Il Primo Libro de Motetti a voce sola* (1672), dedicated to Laura Francesca Fabretti at the convent of Santi Ludovico e Alessio.

30. Vitali, "'La scuola della virtù,'" 115.

31. In 1746 Maria Clementina Anna Maddalena Palazzi entered San Guglielmo for £500 instead of the normal nun's dowry of £2,000. (See ASB, Demaniale 80/814 [San Guglielmo], unnumbered entry dated 13 February 1746.) In 1777 Angela Mengoli (Suor Clementina Maria Teresa) entered the convent of Santissima Trinità for £500 plus £100 for expenses (See BCB, MS B921, 305).

32. ASV, Sacra Congregazione dei Vescovi e Regolari, sezione monache, l'anno 1646 (aprile–maggio) "fano . . . 7 xbris 1646."

33. Ibid., l'anno 1664 (marzo–maggio) A Pesaro . . . 9 maij 1664.

34. Ibid. l'anno 1653 (novembre–dicembre), 7 Nov[em]bris 1653.

35. Ibid.

36. Ibid., l'anno 1654 (settembre–dicembre), 27 nov. 1654.

37. ASV, Sacra Congregazione dei Vescovi e Regolari, posizione 1602, lettere A–B, letter of "8 gennaio 1602."

38. Ibid., two letters of May 1602. By the later eighteenth century the attitude toward outside teachers had relaxed in Bologna. When in 1762, for example, Donna Anna Maria Rosa Geltrude Fontana was accepted *in educazione* at Santa Cristina, with the stipulation that she would eventually become organist, her father agreed to pay for music lessons with a *maestro,* so that she could become adequately proficient in the art. See ASB, Demaniale 21/2822 (S. Cristina), Y10: "Assegnatio Elemosine Dotalis, 1762 Die 8 Mensij Octobris."

39. ASB, Ambasciata bolognese a Roma, positiones 271, n. 49. Cited in Gabriella Zarri, "Monasteri femminili e città (secoli xv–xviii)," in *Storia d'Italia: Annali,* vol. 9: *La chiesa e il potere politico dal Medioevo all'età contemporanea,* ed. Giorgio Chittolini and Giovanni Miccoli (Turin: Rosenberg & Sellier, 1990), 369n.

40. Maria Rosa Moretti, *Musica e costume a Genova tra Cinquecento e Seicento* (Genoa: Francesco Pirella editore, 1992), 131–33.

41. ASV, Sacra Congregazione dei Vescovi e Regolari, sezione monache, l'anno 1730 (gennaro–febraro), 20 febraro 1730.

PART THREE

Empowered Voices

ROM THE CLOISTERED VOICE, we move to the opposite end of the spectrum, where female musicians have transcended the boundaries of performance to assume a commanding position within their society. With voices soaring high above the restrictions of their time, these women have reflected the hope, anger, pride, and longing of their communities. They have not only stirred the emotions, but have also touched the social conscience of their audiences, and in so doing have helped shape the course of history. More potent than any political or military leader, they have become voices of the people.

Some of them have been prominent singers who did not begin as spokeswomen, but over time assumed this role as political and social circumstances dictated. Emanating from various parts of the world, they represent a diversity of musical traditions. Yet these celebrated divas all have two things in common: their strong identification with an important cause and the larger-than-life status they achieved through the power of song.

Marian Anderson, the African-American opera and concert singer, symbolizes such an icon. More than anyone of her time, she broke through the barriers of racial prejudice with her unique voice and noble presence. Forced to pursue her career outside the United States because of racial segregation, she studied and then concertized throughout Europe and Russia, where she was received with unprecedented acclaim. She returned to this country a mature singer, giving, in 1935, a triumphal recital in New York. But Anderson's most historic concert occurred on Easter Sunday of 1939, when, denied the use of Constitution Hall by the Daughters of the American Revolution, she sang at the Lincoln Memorial in Washington D.C. 75,000 people were present at the concert and millions more heard it over the radio. When she stepped up to the microphone on that brisk cold day, the first words she sang came not from an Italian aria, a German Lied, or an African-American spiritual, but from the simple patriotic song, "My Country 'Tis of Thee."

Her biographer, Allan Keiler, writes of that moment: "With her eyes closed and her head raised proudly, a look of determination takes over. . . . And, as she sings 'America' she does not use the word 'I,' 'Of thee I sing' becomes, whether by design or not 'To thee we sing.'"[1] By using "we," Anderson signaled a special bond with the African-American community, but she also declared to the rest of the country, during this momentous occasion, that we were a united nation. The Lincoln Memorial concert stands as one of the great milestones in the struggle for racial equality in America, for what Anderson did for the sake of her art and her beliefs was not only courageous, it was truly incredible.

Another iconic diva, Miriam Makeba, is considered one of Africa's greatest singers. Born near Johannesburg, she was forced to leave South Africa in 1959, after appearing in an anti-apartheid film. Exiled for over thirty years, Makeba spoke out against the racial injustices taking place in her native country. She addressed the United Nations Special Committee on Apartheid in 1963, urging them to declare a complete boycott of South Africa. Even though most of the songs Makeba sang had no obvious political connotations, her performances signified the oppression of blacks in South Africa. As she writes in her autobiography, "when I sing a love song it is, like one critic writes, 'a metaphor for the yearning of a subjugated people to be free.'"[2]

At the same time that individual divas have emerged as agents of political empowerment, songs written in a woman's voice have also provided an outlet for protest by the community at large. Women's laments, as seen in the fourth section of this book, have the power to articulate public pain and discord. In ancient Greece, for example, the unrestrained cries of female lamenters were looked upon as a threat to the social order. While women were denied a public platform to express their views, they did not remain unheard, for Greek writers exploited the authority of the female voice in their poetry and plays. Ritual lamentation by female characters and choruses, appearing at critical moments in the tragedies of Aeschylus, Euripides, and Sophocles, challenged societal institutions and thus exerted a profound influence upon male audiences.[3]

In late sixteenth-century France, political laments called *complaintes* also utilized *la voix féminine* as a form of propaganda. Several songs texts were written from the perspective of Catholic women whose towns submitted to the Protestant "heresy" during the religious civil wars. These anonymous *complaintes*, all sung to a tune known as the *Dames d'honneur* ("Noble ladies"), relate in vivid detail the horrors of war and the hardships of the common people.[4]

Musicians in our own time have also used the lament as a means of political expression. The most spectacular example is the post-modern composer and singer Diamanda Galás. Referred to in the press as the "scream diva" and "spokesperson for the unspeakable," Galás enacts in her performances the grief and rage of women lamenters to protest the horrors of modern society from Armenian genocide to the treatment of AIDS victims.[5] She moves beyond conventional song through her use of wails, cries, whispers, and ululation. Her classically-trained voice, which spans the range of three and a half octaves, provides neither comfort nor solace, but is instead truly unbearable to listen to. Galás talks about the voice as "the primary vehicle of expression that transforms thought into sounds, thought into message. And beyond the words (with all due respect to them), the combinations of vocal and verbal energy can be overwhelming."[6]

The three studies in this section deal with divas whose voices have embodied their communities. In her essay, Virginia Danielson elucidates how the renowned Egyptian singer Umm Kulthūm became a metaphor for her country. Her identity as a national icon was so strong that, for nearly forty years, life would literally stop throughout the Arab world, as families would stay home to listen to her on the radio. She was called the Great Pyramid and the Voice of Egypt. When she died in 1975, over four million people came out in the streets of Cairo, a number larger than for the funeral of the Egyptian leader Jamāl 'Abd al-Nāṣir.

Part of Kulthūm's appeal, as Danielson shows, was her knowledge of ancient and modern Arab poetry and her superb pronunciation. Listeners would refer to her voice as "authentic religious." More important, though, was the special rapport she had with her audience, which went beyond that of a traditional diva. She had the ability to connect with all classes of society, young and old alike; she sang for the whole people.

Mercedes Sosa and Joan Baez, the two divas highlighted in my essay, have used their voices to fight for issues concerning freedom, justice, and human rights. The Argentine singer Mercedes Sosa, like Umm Kulthūm, has been strongly identified with her nation. During the "dirty war" of the 1970s, she defied a brutal military dictatorship by continuing to give concerts all over the country until she was arrested and forced to go into exile. Mercedes Sosa empowered the Argentine people with her personal courage and with her voice. Though the songs she performed during this time could not have overt political messages, their themes of life, unity, and survival resonated deeply in her imprisoned country.

Joan Baez, in turn, became a prominent symbol of political resistance in the United States during the civil rights and peace movements of the 1960s. Very early in her career, her persona shifted from a folksinger, who sang Anglo-American ballads and laments, to an anti-war activist, whose repertory of songs mirrored not only her own beliefs, but those of an entire generation of young Americans.

Tori Amos, the subject of Bonnie Gordon's essay, represents empowerment of a different kind. Instead of protesting such issues as war, poverty, and racial inequality, Amos takes up feminist causes by relating in her music her personal experiences as a woman. Her most revolutionary song, "Me and a Gun," communicates her trauma as a rape victim. Here, she skews the notion of the diva as an object of gaze by offering her voice as a place of identification for other women. Focusing on the "naked" sound of her unaccompanied voice, Amos gets in touch with her feelings and the sensations of a shocking event. As Gordon explains, "by singing of her experience during the rape Amos projects outwards an essentially interior experience. The song becomes a vehicle for articulating pain, recovering and sharing an experience whose destructiveness gains strength from social mandates for silence."

NOTES

1. *Marian Anderson: A Singer's Journey* (New York: Scribner, 2000), 212–13.
2. Miriam Makeba, with James Hall, *Makeba: My Story* (New York: New American Library, 1987), 154.
3. Nancy Sultan, "Private Speech, Public Pain: The Power of Women's Laments in Ancient Greek Poetry and Tragedy," in *Rediscovering the Muses: Women's Musical Traditions*, ed. Kimberly Marshall (Boston: Northeastern University Press, 1993), 93.
4. See Kate van Orden, "Cheap Print and Street Song following the Saint Bartholomew's Massacres of 1572," in *Music and the Cultures of Print*, ed. van Orden (New York and London: Garland Publishing, 2000), 292–95, and "Female *Complaintes*: Laments of Venus, Queens, and City Women in Late Sixteenth-Century France," *Renaissance Quarterly* 54 (2001): 829–32.
5. John Payne, "The Deep End: First AIDS, now Genocide . . . Diamanda Galás Won't Lighten Up," *L.A. Weekly*, 23–29 November 2001, p. 53.
6. Interview in *Angry Women*, ed. Andrea Juno and V. Vale (San Francisco: RE/Search Publications, 1991), 10.

CHAPTER SIX

Voices of the People

UMM KULTHŪM

Virginia Danielson

UMM KULTHŪM was unquestionably the most famous Arab singer of the twentieth century. Born to a poor village family in the delta of Egypt around 1904, she began her career as a precocious child, singing Muslim devotional songs with her father for weddings and special occasions in neighboring villages. By 1926, she had positioned herself at the top of the ranks of professional entertainers in Cairo. She had a voice rich with potential that was rapidly developing into a sophisticated instrument, fine composers and poets who wrote songs for her, an excellent accompanying ensemble, and a lucrative recording contract that allowed her to choose performance opportunities carefully while still building her personal wealth. She remained at the pinnacle of Egyptian musical life until her death in 1975.

Her life and work—her public persona—was huge in Egyptian cultural life, which occasioned over time an enormous discourse, including journalistic reporting, biography and autobiography, and criticism and analysis in print and in everyday talk. This discourse took on particular characteristics over the years. For instance, from early in her career, she was characterized as "essentially Egyptian" (*aṣīl*) by listeners. In the 1920s, journalists wrote that she "excels in her choice of [Arabic] poetry, ancient and modern, which is unparalleled in beauty of style and loftiness of imagery."[1] She was identified as "Bedouin," suggesting a sort of prototypical Arab.[2] Listeners remembered her as "an exemplar of Islamic modesty" whose voice called forth "the authentic religious Egyptian people."[3] At a performance for King Fārūq's birthday in 1937, "everyone noticed her pronunciation and many said it was so good because she could recite the Qurʾān."[4] Calling upon two historically Arab identities, journalist Muṣṭafá Maḥmūd wrote that she was "a Sufi leader in song . . . she struts through a melody like a purebred Arabian horse."[5] In 1966, journalist Kamāl al-Najmī wrote that, following her training with religious singers such as al-Shaykh Abū al-ʿIla Muḥammad, "people began to listen, through the voice of Umm Kulthūm, to songs that brought words and melody together as was the case in ancient Arabic song . . . Under these circumstances, the appearance of Umm Kulthūm became linked to the national artistic revolution, and her voice was one of the most distinctive factors in the success of that revolution" in which public taste turned from Ottoman and Turkish song to historically Arabic song.[6] She was characterized as "an authentic daughter of the people, the highest model of Arabic song, and the highest model of Arab womanhood."[7] In conversations, listeners typically remember her as "authentic" (*aṣīl*), truly Arab and Egyptian. She was a "daughter of the countryside" (*bint al-rīf*). When she performed, she "depicted the state (*ḥāl*) of the people exactly." After her death, obituaries and other encomia described her as "the voice and face of Egypt."[8]

How does one become a "voice of the people"? How does a woman come to occupy such space in a predominantly Muslim society where women are often presumed by Westerners to be oppressed, silent, and veiled? Do societies really "speak" through one voice? How does one understand a culturally exceptional individual? Considering these questions leads to several major issues that surround the study of a single person, here a star performer: the process of constructing a "voice of the people," the relative value of individualism in a society, and the problems of writing biography. After discussing three examples of Umm Kulthūm's "voice," I will return to these issues.[9]

NOTES ABOUT ARAB MUSIC

Historically, Arab music is a linear music that does not make much use of harmony. It relies, instead, upon melodic invention and modulation for musical interest. Rhythmically and melodically modal, Arab music draws upon more than fifty melodic and several dozen rhythmic modes.[10]

The singing of poetry has high cultural value. Good texts should be elegant or clever, featuring allusion, rhyming, puns, and many sorts of plays on words. Words must be treated with care, their letters clearly articulated, and their meanings enlivened and colored with melody. The singer plays the central role in most performance, with instrumental music a distant second. A solo singer leads a performance, driving it forward. He or she is the principal interlocutor with the audience. Instrumental accompaniment is historically heterophonic, following the rendition of lines by the singer.

Audience response shapes performance. It actually appears as a component in many Arabic definitions of song (alongside poetic text, melody, rendition by the solo singer, and instrumental accompaniment).[11] A good audience calls out compliments at appropriate moments, prompting the singer to repeat, vary, and extend lines. Silence from the audience signals dislike. Reacting to each other, singers and audiences produce the length and the shape of a song in performance, collectively extending a twenty-minute composition to as much as two hours. No two good performances are alike. This important practice contrasts with much Western performance practice where, for example, no matter how much an audience likes parts of a symphonic movement, the work ends when it ends, and retains its shape and structure.

Long performances customarily bring together metrical and non-metrical, vocal and instrumental, pre-composed and improvised music. Sometimes these are individual pieces or improvisations chosen and performed together by the artists. Other times, single compositions, like many of Umm Kulthūm's songs, were originally composed (and then extended in performance) along similar lines. Three relevant examples of her work follow.

ASK MY HEART: "SALŪ QALBĪ"

In the 1940s, a time of great turmoil in Egypt, Umm Kulthūm concentrated on two musical styles that eventually became hallmarks of her life's work. She sang a group of neoclassical Arabic poems with weighty historic themes, and she also performed a number of earthy colloquial Egyptian Arabic songs, rooted in Egyptian manners and customs.

"Salū Qalbī" exemplifies the former. Its text was written in 1912 by the then poet laureate of Egypt, Aḥmad Shawqī, ostensibly an ode for the occasion of the birthday of the Prophet Muḥammad. It is a *qaṣīda* (pl., *qaṣāʾid*), a thousand-year-old form of Arabic poetry in which many hemistichs are bound together with a single poetic meter and single end-rhyme. The hemistichs express complete thoughts, making it possible to repeat lines without disturbing the flow of poetic ideas. *Qaṣāʾid* are typically long poems containing numerous allusions to religious or historical events, or to other poems. Like many poems of its genre, its text allows multiple interpretations. One line attracted particular attention:

Wa-mā nīla 'l-maṭālibu bil-tamanni wa-lākin tu'khadha 'l-dunyā ghilāban.

Not through hope will the prize be obtained; the world must be taken by struggle.

The fight in Shawqī's day was against British occupation; in the 1940s, Egypt struggled not only against British and other European imperialist forces, but against the inability of its own government to meet the needs of its people. Foreign soldiers once again became an unwelcome presence in cities and in the region of the Suez Canal. Conscription and taxation increased. A malaria epidemic killed thousands in 1944. Egyptians watched with great trepidation the growing conflict in Palestine. The profligacy of King Fārūq and his perceived immoralities were becoming public knowledge. "There were," recalled journalist Muḥammad Odah, "socialists, there were communists, there were Wafdists, there were nationalists, there were Muslim brothers, you see"—opposition of all stripes—"but everyone in his mind thought a revolution must come. This system cannot survive."[12]

The composer Riyāḍ al-Sunbāṭī set "Salū Qalbī" to music, using classical progressions of historic Arabic melodic modes (*maqāmāt*) and the spare, declamatory style characteristic of sung *qaṣā'id*, as illustrated in the first line. This beginning constitutes a classical exposition of the mode *rāst* (Exs. 6.1 and 6.2).

EXAMPLE 6.1. Maqām rast

EXAMPLE 6.2. Opening of "Salū Qalbī"

The setting was predominantly syllabic, allowing for clear articulation of the words. In performance, Umm Kulthūm rendered one line in a manner very similar to the style of Qur'ānic recitation, that is the reading aloud of the Muslim holy book (Ex. 6.3):

Fa-lam ara ghayra ḥukmi illāhi ḥukman wa-lam ara dūna bāb illāhi bāba

I see no judgment but the judgment of God and I see no door but the door of God.

Fa- lam   a- ra ghay- ra huk- mi 'lla   _   hi huk- man   wa-lam   a   –   ra

du – na ba   –   bi   lla – hi   ba   –   –   ba

EXAMPLE 6.3. Excerpt from "Salū Qalbī"

She typically began the song using a relatively nasal intonation, recalling the vocal tone color often associated with the intensity of Muslim devotional expression. Improvisation occurred only as Umm Kulthūm repeated popular lines over and over at the behest of the audience, infusing them with feeling and meaning.

The effect was to burn poetic lines into the memory of listeners. Although the language and syntax were beyond all but the highly educated, Egyptians of all classes memorized and repeated "Wa-mā nīla 'l-maṭālibu bil-tamanni wa-lākin tu'khadha 'l-dunyā ghilāban." Writer Muḥammad Shūsha described the impact as follows: "When the Second World War ended, and the people proceeded to demand the evacuation of the colonialists from the Nile Valley, [Umm Kulthūm's] concerts resembled political demonstrations in which she ignited nationalist feeling, for she made a point of singing Shawqī's *qaṣīda* 'Salū Qalbī' in each concert, during which she would cry out, in a tempest of national ardor, 'Not through hope will the prize be obtained; the world must be taken by struggle.'"[13]

What tools carried this intensely nationalist message? Umm Kulthūm brought together a classical Arabic poetic genre and a neoclassical musical setting dependent on the historically Arab compositional system with praise of the Prophet Muḥammad cast in elegant literary Arabic. To this she added vocal rendition that gave precedence to the sound and meaning of the words, as would happen in Muslim devotional expression and recitation of Arabic poetry. She applied highly localized vocal color, the sparing use of accompanying instruments typical of sung Arabic poetry, and varied repetition of important lines characteristic of the shaping of Arabic song in performance. These devices constituted a powerful modern Arab Egyptian voice.

IS IT TRUE THAT LOVE CONQUERS ALL?:
"HUWWA ṢAḤĪḤ IL-HAWÁ GHALLĀB"
∼

The new, colloquial songs that Umm Kulthūm sang in the 1940s constituted a second aspect of the turn toward local "rootedness" in cultural expression. Usually dependent on terse, earthy lyrics provided by poet Bayram al-Tūnisī,[14] the music was composed by his close friend and colleague Zakariyā Aḥmad.

Bayram's poems and song lyrics use short phrases, conversational language, and common expressions, often to produce a profound identification with the working class. The beginning of "Huwwa Ṣaḥīḥ" gives voice to the common experience of love lost:

> *Is it true that love conquers all? I don't know!*
> *Abandonment, they said, is bitter and painful and a day feels like a year.*
> *Love came without warning and all its sweetness increased.*
> *I never thought one day it would take me far away.*
> *It raised hopes in my heart for happiness.*
> *I return and my entire heart is a wound.*
> *How, I wonder, could this happen?*
> *I don't know!*[15]

The Arabic phrases for "how could this happen?" ("Izāy, yā ṭará, ahū da illī jará?") and "I don't know!" ("Mā aʿarafshi anā!") are as common in Arabic conversation as they are in English; the former indicates about the same degree of distress in both languages. The short, pithy phrases have great impact in Arabic. The vagaries of the phrases—love is presented as an abstraction that might generalize to love of anything, "this" in "how could this happen?" might be anything—allow listeners (and performers) to infer and to suggest multiple meanings and to apply the sense of the song to many situations of despair. The punctuated rhythm of "how could this happen?" helped render it memorable and affective for listeners (Ex. 6.4).

The song is cast in the musical mode *ṣabā*—in fact it exemplifies classical practice for cadences (here the ending of a section) in the mode. *Ṣabā* is a familiar and historic Arab mode with highly distinctive characteristics. It is also nearly impossible to harmonize. Considering that harmony lies at the

EXAMPLE 6.4. Excerpt from "Huwwa Ṣaḥīḥ il-Haw'a Ghallāb"

heart of modern Western music, the mode *ṣabā* acts as a powerful force in localizing the music as Egyptian and Arab (Ex. 6.5).

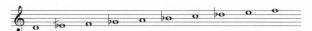

EXAMPLE 6.5. Maqām ṣabā

Typical of Zakariyā Aḥmad's compositions, his sparing use of instrumental interludes and stepwise use of the mode epitomizes historically Arab musical practices. Despite the fashion of large ensembles, Zakariyā, like Riyāḍ al-Sunbāṭī, retains the focus on the singer.

Both "Salū Qalbī" and "Huwwa Ṣaḥīḥ" may be seen as manifestations of cultural resistance to colonial and neo-colonial powers embodied in a turn away from European classicism—and to a lesser extent from European modernism—that characterized the 1940s. Umm Kulthūm's voice supported this movement.

TRACES: "AL-AṬLĀL"

The neoclassical *qaṣīda* "al-Aṭlāl" or "Traces," composed by Riyāḍ al-Sunbāṭī in 1966, proved over time to be one of Umm Kulthūm's most popular songs. She included it in nearly all of her concerts abroad between 1967 and 1972. After her death, it became a signature composition, frequently excerpted to evoke her memory.

Al-Sunbāṭī was known by then as a "genius" at setting *qaṣāʾid*, writing music that helped draw out the meanings and sounds of the words. While using the popular large stage-band-like ensemble, his instrumental writing still gave prominence to the vocal line. The musical setting featured a classical exposition of its melodic mode (*rāḥit al-arwāḥ*), inventive excursions away from the mode, and the declamatory text settings with small melodic excursions for emotional emphasis common to the genre. As a musical genre, "al-Aṭlāl" exemplified the neoclassical *qaṣīda* (Exs. 6.6 and 6.7).

EXAMPLE 6.6. Maqām rāḥit al-arwāḥ

EXAMPLE 6.7. Excerpt from "al-Aṭlāl"

The language, cast in accessible modern standard Arabic, gave form to the intense personal feelings of the poet, Ibrāhīm Nājī, a well-known romanticist writer. Umm Kulthūm derived the text herself from two of Nājī's *qaṣāʾid* ("al-Aṭlāl" and "al-Widāʿ" or "The Farewell"). The song lyrics, opening with the words "Oh my heart, do not ask where love is; it was a castle made of imaginings and it fell,"[16] evokes images of wandering in the desert, coming upon ruins, and searching for something lost—a lover, a family, a home— that is common to the *qaṣīda* tradition. With contemporary and direct language, Nājī voices torment and bereavement. Eventually, the text moves to a painful love relationship in the line "Give me my freedom, set loose my chains; I have given freely, I held back nothing." This line is one of the climactic points of the song, a point that invariably drew prolonged and uproarious approbation.

Originally written as a poem of anguished love, as events progressed in the Arab world, these lines took on new and different meanings. In 1966, some Egyptians perceived them to be relevant to the repressive measures taken by the government of then President Jamāl ʿAbd al-Nāṣir. After defeat at the hands of Israel in 1967, they took on a wider meaning, suggesting the bondage in which many Arabs felt their world to be held. These shifts in meaning are particularly interesting in light of Nājī's romanticism. During the 1940s, he was criticized as escapist and sentimental, wanting a sense of reality and social awareness. Commenting on his oeuvre, the literary scholar M. M. Badawi wrote, "there is remarkably little interest in wider issues, social or political, in his work."[17] It was the audience, not the poet, composer, or singer, who moved the meaning around over time.

GENERAL CHARACTERISTICS OF PERFORMANCE

Umm Kulthūm was heir to a thousand-year-old history of accomplished and respectable female singers. Women, educated in poetry, literature, and song, had been known in Arab society since before the time of the Prophet Muḥammad (d. 632 C.E.).[18] The public space, figuratively speaking, was there to be occupied.

Dress and demeanor, salient in projecting a public persona, were used by performers to signify social affinities. In Egypt, local social values such as modesty and honorable demeanor, informed public performance. While entertainers certainly pushed the limits of respectability simply by displaying themselves on stages and inviting attention, to be really successful in public venues over time, a woman had to appear to be reasonably respectable. The problem was how to perform modestly yet attractively.[19]

Umm Kulthūm set a standard of conservative yet stylish dress, copied, when she was a young woman, from the costumes of the wealthy Cairene Muslim ladies in whose homes she sang. She generally wore long dresses with sleeves, conservative versions of European fashions, or elaborate versions of Egyptian robes. The European aspects of such costumes conveyed cosmopolitan competence; the "coveredness" bespoke the important local value of personal modesty. Richness of fabric and decoration, including elaborate jewelry, indicated wealth and success, a state most female entertainers sought and used in turn to assert accomplished respectability (Figs. 6.1 and 6.2).

Moreover, Umm Kulthūm "always stood still. She didn't dance around," a musician told me, and I learned that this perception was widespread.

Figure 6.1. Umm Kulthūm in Abu Dhabi ca. 1969. Courtesy of Mahmoud ʿArif.

"Standing still," relatively speaking, helped identify her as a singer, not a dancer, which was a much less respectable entertainer in Egyptian society.[20]

The position attained by Umm Kulthūm as a professional musician is not unusual in twentieth-century culture: a talented individual; a seeker of fame and fortune who develops her skills; and, in addition to attaining the status and wealth she initially sought, who also becomes a spokesperson for or representative of a large population. How do we begin to contextualize this person?

LEARNING FROM SOURCES

Musical practice in Egypt includes three related behaviors: performing, listening to performance, and talking about music and performances. "We have much to learn," Stephen Blum writes, "about the ways in which people talk about the dialogues in which musicians and listeners are engaged." "All of the talk relies on tropes, as Goethe recognized: 'We think we are speaking in pure prose and we are already speaking in tropes; one person employs the tropes differently than another, takes them farther in a related sense, and thus

Figure 6.2. Umm Kulthūm in Ewait Hall,
American University in Cairo, 1939.
Courtesy of Mahmoud ʿArif.

the debate becomes interminable and the riddle insoluble.'"[21] "Talking," an anthropologist friend observed, "is a national pastime in Egypt." Musical performance, along with all sorts of other topics, is subjected to detailed discussion, evaluation, and comment. Radio and television broadcasts, for example, are not merely absorbed, they are discussed. They provide a starting point for debating different views.

The central question is not simply what is performed but also what is heard. This talk, this evaluation, locates musical character and value in the larger scheme of Egyptian social life. Speech (and discourses, broadly conceived to include action) provides the means by which musicians and listeners recognize attributes, meanings, and references of sound. Their talk helps to constitute identities of musical styles, as Blum describes: "The definition of stylistic norms evolves from both the actual practice of performing musicians and the verbal statements, evaluations, justifications which attach themselves to practice. Non-specialists participate in several aspects of this process: one chooses what he will listen to, what he will attempt to reproduce, and what he will say about it. . . . Recurrent traits or patterns which result from such procedures for music making might be said to constitute a style."[22] Meaning and value in musical performance is thus co-produced by performers and audiences, by which listening, talking, and writing form part of the creative process. Our source material consists of historically situated performers and performances, as well as listeners who produce, respond to, reproduce, and reuse music—all of which constitute musical practice.

Over time, a discourse may acquire particular characteristics. Talk, along with musical sound, operates in a transformative capacity as well. In the career of a popular star such as Umm Kulthūm, speech about music affects further performances and new productions. Listening practices carried her music into new places and times. The discourse of listeners helps to create a "changing space in which certain possibilities for action emerge, are exploited, and then are abandoned."[23]

Sources of discourse, in twentieth-century Egypt, are voluminous. Brief accounts of Umm Kulthūm's career and commentary on her performances, as well as those of the other entertainers in commercial venues, appeared frequently in the relatively large number of periodicals and columns devoted to music and theater published in Cairo. Many magazines were given entirely to entertainment, music and theater, radio and television performances. Others contained regular articles on music and performance. Stars of music and theater published memoirs. Following the establishment of Egyptian National Radio in 1934, interviews with musicians were broadcast and, beginning in the 1940s, some were kept in sound archives and collected on tape by those aficionados who had the necessary equipment. The advent of recording technologies enabled individual listeners to create their own collections of musical performance.

Fieldwork over a period of years provided an essential addition to this corpus of printed discourse. Talking resulting from interviews with music professionals, music lessons, listening to recordings and performances with acquaintances, and simply living daily life in Egypt added essential depth and nuance to the printed discourse. Access to discourse was not difficult, for music seemed to come from everywhere. Commercial recordings have been available since the turn of the century and played in public places almost constantly since then. Radios, cassette players, and televisions followed and occupied important spaces in community life. Ibrahim Abu-Lughod's description of a radio in a typical Delta grocery shop of the 1960s illustrates the pervasive presence of music (and sound):

> Small in size, limited in stock to the very basic staples, presided over
> by the proprietor assisted by a young boy, usually a relation, it is open
> to the street, equipped with the necessary counter, a few chairs and a

kerosene burner to boil water for coffee and tea. It inevitably contains a radio in constant operation. This radio is a standard prop not only in the grocery store but in the offices of the seed merchant, the grain dealers, the cotton agent, etc. The radio plays constantly not only to entertain the proprietor, for whom business is always slow, but as a service to his friends and customers. Those with business to transact, and even those with no pressing business at all, will stop leisurely to listen for a while, discuss the programs, exchange pleasantries, news and gossip.[24]

In the 1980s and 1990s, in a single block one might hear Western rock music, young Egyptian and other Arab popular music stars, and the recitation of the Qurʾān. Listening to broadcast performances, as indeed listening to broadcast programming of any kind, involves reaction and evaluation among those listening together.

Subsequently, listeners make varying uses of performances. They replay abbreviated and complete performances and move them into new contexts at different times. State ensembles "classicize" older repertory that has retained respectability over time. People "dock" musical performances, as Richard Middleton has said, in different places at different times.[25]

The meaning of Umm Kulthūm's work is not simply expressed, it is produced and re-produced by performers and listeners. To grasp meaning, as Raymond Williams elegantly argues, "we have to learn to understand the specific elements—conventions and notations—which are the material keys to intention and response, and, more generally, the specific elements which socially and historically determine and signify aesthetic and other situations."[26]

Analysis of sound following principles articulated in local music pedagogy presents one viable option for understanding musical performance. Structural analysis, in this case by melodic and rhythmic mode (the systems of *maqāmāt* and *iqāʿāt*), has a strong foundation in Arab music theory dating back to the ninth century. For Umm Kulthūm's repertory, this type of analysis shows us that during the 1920s she sang in a wide variety of *maqāmāt*, some very unusual. In the 1960s, she sang in only eight basic *maqāmāt*; this is perhaps one of the reasons why cognoscenti often characterize her late repertory as inferior and boring.

Structural analysis, however, was only rarely interesting to my Egyptian colleagues and friends, since it failed to account for points in songs that were most affecting for the audiences. This was not the language with which many Egyptian listeners—even sophisticated musicians—evaluated Umm Kulthūm. Linking structural musical analysis to the analysis of discourse opens windows on the dynamics of performance and allows us to see performance and reception as parts of an ongoing musical process embedded in social practice.

BIOGRAPHY AND THE INDIVIDUAL

Talented musicians—notably European classical composers—often have been treated by music historians in the Western modern period as exceptional, sometimes as geniuses, often individuals whose talents and creative processes functioned separately and apart from the society at large.[27] Such an approach directs thought away from the socially and culturally shared toward a concentrated focus on the abilities of one individual.

Anthropologists have long recognized that the lives of individuals offer insights into societies. But the scholarly reconstruction of life histories has, as many have observed, revealed more about the scholar than the individual whose life is represented. For many years, few ethnomusicologists studied individuals (although their fieldwork may depend primarily on contact with one or a small number of people), perhaps to avoid interpretations of culture based on the works of "great men," so long in vogue in the history of European art music. When individuals appear in the foreground of ethnomusicological or folkloric studies, they are rarely famous stars.

Other kinds of sociological analyses treat performers—particularly the highly successful media stars—as creations of corporate businesses such as recording companies and advertising agencies. Again, the society to which the subject belongs is largely ignored, diminished to the point where success is attributed simply to "marketing." Rather than assuming severely limited agency for performers, it makes more sense to ask what their range of movement is within global capitalist commercial environments. What bargains are musicians able to strike with corporate authorities? For, as Richard Middleton wrote, "Composers, performers and other productive agents are not either wholly 'manipulated' or wholly 'critical' and 'free'; their subjectivity—or the positions being continually constructed for that subjectivity—is traversed by a multitude of different, often conflicting lines of social influence, bringing them into multiple, often overlapping identities and collectivities. Neither for them nor for their music are the simple categories of 'mass' or 'individual' appropriate."[28] Furthermore, for very "bright" stars, Simon Frith correctly argues, one wants "to grasp not only the life behind the myth, as many journalists and biographers try to do, but the myth at the heart of the life."[29] From these relationships, one understands what is shared between stars and their audiences and "voices" of people may emerge.

A successful reading of a "voice" such as Umm Kulthūm's comprehends not only the production of music, but also the reception, subsequent productions, and reuses of her songs. Following Anthony Giddens, one views the individual as a "reasoning, acting being," while explaining individual actions with reference to society: neither the actor nor the society has primacy but "each is constituted in and through recurrent practices." Stars, as social actors, "reproduce or transform [systems], remaking what is already made in the continuity of *praxis*."[30] The influential individual may thus be perceived, as Thomas Turino does with Natalio Calderón, the creator of an impressive Peruvian ensemble, as one who made history "but on the basis of political-economic conditions . . . [and] aesthetics *not* of his own making.[31]

Turino and a number of other ethnomusicologists recently examined star musicians through widely varying lenses as illustrated in the recent volume of *Asian Music*.[32] Among social theorists who consider individual "stars," perhaps the most convincing is Raymond Williams, who writes that "even while individual projects are being pursued, what is being drawn on is transindividual, not only in the sense of shared (initial) forms and experiences, but in the specifically creative sense of new responses and formations."[33]

Constructions of stardom certainly will depend on views about individualism held by the relevant society. For instance, Margaret Somerville (referring to Mudrooroo Narogin) points out that requests for autobiographical information tend to "illuminate a collective vision rather than an individual life."[34] Collective concerns would probably also outweigh individual ones in the public expressions of other societies. In the Middle East, value of family or community far outweighs the individualism glorified in the U.S.A. Yet, while in Arab societies speaking about oneself publicly may be viewed as showing bad taste, these societies have produced a thousand-year history of individual virtuosos, usually singers, who have been documented in copious chronicles, notably including Abū 'l-Faraj al-Isbahānī in the ninth-century, *Kitāb al-Aghānī* (Book of Songs).[35] Thus individual "stars" have historic places in Arab life.

THE CREATION OF "VOICE"

As a matter of course in performance, the professional musician chooses musical and other social gestures from any number of precedents, articulating a pattern. Listeners respond in a variety of ways by confirming or challenging the integrity and acceptability of the performance.

Musical performance as a cultural production does not "reflect" social or cultural values but actually helps to constitute them.[36] It advances larger cultural formations, or "conscious movements and tendencies" that are "by no means . . . wholly identified with formal institutions . . . and which can sometimes even be positively contrasted with them."[37]

Viewing Umm Kulthūm's works from this perspective helps to place them in Egyptian society. The affect of her singing might be grasped through its close connections to "meanings and values as they are actively lived and felt," or structures of feeling, explained by Williams as

> characteristic elements of impulse, restraint, and tone; specifically affective elements of consciousness and relationships: not feeling against thought, but thought as felt and feeling as thought: practical consciousness of a present kind, in a living and interrelating continuity. We are then defining these elements as a "structure": as a set, with specific internal relations, at once interlocking and in tension. Yet we are also defining a social experience which is still in process, often indeed not yet recognized as social but taken to be private, idiosyncratic, and even isolating, but which in analysis (though rarely otherwise) has its emergent, connecting, and dominant characteristics, indeed its specific hierarchies.[38]

Artistic conventions and historic musical practices have established musico-social relationships. Written and oral discourse about them define, locate, and attribute cultural value to them that articulates understandings of "virtuosity," "authenticity," "genre," "meaning" and the like and produces "a voice."

Stephen Blum justly warns us that "we have good reason to be suspicious of those who claim that a culture 'speaks' through a single voice."[39] Umm Kulthūm developed musical tools to produce a highly localized sound. She chose to pursue this character of performance. And her audience responded positively. How is a voice of the people constructed? It is created collectively and socially, and not individually, over time. As the elegant Syrian poet Nizār al-Qabbānī wrote after Umm Kulthūm's death, "She was our history and we were hers."

My analysis shows that Umm Kulthūm used tools of music, language, and presentation of self to construct her public persona. She drew from sung poetry, classical and colloquial, essential techniques and practices of classical Arab music, models of female Muslim respectability, and the Arab history of female singers. Her public self developed, as most of ours do, instantiated in time and place. In her case, "Egypt for Egyptians" was a well-known slogan in her youth, the spirit of which carried forward into and through the ʿAbd al-Nāṣir period, that is, for most of her life. Her musical, social, and linguistic articulations of Egyptianness met with welcome and support and her performances fed a river of widespread sentiment in favor of local values.

NOTES

1. *Al-Masraḥ* 13 (8 Feb. 1926): 14.
2. Reported by the poet ʿAbbās Maḥmūd al-ʿAqqād, recollecting an encounter with Umm Kulthūm in 1920 (*al-Muṣawwar* 1306 [21 Oct. 1949]).
3. *Widāʾan ʿan Umm Kulthūm* [Farewell to Umm Kulthūm], ed. Muḥammad ʿUmar Shaṭabī (Cairo: Al-Markaz al-Miṣrī lil-Thaqāfa wal-Iʿlām, 1975), 55.
4. *Ākhir Sāʿa* (21 Feb. 1937): 20.
5. *Rūz al-Yūsuf* (27 June 1966).
6. Kamāl Al-Najmī, *Al-Ghināʾ al-Miṣrī* [Egyptian Song] (Cairo: Dār al-Hilāl, 1965), 56.
7. *Al-Jumhūriyya* (24 Feb. 1968).
8. *Akhbār al-Yawm* (19 June 1967)
9. I will not repeat Umm Kulthūm's life story here, as detailed information is readily available elsewhere. For a variety of perspectives, readers might consult Umm Kulthūm's autobiography as told to Maḥmud ʿAwaḍ, *Umm Kulthūm allāti la yaʿrifuhā Aḥad* [The Umm Kulthūm Nobody Knows] (Cairo: Muʾassasat Akhbār al-Yawm, 1971); and works by Gabriele Braune, *Die Qasida im Gesang von Umm Kultum: Die arabische Poesie im Repertoire der grossten ägyptischen Sängerin unserer Zeit. Beiträge zur Ethnomusicologie*, vol. 16, 2 vols. (Hamburg: Karl Dieter Wagner, 1987) and *Umm Kultum: Ein Zeitalter im Music in Ägypten. Die moderne ägyptische Musik des 20. Jahrhunderts* (Frankfurt am Main: P. Lang, 1994); Virginia Danielson, *"The Voice of Egypt": Umm Kulthūm, Arabic Song and Egyptian Society in the Twentieth Century* (Chicago: University of Chicago Press, 1997); Niʿmāt Aḥmad Fuʾād, *Umm Kulthūm wa-ʿAṣr min al-Fann* (Umm Kulthūm and an Era of Art) (Cairo: al-Hayʾa ʾl-Miṣriyya ʾl-ʿAmma lil-Kitāb, 1976); and Muḥammad al-Sayyid Shūsha, *Umm Kulthūm: Ḥyat Nagham* (Umm Kulthūm: The Life of a Melody) (Cairo: Maktabat Rūz al-Yūsuf, 1976).
10. For good overviews see Stephen Blum, "Hearing the Music of the Middle East," in *The Garland Encyclopedia of World Music*, vol. 6: *The Middle East*, ed. Virginia Danielson, Scott Marcus, and Dwight Reynolds (New York: Routledge, 2002), 3–13; Ali Jihad Racy, "Music," in *The Genius of Arab Civilization: Source of the Renaissance*, ed. John R. Hayes, 2d ed. (Cambridge, Mass.: MIT Press, 1983); also Scott Marcus, "The Eastern Arab System of Melodic Modes in Theory and Practice: A Case Study of Maqam Bayati," in *The Garland Encyclopedia of World Music*, vol. 6, 33–44; Scott Marcus, "Modulation in Arab Music: Documenting Oral Concepts, Performance Rules, and Strategies," *Ethnomusicology* 36 (1992): 171–95; and id., "Arab Music Theory in the Modern Period" (Ph.D. diss., University of California, Los Angeles, 1989) for analytical details.
11. See Kamāl al-Khulaʿi, *Kitāb al-Mūsīqá ʾl-Sharqī* [Book of Oriental Music] (Cairo: Maṭbaʿat al-Taqaddum, 1904), 7.

12. *Umm Kulthūm: A Voice Like Egypt*, prod. and dir. Michal Goldman, 68 min. Waltham, Mass.: Filmmakers Collaborative, 1996. Videocassette. A Wafdist was a member of an entrenched nationalist political party that emerged following the Egyptian Revolution of 1919.

13. Shūsha, *Umm Kulthūm: Ḥyat Nagham*, 59; such a performance may be viewed in Goldman's film *Umm Kulthūm: A Voice Like Egypt.*

14. For a thorough study of the poet's work, see Marilyn Booth, *Bayram al-Tūnisī's Egypt: Social Criticism and Narrative Strategies* (St. Anthony's Middle East monographs, vol. 22; Exeter: Ithaca Press, 1990).

15. The song goes on to recall the joy of seeing a loving glance. A superb rendition of this line may be seen in the Goldman's film *Umm Kulthūm*; see the subtitle "A glance, and I thought it was a greeting—it passed so quickly."

16. "Yā fu'ādī, lā tas'alu ayn al-hawá; kāna ṣarḥan min khayālin fa-hawá." The two words "hawá" are homonyms, allowing for wordplay characteristic of Arabic poetry. Here the "hawá" "hawá-ed" (love . . . fell).

17. M. M. Badawi, *A Critical Introduction to Modern Arabic Poetry* (Cambridge: Cambridge University Press, 1975), 130.

18. See Suzanne Meyers Sawa, "Historical Issues of Gender and Music," in *The Garland Encyclopedia of World Music*, vol. 6, 293–307; and ead., "Sallama al-Qass," ibid., 291–92.

19. Virginia Danielson, "Moving Toward Public Space: Women and Musical Performance in Twentieth Century Egypt," in *Hermeneutics and Honor: Negotiating "Female" Public Space in Islamic/ate Societies*, ed. Asma Afsaruddin (Cambridge, Mass.: distributed for the Center for Middle Eastern Studies, Harvard University by Harvard University Press, 1999).

20. Karin Van Nieuwkerk, *A Trade like any Other: Female Singers and Dancers in Egypt* (Austin: University of Texas Press, 1995).

21. Stephen Blum, "In Defense of Close Reading and Close Listening," *Current Musicology* 53 (1993): 47.

22. Stephen Blum, "Musics in Contact: The Cultivation of Oral Repertories in Meshed, Iran" (Ph.D. diss., University of Illinois, 1972), 4–5.

23. Hubert L. Dreyfus and Paul Rabinow, *Michel Foucault: Beyond Structuralism and Hermeneutics* (Chicago: University of Chicago Press, 1982), 72.

24. Ibrahim Abu-Lughod, "The Mass Media and Egyptian Village Life," *Social Forces* 42 (1963), 101.

25. Richard Middleton, "Articulating Musical Meaning/Reconstructing Musical History/Articulating the 'Popular,'" *Popular Music* 5 (1986): 40.

26. Raymond Williams, *Marxism and Literature* (Oxford: University Press, 1977), 166.

27. For a comparative example see Ali Jihad Racy, "Creativity and Ambience: An Ecstatic Feedback Model from Arab Music," *Worlds of Music* 33 (1991): 7–28.

28. Richard Middleton, *Studying Popular Music* (Milton Keynes: Open University, 1990), 45.

29. Simon Frith, "Essay Review: Rock Biography," *Popular Music* 3 (1983): 276–77.

30. Anthony Giddens, *The Constitution of Society: Outline of a Theory of Structuration* (Berkeley: University of California Press, 1984), 8.

31. Thomas Turino, "The History of a Peruvian Panpipe Style and the Politics of Interpretation," in *Ethnomusicology and Modern Music History*, ed. Stephen Blum, Philip V. Bohlman, and Daniel M. Neuman (Urbana: University of Illinois Press, 1991), 130.

32. "Ethnomusicology and the Individual," ed. Jonathan Stock in *Asian Music* 2001/1. See also Barbara Kirshenblatt-Gimblett, "Authoring Lives," *Journal of Folklore Research* 26 (1989): 123–49, which presents a sensitive critique of life histories from the perspective of a folklorist.

33. Williams, *Marxism and Literature*, 195; see also Raymond Williams, *Culture and Society, 1780–1950* (Garden City, N.Y.: Anchor Books, 1960), wherein he contextualizes the output of a number of British literary "stars."

34. Margaret Somerville, "Life (Hi)story Writing: The Relationship between Talk and Text," *Hecate* 17 (1991): 97.

35. Abū 'l-Faraj Al-Isbahānī, *Kitāb al-Aghānī* (Beirut: Dār Iḥya' al-Turāth al-ʿArabī, 1994).

36. As Raymond Williams writes, "The most damaging consequence of any theory of art as reflection is that, through its persuasive physical metaphor (in which a reflection simply occurs, within the physical properties of light, when an object or movement is brought into relations with a reflective surface—the mirror and then the mind), it succeeds in suppressing the actual work on material—in a final sense the material social process—which is the making of any art work" (Williams, *Marxism and Literature*, 97).

37. Ibid., 119.

38. Ibid., 132.

39. Blum, "In Defense of Close Reading," 52.

CHAPTER SEVEN

"Thanks for My Weapons in Battle— My Voice and the Desire to Use It"

WOMEN AND PROTEST MUSIC IN THE AMERICAS

Jane A. Bernstein

> Not like the brazen giant of Greek fame,
> With conquering limbs astride from land to land;
> Here at our sea-washed, sunset gates shall stand
> A mighty woman with a torch, whose flame
> Is the imprisoned lightning, and her name
> Mother of exiles . . .
>
> EMMA LAZARUS,
> "The New Colossus"

STANDING AT THE MOUTH of New York harbor, the Statue of Liberty has become a symbol of hope and justice for all those arriving from the Old World to the New. As a gift from France to the United States, this female colossus was fashioned after the iconographic emblem of the French Republic. *La Liberté* or "Marianne," as the French call their allegorical figure, was created during the late eighteenth century as a steadfast young woman wearing a Phrygian cap, the symbol of the Revolution. During the political upheavals of the nineteenth century, Marianne came to personify the fighting spirit of the French Republic, appearing after the Revolution of July 1830 in her best-known depiction as *Liberty Guiding the People* in Eugène Delacroix's painting. Here a bare-breasted woman storms the barricades, holding up a tricolor flag with her right hand and carrying a rifle in her left. Her *contrap-*

posto pose contrasts markedly with her static, massively robed American counterpart, who stands calmly poised with torch raised and book in hand. These two representations of liberty present vastly different idealizations of the female form: one an imposing mother welcoming the "huddled masses,"[1] the other a warrior maiden spurring the people into battle.

It is the duality of this female representation as maternal and virginal figures that inaugurates our exploration of women and protest music in the Americas during the mid-twentieth century, for just as these two images have been pressed into service as concrete emblems of national identity, so too have women folksingers come to signify the unified voice of the people. In Argentina, Mercedes Sosa has been transformed into a maternal icon of the Argentine people, who call her "Mother Courage" or *Pachamama* ("Earth Mother" in Quechuan). By comparison, the American Joan Baez has been identified as a virgin warrior, a "pacifist Saint Joan," as one writer dubbed her.[2]

The physical appearance of these two folksingers has also accorded with the virgin–mother ideal. In a culture where the female figure has become the object of the "male gaze," women protest singers have averted this scrutiny by obscuring their bodies and their sexuality. Just as the female form of the Statue of Liberty is concealed beneath heavy drapery, so too has Mercedes Sosa wrapped her monumental frame up in a black poncho—the outfit of the *pueblo* or common folk. Wearing no makeup and her long hair draped around her shoulders, Joan Baez prefigured the feminist counter-cultural aesthetic about feminine appearance by appearing on stage modestly dressed in a skirt and blouse and sometimes without shoes. In order to become activists in a world dominated by men, Baez and Sosa as well as other female folksingers negated their visual presence. Granted, like the mythological figure of Orpheus, the gift of music, their voices emerged as seats of power for their causes and their constituencies during a time of great social and political upheavals across the Americas.

FOLK MUSIC AND POLITICS— NORTH AND SOUTH

In the 1960s and 1970s, songs of social conscious came to the fore as political turmoil and violence grew apace with the dictatorships, military repression, and mass murders in Latin America, and the civil rights and antiwar movements in the United States. Several similarities existed between the protest music of North and South America. Both were connected with left-wing politics, and both were deeply rooted in the folk music traditions of their respective countries.

The protest song emanated from the work of earlier *folkloristas* and ethnomusicologists. While indebted in style to indigenous music, the songs were newly composed. A mimetic process took place whereby the music and texts created by protest writers took on the structure and mannerisms of true folk music. Serge Denisoff calls these works "songs of persuasion," since the simple structure of the melodies and accompanimental harmonies stress the message of the lyrics.[3]

Musical performance also incorporated elements indicative of the folk tradition. Since the words related the message of the song, the singing style of the performer became emblematic of the common people. The voice had to be simple, straightforward, and sound untrained. It meant for women singers a pure, clean tone devoid of excessive vibrato. Low tessitura made the voice sound more maternal, less threatening, and in some cases more androgynous than female. It therefore offered a comforting, soothing presence as in the case of Mercedes Sosa, Ronnie Gilbert, and Odetta's rich contralto timbres. The higher soprano voices of Joan Baez, Jean Ritchie, Judy Collins, and Buffy Sainte-Marie conveyed a reedy urgency and intensity to their performances.

The musical instruments accompanying singers also connected with rural cultures. Brought from Spain to the New World, the acoustic guitar had a long association with folk and popular culture throughout the Americas. Its relative cheapness, portability, and the ease with which one could play simple chordal accompaniments to a song, made it the instrument of choice among self-taught musicians. Some protest singers viewed the guitar as a political weapon—Woody Guthrie had the words "this machine kills fascists" inscribed on his instrument.[4] In Latin America, the guitar also communicated a powerful message as the instrument of the *pueblo*.[5]

In the United States, other fretted and/or plucked string instruments, such as the dulcimer played by Jean Ritchie, the auto-harp, and the banjo, would occasionally double, play counterpoint, or replace the guitar. Latin American musicians also employed instruments native to the Andean regions of northern Argentina, Bolivia, and central and southern Peru. The sharp, high-pitched sound of the charango, a small fretted lute and one of the few *mestizo* or mixed native South American and European instruments, became a favorite. Indigenous wind instruments, such as the panpipes (or zamponas, sikus, or rondeador) and kena or quena (end-blown flute) remained popular as melodic accompaniments by such groups as the Chilean Inti-Illimani and Illapu. Percussion instruments, in particular a large drum, such as the bombo leguero on which Mercedes Sosa accompanies herself, were also used.

Yet despite the striking similarities in the musical character of political songs of the Americas, there were also significant differences between the North and South. In each of their countries, Latin Americans sought a national identity through what they called the *nueva canción* or "new song."[6] They fought at first to free their culture from the commercial "imperialist" influence of North American popular culture by discovering their own indigenous music. Later the *nueva canción* became a powerful weapon against dictatorial regimes. Though protest musicians in the United States, like their southern neighbors, were anti-government, they were not nationalistic. Instead, they struggled for universal concepts of civil rights and peace as personified through the folk music tradition.

One of the most crucial distinctions between the Latin American *nueva canción* and the North American political song, however, turns out to be not one of ideology, but of terminology. Whereas North American singers and songwriters embraced the designation of their politically motivated works as "protest music," Latin American musicians and scholars of the *nueva canción* have tended to eschew this term. In several interviews, the Argentine singer Mercedes Sosa has rejected the protest label, stating that it puts "a stamp on the songs that says 'prohibited' or 'interdicted.'"[7] The *nueva canción,* she says, are "honest songs about the way things really are."[8] The Uruguayan political singer Daniel Viglietti has suggested the word "propose" (*de propuesta*) instead of "protest" (*de protesta*), indicating that the genre rather than being destructive seeks to build bridges.[9] The literary scholar Robert Pring-Mill goes further in coining the term *canciones de lucha y esperanza* (songs of struggle and hope), which he views in the context of Latin American Catholicism.[10] In order to understand these nuanced differences and the important role played by women folksingers, let us take a closer look at the separate movements.

LATIN AMERICA AND THE *NUEVA CANCIÓN*

The *nueva canción* first originated in Chile in late 1950s. It began as an expression of native Chilean culture, countering the widespread domination of North American popular culture in Latin America at the time. The decisive figure in the movement was a woman named Violeta Parra. Known as the "mother of the Latin American folk song," she grew up among the poor of Chile. During the fifties, Parra became a *folklorista,* who, traveling throughout the small towns, mining camps, and Indian villages, collected over 3,000 songs from the different regions of her country.[11] She embarked with her children, Angel and Isabel, on a mission to promote traditional Chilean songs through radio broadcasts and the establishment of folk cafés or coffee houses known as *peñas*.

During this period, Parra, along with Victor Jara, Patricio Manns, and other younger Chilean musicians and political activists, began to compose and sing their own songs in emulation of traditional music. At first these writers of the *nueva canción chilena* focused on the daily life of rural people, but soon they directed their attention to social and political issues. Their songs appealed to urban, middle-class leftists, especially the young, who aspired to create an alternative cultural expression free from foreign "imperialist" influence. The songs also had an impact on the *pueblo*, who identified both with the message, which portrayed them sympathetically, and the music, with its catchy dance rhythms and simple melodies.[12]

The music of the *nueva canción* fused the different aspects of native Indian, European, and *mestizo* genres to create a musical idiom that went beyond class and ethnic lines. Though they mimicked the sound of indigenous song, *nueva canción* composers did not wish to recover their cultural heritage; instead they sought to promote their message and articulate contemporary concerns through a "folk style" that would appeal to the masses.[13]

In 1960, Parra began to shift from *folklorista* to political activist when she composed "Yo canto la diferencia" ("I sing the difference"), which declares her allegiance to the people and the truth. Observers, however, generally point to her song "La carta" ("The Letter") as an important juncture in the *nueva canción* movement.[14] Parra wrote the song in Paris as a response to a violent confrontation between police and workers in Santiago in the fall of 1961, which resulted in the imprisonment of her brother Roberto. The work became the most popular song of the Left.[15]

Parra soon composed other political songs, such as "Me gustan los estudiantes" ("I Like the Students"), which she wrote to show support of the growing militancy of university students against the government. One of her last and most popular songs, "Gracias a la vida," however, transcends her overtly political works. A deceptively simple love song, it became an anthem of the *nueva canción* movement throughout Latin America.

Following Parra's suicide in 1967, Victor Jara and other Chilean folksingers became more politically active. Aligned with the United Popular Front (UP), they wrote campaign songs and performed at meetings and rallies in support of the socialist candidate Salvador Allende, who was democratically elected president in 1970. With the violent overthrow of Allende by a military *junta* in 1973, the *nueva canción* was banned from the country; its performers and composers were jailed, forced to remain in exile, or in the case of its leading proponent, Victor Jara, killed.

It was at this time that the appeal of the Chilean *nueva canción* spread

throughout Latin America. In Cuba, the *nueva trova*, as it was called, represented the Revolution, and as such was recognized and supported by the
government.[16] In other Latin American countries, it remained an expression
of resistance against repressive regimes. This was particularly the case in Argentina, where from 1976 to 1983 one of the most brutal military dictatorships
in the country's history assumed power. The "generals" unleashed a reign of
terror, where thousands of people known as *los desaparecidos* (the disappeared ones) were abducted, tortured, and never heard from again.[17] Fearing
for their lives, few Argentines dissented. One grassroots group that did not
was the Madres de Plaza de Mayo (Mothers of the Plaza de Mayo). Coming
from all walks of life, women, in search of their missing loved ones, began to
gather together one by one to form illegal assemblies. Wearing white head-
scarves, they silently demonstrated every Thursday in front of the presidential palace.[18] The military *junta* tried to suppress them and others they
deemed subversive. Writers, musicians, and artists, in particular, were forced
to go underground or into exile. The singer Mercedes Sosa, however, refused
to remain silent. Like the Madres de Plaza de Mayo, whose visual presence
embodied the Argentine people, she courageously stood up against the dictatorship by empowering her imprisoned nation with her voice.

MERCEDES SOSA: *LA VOZ DE LA GENTE*

It is no accident that the Mothers of the Plaza de Mayo and Mercedes Sosa
were perceived as the guiding spirits of the people of Argentina. In a country
deeply immersed in Roman Catholicism, these women came to represent the
maternal figure of the Virgin Mary—the divine intercessor, who pleads for
the cause of humanity. Fervent Marian veneration has remained a prominent
feature throughout Latin America, where indigenous cultures have had a
long tradition of goddess worship. Each country has its own shrine dedicated
to Mary. In Argentina, the Virgin of Lujan has served as a symbol of both
national and religious identity. The cult of Mary, in turn, has also led to a
secular phenomenon in Latin American *mestizo* cultures known as *marianismo*. Working as a complementary force to *machismo, marianismo* is the
social construction of true femininity, whose characteristics of the ideal
woman consist of "semidivinity, moral superiority and spiritual strength . . .
[with] an infinite capacity for humility and sacrifice."[19] As a *mestizo* of white
and Quechuan (Indian) descent, Mercedes Sosa embodies the positive traits
of *marianismo* in her conviction of freedom and justice and her sense of
social responsibility for the poor and disenfranchised. Her humbleness and

Figure 7.1. Mercedes Sosa in 1980. © Colita/CORBIS.

the personal sacrifices she made during the dangerous years of dictatorship in Argentina also conform to this image (Fig. 7.1).

Sosa was born in San Miguel de Tucum in the northwest Argentine province of Tucuman on 9 July 1935.[20] She came from humble origins; her father was a day laborer and her mother a washerwoman. As a young girl, she began imitating different singers she heard on the radio. Her idol, in particular, was the radio star and *folklorista* Margarita Palacios.[21] Against her father's wishes, she entered and then won, at the age of fifteen, an amateur music contest sponsored by the local radio station. She did not, however, emerge as a professional singer until the early sixties, when she and her husband, the composer Manuel Oscar Matus, gained prominence as performers of the *nuevo cancionero argentino*. She was called "La Negra" for her black hair and the black outfits that she wore.

Sosa's continuing fame during the seventies paralleled the rise in power of the military junta and the emergence of the so-called "dirty war." The dictatorship tried to suppress her public appearances. As early as 1975, she was told that she should not perform on television. Then one by one her recordings disappeared from the stores. Defying the government, she continued to perform until she was arrested while singing the land reform song, "Cuando tenga la tierra" ("When They Have the Land") in a concert in La Plata in 1978. Bomb scares at concerts, threats on her life, and finally a total ban by the government on any further performances forced her to leave her country and to go into exile in Spain. As she explained in an interview about these dark years: "It wasn't specific songs that I sang that were prohibited or specific recordings of mine that were taken out of circulation, but what was prohibited was I myself. What those gentlemen didn't understand was that you could silence Mercedes Sosa force her into exile, but you couldn't take away *La Negra,* her repertory, what she represented in the heart of the people. And that was much larger than me."[22]

Sosa came back to Argentina in 1982, shortly before the fall of the military regime. With the restoration of a civilian government under Raúl Alfonsín, she returned to the stage, giving thirteen sold-out concerts at the Teatro Opera in Buenos Aires. She then issued a double album, *Mercedes Sosa Live in Argentina,* which sold nearly half a million copies, an unheard-of figure in a nation of thirty million people.[23] For the last twenty years, she has continued to concertize in Europe, the United States, and all over Latin America, where she has performed both the classic *nueva canción* repertory as well as works by younger musicians in different popular music genres.

Sosa has been an inspirational singer known for her intensely riveting interpretations of works by others. The composers, whose songs she has carefully chosen, read like a who's who of the movement throughout Latin America—the Chileans Violeta Parra and Julio Numhauser; the celebrated Cuban *trovador* Silvio Rodríguez; the Brazilians Antonio Tarrago Ros and jazz figure Milton Nascimento; and from her own country, such major figures as Atahualpa Yupanqui, María Elena Walsh, César Isella, Victor Heredia, and Armando Tejada Gómez, to name a few.

She has continued to sing about social issues, but themes of renewal and celebration have replaced the solemn subjects of survival and endurance that resonated deeply during "los años negros" in Argentina. These include the young Fito Páez's "Yo vengo a ofrecer mi corazón" ("I Come to Offer My Heart"), Julio Numhauser's "Todo cambia" ("Everything Changes"), and María Elena Walsh's "Como la cigarra" ("Like the Cicada").[24] From her earlier repertory, the two songs "Los hermanos" and "Gracias a la vida" have remained important touchstones throughout her career.

"Los hermanos" ("The Brothers") was written by Atahualpa Yupanqui (1908–92), a composer, poet, guitarist, and singer who is revered as the premier folklorist of Argentina.[25] For over thirty years—long before the *nueva canción* movement of the sixties—Yupanqui collected songs and poems from all over Argentina, which he utilized in his own works. Like Violeta Parra, he worked and lived in the countryside among the *pueblo*. Many of his works use the distinctive forms and rhythms of the gauchos of rural Argentina. Much of his imagery—the oneness with nature and the land, with the common people, and with death—is deeply rooted in native Indian traditions, particularly those of the Quechua.

"Los hermanos" calls for unity among people. The message appears in the *estribillo* or refrain, "Yo tengo tantos hermanos que no los puedo contar" ("I have so many brothers that I cannot count them") that begins the song (see Appendix). Each stanza maps the immensity of this brotherhood—shifting geographically in the first stanza from "the valley, the mountain, the prairies, and the sea" to, in the second verse, "a wide open horizon, just beyond the reaching." By the last verse, the bond between peoples intensifies as "we carry on, toughened by loneliness. And within us come our dead, so that no one's left behind." Here the whole history of the *pueblos* moves ever forward until the final return of the *estribillo,* where Yupanqui provides the true message of the song in the additional line: "Y una hermana muy hermosa que se llama libertad ("And a very beautiful sister named Liberty"). Mercedes Sosa describes "Los hermanos" as having "all the depth and the beauty of that moment of our lives when we open our eyes to our earth and its inhabitants, and we decide to unite with them in perhaps a more important bond than that of nation: to share love, pains, and hope."[26]

Just as the lyrics of the song reflect folk traditions so too does the music, which Yupanqui sets as a *milonga decidora*. The term *milonga* has several musical meanings. It began as an improvised rural song/dance form from the gaucho traditions of Uruguay and Argentina. During the mid-nineteenth century, dance steps were added to the genre, and by the 1880s, its duple meter and strong, syncopated dance rhythm became associated with the urban tango. The *milonga pampeana,* as a folk song accompanied by guitar, has remained popular throughout Uruguay and the Argentine pampas.[27] Yupanqui describes the *milonga decidora* as a meditative form, where "man looks for his necessary solitude to say his things."[28]

The accompaniment of "Los hermanos" follows the familiar syncopated rhythmic dance pattern of the *milonga*/tango (Ex. 7.1). Also typical of the *milonga* is the stepwise descending structure of the melody, which appears in its ur-form in the introduction. In the first couplet of the verse, the melody hovers around the fifth step, and then slowly moves down to third step. In each successive couplet, this melody is subjected to a series of improvised variations by the singer. The use of the minor mode with an occasional inflection on the major third imparts a sad, quiet urgency. The song's restless, searching quality is mainly due to the avoidance of the tonic pitch, which only appears at the end of each refrain as found in the closing *estribillo* of the song (see Ex. 7.2).

EXAMPLE 7.1. Rhythmic pattern of the *milonga* and tango

EXAMPLE 7.2. Closing refrain of the song "Los hermanos"

Just as "Los hermanos" has resonated deeply with the Argentine people, the song that has become most closely identified with Sosa and the *nueva canción* as a whole is "Gracias a la vida" ("Thanks to life"). As previously mentioned, Violeta Parra wrote it shortly before her death in 1967. Many Latin American singers including Parra herself have performed it. Joan Baez first sang it in 1973 as a response to the overthrow of Allende's government,[29] and even the great Mexican-born opera star Placido Domingo has recorded the song. But it is Mercedes Sosa's interpretation that is considered the most powerful and poignant.[30]

The song is a simple strophic one with six stanzas sung to the same music. Set in the tradition of a folk ballad, each stanza begins with the refrain: "Gracias a la vida que me ha dado tanto" ("Thanks to life for giving me so much"). It starts by thanking life for the gift of sight, then hearing, then language; in the fourth verse, the narrator is grateful to life for the strength to walk through cities and rivers, and in the fifth, for her heart. In the last verse, she finally reaches out to connect with the audience with the words:

> *Thanks to life for giving me so much.*
> *It has given me laughter and tears*
> *with which to distinguish good fortune from heartbreak,*
> *and those are the themes which shape my song;*
> *my song which is the same as your song;*
> *as the song of all people; my very own song.*[31]

As Pring-Mill has noted, the *estribillo* does not appear in its traditional position at the end of each stanza but at the start. Serving as a "point of departure" for each successive strophe, this refrain becomes, like that of "Los hermanos," the "conceptual peg on which each stanza hangs."[32] However, it differs from the *estribillo* of "Los hermanos," whose meaning, as we have noted above, remains symbolically incomplete until the very end of the song. The descending stepwise melodic structure of "Gracias a la vida" is also similar to "Los hermanos." Unlike the Yupanqui piece, the tune does not vary with each stanza nor does the accompaniment contain the rhythmic syncopations associated with native folk dance traditions. Parra's song is thus more abstract, and depending on the performer, can be interpreted in several ways. Joan Baez, in her 1974 recording, sings each stanza exactly the same to a driving, duple-meter, Mariachi band accompaniment. Her reading tends to be more martial, more assertive than Sosa's, who treats the work as if it were a private love song. With each strophe, Sosa subtly varies her tone and mood. At first she sounds tentative and introspective, but as the song progresses, her voice (and the accompaniment) change to reveal a more reso-lute, public persona, culminating in the final strophe when she invites the audience to participate in the song.

More than any other performer, Mercedes Sosa has brought the *nueva canción* to the attention of an international audience. As a *mestizo,* she has straddled the two worlds of Argentina—the cosmopolitan, Europeanized urban center and the indigenous culture of the rural areas. She has acted as a mediator for the poor and disenfranchised people of her country both through her actions and her profound musical talent. As such, she has met-onymically become a mother of her nation, emanating from both native Indian cultures and Roman Catholic traditions transplanted in the New World.

FOLK MUSIC REVIVAL AND THE PROTEST MOVEMENT IN THE UNITED STATES

Just before the emergence of the *nueva canción* movement in Latin America, a resurgence in traditional music took hold in the United States. The early sixties was a time of political and social unrest as the baby boom generation came of age. Issues of social concern—civil rights, the threat of nuclear fall-out, and then the Vietnam War—began to capture the attention first of uni-versity students and then the public at large. Protest music played an integral role in the struggle for change as a union emerged between political activism and the urban folksinger.

During the fifties and early sixties—the years of the Beat Generation of Jack Kerouac, Allen Ginsberg, and Lawrence Ferlinghetti—coffeehouses sprang up in large urban centers and small college towns. Offering young students a refuge, they became ideal performance venues for the new protest folksingers. Folk songs that focused on life experiences from a rural past resonated with urban students rebelling against the materialist complacency of the establishment. The counter-culture with its emphasis on experimentation, individualism, and personal self-expression created a haven not just for male performers, but also for women musicians.[33] Urban folksingers such as Ronnie Gilbert, Jean Ritchie, Cynthia Gooding, and Odetta, as well as the later performers Buffy Sainte-Marie, Judy Collins, and Joan Baez, pioneered in a profession dominated by men.

Ronnie Gilbert was a member of the Weavers, the first musical group to popularize the folk music tradition in the United States. Each person in the quartet was well known in his or her own right. Pete Seeger and Lee Hays were founding members of the Almanac Singers, an early forties group who performed a mixture of traditional and topical songs at Communist meetings and union rallies; Fred Hellerman and Ronnie Gilbert sang in a later, politically left, musical organization, the People's Songs Inc.[34] While Seeger was the most vocal and best-known member of the Weavers, Gilbert must be singled out as its only female singer. Recordings by the Weavers sold over four million copies, and their rendition of Leadbelly's "Goodnight Irene" moved to the top of the Hit Parade.[35] Then in 1952, the group was blacklisted from television and radio. At the height of the McCarthy era, they sang at college campuses and in 1955 made a historic recording at Carnegie Hall produced by Vanguard Records.[36]

Other female singers began their careers as soloists specializing in different aspects of the idiom. Jean Ritchie introduced to an urban audience Appalachian songs from her native Kentucky with her natural, flat-sounding soprano voice. Odetta sang the work songs, spirituals, blues, and gospel music of her African-American heritage in a deep, powerful contralto voice.

During the early sixties, Buffy Sainte-Marie and Judy Collins joined the ranks of solo protest singers. Born on a Cree reservation, Sainte-Marie was known for her biting political songs about the treatment of Native Americans.[37] Her antiwar song "Universal Soldier" gained widespread popularity at the height of the Vietnam War. Judy Collins, a classically trained pianist committed to a variety of social and political causes, extended the folk repertory by singing medieval music, cabaret songs by Jacques Brel and Kurt Weill, and works by Leonard Cohen and Stephen Sondheim. All of these women

gained moderate success as folksingers, yet none of them captured the imagination of the public as much and as quickly as Joan Baez.

JOAN BAEZ:
"SIBYL WITH GUITAR"
~

> The expression suddenly appears reverent yet joyous, Indian yet Euro-
> pean, olive-skinned yet white of hue. It is a face that intermingles the
> Christianity of Byzantine Europe with the overpowering naturalism of
> New World Indian; a fitting symbol for all the peoples of the great
> continent.[38]

This passage, which vividly describes the image of Our Lady of Guadalupe,
the national icon of Mexico and the most famous Marian shrine of the Americas, could serve equally well as a portrait of the young Joan Baez (see Fig.
7.2). Of Mexican and Anglo-Scottish descent, Baez represented an intermin-
gling of different cultures. Her modest demeanor and the purity of her voice
contributed to her mystique as a figure of innocence and virtue. Even more
than her public image, her discipline and unyielding commitment to social
and political causes over the past four decades earned her the title of Saint
Joan.

Born in Staten Island, New York, on 9 January 1941, Baez was brought up
in a liberal, academic family.[39] Her father, a research physicist, was born in
Mexico; her mother originally came from Scotland. The family moved
around during Baez's early years. When she was ten they resided in Baghdad
for a year, and during her high school years they lived in Palo Alto, California. After she graduated from high school, the Baez family once more relo-
cated, this time to Belmont, Massachusetts, a well-to-do suburb of Boston.
Baez matriculated as a student at Boston University in the fall of 1958. Attending few classes, she withdrew before the end of her second semester to
become part of the burgeoning folk music scene in Cambridge.[40] She performed regularly at Club 47, a coffeehouse near Harvard Square, picking up
song repertory and guitar technique from a number of amateur and semiprofessional folksingers.[41] Her career took off only a year later when in June 1960
she created a sensation at the Newport Folk Festival. Only a few months after
her Newport Folk Festival debut, the first album she released with Vanguard
Records became a top seller. Practically overnight Joan Baez emerged not
only as a major female performer, but America's premier folksinger.

The repertory she sang on her first album as well as those that followed

Figure 7.2. Joan Baez in 1971. Photograph by Michael Ullman, reproduced with permission.

during the next three years stems from the Anglo-American tradition. The songs consist mainly of strophic narrative ballads and laments. Several appear in Francis Child's anthology *The English and Scottish Popular Ballads* (1882–98) or are broadside ballads. Others are more recent American songs, hymns, and spirituals, some of which were collected and transcribed by Cecil Sharp, the Lomaxes, or newly written by Woody Guthrie, Anne Bradon, and others. Nearly all convey messages of despair and/or death.

In an interview with Charles Fuss, Baez characterized one of these songs ("Wagoner's Lad") as "pre-women's lib."[42] While her description of this lyric dialogue is apt, it does not take into account the fact that the subjects of the songs she performed differed radically from those of her male counterparts, for nearly all of them were concerned with women.

Her early repertory presents a panoply of female life experiences. She sings about women who are faithful ("John Riley"), abandoned ("Wagoner's Lad"), or murdered by rejected lovers ("Banks of the Ohio"). "House of the Rising Sun" is a blues lament of a prostitute, while "Come All Ye Fair and Tender Maidens" and "Silver Dagger" deal with the falseness of men. Other ballads tell the stories of proud and brave heroines: one who pleads for the life of her lover ("Geordie"), another who goes to sea disguised as a sailor ("Jackaroe"), and then there is Mary Hamilton, who hangs for the murder of her illegitimate baby. Most are written in the feminine voice, or if not, Baez changes the pronouns of the lyrics to fit a female point of view. As one reviewer wrote of her 1970 album "One Day at a Time:" "[it is] of a wife, a mother, a lover who sings of liberties and lies, of ghettos and prisons, of bodies and souls. There is the voice of the sorrows of her sisters and herself, each in its place, one at a time, carrying on."[43]

Reviews like this one fed into the myth of Baez as the virgin of sorrows— the *mater dolorosa* who weeps for Christ, her dead son. The ancient, almost eternal quality of the music also fit in with this image. Many of the tunes, while set to major or minor accompaniments, are modally inflected. "House of the Rising Son," "Henry Martin," "East Virginia," and "Lily of the West" are all in the Dorian mode, while "All my Trials" and "Silkie" are Mixolydian. "Wagoner's Lad," "Cherry Tree Carol," and to some extent "Silver Dagger" use the pentatonic scale.

During the mid-sixties Baez became increasingly involved in the civil rights and antiwar movements. Along with Peter, Paul, and Mary, Bob Dylan, Mahalia Jackson, and Harry Belafonte, she performed at the 1963 March on Washington, where she sang the old gospel song "We Shall Overcome," which by that time had been transformed into the unofficial anthem of the civil rights movement.[44] Baez continued to support the cause, joining Martin Luther King in 1966 in Grenada, Mississippi, leading black children in a march to help desegregate an elementary school.[45]

In 1964, Baez began to protest the United States involvement in Vietnam by withholding part of her federal income tax. The following year, she helped found the Institute for the Study of Nonviolence in Carmel Valley, California. Her involvement in the peace movement intensified during the mid-sixties. In 1967 she was arrested twice for blocking the entrance to the Armed Forces induction center in Oakland, California. It was during this time that she met and married David Harris, an antiwar activist, who later served twenty months of a three-year sentence for refusing induction into the armed forces.

Before her marriage, Baez lived the free lifestyle of the counter-culture— having affairs and declaring her bisexuality.[46] Yet her public persona as the "Virgin Mary" continued to play out in the media. She was called the "high priestess of folk song,"[47] the "matron saint of the hippies,"[48] changing over time from "folk madonna to folk matriarch."[49] As Jerome Rodnizky notes, "she blended into the protest tradition, into pacifism, into activism, into a publicized marriage and motherhood into a vicarious martyrdom . . . and finally into a national symbol for nonviolence."[50]

During these turbulent years, Baez's song repertory quickly shifted from traditional Anglo-American ballads to newly composed protest songs. Her first antiwar song, "Last Night I Had the Strangest Dream," was written by Ed McCurdy in 1950.[51] Its naive triple-meter tune conveying a wish for peace fit in well with Baez's public persona. So too did Malvina Reynolds's "What Have They Done to the Rain," which appeared on Baez's third album, *Joan Baez in Concert* (1962). Reynold's child-like melody, however, belies the work's grim message about radioactive fallout.

Songs by other antiwar activists, such as Pete Seeger's popular "Where Have All the Flowers Gone?" and Phil Ochs's "There But for Fortune," also appeared on her early concert programs. But it was Bob Dylan, with whom she was romantically linked in the mid-sixties, who had the most profound effect upon her. The political messages found in his early works, such as "With God on Our Side" and "A Hard Rain's a Gonna Fall," fit well with Baez's intense vocal style.

Dylan based "With God on Our Side" on the earlier Irish Republican Army song "The Patriot Game," written by Dominic Behan in 1957. He borrowed the melody and verse structure, using the second stanza of Behan's lyrics as the inspiration for his opening verse.[52] Dylan's ambivalent message that God will stop a nuclear war can be interpreted as optimistic or bitter cynicism, depending on the performer. Baez's lyrical reading of the song is more full-bodied and less savage than Dylan's. The bittersweet quality of her voice suggests both sadness and hope when she reaches the last stanza.

"A Hard Rain's a Gonna Fall" was written in September 1962, just a month before the Cuban Missile crisis. The five-verse song is structured as a question-and-answer dialogue between parent and son with a chorus containing the title words of the song. As several writers have pointed out, the text of Dylan's song bears a striking resemblance to the traditional ballad "Lord Randal" (Child Ballad No. 12).[53] "Lord Randal" relates the tragedy of a young man who tells his mother he's been poisoned by his lover. Dylan turns this private murder into "the public holocaust faced by the modern world."[54] Using the first line of the folk song as a springboard for his song, Dylan parallels some of the images found in several versions of "Lord Randal." But instead of following the four-line stanzaic structure of the Child ballad, he adds anywhere from five to twelve extra lines to each of the five verses.

Considered one of Dylan's most original early songs, "A Hard Rain's a Gonna Fall" turned out to be an ideal vehicle for Baez, since it became an

effective ballad from a woman's point of view. In comparing Baez's performance with that of Dylan, we notice that a reversal of roles occurs in the
song. Whereas Dylan assumes the persona of the son, Baez takes on the part
of the mother, who queries her son, then offers the same disheartening reply
to his visionary answers. Her reading of the song, while retaining Dylan's
universal message, becomes more personal. In these and other Dylan songs, her
powerful lyrical singing style coupled with her chaste image offended critics
from all sides of the folk music spectrum. Folk purists deemed her voice "too
rich and too grandiose to carry the simplicity of the humble folk song."[55] In
contrast, those in the Bob Dylan–Woody Guthrie camp felt that "she could
not express the heavy contemptuous sarcasm of many of Dylan's songs."[56]

By 1965, Baez and Dylan had moved in opposite directions as she became
increasingly committed to social and political causes, and he, abruptly reject-
ing the protest movement, shifted into rock music. Yet despite their philosophical parting of ways, Dylan continued to have an important influence
on Baez. From 1963 until the present, she has recorded and performed in
concert no fewer than twenty-six of his songs. At his suggestion, she started
to write her own songs.[57] Some of them, such as "To Bobby," "Winds of the
Old Days," and her most popular work, "Diamonds and Rust," are about
him.[58] Even more significant, the changes in musical style that Baez made
later in her career from folk to folk rock and country western had already
been prefigured by Dylan.

During her long career, Baez has written over seventy songs, some with
personal, others with political messages. Her topical works serve as commentaries on the social and political causes in which she has been actively involved. They include such songs as "Where Are You Now, My Son?," written
in 1973 after her visit to North Vietnam; "Warriors of the Sun," her 1982
peace tribute to Martin Luther King Jr., Greenpeace, and the Guardian
Angels; and more recently, "China," written in 1991 about the Tienamen
Square protesters. Yet it is her identity as a voice of spiritual strength and
high morality against political and social injustices that has made her a celebrated icon.

AS THE FOLK REVIVAL and the protest movements have come and gone, Sosa
and Baez have endured as influential musicians. Part of their popularity has
been due to their continued interest in social and political causes. They have
transcended their roles as protest singers through their unceasing advocacy
of freedom, justice, and human rights. Both women have used their musical
gifts as powerful weapons for their beliefs, and as such, have become the
social consciences of their countries: Sosa as an earth mother and symbol of
hope and survival for *la gente del pueblo,* and Baez as a virtuous fighter for

universal nonviolence and racial equality. Yet at the same time that the two singers have achieved iconic status, their feminine power has been negated. No longer real, no longer women, Sosa and Baez have instead become incarnations of the lofty figure of Liberty—fixed in time as immobile symbols of their nations and their causes.

NOTES

∿

The quotation in the title is taken from Joan Baez, *And a Voice to Sing With: A Memoir*, 258. I am grateful to Blanca Rey and Dr. Celian Rey Casserly for their assistance with Spanish translations.

1. Taken from the last stanza of Emma Lazarus's poem inscribed on the base of the statue. On the statue as a maternal icon see Marina Warner, *Monuments and Maidens: The Allegory of the Female Form* (New York: Atheneum, 1985), and Kaja Silverman, "Liberty, Maternity, Commodification" in *Point of Theory: Practices of Cultural Analysis*, ed. Mieke Bal and Inge Boer (New York: Continuum, 1994), 18–31.
2. Jerome L. Rodnitzky, "Joan Baez: A Pacifist St. Joan," chap. 6 in *Minstrels of the Dawn: the Folk-Protest Singer as a Cultural Hero* (Chicago: Nelson-Hall, 1976), 83–99.
3. R. Serge Denisoff, *Great Day Coming: Folk Music and the American Left* (Urbana: University of Illinois Press, 1971), 5–6.
4. Ibid., 4.
5. Jeffery E. Taffet, "My Guitar is Not for the Rich: The New Chilean Song Movement and the Politics of Culture," *Journal of American Culture* 20 (1997): 91–103, at 95.
6. For an excellent general introduction to the *nueva canción* see John M. Schechter, "Beyond Region, Transnation and Transcultural Traditions," in *Music in Latin American Culture: Regional Traditions*, ed. Schechter (New York: Schirmer, 1999), 425–37.
7. Larry Rohter, "Mercedes Sosa: A Voice of Hope," *New York Times*, Sunday, 9 October 1988, sec. 2, 21.
8. Caleb Bach, "Mercedes Sosa, Song with No Boundaries," *Americas* 48 (1996): 40–47, at 42.
9. Mario Benedetti, *Daniel Viglietti* (Madrid: Júcar, 1974), 78, as quoted in Robert Pring-Mill, "*Gracias a la vida": The Power and Poetry of Song* (The Kate Elder Lecture, 1; London: University of London, Department of Hispanic Studies, 1990), 10.
10. Pring-Mill, "*Gracias a la vida,*" 10–15.
11. Albrecht Moreno, "Violeta Parra and 'La Nueva Canción Chilena,'" *Studies in Latin American Popular Culture* 5 (1986): 108–26, at 110.
12. Daniel Ramirez, "The Peña: A Semiological Analysis of the Latin American Folk Music Movement" (Ph.D. diss., University of California, San Diego, 1980), 87.
13. Karen Linn, "Chilean Nueva Cancion: A Political Popular Music Genre," *Pacific Review of Ethnomusicology* 1 (1984): 57–64, at 62.
14. The complete text with some variation appears on several websites, among them "Canciones Interpretadas por Mercedes Sosa" available at http://users.hotlink.com .br/saulob/mercedessosa.htm; also, http://www.ufpel.tche.br/ila/siteletras/espanhol_ cancion_la_carta.shtml; www.olgalara.com; and http://152.42.78.132/pena/chile.html.

15. Moreno, "Violeta Parra," 113.

16. On the Cuban song see Rina Benmayor, "La 'Nueva Trova' New Cuban Song," *Latina American Music Review* 2 (1981): 11–44.

17. For a good introduction to Argentina's dictatorship see Martin Edwin Andersen, *Dossier Secreto: Argentina's Desaparecidos and the Myth of the "Dirty War"* (Boulder, Colo.: Westview Press, 1993).

18. On the Mothers of the Plaza de Mayo see Marguerite Guzman Bouvard, *Revolutionizing Motherhood: The Mothers of the Plaza de Mayo* (Wilmington, Del.: Scholarly Resources, 1993) and Jo Fisher, *Mothers of the Disappeared* (Boston: South End Press, 1989).

19. Evelyn P. Stevens, "*Marianismo*: The Other Face of Machismo," in *Female and Male in Latin America: Essays*, ed. Ann Pescatello (Pittsburgh: University of Pittsburgh Press, 1973): 90–101, at 94.

20. The only full-length study of Mercedes Sosa in English appears in Rebecca Cormier, "The Relationship between Music, Text, and Performer in the Latin American *Nueva canción* as seen the Repertory of Mercedes Sosa" (Master's thesis, Tufts University, 1999).

21. Leopoldo Brizuela, *Cantar la vida: Reportajes a cinco cantantes argentinas, Gerónima Sequeida, Leda Valladares, Mercedes Sosa, Aimé Painé, Teresa Parodi* (Buenos Aires: Librería "El Ateneo" Editorial, 1992), 76–77. On Margarita Palacios see "Intérpretes folklóricos," 2002. Available from http://www.fortunecity.ed/felices/lapaz/124/margpala .htm.

22. Brizuela, *Cantar la vida*, 93–94.

23. Rohter, "Mercedes Sosa," and Don Heckman, "The Voice Heard Round the World," Los Angeles Times, Sunday, 29 October 1995, Calendar sec., 60.

24. On the poet María Elena Walsh see Caleb Bach, "A Child's Wisdom in a Poet's Heart," *Americas* 47 (1995): 12–17.

25. For biographical information see Felix Luna, *Atahualpa Yupanqui* (Madrid: Ediciones Júcar, 1974); Françoise Thanas, *Atahualpa Yupanqui: Essai* (Paris: Le Livre a venir, 1983); and Norberto Galasso, *Atahualpa Yupanqui: El canto de la patria* (Buenos Aires: Ediciones del Pensamiento Nacional, 1992).

26. Brizuela, *Cantar la vida*, 104–5.

27. On the *milonga* see Ercilia Moreno Cha, "Music in the Southern Cone: Chile, Argentina, and Uruguay," in *Music in Latin American Culture*, ed. John Schechter, 265–81.

28. "La milonga es una forma de meditar . . . y está la milonga decidora, donde el hombre busca su necesaria soledad para decir sus cosas." Available from http://argentina .informatik.uni-muenchen.de/tangos/msg06271.html.

29. Joan Baez, *And a Voice to Sing With: A Memoir* (New York: Summit Books, 1987), 170.

30. Robert Pring-Mill offers an in-depth analysis of the song, with particular attention to its poetic structure, in his "*Gracias a la vida.*" For a musical analysis and transcription see Cormier, "Repertory of Mercedes Sosa," 28–32.

31. The full text and best English translation of the song appear in Pring-Mill, "*Gracias a la vida,*" 24–25.

32. Ibid., 31.

33. Sheila Whiteley, *Women and Popular Music: Sexuality, Identity, and Subjectivity* (London and New York: Routledge, 2000), 72.

34. On the Almanac singers and People's Songs, Inc. see Richard A. Reuss, *American Folk Music and Left-wing Politics, 1927–1957*, with JoAnne C. Reuss (Lanham, Md.: Scarecrow Press, 2000), 147–220, and Denisoff, *Great Day Coming*, 77–129.

35. Reuss, *American Folk Music*, 235, and Denisoff, *Great Day Coming*, 146.

36. Vanguard Records, a small but distinguished recording company specializing in folk and jazz as well as classical music, was founded in 1950 by Seymour Solomon and his brother Maynard (the noted musicologist). During the fifties, they had the courage to break with the entertainment industry and record blacklisted performers, including Paul Robeson and the Weavers. In the sixties, they became heavily involved in the folk music revival, serving as the primary recording company of the Newport Folk Festival and of such artists as Odetta, Buffy Sainte-Marie, Ian and Sylvia, and Joan Baez. A brief history of the company is available from http://www.vanguardrecords.com/.

37. On Sainte-Marie as a Native American composer see David P. McAllester, "New Perspectives in Native American Music," *Perspectives of New Music* 20 (1981–82): 440–41.

38. Philip Serna Callahan, *The Tilma: Under Infra-Red Radiation* (CARA Studies on Popular Devotion, vol. 2: Guadalupan Studies, 3; Washington, D.C.: Center for Applied Research in the Apostolate, 1981), 14–15, as quoted in Jeanette Rodriguez, *Our Lady of Guadalupe: Faith and Empowerment among Mexican-American Women* (Austin: University of Texas Press, 1994), 23. Reference to Baez as "Sibyl with Guitar," comes from the title of the cover story in *Time*, 23 November 1962, 54–60.

39. One of the best sources for Baez's life appears in her memoir, *And a Voice to Sing With*. Charles J. Fuss, *Joan Baez: A Bio-Bibliography* (Westport, Conn: Greenwood Press, 1996) offers an excellent concise biography, while David Hajdu, *Positively 4th Street: The Lives and Times of Joan Baez, Bob Dylan, Mimi Baez Fariña, and Richard Fariña* (New York: Farrar, Straus and Giroux, 2001) concentrates mainly on the relationships of these four people during the sixties and seventies. Joan Baez Web Pages (http://baez.woz.org/) provides a wealth of information on the singer, including a chronology of her life, discography, song lyrics, photos, and links to other websites.

40. Hadju, *Positively 4th Street*, 23.

41. On the Cambridge folk music scene, see Eric von Schmidt and Jim Rooney, *Baby, Let Me Follow You Down: The Illustrated Story of the Cambridge Folk Years*, 2d ed. (Amherst: University of Massachusetts Press, 1994).

42. Joan Baez, interview by Charles Fuss in brochure notes to *Rare, Live, and Classic*, Vanguard compact disk VCD3–125–27 (1993).

43. Review of record album *One Day at a Time* performed by Joan Baez, *Saturday Review*, 28 March 1970, as cited in Fuss, *Joan Baez, A Bio-Bibliography*, 66.

44. For the origins of the song and a performance by Baez at the March to Washington see the excellent video *We Shall Overcome*, produced by Ginger Group (Beverly Hills: PBS HomeVideo, 1990).

45. Joan Baez, *And a Voice to Sing With*, 101–10.

46. Ibid., 78.

47. *Billboard*, 30 November 1963, cited by Fuss, *Joan Baez, A Bio-Bibliography*, 58.

48. *Stereo Review*, November 1968, cited by Fuss, 63.

49. Rich Kerstetter, "Joan Baez: From Folk Madonna to Folk Matriarch," *Sing Out!* 41 (August–October, 1996): 36–43.

50. Jerome Rodnitzky, *Minstrels of the Dawn*, 84.

51. Baez, *Rare, Live, and Classic*.

52. Todd Harvey, *The Formative Dylan: Transmission and Stylistic Influences, 1961–1963* (American Folk Music and Musician Series, vol. 7; Lanham, Md.: Scarecrow Press, 2001), 122–24.

53. Among others Wilfrid Mellers, *A Darker Shade of Pale: A Backdrop to Bob Dylan* (New York and Oxford: Oxford University Press, 1985), 132; Harvey, *Formative Dylan,* 4; and Hajdu, *Positively 4th Street,* 119.

54. Mellers, *Darker Shade of Pale,* 132.

55. Rodnitzky, *Minstrels of the Dawn,* 92.

56. Ibid., 93, quoting Alan Weberman and Gordan Friesen, "Joan Baez and the Bob Dylan Songs," review of record album *Any Day Now,* performed by Joan Baez, *Broadside* 97 (March 1969), 1–2, 9–10.

57. Ken Hunt, "Baez Reporting," *Folk Roots* 18, no. 1: 157 (July 1996), 26–31 at 29.

58. Baez, *And a Voice to Sing With,* 241.

APPENDIX
BROTHERS (A. YUPANQUI)

I've got so many brothers, I can't count 'em all.
In the valleys and on the mountains, on the prairies and in the sea.
Each one's got a job to do, each one's got his dreams.
With hope leading the way, memories tagging behind.

I've got so many brothers, I can't count 'em all.

Warm-hearted folks 'cause of that we call friendship.
They've got a prayer for the saying, and tears for the cryin'.
With a wide open horizon, just beyond the reachin'
And the strength to get it, with a doggedness and a will.

It's the farthest, when it seems the closest.

I've got so many brothers, I can't count 'em all.

And that's how we carry on, toughened by loneliness.
We get lost through the world, and then find each other again.
And that's how we recognize each other from afar,
By the ballads that we chew, seeds of immenseness.
And that's how we carry on, toughened by loneliness.
And within us come our dead, so that no one's left behind.

I've got so many brothers, I can't count 'em all,
And a very beautiful sister named Liberty.

TRANSLATION BY BLANCA REY

CHAPTER EIGHT

Tori Amos's Inner Voices

Bonnie Gordon

IN HER 1992 VIDEO ALBUM *Little Earthquakes*, Tori Amos performs "Me and a Gun" on an empty stage. She sits on a barstool wearing an orange sweater that clashes with her red hair. Since a dark background engulfs the performance space, viewers see only her face until a backdrop of an eye comes almost into focus—sometimes closing and sometimes disappearing. Meanwhile her solo voice fills the soundscape, assaulting and mesmerizing the silent audience with blunt gripping words and haunting music. She sings about her own experience as a rape survivor, self-consciously turning a potentially victimizing experience into a powerful performance. The text is graphic and to the point as in her final words, "there's a man on your back and you're pushed flat on your stomach it's not a classic Cadillac." Her solo voice stands alone, in direct contrast to the instrumentally-enhanced texture of the other songs on her album. This performance context renders her naked voice disturbing—its timbre and texture defy expectations of popular music and force its audience to confront the grotesqueness of a violent rape. This is precisely the point for Tori Amos, who asserts that producing the song comprises an act of power. She mobilizes music to "open that door and free myself from being a victim . . . I've smashed all that [victimization]."[1]

Amos made her breakthrough recording of "Me and a Gun" a decade ago on the album *Little Earthquakes*—a song cycle dedicated to finding a personal voice and learning to use it, from which this song stands out as an extreme expression. This essay positions "Me and a Gun" as an artistic vehicle for making silences speak. It takes the song as a point of departure for an exploration of the complex relationships between voice, sexuality, and interiority—that is, a person's most intimate feelings and sensations, which seem impossible to express and to share. After discussing the performance of sexuality and experience in Amos's performance in general, I suggest that "Me and a Gun" exemplifies the ways that the voice can articulate interiority and send messages that contradict words, images, and traditional power relations. The final section of the essay shifts to a second song, "Silent all these Years." Focusing on inaudible and invisible feelings, this work speaks to the special power of music, which communicates so effectively the very interior pain of rape. I choose to focus on Tori Amos and "Me and a Gun," not because I think she consciously embodies concepts of crucial importance to feminist theorists, but rather because her work exemplifies some of the ways in which recent trends in popular music have opened up a space for the female voice to work against traditional power structures and gender dynamics. Thus, rather than giving Amos agency in creating the kind of power reversals I will discuss, I use her work to theorize the subversive potential of the female voice. That she may or may not be conscious of the powers I ascribe to her work is far from my point.

This essay argues that "Me and a Gun" performs a quest for voice and a desire to make accessible very interior sensations and feelings. It realizes the potential of the singing voice to envoice and thus reveal realms of human experience and subjectivity that usually remain beyond the limits of sensibility. The voice can move along such an axis because it emerges from the physical body, serving as a vehicle for self-expression, identity formation, and interaction with others. It also points inwards to realms that cannot be expressed by language and thus cannot be explicitly communicated, making knowable experiences and sensations that otherwise remain completely elusive. The voice is at once material—of the body in the form of air and breath—and immaterial in that it is not something we can touch. This deeply embodied element sounds particularly clearly in "Me and a Gun," with its focus on the raw materials of voice and the sensations of a painful experience. By singing about her experience during the rape, Amos projects outwards an essentially interior experience. The song becomes a vehicle for articulating pain, recovering and sharing an experience whose destructiveness gains strength from social mandates for silence. Working in a more metaphoric realm, "Silent all these Years" emerges as a narrative about normally tacit sounds, singing into phenomenological existence a voice that has been "here," but silent and thus not heard. My focus on voice and performance, as literal not metaphorical constructs, inserts sound into the often-silent discourses of feminist theory. In doing so, it introduces a whole new dimension to the subject of the female voice—a subject that has proved fascinating to scholars of popular music.

Though writers across the disciplines have used voice and performance as rich metaphors for theorizing the silencing and empowering of women, they have remained tacit on the material voice and on musical performances, erasing the physical substance that underscores so many theoretical meta-phors.[2] To foreground voice as an embodied phenomenon is to put the body back into discourses of the voice as a powerful means of expression and a metaphor for agencies and expressive freedoms that have often been denied to women.

Voice emerges from inside the body through the throat, mouth, and dia-phragm, serving as a bridge to invisible and metaphysical realms that define subjectivity. A technology or apparatus palpably worked on the body of the performer and the listener, the singing voice engenders a heightened state of corporeality and thus renders song different from and excessive over speech. Because it is so fundamentally of the body, the reception of sung perfor-mances is always inflected by constructions of gender and of the body. From ancient courtesans to Madonna, the singing voices of women have carried provocative, erotic connotations. Taken as a sign of sublime purity or devilish sexuality, arresting power or devastating weakness, the female voice wields a potentially unruly force. In the last decade, musicologists working particu-larly with opera in the Western classical tradition have taken these paradoxi-cal notions about the female voice as a starting point for understanding the effect of female performers on the stage. This essay gestures toward the rami-fications of the contradictions that surround the female voice.

WHO IS TORI?

Amos's self-proclaimed and erotically inflected vocal power is, to be sure, neither unique nor new. What makes her different from her predecessors, such as Joni Mitchell, is her presence in the mainstream of popular culture and her role in the reconfiguring of the rock world by women. She partici-pated in what might be called the women's rock revolution of the early 1990s, rising to prominence within a cohort of women whose in-your-face style turned female sexuality into something confrontational, challenging norma-tive conceptions and portrayals of female sexuality and identity.[3]

Her quirky stage presence provides a rich site for considering the sexual confrontation of female artists. Her performance stance and her song "Ici-cle," for example, explicitly celebrate female masturbation, thus incorporat-ing her own sexuality within her musical performance. Amos counters and capitalizes on society's tendency to mark the female voice and body as prob-lems by displaying an assertive female sexuality in performance. Playing in the space between danger and desire by simultaneously enacting come-ons and confrontations, she calls attention to her own erotic body. But she uses that attention to claim power and authority over the audience and thus crashes through structures of submission that have historically framed female performers. That she is sexy, but not a sex object, is made abundantly clear in a video performance of "Precious Things," in which she wears a revealing red shirt that helps her flirt with both the camera and the piano. Her high vocal range, crashing dissonances, and occasional screams, combined with lyrics such as "I want to smash the faces of those beautiful boys those Christian boys so you can make me cum that doesn't make you Jesus," claim sexual agency.[4] She makes herself sexually enticing, but retains complete control of the situation.

Her most striking contribution to the 1990s female sexual confrontation comes not from the sheer sound volume of artists like Liz Phair and Kathleen Hanna, but from the basic tenets of her performance style, in which she straddles the piano chair and twists her body to face the audience. By sitting at the piano with her legs wide open to direct not only her voice, but also her genitals at the audience, she violates the protocols of basic girliness that demands closed legs. At the same time, this arresting style works against the classical tradition in which she was first trained—a tradition that her experiments with piano styles and harpsichord playing suggest she has not abandoned. In that milieu, pianists commune only with the piano, and the audience focuses on the instrument, which speaks through its open lid to the silent listener. At the same time, her hard-hitting left hand, honky-tonk style, and outright virtuosity work against the tendency of female popular pianists to underplay their instruments.[5] To be more specific, her curved hands move as her teachers at the Peabody Conservatory taught her, while her active torso and legs do much more than those same teachers probably asked for. In an erotic dance with the piano, she moves her entire body from red lipstick-accentuated lips to bright red platform shoes. Like most pianists, she leans over the keyboard, but her upper body also rotates seductively around her hips. Moving on and off the piano bench, she tosses her head and arms, constantly spreading her legs. Her form-fitting clothes reveal glowing bare skin and highlight her bodily curves and movements.

While such slinky costumes and extreme gestures might seem calculated for the maximum arousal of everyone involved, Amos does not simply present herself as an erotic spectacle or repeat images of women as sex objects. Instead, I read her performance as a manipulation of the relationship between pianist and instrument and between female performer and audience. Rather than displaying a sexual subject, the performance creates a sexual subject with an intense erotic presence and with physical control over the audience and instrument (Fig. 8.1). Of playing her favorite piano—a Bösendorfer—she says: "My back leg gives me support and that's what pulls up

Figure 8.1. Tori Amos singing and playing piano. © Matthew Mendelsohn/CORBIS.

my diaphragm and my body, so I have the power to play and sing. I mean, to play a nine-foot instrument with power, it's not like strumming an acoustic; it's very big, just like a double bass."[6]

Amos's aggressive female sexuality permeates interviews, during which she frequently comments on the sexual energy that fuels her performance. For her, power lies in a sexual and physical relationship with the music. She remarked in a 1992 *Hot Press* interview that, "sexual energy is where I sing from."[7] In a response to critics who demonized her playing as overly "sexy," she speaks of turning her sexuality into musical passion: "I am not offensive, that's just passion. I want to show my power. Many women think that when they are intelligent or show their passion they are considered to be bitches. And to justify themselves, they sit there with dry, closed legs and condemn me for that. I have a conscience, a heart, a spirit, but also my sex. I am a sexual, emotional being. When you describe the appearance with one word, I would consider confrontation the right word."[8] This statement self-consciously inflects her performance with sexual confrontation and suggests a conflation of sexuality, power, and intelligence. Such an adamant assertion of female sexuality in conjunction with creativity works against social norms that in Western culture have often mandated the policing of women's desires.

CONFESSIONAL?

Like many female singer-songwriters Tori Amos's songs deliver an intensely personal message and, I would argue, a performance of privacy contingent on a particular space. The creation of this space, which is simultaneously public and private, collapses distinctions between intimate revelation and public display. With a vocal mix that accentuates her lips smacking, tongue clicking on teeth, heavy breathing, and sighing, her songs suggest a sonic intimacy usually reserved for personal conversation. The effects of a microphone, revelations that seem too personal to share with strangers, and a dark space blur distinctions between private and public. In other words, the audience hears her speaking and singing as if she engages them as individuals, whispering in their ears, yet they sit in a club, auditorium, or even a huge stadium.

The illusion of direct communication gains strength through the content of her song, which tends to reflect her own experiences as well as the self-reflexive language that she uses to promote them. "Me and a Gun" offers a key example of singing as a mechanism for achieving self-awareness. In it, the voice becomes a medium for uttering otherwise inexpressible selves and thoughts. In the opening sequence of the *Little Earthquakes* video, she declares, "Songs are almost like my teachers. I have to be willing to open that closet and be willing to bring out my little party hats."[9] Singing for Amos creates both an expressive voice as well as an identity. "I take the stage and that piano and demon girl comes out. There are things that I refuse to deal with except through my music; things I will only deal with through my music because I just don't trust humanity that much, and I don't know if I trust me that much. But I trust the songs."[10]

To be sure, self-consciously representing inner emotions and processes does not make Tori Amos unique. Popular lyrics, especially those by women, historically depend largely on an ideology of authenticity that creates the illusion of the performer speaking directly to the audience and telling a true story about herself. Ancient laments, blues tunes, and torch songs all tell personal stories of the perils of love. Perhaps most relevant for Amos, female folk singers of the 1960s and 1970s staked their reputations on telling deeply personal stories. Joni Mitchell's *Blue*, first released in 1972, which described two years of her life, ushered in a musical trend emphasizing individual experience—a trend that has more recently been picked up by artists as diverse as Björk, PJ Harvey, and Madonna.

Such music has often been derogatively called confessional. Simon Reynolds and Joy Press write that "At the opposite extreme from the tough rock chicks is the female tradition of confessional song writers, whose soul-baring turns suffering into an affirmation; a kind of strength through vulnerability."[11] They understand the music of Amos and others like her as projecting individualized experiences. About *Little Earthquakes* they write, "The whole album is based around the idea of the talking cure, of finding one's voice and turning suffering into a story."[12] To label her music confessional without theorizing the term seems problematic. First the label most often refers uncritically to women. It suggests that the issues Amos raises relate only to herself. Such an assumption obscures the very public interrogation of sexuality and voice inherent in her music. On a more personal note, Amos's music, with its embracing of sexuality, seems determined to challenge the dominant ideology of confession that often conflates sexuality with sin.

Rather than calling Amos's music confessional, I prefer to read her self-expression as a calculated use of her voice to claim power. Amos represents an experience for a very specific purpose that differs from simply miming or repeating a past event.[13] Instead of just telling a story about herself, she expresses her experience with a clear interactive and political agenda. Because repetition always involves a change, telling her story ultimately alters the meaning of that story. The violation of the actual event, then, turns into a source of power and a statement for rape survivors. In this situation, the act of representation differs from the thing it represents. Amos does not just portray her isolated experience in isolation but instead self-consciously puts herself in relation to others. Celia Lury has called this kind of performance and text "strategic expression."[14] In other words, self-expressions, like Amos's, do their work by allowing audiences to identify with them both as women and as individuals and thus place personal stories in larger contexts. Feminist texts or performances capitalize on distinctions between the representation of an experience and the experience itself. This difference opens up a space that allows for the reinterpretation of an experience or event. In these terms, Amos uses her "experience" to create representations that claim a distinctly female power. Thus, for instance, thoughts on sex without love in leather or self-torment in "Crucify" become larger commentaries on the construction of female sexuality. Amos's discussions of her life create a distinct space between the experience and the representation of that experience—the latter has aesthetic and political purpose.[15] Experiences happen to everyone but some use those experiences in a socially productive manner.

TELLING HER STORY

After playing in a nightclub one evening in 1984, Tori Amos offered a fan a ride home. He raped her. She emerged from a seven-year period of silence a very vocal advocate for rape and incest survivors. In the mid-1990s she co-founded, along with her record company Atlantic, RAINN—the Rape, Abuse, and Incest National Network—a crisis hotline. Her own 1996 Madison Square Garden concert raised $250,000 for the network. "Me and a Gun," as she tells it, has been a particularly important part of her recovery, an inspiration for countless other women, and a nexus for rape-survivor action. Coupled with verbal accounts of her experience, the song appears on numerous rape-survivor web pages.

In the song, Amos sings about her own rape in a musical analogue to whispering, producing a sound whose mutedness commands attention. The text tells a vivid and believable story that moves painfully between the remembered past and its traumatic revival in the narrative present. This telling of her own story marks a crucial action in the context of rape, the reception and representation of which still remains deeply entrenched in who said what, who gets to speak, and who defines reality. Rather than erasing the rape, she explicitly writes it into existence with terse but powerful language that confronts its unpleasant particularities.[16] By singing and not just writing or speaking these words, Amos uses the intimate connection between voice and body to project a painful event outwards. She thus turns the experience of rape on its head by making something inherently disempowering into a powerful performance gesture.

Amos describes "Me and a Gun" as a vehicle for recovery, asserting that performance allowed her to overcome the guilt and disempowerment she felt after the event. She talks of a long period of denial during which she refused to discuss her rape or seek help. But an hour after seeing the film *Thelma and Louise*, in 1991, she relived the experience. Amos went home, wrote the song, and performed it that very night in a club. Since then she has claimed the song as a vehicle for reaching out, literally and figuratively, to others with similar experiences.[17]

In a 1992 interview she offered very specific reflections on the song and its relation to her experience:

> Why have I survived that kind of night, when other women didn't? How am I alive to tell you this tale when he was ready to slice me up? In the song I say it was "Me and a Gun" but it wasn't a gun. It was a knife he had. And the idea was to take me to his friends and cut me up, and he kept telling me that, for hours. And if he hadn't needed more drugs I would have been just one more news report, where you see the parents grieving for their daughter. And I was singing hymns, as I say in the song, because he told me to. I sang to stay alive. Yet I survived that torture, which left me urinating all over myself and left me paralyzed for years. That's what that night was all about, mutilation, more than violation through sex. I really do feel as though I was psychologically mutilated that night and that now I'm trying to put the pieces back together again. Through love, not hatred. And through my music. My strength has been to open again, to live, and my victory is the fact that, despite it all, I kept alive my vulnerability.[18]

Amos's words here make it clear that instead of repeating the rape experience the song reenacts an experience.

As a representation that contains traces of reality, "Me and a Gun" allows Amos to reclaim her voice and establish connections with others. The lyrics guide the listener into her experience through images of bizarre thoughts that rush through the mind at a moment of trauma—the out-of-body experience that allows survival. The constant shifts in pronoun from "I" to "You" blur the subjective line between singer and listener and enhance her connection with other survivors by suggesting that the individual story is a particular incidence of something that happens to lots of women: "You can laugh / Its kind of funny / Things you think / Times you think / Times like these / Like I haven't seen BARBADOS so I must get out of this." Amos moves between the "You" of a universal trauma survivor and the "I" of her experience to illustrate the mind's ability to literally flee the situation, in her case by thinking of Barbados.

Through music, the voice reclaims the body lost during the experience of rape. The material voice then creates a metaphoric voice. The song begins with soft and halting phrases devoid of vibrato. It moves in very small gestures with a chant-like texture, repetitive structure, narrow range, and rhythmic consistency. As she tells her story, Amos adds volume, vibrato, and increasingly sustained notes to create the effect of growing vocal strength.

She often articulates her own presence by emphasizing the word "I." The line "Like I haven't seen Barbados" becomes a refrain replacing the words "And I sang Holy Holy as he buttoned down his pants," as if singing allowed her a vision that in turn made possible survival. The form expands with the gradual elongation of eight-bar phrases.

The words confront head-on the ideology of blame and culpability that often surrounds rape as she juxtaposes a "slinky red thing" with a reference to the religious confessional realm "Me and Jesus":

> *Yes I wore a slinky red thing*
> *Does that mean I should spread for you, your friends*
> *Your father, Mr Ed . . .*
> *Me and Jesus a few years back used to hang*
>
> *And he said "it's your choice babe just remember*
> *I don't think you'll be back in three days time so you choose well"*
> *Tell me what's right*
> *Is it my right to be on my stomach of Fred's Seville*

The progressive strength of the music can be read as an adamant rejection of culpability so that the sound defines a submissive relationship to the rapist and Jesus. She begins adding vibrato and volume when she sings of the red dress, and as she reaches the chorus, her voice becomes less staccato and less strained. As if to reassert herself she sings the largest leap of the song thus far, an octave on the "I" of "And I know." When she asks, "Is it my right," it is clear from the strength of her sound that it is NOT her right. At the same time, by taking on the voice of Jesus she infuses her own voice with a kind of sacred power.

Since this is a song and not just a text, it creates a world of its own—one that is temporarily inescapable for the listener. Music entraps the listener by surrounding her with sound. It does not work like a novel or an epic present-ing a tale told later by a detached narrator who survived. Music is a temporal art—it moves. Since it constantly progresses, it ensnares the listener in the beat of passing time, miming the world in present time and thus refusing to pacify with an insistence on the story already being over.[19] In this case, it is as if listeners are inside the experience of rape. The endless quasi-repetitions of "Me and a Gun" heighten the effect of a never-ending present. With the exception of two phrases, the entire song hovers within the very small inter-val of a fourth, moving predominantly between the A below middle C to D. Rhythms and pitch patterns repeat over and over again, varying just slightly with each phrase. Amos's singing style accentuates this effect as she elides

words and phrases. The excessive near repetition creates a feeling of timeless-
ness akin to an altered musical state. You think you've heard the rhythm
before, but what you hear has changed ever so slightly (Ex. 8.1). The first and
third phrases differ only minutely. The pitches are the same with the exception of a skipped passing D on the penultimate note, but rhythmic variation
changes the emphasis. Meanwhile phrases and words elide at odd moments,
making you feel that just when you've grasped a pattern, it quickly transforms itself. Phrases never actually conclude but simply run into one another.
In the phrase "And I wanna live got a full tank of gas . . . ," for example, the
word "live" runs directly into the beginning of the next line of text "got
a . . ." (Ex. 8.2).

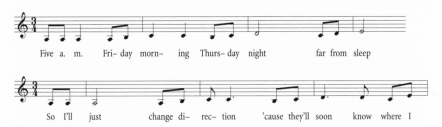

EXAMPLE 8.1. Tori Amos, "Me and a Gun," mm. 1–4 and 8–11

EXAMPLE 8.2. Tori Amos, "Me and a Gun," mm. 12–16

OBJECTS AND PAIN

"Me and a Gun" moves in fragments that while revealing evocative details
eschew narrative. Amos never actually mentions emotional or physical pain,
or describes her feelings. Listeners grasp the reality of her experience through
the speaking, or more precisely singing, of specific things. Things make histories, mark events, and perhaps most crucially translate memory into a material process. Within the song, objects exist as visual realities through the
constitutive power of sound and language. The song animates objects hidden
in Amos's memory. As material things these sung objects transform the past

into a present that is established by the performance. As silent witnesses to the event, they testify to its veracity. Their existence in song allows Amos to recreate the imaginary realm of the rape.

Such a predilection for material goods makes sense in a song that recasts a painful experience. Elaine Scary argues that objects take on specific significance in remembering and projecting pain. Pain occurs deep in the interior of a person's body, thus remaining invisible to anyone else. It is fundamentally unshareable and resistant to language, for to understand someone else's pain is to understand what happened inside her body. In order to express pain, the person must externalize it by making it into something that others can grasp.[20] It depends on turning the immaterial and invisible experience of pain into an experience grounded in materials that others can see in their imagination. Moreover, the act of turning a painful experience into a shareable one empowers the survivor.

"Me and a Gun" explodes with things: the buttons on the jeans, the car where the rape occurred, the classic Cadillac that the car was not, the biscuits, and the gun—always there and always threatening. These things allow listeners to see in their imagination and thus identify with Amos's experience. With their intimate connection to his body, the man's pants seem particularly potent. "I sang Holy Holy as he buttoned down his pants." This fragment of information suggests hands that unbutton, legs that live inside the pants, and finally an entire menacing body. Clothes constitute the man, projecting both the body that inhabits them and the actions of that body. Similarly, Tori Amos alludes to her own body through clothes, "so I wore a slinky red thing." These semantics evoke visions of close-fitting clothing that emphasizes the body underneath—the body that never actually gets mentioned in words. Ripped from their musical context, the words work only as metonymic representations. However, within the performance their bodies take on very different presences. The man remains fractured through the litany of disjointed things attached to his body: pants, guns, buttons, etc. He is never really there. In contrast to his menacing fragments, Amos becomes powerfully present. She makes music: her lips move; her hands clutch the microphone, her stomach takes in air. Her body has a material presence. His does not.

Through musical performance, Tori Amos extends her body out into the world and thus remakes the violation of her rape.[21] The sound of her voice becomes the enunciation of her painful experience, linking the physical body seen and heard with the physical body involved in the tale. Amos's voice is transported through time as the voice that sang "Holy Holy" now fills the performance space. Since her voice comes from inside the body, it allows her to express sensations and feelings occurring in her body's interior, including her pain and the violence done to her during the rape. While language can articulate what happens on the body's surface (cuts, scrapes, kicks, etc.), song, with its special access to the interior, can articulate the seemingly unshareable experience of pain. Song uses the materials of the body—the mouth, the breath, the tongue, and the teeth—to project internal experiences outwards. It is at once tangible, made of air and breath, and intangible in its total lack of tactibility. Thus it can link internal experiences and external world. It, like pain, thus breaks down boundaries between inside and outside.

Tori Amos's bodily sounds, breaths, and words represent condensed local instances of destruction and regaining of language that accompany pain and its recovery. Pain, because it is such an interior experience, defies language and in its most extreme cases destroys the sufferer's ability to string together coherent words. Amos projects outward cries and groans—the moment where pain destroys language—within a sung gesture that begins to enable her own very private experience of pain to enter the very public domain of the concert stage. Her solo singing voice acts as an interpreter for pain most obviously when moments of pure sonic force emanate from her body, when we hear her body, her breathing, her sighing, her moaning, and her "noise." The recorded version of this song, for example, emphasizes her breathing between words, especially when she sings "Me and a Gun." She almost grunts on the word "yes" in "Yes I wore a slinky red thing." And she chokes on the word "Jesus" in "Me and Jesus." These are the characteristic traces of the body contained within the sound, the moments that emphasize the limnality of voice and give such special access to pain and other interior realms. At the same time the song itself gives voice to her pain, allowing her a power of articulation that exceeds pure grunts and groans.

"SILENT ALL THESE YEARS"

Tori Amos insists that though it is hard for her to talk about being raped, the experience of singing permits her to voice her own unspeakable thoughts. "Silent all these Years" exemplifies what it is about singing that allows for such an intense expression of interiority. In a 1999 interview with Connie Chung and three other rape survivors on the television show *20/20*, Amos punctuated her comments with phrases from "Me and a Gun" and "Silent all these Years." She sang, in response to "Shannon" discussing her inability to talk about rape, "I've got something to say, I know, but nothing comes."[22] On that show, Elizabeth Vargas confirmed that "Silent all these Years" describes the feeling many victims have of "being boxed in by their silence."[23]

I bring in this song because its focus on making audible the invisible further enlightens the expression of interiority that Tori Amos enacts in "Me and a Gun." While "Me and a Gun" gives voice to a specific traumatic experience, "Silent all these Years" puts the more general formation of self-voice on display. The song foregrounds the existence of a voice beneath the surface. It does this through a disjunct narrative about finding a personal voice and hearing one that has been there all along. In contrast to the blunt words and stark texture of "Me and a Gun," "Silent all these Years" traffics in metaphors and derives musical meaning from a variety of vocal timbres, piano motives, and orchestral accompaniments. In the song, Amos's words articulate silence but her voice and piano-playing strike a dissonance between an enunciated silence and a palpable vocal presence. Further heightening this tension, the video presents images of her body trapped inside a revolving box and shrinking video frames move by like snapshots while the sonic presence of her voice renders her audible and thus tangible.

By uncovering a previously submerged, inaudible, and invisible voice, "Silent all these Years" makes explicit the potency of the singing voice and thus reveals realms of human experience and subjectivity that usually remain beyond the limits of sensibility, like the experience of rape.[24] Singing into existence a voice that has been "here" but "Silent all these Years," the song and video explicitly explore the unconscious, by putting voice at the point of intersection between inside and outside the body.

The lyrics allude to abandonment by a lover, teen pregnancy, abortion, family and class conflicts, and of course the experience of crippling self-censorship. An association of the mother with the Antichrist, "I got the anti-Christ in the kitchen yellin' at me again," suggests a religious background where all these issues would become a very big deal, which is not surprising given Amos's preacher's daughter roots. In the video, visual images do not narrate or follow the words in a conventional story line. Instead they move in snapshots and slow motion: Amos sitting in a box, a small child running across the screen, Amos wearing a number of different outfits and myriad facial expressions. Formally, the song is in verse-chorus structure with a bridge. Like "Me and a Gun," Amos sings in a narrow range, but she also plays the piano with orchestral accompaniment as well as overdubbing for special effects.

Amos is exactly the opposite of silent in this song about silence. As she sings, "I got something to say but NOTHING comes," something does come: the music. After a brief rest between "but" and "Nothing" she enters on a G, the highest pitch and largest leap thus far in the song—a fifth. In this, the music continually challenges the words or the images. The song's assumption of a radical distinction between *here* and *hear* suggests that a voice can be present without being heard. Silences can speak. The chorus, "But what if I'm a mermaid," suddenly adds an overdubbed scalar ascent and off-beat triangle that destabilizes rhythmic motion. This texture, in particular, emphasizes the word HERE. "I don't care 'cause sometimes I said sometimes I hear my voice and it's been HERE Silent All These Years." Besides the added orchestration, the "here" is accented, like the word "nothing," with a rest that obscures the leap of a sixth—a large leap in the context of a narrow-range song (Ex. 8.3). It also is accompanied by the most interesting harmonic inflection in the song: a C♯ in the bass line destabilized with D♯s in the piano and vocal inflections that move between G♯ and F♯. At this moment the cadence comes alive, suggesting a musical revelation that momentarily transforms the quotidian silence embodied in the music by the repetitive and almost trite style of the previous verses.

The bridge exhibits a similar disjuncture between lyrics of confinement and sounds of something else. The words "years go by will I choke on my tears till finally there is nothing left" suggest a sense of inevitable loneliness and disempowerment, yet musically this moment feels more intense and less fettered than any other passage in the song. The end of the chorus, "Silent all these Years," elides with the next line of text, "years go by." She elevates the word "years" an octave above the listener's expectations, producing a

EXAMPLE 8.3. Tori Amos, "Silent all these Years," mm. 27–33

striking leap in a song predominantly limited to a very narrow range, and then continues singing in this higher range. Suddenly, the soundscape thickens in range, timbre, and tessitura: she sings with much more vibrato and adds strings and extra vocal tracks to her voice. At the same time that her voice is freer and more lyrical, the overdubbing creates the uncanny effect of hearing too many voices, as if voices are straining to get out—and they are out of sync, chasing one another. These two examples illustrate that by carefully listening to the disjuncture between word and sound one can see that the act of singing and making music can overturn disempowerment and silence. Thus musical performance gives a material presence to the claiming of personal voice that underlies both feminist theory and traditionally female creative endeavors.

SOUND TRUMPS VISION

The video version of the song dramatizes the ways in which song can allow women to overcome disempowered states. It does this most clearly when sound trumps vision and at moments of disjuncture between the visual, verbal, and sonic spheres of the video. In the video, splits between visual and acoustic elements reinforce the disparity between sound and other kinds of discourse and allow a reversal of verbal and visual images of passivity. This reversal provides symbolically the more literal power reversal in "Me and a Gun," in which musical performance rewrites a traumatically disempowering experience.

The video includes striking instances of misspeak lip-synching where Amos appears to mouth unintelligible words, but the continuous song always ensures that the viewer hears precisely what she says. Giving control to vocal sonority overturns a cultural tendency that usually privileges the visible.[25] Specific moments in the video play ironically on this tension. For example, as she sings the words "I love the way we communicate," her mouth forms words that the listener cannot hear and thus cannot communicate with.

The video's visual progression follows the contraction between words about silence and the palpable presence of her voice. Words about silence accompany images of Amos inside increasingly less restrictive frames. This visual series, on the one hand, illustrates society's control of women and Amos's overcoming of these constraints. On the other hand, they represent a peeling away of layers from an interior voice that has always been there but could not break out. The boxes then symbolize the closet from which her voice spoke—a closet that eventually vanishes. It begins in the first chorus when Amos appears trapped inside a rolling box screaming something inaudible. At the second chorus, her face materializes in a gray shaded region of the video screen. By the third chorus, her large black shoes lead her entire body both into and out of a long rectangular shaded region. Finally, at the end of the video, she breaks free of all boxes and remains trapped only by the constraints of the screen.

Throughout the video, song compels a confrontation between the audio and the visual—marked by Amos's final, off-center stare, during which she confronts the viewer's gaze. She constructs the viewer as an object of her own gaze, which necessarily challenges any active/passive dichotomy. From a theoretical perspective, opening up a space between sound and vision overturns traditional concepts of the gaze, which define the spectator as male and the thing observed as female. Men are active creators and women are passive objects, men are powerful and women are disempowered.[26] By manipulating both sides of the gaze, Amos's production problematizes such a rigid model. It thus creates a performance that reverses binary oppositions that would pit the gazing male subjects against the gazed-upon female object. Amos may seem, with her waif-like appearance, skimpy clothes, and averted gaze, to put herself in the position of an object to be stared at (the visual version of the silence her words describe). But by the end of the song, she has become the active observer and the source of power in the video.[27] Again this reversal suggests a discursive version of the manipulation of a physical power dynamic performed in "Me and a Gun." It is another instance in which Amos uses performance to turn a fundamentally disempowering moment into a powerful form of expression.

VOICING THE INVISIBLE

Amos further complicates the relationship between vision and sound by playing with the relationship between her own body and the sounds it makes. Her body, throughout the video, appears and disappears, but her voice always remains powerfully present.[28] The constantly shifting relationship between Amos's body and voice calls attention to the link between voice and invisible realms, the relationship between presence and absence. Since the video first presents her material body and voice together, the audience knows where the sound comes from; but they can't actually see it. They hear an ever-present disembodied voice. The ensuing desire for the return of Amos's body—the source of sound—grants the invisible a compelling force that places her body at the center of the video. When Amos (like many other video makers) shows herself as the sonic producer and then removes her body from the picture, distinctions between sounds that are always there and sounds that are supposed to be explicitly sung blur. It becomes hard to tell the difference between sounds characters make and hear and those that they are not conscious of but which create the musical milieu that encircles them. When we actually see Amos creating the music that should be part of the video's sung world—that is when her body and voice are *both* present, we see her making the sounds that constitute the video's background soundscape.

When her body disappears, Amos exists largely through her voice, which is heard outside of and over the video's narrative as sheer sonority and physical volume. Filling the void with only sound marks the voice as the crucial instrument of self-formation and makes the presence of her body palpable even when it seems most absent. Even when you can't see her body you know that she is physically there. Most often her voice fails to hold a visual presence but I would argue that it maintains a material one. In these invisible but very audible moments the voice adamantly reveals that which might otherwise lie beyond the limits of perception. It quite literally gives voice to the invisible and the unspeakable. Similarly, the song's chorus can be read as revealing these usually unheard realms, bringing to the surface sounds that usually exist at some deeply invisible and inaudible level. It is the sound of silence. The musical and textual phrase "sometimes I hear my voice and it's been HERE 'Silent All These Years'" recurs until the very end of the song, when Amos finally says "yes I can hear," and then repeats the words "I hear my voice" four times and the words "Silent All These Years" three times. The supposedly silent voice keeps making itself heard.

She begins the video seated at the piano playing a rhythmically destabilizing coiled up figure that recurs through the video (Ex. 8.4). This motive elides into the first line of text, which begins on the center pitch of the initial motive. "I got something to say you know but nothing comes." But something does come: the music. This motive could represent a sonorous incantation of Amos's unconscious, the unconscious that ultimately brought forth "Me and a Gun." The figure exists suspended at first without harmony. When the coiled up figure, a pitch bounded by half steps on either side, finally leaps up a third it sounds liberating but still ambiguous since there is no tonality within which to understand it. The moment then resonates with feelings of confinement and the desire to soar into voice, agency, and freedom. Appearing three times, this motive offers structure to the song, and, more significantly, becomes the voice that she supposedly could not find. When she finally and obsessively repeats her verbal proclamation of silence, the chromatic motive running through the song ends with three tonic chords. The body escapes boxes and frames for the last time. The constant repetition of this musical motive and of her words about silence continually reinterprets the narrative, representing a musical incantation of Amos's unheard voice.

The singing voice in both "Silent all these Years," and "Me and a Gun"

EXAMPLE 8.4. Tori Amos, "Silent all these Years," mm. 1–4

animates sounds that have been here all along. Its supersensuousness allows the voice to perform experiences that otherwise lie beyond the limits of sensibility—whether it is a silenced internal voice or the visceral experience of physical and emotional pain. This special capacity of the voice comes, I would argue, from the intense materiality of the human voice, its liminal position between the physical body and the discursive world that constructs it, between the body's tactile surface and immaterial interior sensations. The best of today's female performers have figured out, consciously or not, how to access that liminal space and how to claim sexual but assertive female bodies with powerful voices.

NOTES

~

I would like to thank the following people for their careful readings of this essay: Joseph Auner, Jane Bernstein, Matthew Butterfield, Deborah Heckert, Jeffrey Kallberg, Nathan Macbrien, Megan Prado, and Deborah Wong. I am also grateful to Sword and Stone Publishing for granting me permission to reproduce lyrics and musical extracts from the songs "Silent all these Years" and "Me and a Gun."

1.   Amos, *Little Earthquakes,* videocassette (New York: A*Vision Entertainment, 1992).
2.   The collection, *Embodied Voices: Representing Female Vocality in Western Culture,* ed. Leslie C. Dunn and Nancy A. Jones (Cambridge: Cambridge University Press, 1994), is an exception. The editors theorize vocality as a broad spectrum of utterances that stretch beyond language.
3.   See Sarah Cooper, *Girls! Girls! Girls! Essays on Women and Music* (New York: New York University Press, 1996); Simon Reynolds and Joy Press, *The Sex Revolts: Gender, Rebellion and Rock 'n' Roll* (Cambridge, Mass.: Harvard University Press, 1995); Evelyn McDonnell and Ann Powers, *Rock She Wrote* (New York: Delta, 1995). Lucy O'Brian, *She Bop: The Definitive History of Women in Rock, Pop and Soul* (New York: Penguin, 1995). For more recent work see Gayle J. Wald, "Just a Girl? Rock Music, Feminism, and the Cultural Construction of Female Youth," *Signs* 23 (1998): 585–611; Sheila

Whiteley, *Sexing the Groove* (London and New York: Routledge, 1997); Laurie Burns and Mélisse Lafrance, *Disruptive Divas: Feminism, Identity and Popular Music* (New York and London: Routledge, 2002); Sheila Whiteley, *Women and Popular Music: Sexuality, Identity and Subjectivity* (London and New York: Routledge, 2000).

4. Tori Amos, "Precious Things," on *Little Earthquakes,* videocassette.

5. Though she uses her instrument differently from most female musicians, Amos follows a long tradition of keyboard players for whom the demands of performance and virtuosity have led to extreme measures. Elton John stands over the keyboard; Keith Emerson used a grand piano that lifted up and spun around; and even the nineteenth century virtuoso Franz Liszt played with such force that he broke piano strings.

6. Ann Powers, "A Poet with a Piano and a Lot of Bravado," *New York Times,* Sunday, 14 January 1996, sec. H, pp. 27–28.

7. Gene Stout, "Tori Amos and a Man Called (E)," *Seattle Post-Intelligencer,* 28 August 1992, What's Happening, p. 11.

8. Ulrich Grepel, "Grace, Feeling and Passion," September 1993 *Vision—Crossover,* translation of German interview transmitted over email to Tori Amos newsgroup on 29 November 1993.

9. Introduction to *Little Earthquakes.*

10. Kalen Rogers, *Tori Amos All These Years: The Authorized Illustrated Biography* (New York: Omnibus, 1994), 29.

11. Reynolds and Press, *Sex Revolts,* 249

12. Ibid., 265

13. Celia Lury, "Reading the Self: Autobiography, Gender and the Institution of Literacy," in *Off-Center: Feminism and Cultural Studies,* ed. Celia Lury, Sarah Franklin, and Jackie Stacey (London: Harper Collins Academic, 1991), 102.

14. Ibid., 107.

15. In 2000, Sheila Whiteley made a similar point, but without the notion of strategic expression, in *Women and Popular Music,* 197–205.

16. She undermines generations of cultural texts that have "obsessively made rape both so pervasive and so invisible a theme—made it unreadable." Lynn A. Higgins and Brenda R. Silver write about the history of representations of rape in their introduction to *Rape and Representation* (New York: Columbia University Press, 1991).

17. Bob Frost, "The West Interview," *San Jose Mercury News West Magazine,* 22 November 1992.

18. Amos, "The Hurt Inside," *Hot Press Magazine,* 23 February 1994.

19. This idea is taken from Carolyn Abbate, *Unsung Voices: Opera and Musical Narrative in the Nineteenth Century* (Princeton: Princeton University Press, 1991).

20. Elaine Scary, *The Body in Pain: The Making and Unmaking of the World* (New York: Oxford University Press, 1985), 164.

21. Scary makes an argument almost identical to this; however, she deals more directly with the concept of sentience.

22. Interview with Tori Amos, "Chasing away the Demons," *20/20,* 15 February 1999.

23. Ibid.

24. The following discussion of the supersensuous nature of the human voice is heavily influenced by Gary Tomlinson. I have drawn much from and adapted the vocabulary of his *Metaphysical Song: An Essay on Opera* (Princeton: Princeton University Press, 1999).

25. Carolyn Abbate writes very convincingly about this tendency in "Opera or the En-

voicing of Women," in *Musicology and Difference: Gender and Sexuality in Music Scholarship*, ed. Ruth A. Solie (Berkeley: University of California Press, 1993), 225–59.

26. Laura Mulvey, "Visual Pleasure and Narrative Cinema," *Screen* 16 (1975): 6–18. Also see Alice Kuzmiar, "Ears Looking at You: E. T. A. Hoffmann's *The Sandman* and David Lynch's *Blue Velvet*," *South Atlantic Review* 54 (1989): 7–21.

27. Here, I am speaking of necessarily generalized discursive effects and do not mean to assume anything about what actual men and women feel when they watch this video.

28. For a discussion of the separation of sound from body see Mary Anne Doane, "The Voice in the Cinema: The Articulation of Body and Space," *Yale French Studies* 60 (1980): 33–50.

PART FOUR

Lamenting Voices

For he has conquered all Hellas by his skill
In the art Athena once invented,
when she wove
the grim death chant of the cruel Gorgons,
which she heard pouring out
in streams of bitter anguish
under the maidens' repulsive serpent heads

PINDAR,
Pythian Ode 12

AMENTING REMAINS one of the oldest forms of female vocality, and as such, one of the few musical traditions in which women
have played a dominant role as public performers. As a musical genre,
it existed as far back as ancient times. It surfaces in nearly all societies throughout the world, appearing in different guises as dirges, keens, ele-
gies, and wailing songs. The lament has also served as a topos in Western
civilization from ancient Greek tragedies to present-day pop songs.

Most of the ethnomusicological studies on the lament have dealt with life-
cycle events in various cultures.[1] In rituals associated with birth, puberty,
marriage, and death, women have taken an active part in musical performances. While holding a strong and obvious connection with celebrations of
birth, infancy, and initiation into adulthood, women maintain an even more
intense musical presence in rites for the dead and other leave-taking rituals.
As part of wedding ceremonies in some societies, women sing laments to
mark the separation of brides from their families. They also publicly mourn
the departure of individuals from their community or, conversely, as exiles,
sing of longing for the past and for their homeland.

Female lamenters often serve as intermediaries, making public the private
grief of an individual. In so doing, they turn personal mourning into a communal experience. In some cultures, they take on magico-religious powers,
where their musical performances act as a link between the living and the
spiritual world of the dead.[2]

Though lament traditions of different cultures vary widely around the
world, they exhibit certain striking similarities in vocal expression and me-

lodic construction. In many cases, the prominence of intermediary sounds, such as cries and wails, blur the boundaries between speech and song. More melodic than speech-like, the lament is punctuated with sobbing and shouts to express grief. Often the melody hovers within a limited range of a fifth or less. The songs generally consist of a series of improvised variations on a pattern of narrow melodic intervals that begin on a high pitch and cascade downwards three or four notes, as seen in the ritual wailing called *sa-yalab* sung by women of the Kaluli people in the rain forests of Papua, New Guinea.[3]

Women have sung funeral laments in various rural communities throughout Europe—from the Baltic region in the north to the Mediterranean in the south. In Scotland and Ireland, public lamenting known as *caoine* or keening has had a long history, dating back to the seventh century.[4] Women have also played a central role in the lament tradition of various societies in the Middle East and Africa. Among the Druze of Lebanon, singers known as *naddāba* have performed *firāqiyya* or songs of departure for the dead.[5] Female lamenting also takes place in several West African communities. The funeral songs of the Akpafu people of southeastern Ghana, for example, are sung by women in a call-and-response form.[6] And across the globe, the Eipo women from West Irian, New Guinea, almost exclusively take charge of singing spontaneous laments intermingled with weeping or crying, which they sometimes perform in multi-part fashion at the interval of a second.[7]

While women's dominant position as lamenters has been primarily associated with life-cycle phenomena, they have also transcended the confines of private ritual by expressing the grievances and complaints of the community as a whole in a wider public sphere. In Greece and more recently in South Africa and the Middle East, lamenting has turned into a powerful form of social and political protest.[8] It has extended to other musical idioms—as female folksingers have appropriated narrative ballads and other traditional songs with mournful texts.

The lament has also figured prominently as a topos in Western culture. Laments, sung mainly by women to articulate unbridled emotion, took center stage in ancient Greek tragedies. And in the works of Roman poets, abandoned heroines, such as Ariadne and Dido, served as prototypes for the lamenting characters of later musical genres. During the Renaissance, lament texts from Classical literature through the contemporary epic romances of *Orlando furioso* and *Gerusalemme liberata* inspired countless musical settings. But it was with the advent of opera in the early seventeenth century that the lament came to the fore.

Even from the very beginning, the power of the lament to move audiences signified the very essence of the operatic ideal. While it epitomized the new art form, the lament also stood apart from other operatic conventions in its intensity of expression. Indeed, in some cases, it became equated with affective excess verging on madness. Thus, the lamenting figure tended to be gendered, usually representing a female character or a male character in an aberrant state. It also stood for the excess of the opera genre itself.

The emotional, often violent shifts of the texts barred the operatic lament from following the prescribed musical structures of other arias. The flexibility of a recitative style alternating with more melodic sections, as found in the popular and highly influential *Lamento d'Arianna* by Claudio Monteverdi, graphically depicts the state of mind of the abandoned Ariadne. In addition to the recitative model, composers would construct laments over a repeating descending tetrachord in the bass.[9] This descending ostinato became synonymous with operatic laments well into the eighteenth century, appearing in such well-known works as Henry Purcell's *Dido and Aeneas*.

The two essays presented below engage in two unusual expressions of the lament. Ellen Harris approaches the operatic lament through the study of voices in the Italian cantatas of George Frideric Handel. She delves into distinctions made by the Baroque composer between male and female characters in his musical settings, focusing in particular on the convention of the abandoned woman. Tammy Kernodle turns her attention to the lament as a genre of empowerment. In her essay, she views the African-American blues as a type of lament that envoiced black women, who, through music, cut through racial and sexual politics to make public their private expressions.

NOTES

1. An excellent overview of the secondary literature on the lament as a life-cycle ritual appears in Jane Bowers, "Women's Lamenting Traditions around the World: A Survey and Some Significant Questions," *Women & Music* 2 (1998): 125–46.

2. See, for example, Elizabeth Tolbert, "Magico-Religious Power and Gender in the Karelian Lament," in *Music Gender, and Culture*, ed. Marcia Herndon and Susanne Ziegler (Wilhelmshaven: Florian Noetzel, 1990), 41–56.

3. Steven Feld, *Sound and Sentiment: Birds, Weeping, Poetics and Song in Kaluli Expression*, 2d ed. (Philadelphia: University of Pennsylvania Press, 1990).

4. John MacInnes, "Caoine," *The New Grove Dictionary of Music and Musicians*, ed. Stanley Sadie and John Tyrrell, 2d ed. (London: Macmillan, 2001), 5:82–83.

5. Ali Jihad Racy, "Lebanese Laments: Grief, Music, and Cultural Values," *World of Music* 28 (1986): 27–40.

6. V. Kofi Agawu, "Music in the Funeral Traditions of the Akpafu," *Ethnomusicology* 32 (1988): 75–105.

7. Artur Simon, "Types and Functions of Music in the Eastern Highlands of West-Irian (New Guinea)," *Ethnomusicology* 22 (1978): 441–55.
8. Anna Caraveli, "The Bitter Wounding: The Greek Lament as Social Protest in Rural Greece," in *Gender and Power in Rural Greece,* ed. Jill Dubisch (Princeton: Princeton University Press, 1986), 169–94.
9. Ellen Rosand, *Opera in Seventeenth-Century Venice: The Creation of a Genre* (Berkeley and Los Angeles: University of California Press, 1991), 361–86.

CHAPTER NINE

Having Her Say

THE BLUES AS THE BLACK WOMAN'S LAMENT

Tammy L. Kernodle

In 1981, the composer Undine Smith Moore, in a keynote address to the First National Congress on Women in Music, related how as a child in southern Virginia she had witnessed her aunts lamenting over a dead relative:

> I remember the weeping as we went across the fields to see cousin Johnny—"Cousin Johnny dead"—the nearest cousin, the clock stopped. My aunts dressed in black with long veils, but dancing in a corner, dropping deeply and rising rhythmically from the floor—Aunt Sarah with her hair always corn rowed. The timbre of the voices of my aunts passing the farm at night, giving their special hollers. . . . About five or six years ago, in the archives of the Library of Congress, I sat listening to a recording of early blues and hollers. Suddenly, I found myself weeping, weeping almost to the point of embarrassment. The timbre of the voices of my aunts had come to me from some place deep in myself, which I did not know existed.[1]

Those special hollers and the ritualized manner in which her aunts performed them resonated with a tradition that emanated from West Africa, developed out of the African's experience in America, and had a direct relationship to the early blues. Like the African lament, the blues gave women the means to convert private expression into public music making. Through her "wailing," "moaning," and "crying," the rural blues singer established the environment for public utterance, by drawing other members of the community into the ritual. She articulated the black woman's perspective of life in America and provided a voice for a segment of the population that through racial and sexual politics had been suppressed.

Since the early 1920s there has been a fascination with black rural practices, especially the blues. The result is a vast literature that documents the early blues, mainly from the point of view of the southern black male experience. Only during the past decade has much attention been paid to female blues singers. Scholars have focused on the life experiences and songs of women who sang the urban, classic blues in the 1920s and early 1930s. Through their readings of song texts, they have placed classic blues at the center of black feminism in early twentieth-century America.[2] While these analyses have provided depth and dimension to the blues discourse, there is still a facet of the blues tradition that scholars have ignored: the role women played in the antecedents of the classic blues, most specifically the rural blues tradition.

In this essay I will explore the blues as a direct descendent of the lament tradition of both West Africa and the Caribbean by way of the Atlantic slave trade. I will examine how the performance practices of both rural and classic blues women paralleled the ritualistic functions of the lamenter. Finally, I will discuss how the rural women's blues tradition served as an important link between the traditions of Africa, the Caribbean, and antebellum America, and the bourgeois, sophisticated classic blues of the 1920s and 1930s.

THE AFRICAN LAMENT AND THE BLUES

The tradition of lamenting found in West and Sub-Saharan Africa provides the earliest cultural basis for the public, communal music making and narrative text structure that defines the early rural blues tradition. Having developed into various traditions in the Caribbean and South America, the lament was first brought to America via the Atlantic slave trade.[3] During the seventeenth century, most of the English slaveholdings were transported to the islands of Jamaica and Barbados first, to undergo "seasoning" before being shipped to the American colonies. The interaction between West African slaves, European landowners, and slave masters and the indigenous people of these islands accounted for the creolized forms of music, language, and dance that developed in the Caribbean.

By the early eighteenth century, American slaveholders began receiving shipments of slaves directly from the African continent. Most were deposited in specific geographic locations because of the region they were extracted from or their work capabilities. Such practices enabled distinct cultural groups to establish strong kinships. Concentrations of Africans from the same ethnic group in certain geographic areas meant that a number of African musical traditions were preserved or adapted into new forms. Music making, an integral part of the slave's daily life, became central to survival in the New World. Not only were funeral ceremonies, ritualistic songs, native African instruments such as the banjo and fiddle, work songs, and dancing vital components of these traditions, but new forms of expression, such as the spiritual, also emerged. While the prohibition of some musical practices brought about the eventual disappearance of many of West African traditions, others survived as rituals practiced in secret.

The delay in converting slaves to Christianity may well account for the continuation of certain African religious customs among the slaves, including the lament. Practices similar to those described by Nketia in his research on lament traditions in West Africa or in the Caribbean have been documented in regional black communities throughout the southern United States during the early twentieth century.[4] Indeed, Undine Smith Moore, as we have already seen, testifies to the retention of such traditions.

Communal music-making practices such as the work song and the spiritual defined the earliest form of African-derived music in the colonies. While these forms emphasized group musical performance, the field holler, which centered on individual performance, is the most direct musical link with the lament. According to Lawrence Levine, "the field holler arose out of spatial isolation. With the end of slavery, the percentage of Negroes who worked alone or in very small groups increased and the use of field hollers unquestionably increased as well."[5] The holler can be divided into two categories: calls and cries. Cries were a form of self-expression where one verbalized his or her feelings, while calls were used to communicate messages to the larger community.[6] Both forms contributed directly to the development of the blues.

Evolving primarily out of the need to express one's emotions in secular terms, the blues reflected the social changes that blacks encountered following Emancipation. The early blues was not highly structured and although it featured some musical accompaniment, the emphasis was placed on the voice. The power of this early form of the blues rested on the performer's ability to express effectively the emotions of the text. A singer would often infuse moans, groans, cries for mercy, and vocal inhalations into performances, which took place in the rural areas of the Mississippi Delta region and Texas.

Several ethnographic and cultural studies from the early twentieth century document the blues as a vital component of everyday life in these regions. Howard Odum, as early as 1905, published collections of black folksongs he transcribed in Mississippi and Georgia. Many of the texts of the songs appeared later on blues recordings, and were performed, according to Odum, after work or church for dances and other social gatherings.[7] The folk music of this region that evolved into the blues employed many traditional verses that were common property of singers. These texts were arranged in a variety of stanza patterns that ranged from a single line being endlessly repeated to groupings of three or four lines. Singing was often accompanied by one or more musical instruments, generally a guitar or small string ensemble in the small towns, or the piano in the larger cities.[8] Most of these early practitioners were nomadic and often traveled consistently throughout the region. They lived by their own wits and often offered their services as laborers during the day. At night these individuals served as conduits for the community's hopes, desires, and despairs by mediating the open exchanges of human expression that generally occurred with their audiences. Their songs often recounted the happenings of other close geographic areas or discussed in frank and profane terms the common struggles of everyday life. Songs of the latter genre ranged in topic from boll weevil infestations, poverty, and lost loves to ill health, death, and the desire to start life anew somewhere else. Just as the minister captured the attention and emotions of his parishioners on Sunday mornings, the blues performer navigated his or her "congregation" through a series of emotional highs and lows.

While the rural blues has been associated primarily with male performers, there are a few exceptional women who have earned a distinct place in the early history of the genre. Before Mamie Smith arrived at the Okeh Recording studio in 1920 and launched the age of the classic blues, there already existed a strong but undocumented history of women blues singers in the Mississippi Delta and Piedmont regions. As early as the 1890s, an amateur folklorist in Frankfort, Kentucky, reported hearing a black woman in the county workhouse perform a melancholy song called "jailhouse moan." Ma Rainey would claim, in 1902, to have witnessed a woman in Missouri sing a "strange [but] poignant" song.[9] These singers and instrumentalists adopted the same verse, harmonic, and melodic forms as their male counterparts, but they developed their own highly personal, often improvisatory rural blues style. The songs, though not performed widely, spoke of the experiences of the women of these regions, provided documentation of life in the rural South from a female perspective, and captured the unspoken sentiments of the community. The sound of these blues differed greatly from the highly sophisticated classic blues of the 1920s, as it drew heavily on the African-American musical forms of the antebellum period as well as those from the years following Emancipation. The approach to vocal timbre, text delivery, and interaction between the instrument and voice evolved from regionalized traditions of the shout, ballad, work song, field holler, and instrumental music. It is the social uses of these songs and the cultural narrative emanating from them, however, that is most important to this discussion.

THE RURAL BLUES WOMEN
〜

Unlike many of the women of the classic tradition, the rural blues woman wrote much of her own material and often accompanied herself. Most importantly, her desire for a more intimate relationship with her audience dictated that she reject the tent show and theater circuits that had elevated the status of the classic blues woman. Instead she played at juke joints, fish frys, barn dances, or in the case of the Memphis blues woman Memphis Minnie (née Lizzie Douglas), participated in competitions that pitted her musical talent against a male counterpart. It is in the recordings of guitarist Memphis Minnie, blues singers Bessie Tucker, Lottie Kimbrough, and others that we find concrete examples of blues women who created music that was unaffected by the "bourgeois" culture of middle-class blacks, or displayed any of the traits commonly associated with classic blues women, who, because of their commercial appeal with mainstream audiences, elevated the blues out of the stigma of cultural marginality and geographic seclusion.

Yet despite these differences, there were many similarities in the life experiences of the rural and classic blues women. The majority were born in the South and reared in fundamentalist churches. Most ran away from home at an early age to make a better life for themselves. All made music the vehicle for change and advancement beyond the common experiences of black women. The formation of their respective styles rested in the cultural roots of their local communities, but for many, especially the classic blues women, they became less and less the *creators* of their songs and more and more the *interpreters* of material crafted by musicians the likes of J. Mayo Williams, Perry Bradford, and Clarence Williams. Though this raises questions regarding the authenticity of the sentiments conveyed in these blues, it does not undermine their importance nor the function these songs had in chronicling the life experiences of certain segments of the black population. Rural blues women, especially those who accompanied themselves or wrote their own songs, provide the stronger link with the lament tradition.

Bessie Tucker, Ida May Mack, Geeshie Wiley, Josie Bush, Bertha Lee, and Memphis Minnie sang the blues before and after the classic blues craze of the 1920s and were significant in spreading rural music traditions throughout the Mississippi Delta region, Texas, and beyond. Bessie Tucker, who performed and lived in Dallas, was one of the few singers who recorded commercially in the free style of an unaccompanied field holler. Ida May Mack, who made her first and only recordings at age twenty-five in 1930, ran away from her Baptist home in Tchula, Mississippi, in search of fame and fortune on the tent show circuit. Bertha Lee, who moved to the Lula, Mississippi, area as a young girl, began a long association with the proclaimed "Father of the Mississippi Blues" Charley Patton. Geeshie Wiley, considered the greatest recorded rural blues singer, was from Natchez, Mississippi, and often performed with fellow blues woman Elvie Thomas.

These women and others, who have not been documented extensively, modeled themselves after the male blues performers who traveled throughout the Mississippi Delta region. Their extant recordings reveal a mode of singing and playing that conveyed a special connection to the songs they sang. It was a highly personal style of delivery drawn from the melismatic and guttural inflections of the field hollers and work songs, as well as the lyricism of the ballad. The rural blues woman sang with an impassioned voice that had a raspy, harsh quality and in regional dialects that often made various portions of the text difficult to understand. The melodies were often pentatonic with a very strong structural link to the improvised field hollers. Characteristically these melodies were constructed on a melodic progression that began on a tone usually sung at the top of the singer's range and descended to lower pitches in the intervals of a third as the statement of the text progressed. Some blues songs consisted of adapted verse forms from other traditions. In general, texts adhered to an AAB verse form. This structure enabled the singer to capture the attention of the listener by repeating the opening line and then concluding each verse with a contrasting line of text. The women would, in some cases, sing the verses in an order that occurred to them at the spur of the moment. They would also adapt the structure of the song to fit the mood of the text. If the lyrics, for example, conveyed several different emotions, the singer, wishing to highlight each emotion, would often separate the verses of a song by inserting an instrumental solo as a chorus.

Tucker, Mack, Bush, and Lee, like most of the classic blues singers of the 1920s, often relied on musical accompaniment by solo male performers, or established groups such as the Memphis Jug Band, which became important in the documentation of early African-American instrumental and regional musical forms. But other rural blues women such as Mattie Delaney, Elvie Thomas, Geeshie Wiley, and Memphis Minnie often accompanied themselves, thus adding another dimension to their blues performances. All of these women used the guitar as an extension of their voices and often played intricate melodic lines over the powerful, driving rhythms that define the sound of Mississippi Delta and Texas blues. In the case of Memphis Minnie, another guitarist often supported her guitar playing during the 1920s, and in her later years she was accompanied by piano. It is evident in her extant recordings, however, that she often played the lead while the other played rhythmic backup. Memphis Minnie, like most guitarists from this region, played very percussively, often bending the strings of the instrument in order to mimic the flexible timbre of her voice. She developed this style of playing while performing on the streets, alleyways, and parks of her hometown Memphis, which cultivated a very active music scene.

The mournful sound of the early twelve-bar blues was solidified with its emphasis on subdominant harmonies. "Blue notes" in the melody also enhanced this doleful quality. These altered chromatic pitches, which often clashed with the fixed major tonality of the chords, confirmed the deep-rooted connection between the blues and the African musical aesthetic. In "Penitentiary Blues," Bessie Tucker, a noted early improviser of the Texas blues, employs vocal devices that display the agony she feels over unrequited love. The performance begins with Tucker moaning. She drags out the text with moans and groans reminiscent of field hollers. Throughout the song, she bends notes and "corrupts" the rhythm to the point that no real metric pattern can be detected. The mood of the piece is initially established by the piano, played by K. D. Johnson, one of the few exponents of the early Texas style of barrelhouse piano to be recorded. Johnson presents a very slow and deliberate rhythmic pulse that foreshadows the melancholy nature of Tucker's voice. His playing is defined by his navigation of the blues progression via a blues-inspired ragtime style, which developed shortly before the classic ragtime tradition of Scott Joplin. It features a "boom-chuck" bass pattern (bass note chord rhythmic pattern) juxtaposed against simple but highly syncopated riffs in the right hand. Tucker's voice interrupts this piano solo with high-pitched but resonating moaning that mimics crying. This segues immediately into the first phrase of the first chorus of blues: "What's the matter with my man today?" Tucker begins on a high pitch that descends to lower pitches in the course of the statement of the first line of text. The pianist switches to an accompaniment style of pulsating chords in the left hand (similar to the strumming guitarists rely on as the rhythmic pulse) and improvised riffs in the right. He fills the space between statements of the text with a series of motivic ideas that are confined to the upper registers of the piano. Johnson's style of playing is almost a complete duplication of the accompaniment approaches played by rural guitar players. Although sources indicate that it is this piano approach that gave way to the rural guitar style, one would assume the opposite in light of the lack of extensive documentation of these early piano styles. When Tucker sings the last line of the verse: "I ask him if he love me and he walked away," she forgoes moaning in favor of a type of crying-singing, where she stretches out various lines of text through the use of melismas and guttural effects. As the performance continues it becomes apparent that Tucker's vocals and Johnson's piano are two varying performances juxtaposed against each other in the manner of an antagonistic dialogue. However, Tucker's vocals seem totally unaffected by the pulsating piano, which at times begins to overshadow her as if it is the focus of the performance. There is seemingly no motivic connection between Tucker's voice and the piano, although the latter provides the rhythmic and harmonic stability. Tucker continues to become more and more improvisatory as the song continues:

> *Penitentiary, penitentiary. Ahh, gonna be my home*
> *Penitentiary, penitentiary. Ahh, gonna be my home*
> *Because my man mistreated me—he done me wrong.*
>
> *The man that I'm a loving, he gonna get me killed.*
> *The man that I'm a loving, he gonna get me killed.*
> *Because love is a proposition that got many poor girls killed.*
>
> *I love you and you won't behave.*
> *I love you and you won't behave.*
> *You gonna keep on a piling gonna wake in your grave.*[10]

MEMPHIS MINNIE'S BLUES

It is in this rural performance style that a few women managed to gain a level of financial and artistic autonomy normally reserved for male singers. They avoided the pressures of male management and the exploitative nature of male songwriters, who often penned the songs of the classic blues women and dictated the musical sound of their recordings. Some of the rural blues women formed partnerships with male performers that allowed them to operate in leadership roles: "Signifyin" Mary Johnson and Lonnie Johnson, Bertha Lee and Charley Patton, Memphis Minnie and Kansas Joe McCoy, to name a few. In the case of Memphis Minnie, her authority as a performer drew many male admirers to her singing and guitar playing.[11] In Chicago during the 1930s, she would often participate in contests between blues singers. Blues man James Watt recalls one instance where she battled Muddy Waters: "Playing that guitar, her and Muddy. They used to have these contests, the one who win the contest, they would get the fifth of whiskey. And Memphis Minnie would tell Muddy. 'I'm getting this fifth of whiskey.' She'd get it every time, though. She would get it *every time*. Muddy just couldn't do nothing with Memphis, no, uh, uh, not back then . . ."[12]

By the time of her first recordings in the late 1920s, Memphis Minnie was a notable musician, songwriter, and singer. She often played lead guitar, and performed most of the solo vocals in her duo combos. Her partners, who mostly consisted of her husbands, provided her with a musical identity that had been reserved primarily for men and earned her a distinct position in the vaudeville tradition.

The diversity of themes in the blues of Memphis Minnie indicates the role that these songs had in documenting the sentiments of the community as well as in providing a philosophical connection between women's blues and lament. She sings about life on the farm in "Sylvester and his Mule," making sarcastic references to Franklin Delano Roosevelt and the promises of the New Deal. "When the Levee Breaks," one of the first songs she recorded with her first husband Joe McCoy, is about the devastating 1927 flood that destroyed many of the outlying areas of Memphis. For Memphis Minnie and McCoy, this piece not only documented a tragic event, but also served as a metaphor for the new life they were beginning in Chicago at this time.

Most of Memphis Minnie's blues drew heavily on her own background as a southern black woman. Her song "Hustlin' Woman Blues" pays testament to her experience as a prostitute long before her recording career began. The musical style of this performance is typical of her recordings with McCoy. Minnie played lead guitar, which consisted primarily of treble-based riffs played over an ostinato progression strummed by McCoy. By peppering her singing with spoken discourse, she vividly portrays the relationship between pimp and prostitute:

> I stood on the corner all night long, counting the stars one by one.
> I stood on the corner all night long, counting the stars one by one.
> I didn't make no money, Bob, and I can't go back home.[13]

The subjects of Minnie's blues were not the only unusual aspect of her performances. She never referred to her physical attributes in her songs as other blues women did. Instead, she preferred to use the songs as vehicles that acknowledged events that impacted the black community. She even refused to move to Chicago, as so many blues women did, traveling there only to record. During the times when she wasn't recording, Minnie toured the South or just around the Memphis area.

By 1935, as evidenced in her extant recordings, Minnie began experimenting with new sounds, which enabled her to survive the commercial music shift that would displace classic blues women in a short time. Although she retained the rural flavor of her previous recordings, her accompanying lines became less intricate. This can be accounted for by the absence of McCoy's second guitar that had aptly supported her treble runs. Now forced to maintain both her own bass lines as well as her treble riffs, Memphis Minnie found it more difficult to play the complex runs that had defined her early playing. The piano accompaniments she employed throughout the mid- to late 1930s allowed her to make a switch from the elaborate picking style of her early recordings to a more reserved style that placed the guitar in a more supportive role. It was a style better suited for the northern popular music scene, which was quickly embracing the jazz sounds of the emerging dance band orchestras. Minnie's ability to change with the musical times meant that her career would survive the eventual death of the classic blues craze.

THE CLASSIC BLUES ERA

At the time of the rural blues, life in the South was becoming increasingly difficult as boll weevil infestations, increasing poverty, and violence at the hands of terrorist groups came to characterize black life. From 1916 to 1930, thousands of rural blacks left the South and migrated to the North in what became known as the Great Migration. Hoping to escape forced labor, poverty, and the Ku Klux Klan, blacks answered the North's call for unskilled laborers. Good news and talk of the "Promised Land" from relatives who had resettled in the North spurred southerners to pack up and move. Black males relayed stories of jobs that paid double, or even triple the amount they had made in the fields in the South. The majority of these migrants found jobs in slaughterhouses, foundries, and steel mills such as Carnegie Steel, American Wire and Steel.[14] Most women found temporary positions at department stores and factories, as well as in domestic work. Work opportunities, however, were greater for men resettling than for women, and living conditions proved more conducive to single traveling men than families.[15]

Although cities such as Chicago, New York, Pittsburgh, and Cincinnati held promises of a "new life" for southern blacks, there were pitfalls in the North. Migrants were often herded into the most populated and most unsanitary areas of the city. They were often denied union wages or jobs. The discrimination that had defined life in the South still manifested itself in the North—sometimes coming from the blacks themselves. Nevertheless, southern migrants persevered and created their own cultural "spaces" where they could hear the music of home.

Although initially unaffected by the culture of the North, in time the blues began to show the influences of other musical traditions. The new blues style featured sophisticated vocal performances, expanded instrumental accompaniment, and salient features of vaudeville. Its leading exponents were women, who like their male counterparts had migrated to the North in search of new lives. Although, as we have seen, women did perform the earlier rural blues, they became synonymous with the new style, known as the classic blues. The classic blues, which came into vogue in the 1920s, marked a transition in idiom. For the first time, black music did not exclusively center on the concerns of black society. Instead, this new form of the blues would signify the evolving concepts of identity in the post–World War I black community. As the noted scholar and playwright Amiri Baraka asserts, "the emergence of the classic blues indicated that many changes had taken place in the Negro. . . . [Their] sense of place, or status, within the superstructure of American society had changed radically since the days of the field holler."[16]

The ascent of the classic blues singers from the south and the southern black enclaves of northern cities also reflected the evolving role of the black woman as a musician. Prior to the 1920s, black women were limited to composing and performing music primarily in the church. For those women like Memphis Minnie, acceptance into social and church circles was often denied as the blues was seen by middle-class and church-going blacks as the "Devil's Music." The rich and vibrant musical scene of Memphis and other cities such as Dallas provided early rural blues women with a means to perform without having to travel constantly from town to town and city to city. These guitar-playing women bridged the gap between the urbanized classic blues woman on one side and the progressive aspects of the male country blues men on the other.[17]

The "opening" of American theaters to women of color and the interest of the recording industry in their music provided new ways for the blues singers to shift from the private to the public sphere. First the tent and medicine shows and then the vaudeville theaters offered black women opportunities to perform. Only the most celebrated and talented black performers initially had access to the big-time vaudeville circuits. The lack of financial sponsorship for black shows and the racism performers encountered from some of the owners and managers led to the creation of a separate circuit known as the Theater Owners Booking Association.[18]

The TOBA, or "Tough on Black Actors or Asses," as the performers dubbed it, became the main vehicle to handle vaudeville bookings for African Americans. The circuit stretched from Cleveland to Galveston and Kansas City to Jacksonville. The shows featured on the circuit were tabloid editions of musical comedies. TOBA audiences were outspoken and inhospitable to acts that were either lackluster or strayed too far from preferred black performance style. There was no "hook" to drag inept performers off the stage when the boos reached a crescendo, but the audience would greet unpopular acts with derisive catcalls and an occasional flying missile. The TOBA, with its all-black audiences and often shabby, ill-kept theaters, became the perfect venue for the developing forms of black music, dance, and comedy. It gave many blues women their first performance opportunities.[19]

The pivotal figure in launching the classic blues onto the vaudeville stage was Ma Rainey. Born Gertrude Pridgett in 1886, Rainey had already established herself as a powerful vocalist and entertainer long before the classic blues craze of the twenties. She and her husband William "Pa" Rainey performed together in minstrel shows as early as 1904. Ma Rainey was one of the last of the great minstrel show artists, and one of the first performers to showcase blues songs on the stage.[20] In this early articulation of the classic blues, there was generally a thin line separating song and speech as performers such as Rainey would often move freely between the two. Rainey's rich contralto voice embodied the rural, southern blues with its "underlying seriousness and melancholy."[21] Her performances blended the southern black experience with that of the migrants in the North. Her importance in the development of the classic blues earned her the moniker "Mother of the Blues."

The songs that Rainey and others sang generally followed the AAB verse form of earlier blues idioms. But unlike the rural blues, they displayed a more sophisticated sound. The accompaniments ranged from Ma Rainey's jug band to early jazz groups, which, along with the solo piano, became the standard accompaniment. The infusion of the early jazz sound into the blues tradition helped reposition the classic blues, taking it from cultural marginality to mainstream acceptability among middle-class blacks and whites. Highly controlled, these blues allowed very little deviation from the established tempo, rhythmic structure, or verse form. Even improvisatory moments were clearly well thought out. As in the rural tradition, the emphasis in the classic blues was placed on the voice. The classic blues singer, like her rural counterpart, often employed moans, groans, and melismas in order to advance the emotional content of these songs.

The blues woman's charismatic persona, her sexuality, and her exhibition of sensual power stirred the imagination of her poor black audiences. Her glamorous stage presence demonstrated to black women that they could be celebrated as being beautiful and that they did not have to remain silent about their experiences.[22] At the same time that she presented to black women an alternative to domestic life, the blues singer could also relate to the experiences of southern black women and recent migrants to the North. The typical blues woman left home at an early age in search of a better life; she eventually discovered that more money was to be made singing in the brothels and speakeasies of the urban North than in domestic service. Despite the physical separation of her voice, whether on the distant stage or on phonograph records, the blues singer created a spiritual link, by speaking directly to the emotions of her listeners. Oakley recounts Carl Van Vechten's experience of seeing Bessie Smith performing at the Orpheum Theatre in 1925. "The black and blue-black crowd, notable for the absence of mulattoes, burst into hysterical, semi-religious shrieks of sorrow and lamentation. Amens rent the air, little nervous giggles, like the shattering of Venetian glass, shocked our nerves. When Bessie proclaimed, 'It's true I loves you, but I won't take mistreatment any mo',' a girl sitting beneath our box called 'Dat's right! Say it, Sister.'"[23]

THE BLUES WOMAN AS LAMENTER

Although scholars have focused on the explicit sexual content of the texts, other extra-musical messages may be found in the songs. These lyrics, from the earliest blues sung by Ma Rainey to the more sophisticated songs of Ethel Waters and Alberta Hunter, document the evolving aspects of black life in America, especially in relation to black women. Through the songs, the blues woman could simultaneously speak to her own experiences and those of the collective whole. Expressions of love, sorrow, joy, as well as pain and despair are all expressed in the blues.

The appeal of the classic blues woman was her ability to identify with her audience, to put a finger on their deepest concerns, and to offer them advice and solace.[24] In Clara Smith's "Strugglin' Woman's Blues," the singer recounts how her life is a struggle as she works hard to try and keep a man who doesn't love her. The stylistic differences between Smith's recording and those discussed earlier are quite remarkable. Here the jazz band of clarinet, cornet, piano, bass, and guitar, and not Smith's voice, establishes the emotional mood of the song. Smith's delivery of the text is devoid of the high-pitched nasal sound, as well as the moans, groans, and guttural effects that were often employed by rural singers.

> *Every morning, early every morning.*
> *I have to rise with the morning sun.*
> *I have to rise with the morning sun.*
> *A poor struggling woman, her work is never done.*
>
> *Folks say I'm a fool just a working fool for that man of mine.*
> *Folks say I'm a fool just a working fool for that man of mine.*
> *But what he's done to me will come back to him in time.*
>
> *My man don't want me, trouble haunt me, I always lose.*
> *My man don't want me, trouble haunt me, I always lose.*
> *Hard working hurtin' me, but I'm just dying with the blues.*

> *But I'll keep on struggling, always struggling with my heavy load.*
> *But I'll keep on struggling, always struggling with my heavy load.*
> *I may find a happy home, but further down the road.*

Several blues songs highlighted the unhealthy conditions that flourished in black neighborhoods. Life in the North brought various diseases that often left women and men to die in sanitariums or hospitals isolated from loved ones. During the period from 1923 to 1927, a black woman was 50 percent more likely to die in childbirth than her white counterpart in the Northeast. In general, deaths in Harlem were 42 percent higher than in the rest of New York City; the tuberculosis mortality rate alone was three times greater. In 1930, Memphis Minnie recorded the "Memphis Minnie-Jitis Blues," where she details the horrors of being infected with meningitis and the substandard medical care most received. Despite the humorous pun in the title, the song tackles a tragic topic. Bacterial meningitis was fatal in the 1920s and 1930s and lower classes in the ghettos were especially vulnerable to the disease.

> *Mmmm, the meningitis killing me.*
> *Mmmm, the meningitis killing me.*
> *I'm bending, I'm bending, baby, my head is nearly down to my knee.*
>
> *I come in home one Saturday night, pull off my clothes and I lie down.*
> *I come in home one Saturday night, pull off my clothes and I lie down.*
> *And next morning just about day, the meningitis begin to creep around.*
>
> *My head and neck was paining me, seem like my back would break in two.*
> *My head and neck was paining me, seem like my back would break in two.*
> *Lord, I had such a mood that morning, I didn't know what in the world to do.*
>
> *My companion take me to the doctor, "Doctor, please tell me my wife's complaint."*
> *My companion take me to the doctor, "Doctor, please tell me my wife's complaint."*
> *The doctor looked down on me, shook his head, said, "I wouldn't mind telling you,*
>   *son, but I can't."*
>
> *"You take her round to the city hospital, just as quick, quick as you possibly can.*
> *"You take her round to the city hospital, just as quick, quick as you possibly can.*
> *Because the condition she's in now, you never will get her back home 'live again."*
>
> *He rode me round to the city hospital, the clock was striking ten.*
> *He rode me round to the city hospital, the clock was striking ten.*
> *I heard my companion say, "I won't see your smiling face again."*[25]

Memphis Minnie used her own ordeal with the disease as the basis for this song. She was stricken with both meningitis and yellow fever while living in Memphis. The doctors gave up on her and said that there was no cure. The incident commonly recounted by Memphis Minnie states that her husband went and got a quart of corn whiskey. She claims it was the alcohol and not the medicine that saved her. According to several sources, she went into a coma and was placed in a room to die. The hospital staff had even gone as far as to cover her with a sheet. The next morning, having sweated the fever out through the whiskey, Memphis Minnie awoke fully recovered.[26] Seeking medical attention on charity, the norm for most working-class blacks, had exposed her to inconsistent and outdated medical treatment. She actually penned the song and recorded it in the hospital.

Although the majority of the composition is consistent with its performance of treble-based riffs as fill-ins and extensions of the voice, there is one instance in which she attempts to represent musically the content of the text. In the sixth chorus of the blues, the second phrase of the first line ("He rode me round to the city hospital, the clock was striking ten") Memphis Minnie plays a motive that mimics the sound of clock bells tolling. It is one of the most vivid forms of word painting found in her compositions.

In "Dirty T.B. Blues," the classic blues singer Victoria Spivey describes the experiences of women who migrated to the city alone and had the misfortune of contracting tuberculosis:

> *Here I lay a-crying, something on my mind.*
> *It's midnight, wonder where the nurse could be.*
> *I feel down, not a friend in this town, I blew in all alone.*
> *Sisters are gone, brothers are too, nowhere to call my own.*

The performance uses a narrative lyric structure and is characterized by its close stylistic relationship with the early New Orleans style taken up in Chicago by Joe "King" Oliver, Jelly Roll Morton, and Louis Armstrong. Prominent are the flat four rhythm indicative of early jazz and collective improvisation between cornet, clarinet, and trombone. The cornet, which serves as the primary instrument, initially offers musical responses to Spivey's statements, but as the song progresses the clarinet and trombone join in the dialogue too. Spivey builds the emotion of the story by becoming more agitated vocally during the performance. By the statement of the second verse, "I can't keep from crying, left alone while I was dying. Yes, it may look crazy for me to be on my knees. But it's the Lord's difference between grace and TB—Oh, Lord," Spivey takes to a moaning, crying type of singing that creates rhythmic tension with the accompaniment. The third verse is set apart from the previous through the use of stop-time rhythm, which emphasizes the climactic points of the following text:

> *Yes he railroaded me to the sanitarium, it's too late, I've finished my run.*
> *This is the way all women are done when they've got the dirty TB.*

Following an instrumental break, in which the cornet improvises on the vocal melody, Spivey returns with the last stanza of text:

> *Yes, I run around for months and months from gin mill to gin mill to Honky tonks.*
> *Now its too late, look what I've done done now. I've go the dirty TB.*[27]

She punctuates the verses with moans of "Oh, Lord" as well as a call and response between her moans and the cornet. Her use of the narrative form instead of the typical AAB structure draws the listener in as she recounts what brought her to the point of death from tuberculosis.

Disease was not the only condition the blues spoke about; poverty and the uncertainty brought on by the Great Depression were also popular themes. In "Outdoor Blues," Memphis Minnie sings of the homelessness that plagued many in the Depression years. Her account of life on the streets is structured into six stanzas of twelve-bar blues set in AAB verse form. Typical of her guitar-duet performances, it begins with a short introduction where one guitar (Joe McCoy) plays the chord changes and establishes the moderate swing of the tempo. Minnie's guitar functions as a second voice, often entering in call-and-response dialogue with the singer's voice. Her high-pitched nasal sound conveys a stronger connection with the sound of the rural blues man than with the rough-toned classic blues women. The descending melody immediately grabs the attention of the listener. During the first chorus Memphis Minnie uses her guitar to emphasize the portions of the text she deems most important. For instance, in the first chorus, "One cold night I's out in the frost and snow, / One cold night I's out in the frost and snow, / I didn't have a penny, I couldn't find no place to go," she plays one-stringed fill-ins that bridge the first and second statements of the first line. When she reaches the word "penny," Minnie's guitar repeats the exact pitches she just sang, thus placing emphasis on the word denoting her situation—the lack of money. As the performance continues, Minnie's accompaniment becomes more elaborate, while the second guitarist hardly deviates from the simple strums of the basic chord progression. Unlike many rural blues tunes, the tempo does not follow the traditional practice of speeding up, but remains constant throughout the song. During the third stanza, "I was so cold, my face was near 'bout froze, / I was so cold, my face was near 'bout froze, / And I didn't have a penny, I couldn't find no place to go," her guitar playing shifts from the one-string figures to full-chord punctuations, which again emphasize the word "penny." In the fourth chorus, she plays a series of percussive ascending and descending chords, depicting the text: "I come to a house, I knocked upon the door, / I come to a house, I knocked upon the door, / They wouldn't accept my company because I didn't have on no clothes." By the fifth chorus Memphis Minnie, reaching the extremes of her emotions, starts to moan. This moaning encompasses the first section of the phrase and is followed by a verbal response that describes her condition.

> *Hmmm, my face was near 'bout froze.*
> *Hmmm, my face was near 'bout froze.*
> *I didn't have a penny, I couldn't find no place to go.*

The entrance of the final chorus deviates from the previous choruses in that the first four measures are a guitar solo with an ostinato accompaniment by the second guitarist. Minnie concludes this final chorus with the following text and a concluding guitar flourish:

> *I looked and saw an old lady standing in the door.*
> *She said come here daughter honey where's that you trying to go?*

FROM EMANCIPATION TO THE GREAT DEPRESSION, blacks created new musical traditions and revamped existing ones in an effort to communicate the social, economic, and physical changes they were undergoing. The blues idiom documented these experiences by presenting the most vivid descriptions of black life in America during the early twentieth century. Pivotal to the understanding of the blues is the role women played as performers. Much like the laments of Africa, both the rural and classic blues style provided a "voice" for women of color. It captured the collective feelings of the black community, while at the same time it expressed the personal sentiments of the women performers. Most significantly, the blues enabled women to make the transition from private to public music making, and in so doing redefined black womanhood.

NOTES

1. Undine Smith Moore, "My Life in Music," *IAWM Journal* 3 (1997): 9–10.
2. See, for example, Angela Y. Davis, *Blues Legacies and Black Feminism: Gertrude "Ma" Rainey, Bessie Smith, and Billie Holiday* (New York: Pantheon Books, 1998); Hazel Carby, "It Just Be's Dat Way Sometimes: The Sexual Politics of Women's Blues," in *Feminisms: An Anthology of Literary Theory and Criticism,* ed. Robyn R. Warhol and Diane Price Herndl (New Brunswick, N.J.: Rutgers University Press, 1991), 746–58.

There are, however, other works that speak to the cultural importance of the classic blues woman and her rural counterpart. They include, but are not limited to, Alan Lomax, *The Land Where the Blues Began* (London: Minerva, 1997); Houston Baker, *Blues, Ideology and the Harlem Renaissance* (Chicago and London: University of Chicago Press, 1987); and Giles Oakley, *The Devil's Music: A History of the Blues* (New York and London: Harcourt Brace Jovanovich, 1976).

3. For more information on the lament traditions of the Caribbean and South America see Virginia Kerns, *Black Carib Kinship and Ritual: Women and Ancestors* (Urbana and Chicago: University of Illinois Press, 1983) and Greg Urban, "Discourse, Affect and Social Order Ritual Wailing in Amerindian Brazil," *American Anthropologist* 90 (1988): 385–400.

4. J. H. Nketia, *Funeral Dirges of the Akan People* (Exeter, N.H., 1955), 68.

5. Lawrence W. Levine, *Black Culture and Black Consciousness: Afro-American Folk Thought from Slavery to Freedom* (New York: Oxford University Press, 1977), 218.

6. Ibid., 219.

7. David Evans, "Goin' up the Country: Blues in Texas and the Deep South," in *Nothing but the Blues: The Music and the Musicians*, ed. Lawrence Cohn (New York and London: Abbeville Press, 1993), 35–36.

8. Ibid., 36.

9. Don Kent, brochure notes for *I Can't Be Satisfied: Early American Women Blues Singers,* Vol. 1: *Country;* Vol. 2: *Town.* Yazoo compact disks B000000G92, B000000G93 (1997).

10. Bessie Tucker, "Penitentiary," in *I Can't Be Satisfied: Early American Women Blues Singers,* Vol. 1: *Country.*

11. On her life see Paul and Beth Garon, *Woman with Guitar: Memphis Minnie's Blues* (New York: Da Capo Press, 1992). In addition to her biography, the Memphis Minnie website (http://www.ping.be/ml-cmb/mmindex.htm) includes an excellent "sessionography" listing all recording sessions and first issue recording labels and numbers.

12. Garon, *Woman with Guitar,* 59.

13. Memphis Minnie, "Hustlin' Woman's Blues," Bluebird B-6202 (1935), "Fly Right" LP 108, Stash LP 117, and *Memphis Minnie 1935–1941, Volume 1 (10 Jan. 1935–31 Oct. 1935),* RST Records compact disk BDCD-6008 (1991).

14. Peter Gottlieb, "Reaching Pittsburgh," in *Making Their Own Way: Southern Blacks' Migration to Pittsburgh, 1916–1930* (Urbana and Chicago: University of Illinois Press, 1987), 39–42.

15. Ibid.

16. Leroi Jones (Amiri Baraka), *Blues People* (New York: Morrow Quill Paperbacks, 1963), 87.

17. Garon, *Woman with Guitar,* 10.

18. There are many conflicting accounts as to the genesis of the TOBA. Some attribute the circuit to F. A. Barrasso, a Memphis-based Italian businessman who owned several theaters in the South. It is believed he started the TOBA in 1907. Other sources attribute the circuit to Sherman Dudley. Dudley was connected with the administration of the circuit and may have been a manager or booking agent but he was not the creator of the TOBA. For information on TOBA, see Mel Watkins, *On the Real Side: Laughing, Lying and Signifying. The Underground Tradition of African American Humor that Transformed American Culture, from Slavery to Richard Pryor* (New York: Simon and Schuster, 1994), 155–56; Daphne Duval Harrison, *Black Pearls: Blues*

Queens of the 1920s (New Brunswick, N.J.: Rutgers University Press, 1998), 17–41; Athelia Knight, "In Retrospect: Sherman H. Dudley: He Paved the Way for TOBA," *The Black Perspective in Music* 15 (1987): 152–81; Marshall and Jean Stearns, *Jazz Dance: The Story in American Vernacular Dance* (New York: Schirmer Books, 1968), 75–84; Langston Hughes and Melton Meltzer, *Black Magic* (Englewood Cliffs, N.J.: Prentice-Hall, 1967), 67–72.

19. Watkins, *On the Real Side*, 367.
20. Derrick Stewart-Baxter, *Ma Rainey and the Classic Blues Singers* (New York: Stein and Day Publishers, 1970), 38.
21. Oakley, *The Devil's Music*, 101.
22. Carby, "It Just Be's Dat Way Sometimes," 756.
23. Oakley, *The Devil's Music*, 117.
24. Henrietta Yurchenko, "Mean Mama Blues: Bessie Smith and the Vaudeville Era," in *Music, Gender and Culture*, ed. Marcia Herndon and Susanna Ziegler (Wilhelmshaven: F. Noetzel, 1990), 241–51.
25. Memphis Minnie, "Memphis Minnie-Jitis Blues," Vocalion LP 1588 (1930).
26. Paul and Beth Garon, *Woman with Guitar*, 147.
27. Victoria Spivey, "Dirty TB Blues," *I Can't Be Satisfied: Early American Women Blues Singers*, Vol. 2: *Town*, Yazoo 1997.

CHAPTER TEN

Abandoned Heroines

WOMEN'S VOICES IN HANDEL'S CANTATAS

Ellen T. Harris

IN 1706 GEORGE FRIDERIC HANDEL (1685–1759) left his homeland of Germany and traveled to Italy. After four years there, he accepted a position at the court of Hanover, Germany, but quickly proceeded to London, where he settled for life, moving into his own house in 1723. These seventeen years (1706–23) mark the only period in Handel's life during which he regularly lived in the houses of his patrons—such as the Medici court in Florence, the villas and palazzos of the Marquis Ruspoli, and the Cardinals Pamphili and Ottoboni in Rome; the German Hanoverian court, the London mansion of Lord Burlington, and the Cannons estate outside London of the Earl of Carnarvon (named Duke of Chandos in 1719).

The period is distinguished artistically by Handel's composition of small-scale vocal works to be performed at the private musical or social gatherings of his hosts. These cantatas, written for a single voice or group of soloists and accompanied by instrumental groups of various sizes, ranging from simple continuo (a combination of harpsichord and cello) to larger instrumental groups including strings and wind instruments, represent private music written for private performance. After moving into his own house in 1723 at the age of thirty-eight, Handel stopped writing these small vocal works and dedicated himself to composing for the public stage. Of all the genres in which he composed, only the cantatas remained unpublished in his lifetime.

Overall, Handel's more than one hundred cantatas can be divided into two unequal groups by performing forces: cantatas for solo voice and continuo accompaniment (about seventy) and cantatas with additional instrumental accompaniment (about thirty). This second group can be further divided between works for solo voice and works for two or more voices. The cantatas can also be distinguished geographically, the vast majority having been written in Italy (1706–10). Although he also wrote two operas (*Rodrigo* and *Agrippina*) and two oratorios (*Il trionfo del tempo* and *La resurrezione*) during these four Italian years, Handel was most often engaged in writing cantatas: at least seventy-three can be dated to this circumscribed period. The cantatas, therefore, offer the best evidence of Handel's compositional development.

Examination of the cantatas in light of his later compositions reveals that the early crafting of distinct musical styles for men's and women's voices played a critical role in Handel's growth as a composer. Gender differentiation in Baroque music had to be largely compositional, since male and female characters were not identified by the natural ranges of male and female voices. Rather, most male and female roles were written in the same treble ranges and were sung interchangeably by male castrati or female sopranos. That is, treble-voiced roles did not need to be performed by singers of the same sex as the character: male castrati often played female roles and female sopranos similarly played male roles ("trouser roles"). Clear examples of such cross-dressing in performance exist in Handel's Italian works. The cantata *Delirio amoroso* (1707), which depicts a distraught woman after the death of her lover, was written for a male singer (castrato), while the role of the shepherd Olinto (depicting Handel's patron the Marquis Ruspoli) in the cantata *Oh, come chiare* (1708) was played by the female soprano Margherita Durastante. Exceptions to the dominance of treble voices in Italian operatic music occur in roles depicting old men and some villains, which parts were often given to natural basses. Tenors were still more rare but, when used, typically depicted monarchs or military commanders in opposition to the leading male role for treble voice. The cantata texts include no such characters. Rather, they present the voices of young men and women who express the passion and anguish of love. The treble voice prevails in the approximately ninety cantatas Handel wrote for single solo voice. Only four are for bass; none is for tenor.

The solo voices of Handel's continuo cantatas are rarely identified in the text by name or gender, and the sex of the beloved of whom they sing often is obscured as well by referring only to the lover's beautiful qualities of person and spirit. By contrast, Handel's eighteen solo instrumental cantatas composed in Italy typically name the character (and thus the sex) portrayed by the singer.[1] Of these, fourteen can be dated to Handel's earliest Italian period—1707 or before. This group of cantatas offers a means of examining Handel's early stylistic development through his use of specific and clearly distinguished voices for women and men.

The texts of Handel's cantatas for women differ strikingly from those written for or about men. The women, even when placed in a brief narrative frame, speak in their own voices. In *O numi eterni* (*Lucrezia*) the raped Lucrezia cries out for vengeance as she takes her own life. In *Delirio amoroso,* Clori, rejected by Tirsi during his life and delirious after his death, follows him in her dreams to the Underworld. *Diana cacciatrice* ("Alla caccia") celebrates the hunt in the voice of the goddess Diana. In *Tu fedel? tu costante?* an unnamed woman complains of the faithlessness of her lover Fileno and threatens to leave him. The sorceress Armida hurls threats at her departing lover Rinaldo in *Armida abbandonata,* but finds that her love leaves her powerless to harm him. In *Ero e Leandro* ("Qual ti riveggio"), Hero finds Leander, her beloved, drowned on the shore, tears out her hair (symbol of her earthly beauty, which had bound the heart of Leander), and then drowns herself. In *Agrippina condotta a morire,* Handel depicts the mental anguish of the former Roman empress immediately before her execution.

Handel's men, by contrast, are distanced by a narrative structure. In *Abdolonymus* ("Figlio d'alte speranze"), for example, the changing fortunes of King Abdolonymus are described in the third person. (Abdolonymus's own voice may perhaps sound once, but only in an aria that expresses no emotion concerning the king's debased condition and can be heard as a quotation of what Abdolonymus said by the singer/storyteller rather than direct address.) *Tra le fiamme,* composed shortly after *Armida,* narrates (rather than dramatizes) the story of Daedalus and Icarus, who fashion wings for themselves in order to fly. In *Nel dolce dell'oblio* (also titled *Pensieri notturni di Filli*), the male character describes Phyllis, his beloved, sleeping and dreaming, but not his own emotions. In *Notte placida* the (same?) man prays for sleep so that he can dream of Phyllis. Although told in the first person, *Notte placida* barely explores the character's emotional state; the clearest musical image in this cantata is Handel's depiction of the "gentle zephyrs" that the singer calls upon to rock him to sleep.

Whereas the lamenting Clori, Armida, and Hero place love at the center of their being so that abandonment destabilizes them, the unnamed male lovers in *Nel dolce dell'oblio* and *Notte placida* seem to be able to hold love as a thing apart or, at least, to keep their emotions under rational control. Indeed, in many cantatas about men, the topic often turns away from love altogether and depicts man's life in terms of fame and glory. The story of Abdolonymus concerns not love but station; the story of Icarus, ambition. In the only instrumental cantata to depict one of Handel's patrons explicitly, the multi-voice *Oh, come chiare,* Ruspoli is portrayed not as a lover but as a warrior.

In contrast, Handel rarely depicts women who are not lamenting. The only two such instrumental cantatas, both written in spring 1707, portray women who have given up the company of men. In *Tu fedel? Tu costante?* an un-

named woman rails against the inconstancy of her fickle lover Fileno, but
then decides either to find a new lover or give up men entirely "to be free
again, loveless as before." *Diana cacciatrice* depicts the virgin goddess Diana
summoning her nymphs to banish love and join the hunt. According to
myth, Diana was surprised while bathing by the mortal Actaeon; in retribu-
tion for his seeing her undressed, she changed him into a stag, whereupon
he was killed by his own dogs. The manuscript of *Diana cacciatrice* contains
an "arietta" in which the goddess sings a tribute to Melampus, one of Actaeon's dogs,[2] implicitly celebrating the death of Actaeon. In its reference to
Melampus, Handel's Diana cantata portrays the goddess, like an abandoned
woman, as a life-threatening danger to men.

The women in Handel's cantatas always express themselves directly and
with vehemence; in contrast, the strongest expression in first-person cantatas
for men's voices comes not from direct emotion but from nature as a metaphor for emotion. *Ah! crudel,* probably composed late in 1707, reaches its
emotional peak in an *accompagnato* describing lightning, a storm, and a
clearing as a metaphor for the singer's hope that his sorrows will turn to joy.
Cuopre tal volta, composed in Naples in 1708, uses a depiction of a storm for
its entire text, saving only the last six lines to explain the metaphor. *Alpestre
monte* depicts instead a "wild mountain and lonely forest, melancholy abode
of horror, lair of wild beasts," to which place the singer has come to seek
death as his heart is surrounded by "evil shadows and spectres." Although
unpredictable, nature provides the men's cantatas with an equivalent to and a
substitute for the uncontrolled woman's voice; the disturbing natural images
cannot match the power and emotion directly expressed by an abandoned
woman. In *Armida,* and again in *Agrippina,* written around the same time as
Alpestre monte, storms do not happen externally, as they do to the men, but
rather exist within the women and are transformed by them into curses upon
their betrayers. Indeed, in the cantatas for men, the storms are echoes of
women's voices and represent a "feminine" disruption in the men's lives. The
first-person, distraught voices of the women themselves bring to Handel's
music a passion and emotional depth largely lacking in the cantatas for men.

The despair of Lucrezia, Clori, Armida, Hero, and Agrippina significantly
affects their musical utterance, and Handel depicts their distress by tearing
at the musical fabric with dissonance, disjunct motion, chromaticism, and
rhythmic and formal irregularities. The normal structural pattern in Handel's
cantatas, as in his mature operas, is a succession of recitative–aria pairs,
where the aria is typically in da capo form. The instrumental cantatas, following the typical pattern in continuo cantatas, sometimes limit themselves to
two pairs, as in *Nel dolce dell'oblio* and *Alpestre monte,* but it is also common

to see the pattern extended to three pairs, as in *Abdolonymus* and *Cuopre tal volta*, or even four pairs, as in *Notte placida* and *Clori, mia bella Clori*. All these examples, however, represent men's voices. The women's cantatas regularly break this formal pattern, being, like the women themselves, neither contained nor predictable. *Lucrezia*, for example, begins with two recitative–aria pairs, but then dissolves into a unique sequence of recitative and arioso for an equivalent length of text. In places, successive, individual lines of text are singled out for distinct treatment, rapidly shifting, as occurs in *Lucrezia* from *furioso* to *adagio* to *larghetto*. In four of the six women's cantatas, the voice ends in recitative: *Lucrezia, Delirio amoroso* (for Clori, where the vocal recitative ending is followed by an instrumental minuet), *Ero e Leandro*, and *Agrippina*. All the cantatas for men's voices end with an aria. That is, whereas the men's cantatas end with a complex and complete musical period, the women's cantatas tend to collapse into musical recitation.

The women's cantatas, more flexible in overall structure, also exhibit more freedom in individual aria form. Of course, da capo form, which dominates Italian operatic music at this time, prevails in all the cantatas. In the cantatas for men, there is only one aria not in this form: *Notte placida* ends with a free fugue for voice and instruments. The women's cantatas offer more variation. *Diana* and *Delirio amoroso* both contain ariettas (short arias in two-part form). *Tu fedel? tu costante?* ends with a binary dance movement. In contrast, the final movement of *Un alma innamorata*, a male-voice cantata, takes the binary dance form and expands it into a da capo.

In instrumental cantatas generally, as in opera, recitatives are usually accompanied only by continuo—that is, *recitativo semplice*. Recitative with additional accompaniment, or *accompagnato*, tends to be used for heightening of emotion or description, and, not surprisingly, accompanied recitatives in the women's and men's cantatas differ. In the men's cantatas such recitatives occur relatively rarely, in only three of ten cantatas: *Ah! crudel, Alpestre monte*, and *Notte placida*. In *Ah! crudel* the agitated *concitato* paints a storm; in *Alpestre monte* sustained chromatic chords depict the mystery of the "lonely forest, melancholy abode of horror," and in *Notte placida* the sustained triads in the violins represent the peaceful state of sleep. Despite their enhanced expression, these accompanied recitatives continue to function as musical declamation, unchanged from simple recitative other than by the addition of instrumental support.

The situation is quite different in the women's cantatas. Here the *accompagnato* passages function less as recitative than as an aria fragment. This concept is particularly strong in *Agrippina condotta a morire*, where the abandoned arias metaphorically depict Agrippina's own abandonment. The former empress, condemned by her son Nero to die, expresses her fluctuating emotions in an extended scene that forms the mid-point of the cantata. She begins as if in an *adagio* aria saying that she cannot desire the death of one to whom she gave life. Then cutting herself off in recitative, she calls herself a madwoman for having such tender feelings and begins a *presto* aria calling for Nero's death. However, she is again unable to complete her "aria" thought, and falls back into recitative, moving to a complete recitative cadence in order, once again, to start afresh, this time with an aria fragment in 3/2 asking that death be hers alone. This pattern continues through yet another vengeful *allegro,* again abandoned. Agrippina now returns to her opening *adagio* and thereafter concludes the scene in simple recitative.

Lucrezia, in its use of continuo accompaniment, demonstrates that the stylistic issue cannot be reduced to accompanied versus simple recitative, but rather encompasses recitative and aria function. After two recitative–aria pairs of seething emotion, Lucrezia can no longer maintain this formal façade. The remainder of the cantata consists of recitative and aria fragments in one extended *scena* leading to her death: the cantata ends in recitative. As in *Agrippina,* the dependence on musical declamation lends this cantata a stronger forward momentum than is possible in the more formal progression of successive recitative–aria pairs typical of the cantatas for men.

The differences of musical structure and idiom that distinguish Handel's cantatas for women's voices from those for men's voices can be illustrated by a musical comparison of *Lucrezia* and *Abdolonymus,* both of which are among the earliest works Handel wrote in Italy. Whereas *Abdolonymus* is narrative, *Lucrezia* is a first-person *scena. Abdolonymus* consists of three recitative–aria pairs, in contrast to *Lucrezia*'s flexible and fragmentary sequence. Lucrezia's recitative throughout is imbued with dissonant and disjunct angularity expressive of her wild passion and abandon; minor seconds, augmented fourths, diminished fifths, and diminished sevenths abound in the vocal line and harmony (Ex. 10.1).

A voi, tremende Deità,	To you, fearful gods
Del abisso, mi volgo a voi s'aspetta	Of the abyss, I turn, [and] wait for you
Del tradito onor mio far la vendetta.	To avenge my betrayed honor.

In contrast, Abdolonymus's recitative, comparing the king's calm to that of a sailor amid storms, proceeds in a bland and formulaic setting. A diminished seventh in the voice perhaps describes the dire extremity of the sailor (*nocchier*) in the metaphor, but the storm (*le tempeste*) is depicted by a well-behaved and non-tempestuous, if expressive, cadence (Ex. 10.2).[3]

EXAMPLE 10.1. Handel, *Lucrezia*, second recitative (ending)

EXAMPLE 10.2. Handel, *Abdolonymus*, opening recitative

Lo spirto suo godere	See his spirit find contentment
tra disastri vedete,	amid disasters,
qual che posa nocchier	such as brings calm to the helmsman
fra le tempeste	amid storms.

The arias in *Lucrezia* exhibit continual variation and asymmetry, and even the long vocal melismas are angular and irregular, resisting any tendency to fall into patterns or sequences, as is clear in the settings of *infetti* in the second aria (Ex. 10.3).

Il suol(o) che preme, l'aura che spira	May the ground beneath his feet open up,
L'empio Romano, s'apra, s'infetti.	And the air the evil Roman breathes grow foul!

By comparison, Handel chooses in all three arias of *Abdolonymus* to depict not the king's emotional state, but fortune's wheel, creating each accompani-

EXAMPLE 10.3. Handel, *Lucrezia*, "Il suol che preme"

ment out of different and distinct turning motives. In the first aria, for example, he paints the wheel with two motives: by motion up and down an octave decorated with small melodic turns and by a threefold repetition of a descending four-note pattern (Ex. 10.4). Turning motives occur in the vocal line as well, leading to repetition, regularity, and sequence. Even on words like *tormento*, Handel maintains strict sequential patterning coupled with a circle of fifths motion in the harmony (diametrically opposite to his irregular setting of *infetti* from *Lucrezia*), as shown in Example 10.5.

e non è che tormento   and it is nothing but torment

EXAMPLE 10.4. Handel, *Abdolonymus*, first aria, opening ritornello

EXAMPLE 10.5. Handel, *Abdolonymus*, first aria, B section, mm. 41–44

Lucrezia and *Abdolonymus* clearly illustrate the striking musical differences between the cantatas for women's and men's voices in Handel's cantatas. The underlying reasons for these differences reside in three central and closely related influences: (1) the distinctions in the texts themselves, which, however, can be shown not to be overriding; (2) an earlier musical style largely abandoned at the turn of the eighteenth century; and (3) a tradition of speaking metaphorically in the voice of abandoned and/or dangerous women. Each of these will be discussed in turn.

Cantata texts featuring a historical or mythological woman (Lucrezia, Diana, Armida, Hero, and Agrippina) derive from a long tradition of cataloging and impersonating celebrated women. The classical heritage of this tradition can be traced to Ovid's *Heroides,* a set of poems depicting letters abandoned women might have sent to their beloveds and the first poetic collection written in the imagined voices of women (Fig. 10.1) Ovid's heroines include Hero (writing to Leander), whose voice is heard in one of Handel's cantatas, and women Handel depicted later in his career: Medea (*Teseo*), Ariadne (*Arianna*), and Dejanira (*Hercules*). The list also contains other popular operatic heroines such as Dido and Penelope. Through the writings of Giovanni Boccaccio and others, this tradition of heroic epistles was revived

Figure 10.1. *Ariadne Abandoned by Theseus on Naxos* (1774) by Angelica Kauffmann (1741–1807). The Museum of Fine Arts, Houston; Gift of Mr. and Mrs. Harris Masterson III in memory of Neill Turner Masterson Jr.

in medieval Europe. Boccaccio's catalogue of 104 women reflects Ovid's *Heroides* and previews Handel's cantatas and operas by including Medea, Dejanira, Penelope, Lucrezia, Athaliah, Berenice, Cleopatra, and Agrippina. Boccaccio's path-breaking work gave rise to other, similar works concerning women even as his own book continued to be published in both Latin and the vernacular into the seventeenth century, by which time the voices of abandoned and celebrated women had become inextricably associated with opera.[4]

Women's disruptive effect on men's lives was a repeated and particularly common element in classical stories of abandoned women. Ariadne, deserted by Theseus on the island of Naxos, curses Theseus and asks the gods to make Theseus treat himself and his dearest love with the same carelessness he showed to her; the gods intervene, and Theseus's forgetfulness causes the death of his father. Virgil's Dido, deserted by Aeneas, is more vindictive; she begins her tirade with vile imaginings of killing Ascanius, Aeneas's son, and serving "him up for his father to banquet on," and ends with the curse that is fulfilled—that Aeneas "fall before his time and lie on the sands, unburied."[5]

Seventeenth-century abandoned women follow this classical model up to a point but, then, "with a curious schizophrenia," immediately recant.[6] In Ottavio Rinuccini's 1608 libretto for Monteverdi's *Arianna* (1608), Ariadne calls forth the ocean and the winds to sink Theseus in the abyss, but then cries, "What am I saying, alas, what raving! Unhappy one, ah me, what am I asking for? O Theseus, O my Theseus, it is not I who spoke those wild words; it was my anguish that spoke . . ."[7] In *L'incoronazione di Poppea* (1642), the lament that Busenello gives Octavia concerning Nero's abandonment of her follows the same pattern; she urges Jove to punish her husband Nero with thunderbolts, but then realizes "Ah, but I go too far, and I repent." That is, the seventeenth-century woman was not only depicted, like her classical forebears, as a disruption to others, but she became internally disturbed as well. By the end of the seventeenth century, such "hysteria" was considered an ailment characteristic of the majority of women.[8] The symptoms were typified by "wavering and unsteady" judgment, whereby such women "resolve to do such an Action, a Moment after they alter their Purpose,"[9] and as one leading physician put it, "As to females, if we except those who lead a hard and hardy life, there is rarely one who is wholly free from it [hysteria]."[10]

Handel's abandoned women often voice their curses (and schizophrenia) in language that strikingly parallels the seventeenth-century models. Armida's curse (and recantation) echoes Rinuccini's *Ariadne,* first calling forth the winds and sea monsters, and then recanting: "O you dread monsters of the inconstant and stormy sea, come out from your deepest lairs to avenge me, and be merciless towards that cruel man . . . Ah, no! Stop! O winds, yes, stop, do not engulf him, no!"[11] Agrippina, abandoned and condemned to die by her son Nero, also vacillates between revenge and forgiveness: "Immortal Jupiter, you who from the sky empty the quiver of wrath upon the head of the guilty . . . , avenge these tears . . . ; thunder, immortal Jupiter, and let loose your lightning. May your cruel thunderbolt turn the tyrant to ashes, Jupiter in heaven, if you are just! . . . let my unworthy son die—ah! at that name I still remember that I am a mother, and my fury abates, I cannot say how."[12]

The emotional turmoil of these women distinguishes their texts from those for men and offers an opportunity of a musical setting that is equally distinctive. However, Handel's decision to differentiate men's and women's voices not only results from opportunities presented by the texts but has an important chronological basis as well. That is, from a musico-historical point of view, Handel's cantatas for women adhere to an earlier, seventeenth-century concept of the cantata (and opera) as a recitative monologue (or dramatic recitation) interrupted by lyrical passages. In early opera and cantata, this form was especially favored in women's laments, and Ellen Rosand identifies the locus classicus of this style in Monteverdi's lament for the abandoned Ariadne. As she writes: "The lament is self-contained, but it is not closed: it is not an aria. Arias, being fixed, predetermined musical structures, were inappropriate to the expression of the uncontrolled passion of a lament. . . . In writing their laments, librettists and composers in Venice were clearly responding to the model of *Arianna*. . . . Typically the texts are long . . . [and include] particularly vivid, often violent, imagery. . . . Finally, they all fall *Arianna*-like into multiple sections that mark the vicissitudes typical of a lamenting heroine in extremis."[13]

By the beginning of the eighteenth century, more regular structures replaced the flexible and free forms of the seventeenth century. Textual and musical reform, most often discussed in terms of the development of *opera seria* in the librettos of Apostolo Zeno and Pietro Metastasio, was fundamental to the mission of the Arcadian Academy of Rome as it sought to abolish the excesses of seventeenth-century poetry. This reform affected the cantata as well.

The long, flexible form found in *Lucrezia* (1706) has parallels in the structures of a number of Handel's early works, including *Udite il mio consiglio* (composed 1706?), whose large-scale structure follows the pattern recitative–fugal arioso–aria–recitative–aria–arioso. Cantatas that end in recitative or arioso can mostly be dated to 1707 or before; examples include *Udite il mio consiglio*, *Sarei troppo felice*, *Venne voglia*, and *Vedendo amor*. By 1708, Handel's continuo cantatas generally fall into the strict pattern of two recitative–aria pairs, where the arias are both da capo. Arias in binary and other non-da-capo forms typically date from the earlier period: examples can be found in *Aure soave* (1707), *Menzognere speranze* (1707), and *Irene, idolo mio* (no date). Disjunct motion and nonsequential dissonant harmonies and melodies tend to disappear.

Handel has left clear evidence of his stylistic shift in six cantatas he composed in Italy and revised later in England. His revisions all work toward controlling the violence and exuberance of his earlier compositional style. He eliminates wide leaps, clarifies harmonies, removes redundancies, and generally tightens the formal structure; arioso endings of recitatives are typically replaced and longer cantatas are reduced to the pattern of recitative–aria alternation.[14] A particularly good example exists in *E partirai, mia vita?*, a cantata that depicts the voice of an abandoned lover (without identifying the sex of the singer or the beloved). Handel's first version partakes of the tradition of women's passionate and unstable voices, while the later version depicts the same text more through rational artifice than passionate outburst. For example, he reduces the disjunct motion and overall range of the first recitative (Ex. 10.6a and b). The arioso ending of the second recitative was replaced by a more "sharply declaimed" version (Ex. 10.7a and b).[15] The irregular bass and vocal lines of the second aria are made regular and sequential (Ex. 10.8a and b). With this chronological style shift, as witnessed in the cantatas of Alessandro Scarlatti (1697), Francesco Mancini (1700), and Handel (1707), the seventeenth-century recitative frame that allowed for freer structures and recitative endings was judged to be unformed, incomplete, and unfinished in comparison with the newer aria-dominated, recitative–aria building block. Handel's revisions illustrate his adoption of the newer idiom.

Given Handel's early use and later abandonment of freer formal and stylistic patterns in his continuo cantatas, one could simply conclude that in writing his early cantatas for women the young German composer had not yet caught up with style changes adopted earlier by contemporary Italian composers. Yet such structures occur among the instrumental cantatas only in

EXAMPLE 10.6a. Handel, *E partirai, mia vita?*, opening recitative: original version

EXAMPLE 10.6b. Handel, *E partirai, mia vita?*, opening recitative: revised version

EXAMPLE 10.7a. Handel, *E partirai, mia vita?*, second recitative: original version

EXAMPLE 10.7b. Handel, *E partirai, mia vita?*, second recitative: revised version

those for abandoned women. From the outset, the cantatas for men are more rational and more modern; based on the recitative–aria pair, they include, with the rarest exceptions, only da capo arias. Not only do they all end with aria, but *Tra le fiamme* even builds an aria frame with the repetition of the da capo from the opening aria to end the cantata. Although chronology explains some of these differences—the women's cantatas are by and large earlier than the men's—the overall shift can only be understood by examining both chronology and the use of gendered voices. That is, not just in the composition of cantatas, but in rewriting *E partirai, mia vita?* and in the evolution of his cantata style more generally, Handel largely gave up the passionate voice of an abandoned woman for the more controlled (masculine) voice of reason. Although he clearly makes a distinction in his early cantatas between the fragmented voices of disruptive, lamenting women and the rational controlled voices of men, after 1708 his style shifts away from the

EXAMPLE 10.8a. Handel, *E partirai, mia vita?*, second aria: original version

EXAMPLE 10.8b. Handel, *E partirai, mia vita?*, second aria: revised version

use of the "feminine voice" even in texts, like *E partirai, mia vita?*, that would seem to call for it.

In his book *Abandoned Women and Poetic Tradition*, Lawrence Lipking analyzes the role of the abandoned woman's voice in poetry. He writes, "Almost every great male poet has written at least one poem in the voice of an abandoned woman. . . . Often these crossed-dressed poems have a crucial place . . . in the poet's development." Later he adds, "Again and again men have turned to abandoned women during a stage of poetic self-definition."[16] The history of operatic development in the Baroque offers a parallel example, where over and over again abandoned women provided a voice for composers struggling with the nexus at which music intersects with drama. It is Ariadne's lament that takes Monteverdi from the formal pageantry of *Orfeo* to the passionate expression of *Il ritorno d'Ulisse* and *L'incoronazione di Poppea*, each opera buttressed respectively by the laments of Penelope and Octavia. Nicholas Lanier transferred the Italian achievement of passionate musical expression to England around 1630 in his *Hero and Leander*, a solo lament by Hero that "expresseth passion, hope, fear, and despair, as strong as words and sounds can bear, and saving some pieces by Mr. H. Purcell, wee have nothing of this kind in English at all recommendable."[17] Purcell's own epiphany comes with Dido's lament, his operatic masque *Dido and Aeneas* preceding all his great "dramatic operas," such as *King Arthur* and *The Fairy Queen*. For Handel, too, the adoption of a woman's voice during the early part of his Italian period represented a critical moment in the evolution of his musical style, teaching him how to plumb the depths of passion and extremes of emotion.

The voices of abandoned women do not simply offer a pathway to stylistic self-definition, however. As Lipking further demonstrates, poets often adopt the voice of an abandoned woman to express personal or public loss, since no parallel tradition exists for an "abandoned man."[18] Ovid's Orpheus, perhaps the prototype for male loss, does not wail or curse, nor does he waver; instead, he conceives a plan and acts on it.[19] Orpheus's song for the gods of the Underworld is not an uncontrolled lament, but a carefully conceived artwork with clear purpose. Rather than trying to depict an abandoned man, then, male poets from the time of Ovid have typically put on the mask of a woman in order to lament.

Because music offers less obvious biographical information than words, it is particularly difficult to assess when a composer might be using the voice of a woman as a form of self-expression. In the case of Handel, the difficulty is compounded by the dearth of personal and biographical data to provide a key. However, the individual abandoned woman in music frequently symbolizes a large category of human loss or abandonment, perhaps most obviously in sacred compositions where the soul abandoned by God or Christ is conventionally portrayed with a woman's voice. Understanding the artist's use of the abandoned woman as metaphor offers a way of approaching the artist's own voice.

The texts of Handel's cantatas for abandoned women can be divided into three distinct metaphorical categories. Armida and Agrippina portray the irrationality associated with all women, which is not only dangerous and fear-inspiring, but contagious to men who love women; Lucrezia represents a political metaphor, as when liberty, or the populace generally, is (raped and) abandoned by those in power; and Clori and Hero may represent the metaphor of a soul deserted by God.[20] All three types of abandoned women continue to appear in Handel's later works depicting not just a specific female character but, metaphorically, a more general sense of human loss. Further, in rare instances, Handel moves beyond metaphor by having his male characters speak directly in the voice of an abandoned woman.

Armida and Agrippina are the most obvious viragos among Handel's cantatas. Both reappear almost immediately in his operas: Agrippina as the title character of his opera for Venice (1709) and Armida in his first opera for London, *Rinaldo* (1711). In addition, sorceresses with magical powers, such as Medea (*Teseo*), Melissa (*Amadigi*), and Alcina (*Alcina*), are among Handel's most interesting operatic characters, and strong, dangerous mortal women, including Poppea (*Agrippina*) and Delilah (*Samson*), continue to populate his operas and oratorios as well. Handel's dramatizations of these women are not just structurally related, however; sometimes the women share the same musical voice. The first aria in *Agrippina condotta a morire*, "Orrida, oscura," where Agrippina calls on the heavens to lour with thunder and lightning, for example, is transferred with new text ("Sibillando, ululando") to the sorceress Medea in *Teseo* as she calls forth spirits to torment her rival.

The depiction of magical and mortal viragos serves not only to illustrate a specific character (such as Medea) but to represent the volatility of women and the dangers of loving them. As repeatedly stated in multiple cantata texts, women entrap and torture their prey, and men are urged to flee them. In *Dalla guerra amorosa* (before 1709), where "reason" calls the singer away from the "war of love," the stated danger of loving women is that men in love lose their rational sense (thereby becoming more like women). The idea that by loving women a man is subdued, weakened, and made effeminate (and thus irrational) continues to appear in Handel's later works. Samson provides the most obvious example: by trusting Delilah, he loses his God-given source of masculine strength.

In his opera *Orlando*, Handel musically depicts such "effeminate" love madness in a man by giving Orlando the voice of an abandoned woman. At the opening of *Orlando* (premiered 1733), the magician and mentor Zoroaster shows the valorous knight Orlando the two paths he can follow: that of love or battle. He urges Orlando to purge from his heart all effeminate passions ("Purgalo ormai da effeminati sensi") and follow glory. Nevertheless, Orlando chooses love and becomes a prisoner of his emotions. He strips himself of the outward signs of his masculinity and power by discarding his shield and sword, and, similarly, Handel strips him musically of his masculinity by having him sing like an abandoned woman in free forms that combine recitative and aria fragments. He does not regain control of himself or of his music (by returning to da capo form) until Zoroaster restores his senses, at which time he vows to abandon love and follow valor. Whereas the instrumental cantatas depict the danger posed by irrational, abandoned women, the story of Orlando and Handel's setting of it depicts the danger that by loving a woman too much a man may become irrational and effeminate himself.

In contrast to the viragos, Lucrezia offers an example of a betrayed woman whose situation has political ramifications. Raped by Sextus Tarquinius, son of the Etruscan king of Rome, she commits suicide to expiate the dishonor that her loss of chastity, although not of her doing, has brought upon her family. Her husband and father avenge her honor and her life by overthrowing the Tarquins, thereby ending the tyranny of Etruscan rulers and establishing the Roman Republic. Lucrezia thus represents more than herself: she stands for all of the populace tyrannized and mistreated by the Tarquin kings, and, true to her role as a political metaphor for an oppressed people, she— unlike Armida and Agrippina—never wavers in her condemnation of her betrayer.

Abandonment or endangerment as a result of political circumstance or intrigue in Handel's later works is often depicted by women, as in *Susanna* (1748) and *Esther* (1718), and these women, like their virago cousins, are musically associated with their cantata predecessors. For example, Susanna, under threat of death on false premises, sings "If guiltless blood be your intent," borrowed (Ex. 10.9a and b) from *Lungi n'andò Fileno,* a continuo cantata for an unnamed abandoned woman who says that she is "not permitted to hope except for the tyranny of a cruel death." In some cases, the borrowings indicate the permeable boundaries between categories of abandoned women. Although Agrippina may be a virago, she is also abandoned politically (and ordered killed) by her son Nero. Handel uses her music in *Esther* (transmitted through the Brockes Passion; see below), where Haman, the chief minister of King Ahasuerus of Persia, has ordered the execution of "all the Jewish race." Esther, herself a member of the Israelite community, not only is personally threatened by the edict, but she risks death by approaching the king, her husband, without a summons to plead for her people. Entering the throne room under this double threat of death, she sings "Who calls my parting soul" as she sinks into a faint, the opening motive derived from the beginning of Agrippina's scena, "Come, o Dio" (see Ex. 10.10a and b).

Men rarely take on the voice of political abandonment directly, but, once again, there is at least one clear instance in Handel's works. In *Tamerlano,* the Turkish sultan, Bajazet, has been taken prisoner by Tamerlane, emperor of the Tatars. Finding no way to escape, Bajazet commits suicide, and in an extended *scena* at the end of the opera, the dying sultan alternately comforts his daughter and calls on the Furies to avenge him. His words echo those of Lucrezia, another victim whose death is politically charged:

EXAMPLE 10.9a. Handel, *Lungin'andò Fileno*, "Dunque se il tanto piangere"

EXAMPLE 10.9b. Handel, *Susanna*, "If guiltless blood be your intent"

EXAMPLE 10.10a. Handel, *Agrippina condotta a morire*, "Come, o Dio" (voice and bass only)

EXAMPLE 10.10b. Handel, *Esther*, "Who calls my parting soul" (voice and bass only)

Bajazet: *Io sarò la maggior furia d'averno.*

I will be the greatest fury in hell.

Lucrezia: *Nell'inferno farò la mia vendetta.*

I will wreak my vengeance in the Underworld.[21]

The musical relation of Bajazet's suicide scene to the musical topos of feminine instability is highlighted by Handel's borrowing from it the accompanied recitative at the climax of the scene, "Si, figlia, io moro" for the feigned mad scene of the heroine Rosmene, "Ahi! che mancar mi sento" in his penultimate opera *Imeneo*.[22]

Finally, the cantatas of Clori (*Delirio amoroso*) and Hero (*Ero e Leandro*) seem to hint at the idea of the holy spirit or soul as an abandoned woman. That these are the only two cantatas about abandoned women that derive from the houses of cardinals (Clori was written by Cardinal Pamphili and composed for him; Hero was possibly written by Cardinal Ottoboni and composed for him) may therefore be significant. Clori, distraught over the death of her beloved Tirsi, descends into the Underworld to find him, but he does not welcome her there. She thereupon determines to transport them both to blessed Elysium (heaven), where they can live united. Hero, distraught over the death of Leander, unites herself with him in death. In each case there is a possible religious metaphor. In *Deliro amoroso* the holy spirit or soul (Clori), separated from Christ, descends into hell (where they cannot live united), and rises into heaven to be joined with him. The image of the soul seeking Christ can be viewed as a reversal of the typical metaphor of Christ pursuing a reluctant soul, but it adheres to the common portrayal of the soul thinking (incorrectly in Christian theology) it has been abandoned. Whether an abandoned lover or a metaphor for an abandoned soul, Clori is delusional; she thinks she is descending into hell, believes she is rejected, but longs to be united with her beloved/Christ in heaven. In *Ero e Leandro* the soul/woman (Hero) seeks to become the bride of Christ (and she tears out her hair as a symbol of the earthly pleasures she is abandoning). In a religious reading, the suicide of Hero cannot, of course, be understood literally, but Hero's language is not wholly distinct from such religious texts as the *Salve regina,* which Handel also set in 1707, in which the soul exclaims: "To thee do we cry, poor banished children of Eve, to thee do we send up our sighs, mourning and weeping in this vale of tears, . . . and after this our exile [life on earth] show unto us the blessed fruit of thy womb, Jesus [in life after death]."

Certainly the language of the lost soul and the abandoned lover are closely parallel. The first aria text in Handel's cantata *Figli del mesto cor* reads:

Son pur le lacrime	Tears are still
Il cibo misero	The wretched food
Ch'io prendo ognor.	That I always take.
Sempre tra gemiti	Always groaning,
Non spiro altr'aere	I breathe no other air
Che del dolor.	Than that of sorrow.

Psalm 42, the text that Handel chose to set both for his first Chapel Royal Anthem (1714) and his first Chandos Anthem (1716), begins in the Chandos version:

> As pants the hart for cooling streams
> So longs my soul for thee, O God.
> Tears are my dayly food:
> While thus they say, where is now thy God?[23]

Musical as well as textual parallels exist between the cantatas and the Chandos Anthems. In *The Lord is my light* (Chandos Anthem 10) the setting of "They are brought down and fall'n" is modeled on Lucrezia's "Alla salma," and the musical setting of Armida's directions to the winds, "Venti, fermate," is used to set the text "It is the Lord that ruleth the sea."

The Brockes Passion (1715?) offers the prime example of a man taking on the voice of an abandoned soul. After Jesus is betrayed by Judas and taken away, the crowd flees for its life, but the apostle Peter remains alone and asks to be taken with Jesus (and not abandoned). His aria "Nehmt mich mit, verzagte Scharen," borrows its musical incipit from the aria of Clori in *Delirio amoroso*, "Lascia omai le brune vele," as she imagines sailing with her lover (Christ?) to Elysium Fields. After Peter denies Jesus three times, his distress deepens. "Heul, du Fluch!," in which he berates himself (and declares that he should weep blood rather than tears of water), is based on the 1712 version of "Tears are my daily food" from *As Pants the Hart*, and "Schau ich fall in strenger Busse," which refers to the Prince of Night laughing at his fall, on Lucrezia's first aria, "Già superbo del mio affanno."

In sum, Handel's instrumental cantatas for women's voices hold a special, and somewhat complex, place in his compositional practice. First, their passionate expression reflects a long literary tradition depicting women in extreme situations, and their irregular structure can sometimes be attributed to the texts themselves. However (and secondly), the overall musical traits associated with women's voices also represent an early style both historically and within Handel's own composition; that is, as his own revisions of *E partirai, mia vita?* illustrate, the texts themselves do not govern absolutely the instability of the setting no matter how strongly they might suggest it. Finally, the voices of abandoned women do not disappear from Handel's music altogether but continue to resonate metaphorically in depictions of human loss, for Handel often returns to the voices of his early cantata women to portray political or spiritual suffering.

The question may still be asked whether this extraordinary set of cantatas for abandoned women had any personal resonance for Handel. That is, if his male characters Orlando, Bajazet, and Peter speak with the voices of women, does he? Although it is easy to imagine that Handel, as a bachelor, German expatriate, and devout Lutheran in Catholic Italy, not only experienced but could have expressed a sense of emotional, political, or spiritual abandonment, it is not possible to make specific, biographical connections between his life and the voicing of such feelings. However, Handel's developing compositional voice can surely be heard in his cantatas for women, providing an example of the special connection advanced by Lipking between young poets' development of style and their use of abandoned women's voices wherein "the art of the exercise consists of knowing which rules to break."[24] Handel exercised this impassioned and unrestrained voice for the first time in Italy (his Hamburg opera *Almira* [1704] betrays barely a glimpse of it), but also in Italy, especially under the influence of leading members of the Arcadian Academy of Rome, he had to learn to control this feminized voice with rational (masculine) principles of style and structure. Like Orlando, he had to master the woman's voice within. Handel's Italian cantatas for Lucrezia, Clori, Diana, Armida, Hero, and Agrippina offered the young composer an opportunity to push the boundaries of standard practice early in his career and provided a resonant resource for dramatic writing throughout his life. Handel found the breadth and depth of his own expressive voice by trying on the voices of abandoned women.

NOTES

This essay is adapted and condensed from "Women's Voices / Men's Voices" in *Handel as Orpheus: Voice and Desire in the Chamber Cantatas*. It is revised and reprinted by permission of the publishers, Harvard University Press, Copyright © 2001 by the President and Fellows of Harvard College.

1. I am including in this tally the cantata O numi eterni for Lucrezia, the Roman noblewomen raped by the son of the Etruscan king of Rome. Although primarily for voice and continuo, the cantata includes a section with an additional instrumental part marked *si suona* ("one plays"). It is also the only continuo cantata with a named historical character similar to those in the instrumental cantatas from the same period.

2. This arietta may have been at some point added or deleted, but its origin as part of the Diana cantata seems clear. For a different view, see Handel, *Kantaten mit Instrumenten* I–III, ed. Hans-Joachim Marx (*Hallische Händel-Ausgabe*, series 5, vols. 3–5; Kassel: Bärenreiter, 1994, 1995, 1999), 1:xvii, who nevertheless provides manuscript information that ties the single sheet of the arietta to the cantata as a whole (III, 142).

3. Translations of *Abdolonymus* ("Figlio d'alte speranze") by Terence Best from Marx, *Kantaten mit Instrumenten,* II, xli.

4. Giovanni Boccaccio, *Concerning Famous Women,* trans. Guido A. Guarino (New Brunswick, N.J.: Rutgers University Press, 1963); Wendy Heller, "Chastity, Heroism, and Allure: Women in Opera of Seventeenth-Century Venice" (Ph.D. diss., Brandeis University, 1995), 18.

5. The story of Ariadne appears in Catullus, *Carmina,* ed. and trans. Guy Lee (Oxford: Oxford University Press, 1990), ll. 192–250, 90–95; Dido's story appears in Virgil, *Aeneid,* trans. C. Day Lewis (New York: Doubleday, 1953), bk. 4, ll. 591–629, pp. 99–100.

6. Heller, "Chastity, Heroism, and Allure," 140.

7. As quoted and translated ibid.

8. David Hurley, "Dejanira and the Physicians: Aspects of Hysteria in Handel's *Hercules,*" *Musical Quarterly* 80 (1996): 548–61.

9. Nicholas Robinson, *A New System of the Spleen, Vapours, and Hypochondriack Melancholy* (1729), as quoted in Hurley, "Dejanira and the Physicians," 551.

10. *The Works of Thomas Sydenham, M.D.,* trans. from Latin by R. G. Latham (London: Sydenham Society, 1848–50), 2:85, as quoted in Hurley, "Dejanira and the Physicians," 550.

11. As translated by Best in Marx, *Kantaten mit Instrumenten,* II, xxxiii, with slight alteration.

12. Ibid., xxxv.

13. Ellen Rosand, *Opera in Seventeenth-Century Venice: The Creation of a Genre* (Berkeley: University of California Press, 1991), 363–64.

14. The revisions have been discussed by John Mayo, "Handel's Italian Cantatas" (Ph.D. diss., University of Toronto, 1977), chap. 3, "Alternative versions and revisions," 145–94, and "Einige Kantatenrevisionen Händels," *Handel Jahrbuch* 27 (1981): 63–77. *E partirai, mia vita?* is discussed by Mayo in "Italian Cantatas," 151–55.

15. Mayo, "Italian Cantatas," 153.

16. Lawrence Lipking, *Abandoned Women and Poetic Tradition* (Chicago: University of Chicago Press, 1988), xx and 128.

17. Roger North as quoted in Ian Spink, *English Song: Dowland to Purcell* (London: B. T. Batsford Ltd., 1986), 103.

18. Lipking, *Abandoned Women,* xviii, writes: "The stereotype is so firmly established, in fact, that an abandoned man may begin to feel his sexual identity waver. Some cultures exclude the possibility of male abandonment."

19. In some, especially musical versions of the story, Orpheus is allowed to lament. However, as Susan McClary writes in her discussion of Monteverdi's Orfeo, the lamenting Orpheus becomes a feminized hero. She notes that the "mistake" of depicting a lamenting man was "rarely repeated" in the history of opera and associates some coolness in the reception of *Orfeo* with this problem (*Feminine Endings: Music, Gender, and Sexuality* [Minneapolis: University of Minnesota Press, 1991], 46–48).

20. My categorization is indebted to Lipking, *Abandoned Women,* chap. 1: "Ariadne at the Wedding: Abandoned Women and Poetic Tradition," 1–31.

21. The sentiment is not rare in Handel's works, but frequently occurs in similar circumstances; examples include Cleopatra (*Giulio Cesare*) after she is taken prisoner by her brother ("Piangerò") and Ariodante (*Ariodante*) after Polinesso has convinced him (falsely) that his beloved Ginevra is untrue ("Scherza infida"). In both these cases, however, the danger passes. Lucrezia and Bajazet are uniquely related in that both are suicides.

22. Handel alters the vocal line where necessary to accommodate the different text; Roger L. Lustig, "An Unusual Handelian Self-Borrowing and Handel's Dramatic Designs" (unpublished typescript).

23. See Graydon Beeks, "'A Club of Composers': Handel, Pepusch and Arbuthnot at Cannons," in *Handel Tercentenary Collection,* ed. Stanley Sadie and Anthony Hicks (Ann Arbor: UMI Research Press, 1987), 215–17.

24. Lipking, *Abandoned Women,* 25.

PART FIVE

Gendered Voices and Performance

How you please me, oh strange timbre!
Double sound, man and woman in one,
Contralto, bizarre mélange,
Hermaphrodite of the voice!

THÉOPHILE GAUTIER,
Contralto

ENDER IS TRADITIONALLY PRESENTED as a cultural and social construction of sexual difference. It has been commonly defined, like sex, its biological counterpart, as a binary division between male and female. While this dichotomous viewpoint may seem obvious to us, an exploration of diverse societies throughout the world and throughout history has demonstrated that gender is not a fixed entity. It is instead a fluid phenomenon that can change over time, conveying different meanings in different historical and cultural milieus.

Musical performance has played an important role in reflecting and constructing gender roles in societies around the world. Ethnomusicologists, using anthropological models, have examined the significance of performance traditions as part of the process of socialization. Music performed in rituals and ceremonies, in particular, helps bring a community together by supporting common beliefs and values. One way it does this is by providing models of social behavior.

In cultures that promote a binary opposition of male/female, musical performance can encourage the inculcation of gender identities. This may occur when a distinction is made between men and women in performance styles, musical repertories, or the playing of specific musical instruments. Contrasting singing styles by men and adolescent girls in the Brush Dance ceremony of the Yurok, Hupa, and Karok Indians of northwestern California, for example, mirror the marked polarity between male and female role models.[1] In the rural communities of Slavonic countries, certain vocal forms, such as lullabies, laments, and wedding and harvest songs are identified closely with women.[2] Among the gypsies who perform at wedding ceremonies in rural Turkey, the playing of musical instruments is gender-specific, with women accompanying themselves only with a frame drum or *delbek* and men playing the double-skin drum called the *davul* and the *zurna* or shawm.[3] And in the traditional music of Sweden, fiddle playing is associated with men, while women, who, in rural areas, are in charge of cattle-herding, blow animal horns and lurs (long trumpets made of wood and birch bark).[4]

In recent years, feminist scholars have called into question the rigorous binary opposition that has defined gender in Western society. They have noted that gender is not classified on the basis of biological factors, but is instead a product of social behavior and perception, which Teresa de Lauretis characterizes as "both a sociocultural construct and a semiotic apparatus, a system of representation which assigns meaning . . . to individuals within the society."[5] While de Lauretis stresses gender as representational, Judith Butler emphasizes its "performative" nature, whereby gender is created through performances of behavior and dress that can either reflect the binary organization of male/female or subvert it.[6]

Music, theater, and dance can inflect performativity by providing, as Laurence Senelick notes, "the most direct, most graphic, often the most compelling representations of gender."[7] We have already observed how musical performance in rituals and ceremonies can uphold traditional gender divisions. At the same time, it can undo the dialectical strictures of gender by means of on-stage cross-dressing and multi-role performance.

Stage transvestism is a phenomenon that occurs in musical theater of many cultures. The most common form, male cross-dressing, ostensibly came about because of the prohibitions against women appearing on the public stage. We have already come across the *onnagata* and *dan* roles of Japanese kabuki and Beijing opera. Western counterparts of these travesty roles can be traced as far back as ancient Greek drama.[8] In the Renaissance, boy actors and singers played female characters in Elizabethan theater.[9] With the advent of opera in the early seventeenth century, castrati, who first sang in church choirs, were called upon to perform both male and female roles (particularly in Rome, where the Church upheld the proscription of women performing in operas until 1798).[10]

Not long after women finally made it onto the public stage as singers, they also appeared *en travesti*, when, in 1639, opera went public in Venice. These cross-dressed roles generally occurred in situations where female characters would disguise themselves as males—a plot device derived from earlier *commedia dell'arte* scenarios (and known to us through Shakespeare plays).[11] Female cross-dressing has continued in opera up into the twentieth century, with divas playing women disguised as men, who look for or save their be-loved (as in Handel's *Serse* or Beethoven's rescue opera, *Fidelio*) or in trouser parts, as they are commonly called, where the female singer actually assumes a true male identity such as the adolescent pages, Cherubino in Mozart's *Nozze di Figaro* and Oktavian in Richard Strauss's *Der Rosenkavalier*. Female mezzo-sopranos and contraltos have also sung heroic roles originally in-tended for castrati, such as Pauline Viardot's famous mid-nineteenth-century portrayal of Gluck's Orpheus or, closer to our own time, Janet Baker's interpretation of Handel's Julius Caesar. Finally, there are heroic male roles, such as Rossini's Tancredi, that, as Heather Hadlock elucidates in her essay below, were composed explicitly for women singers during the early nineteenth century—a transitional period when the operatic castrato voice was near extinction.

The three studies in this section illustrate the various ways in which gender roles and identities occur in performance. Jane Sugarman looks at traditional gendered discourse in the wedding songs of Prespa Albanians. Contrasting singing styles, song texts, and vocal timbres, as she argues, not only serve as vehicles in which to represent gender differences, they also play a crucial role in shaping the community's accepted concepts about masculinity and femininity. With Heather Hadlock's essay on the *musico*s, we shift to the gender ambiguities of cross-dressed performance on the operatic stage. Here, Hadlock reveals how male heroic roles for female singers *en travesti* altered dramatically during the first half of the nineteenth century as the taste of the time changed.

In the final essay, Tomie Hahn moves even further afield by considering the transformation of a single female performer of traditional Japanese dance into multiple characters. With only a fan and the kimono she wears to use as her props, the dancer must depict each persona with great clarity in order to convey the narrative. Hahn argues that shifting or codeswitching between characters in dance "metaphorically mirrors a social coordination of self present in daily life in Japan, where clear delineations between men and women, various social circles, and the young and old are reflected in encultu-rated behavior and speech." In a sense, we have come full circle in our discus-sion of gendered voices, for *nihon buyo*, which presents gender ambiguities that are meant to subvert social order, paradoxically embraces traditional gender roles imbued by Japanese society.

NOTES
〜

1.   Richard Keeling, "Contrast of Song Performance Style as a Function of Sex Role Polarity in the Hupa Brush Dance," *Ethnomusicology* (1985): 185–212.

2. Anna Czekanowska, "Towards a Concept of Slavonic Women's Repertoire," in *Music, Gender, and Culture,* ed. Marcia Herndon and Susanne Ziegler (Wilhelmshaven: Florian Noetzel, 1990), 57–70.

3. Susanne Ziegler, "Gender-Specific Traditional Wedding Music in Southwestern Turkey," in *Music, Gender, and Culture,* 91–92.

4. Anna Johnson, "The Sprite in the Water and the Siren of the Woods: On Swedish Folk Music and Gender," in *Music, Gender, and Culture,* 34–37.

5. *Technologies of Gender: Essays on Theory, Film and Fiction* (Bloomington: Indiana University Press, 1987), 2–3.

6. *Gender Trouble: Feminism and the Subversion of Identity* (New York and London: Routledge, 1990) and *Bodies that Matter: On the Discursive Limits of "Sex"* (New York and London: Routledge, 1993).

7. *The Changing Room: Sex, Drag and Theatre* (London and New York: Routledge, 2000), 6.

8. Froma I. Zeitlin, "Playing the Other: Theater, Theatricality, and the Feminine in Greek Drama," *Representations* 11 (1985): 63–94.

9. There is a large number of recent works on this topic. See, for example, Stephen Orgel, *Impersonations: The Performance of Gender in Shakespeare's England* (Cambridge and New York: Cambridge University Press, 1996); Peter Stallybrass, "Transvestism and the 'Body Beneath': Speculating on the Boy Actor," in *Erotic Politics: Desire on the Renaissance Stage,* ed. Susan Zimmerman (New York and London: Routledge, 1992); and Marjorie Garber, *Vested Interests: Cross-Dressing and Cultural Anxiety* (New York and London: Routledge, 1992). On boy singers in Elizabethan dramas see Linda Phyllis Austern, "'No Women Are Indeed': The Boy Actor as Vocal Seductress in Late Sixteenth- and Early Seventeenth-Century English Drama," in *Embodied Voices: Representing Female Vocality in Western Culture,* ed. Leslie C. Dunn and Nancy A. Jones (Cambridge: Cambridge University Press, 1994), 83–102.

10. On the castrati see Angus Heriot, *The Castrati in Opera* (London: Calder and Boyars, 1975); John Rosselli, *Singers of Italian Opera: The History of a Profession* (Cambridge: Cambridge University Press, 1992), 32–55; Joke Dame, "Unveiled Voices: Sexual Difference and the Castrato," in *Queering the Pitch: The New Gay and Lesbian Musicology,* ed. Philip Brett, Elizabeth Wood, and Gary C. Thomas (New York: Routledge, 1994). On the castrato as portrayed in the film *Farinelli,* see Katherine Bergeron, "The Castrato as History," *Cambridge Opera Journal* 8 (1996): 167–84; Ellen Harris, "Twentieth-Century Farinelli," *Musical Quarterly* 81 (1997): 180–89; and Felicia Miller, "Farinelli's Electronic Hermaphrodite and the Contralto Tradition," in *The Work of Opera: Genre, Nationhood, and Sexual Difference,* ed. Richard Dellamora and Daniel Fischlin (New York: Columbia University Press, 1997), 73–92.

11. On gender ambiguities in seventeenth-century Venetian opera see Susan McClary, "Gender Ambiguities and Erotic Excess in Seventeenth-Century Venetian Opera," in *Acting on the Past: Historical Performance across the Disciplines,* ed. Mark Franko and Annette Richards (Hanover, N.H.: Wesleyan University Press, 2000), 177–200, and Wendy Heller, "The Queen as King: Refashioning Semiramide for *Seicento* Venice," *Cambridge Opera Journal* 5 (1993): 93–114; in early eighteenth-century Neapolitan opera see Nina Treadwell, "Female Operatic Cross-Dressing: Bernardo Saddumene's Libretto for Leonardo Vinci's *Li zite 'n galera* (1722)," *Cambridge Opera Journal,* 10 (1998): 131–56.

CHAPTER ELEVEN

The Nightingale and the Partridge

SINGING AND GENDER AMONG PRESPA ALBANIANS

Jane C. Sugarman

"I'm going to capture you, my fair one,
I'm going to capture you this summer:
I won't leave you uncaptured!"

"I'll turn myself into a moon, and I'll hide in the sky:
O bey,[1] you'll never capture me."

"I'll turn myself into a sun, and I'll come after you:
I won't leave you uncaptured!" . . .

"I'll turn myself into a partridge and I'll fly away:
O bey, you'll never capture me."

"I'll turn myself into a nightingale, and I'll come after you:
I won't leave you uncaptured!"

SONG SUNG BY BRIDE'S RELATIVES,
PRESPA, 1981

THE WEDDING SONGS of Albanian women from the Lake Prespa district of Macedonia often portray young men and women as birds. The young man as suitor is most often depicted as a nightingale (*bilbil*), a bird known for its rapturous singing. A young woman, however, is depicted as a partridge (*fëllënxë*) or turtledove (*guguçe*), birds that are thought of as beautiful, vulnerable, and quiet in demeanor and song. By combining attributes of physical appearance, bodily demeanor, and singing style in a single image, the women's songs present these features as inextricably related. And by associating them with creatures of nature, the songs imply that such attributes are as natural for young men and women as they are for birds.[2]

Concepts concerning gender have been instrumental in structuring virtually every facet of the daily lives of Presparë, as Prespa Albanians call themselves, and they have had a pervasive effect in shaping Prespa expressive forms. Gender-related notions can clearly be "heard" in the structure of Prespa singing, which is premised upon gender segregation. They can also be heard in the polarized vocal timbres and singing styles of women and men and in the contrasting themes of their song texts. The sound of Prespa singing, however, is merely the aural component of a broader community-held approach to self-presentation and social interaction, which encompasses both physical demeanor and the emotional atmosphere that is encouraged at social gatherings. In this study, I will thus analyze Prespa singing as both a visual and aural embodiment of aspects of the community's conceptualization of gender.

Specific beliefs and attitudes regarding gender form an inextricable component of a community's notions of social order. For individuals within a community, the internal consistency and logic underlying those notions may be so pervasive that concepts regarding gender may appear to be utterly natural and unquestionable. Many Presparë, particular those of older generations, do indeed regard the differences that they perceive between women and men as natural phenomena, and they extend this attitude toward the complex of features that distinguishes women's and men's singing. For them, the activity of singing encapsulates gender distinctions in an all-encompassing and abstract way to which they respond intuitively rather than analytically. My first aim in this essay is to explicate the logic through which singing is able to serve Presparë as such an apt vehicle for the representation of gender difference. Secondly, I wish to emphasize that singing, rather than merely reflecting notions of gender, also shapes those notions in return. Singing provides Presparë with a means of tangibly living out their strongly contrasting notions of femininity and masculinity. Through singing they are temporarily able to mold their individual selves into the form of a community ideal. In the process they may choose to affirm that ideal, by following closely the norms of musical practice, or they may use their singing to suggest its revision. In short, gender concepts and musical practice may be seen to exist in a dialectical relationship to each other.

GENDER AND THE PRESPA SOCIAL ORDER

∼

Albanians from the eastern shore of Lake Prespa form one of three communities of south Albanians hailing from the southernmost districts of Macedonia.[3] Due to large-scale emigration since the 1950s, today the majority of families live outside Prespa, in towns in Macedonia and elsewhere in the former Yugoslavia, as well as in Western Europe, North America, Australia, and Turkey. My comments here refer primarily to Prespa families living in Canada and the United States, but the features that I analyze are also characteristic of communities in other locales.

Presparë place an emphasis on patrilineal descent and, as a consequence, regard male and female children differently from the moment of their birth. The birth of a son signals the continuity of the household and is cause for a large celebration. He is hailed as "the foundation of the house" (*temeli i shtëpisë*), and family members begin looking ahead to his wedding and speaking to him about it before he can talk: telling him what a nice bride they will find for him, or promising him that the best Rom (or Gypsy) band will play for his wedding. A daughter, however, is considered to be the family's "doorway to the world" (*dera e botës*), for she is expected to leave the household at marriage, thus establishing ties of kinship and obligation to heretofore unrelated families.

Until the period of massive emigration began, the experiences of young women at marriage were highly predictable. A woman entered her husband's household on the basis of a marriage contracted by the couple's parents and other relatives, and lived with him, his parents, and his brothers and their families. She was considered to be subordinated first to her husband's father, then to her mother-in-law, and then to her husband and his brothers. Her principal duty was to bear children, particularly sons, and secondarily to add to the family's workforce. Her virginity at marriage was insisted upon, as was her chaste behavior as a married woman, in order to insure that her offspring were genuine heirs. As Juliet du Boulay has remarked of Greek brides, she was expected to "bring to her marriage a chastity that reaches far beyond sexual fidelity and involves, without exception, all areas of her behavior."[4] Any breach of the code of conduct stipulated for her had the potential of dishonoring her household, and thus her behavior had to be beyond reproach. In particular, it was her responsibility to avoid any intimate contact with men outside her household and to suppress any hint of sexuality in her demeanor. The type of conduct stipulated for her during her reproductive years was far stricter than that expected of males.

In general, work activities within the village were segregated by gender. Women performed most of the chores centered around the house, while men performed most of the fieldwork, cared for livestock, went to market, and conducted business transactions. The women's domestic sphere was thus included within that of the men, who were held responsible for the welfare of their household in all interfamilial matters. This responsibility was ascribed to men primarily because they were perceived as being physically stronger by nature than women. They were also regarded as having greater social savvy because of their activities within the public sphere, and their esteem within the community increased as they gained in experience. While perceived by men as lacking in knowledge of broader societal affairs, adult women were nevertheless in charge of domestic matters, and here too esteem increased together with experience. As a woman bore children and took a greater part in the management of the household, she established her legitimacy within the family and was no longer viewed as an outsider.

In the past few decades the daily life of Presparë has undergone dramatic changes. Many of the adults in North America emigrated as young couples, leaving their parents behind. Now many women work outside the home, in factory or service jobs. As a result of these processes, women have often taken on the role of partner with their husband in decisions regarding the household. Likewise, although most young Presparë still marry within the community, they are now given more of a say in the choice of a marriage partner. Nevertheless, many younger Presparë retain attitudes toward gender relations and concepts of social ordering that developed among prior generations.

Within the realm of interfamilial relations Presparë maintain an egalitarian stance between households, with the oldest male of each household serving as its symbolic head. Recognized categories of social differentiation are limited to those that distinguish personnel within each household. A boy is regarded as a *djalë* until he marries, when he becomes a "man" (*burrë*). When his children begin to marry, he becomes a male elder, or *plak*. Likewise, a girl is a *çupë* until she marries and leaves the family home. She remains a "bride" (*nuse*) until her children begin to marry, when she becomes a female elder, or *plakë*.

Within this schema, young married adults are seen as the generation responsible for producing children. Sexual activity is expected of them, but only as a means of procreation; sexuality in any other context is dangerous and not to be alluded to in any public situation. Once a couple's children have married, however, they are viewed as having passed on reproductive responsibilities to their children, and they are no longer regarded as sexual beings. One way in which their perceived loss of sexuality and fertility is marked, especially for women, is by a change in dress: from bright, open colors such as white, red, or royal blue to subdued, "closed" ones such as navy blue or dark brown. In any social situation, an individual is expected to dress and to behave in a manner consistent with his or her social category. Considerations of gender are thus always mitigated by age and marital status.

Views regarding gendered social roles serve as the basis for patterns of

deference that are still observed between household members and, by extension, between any persons of different social categories. Between generations
all children are expected to defer to all adults, and all younger adults to all
elders. At a social gathering such deference may involve, for example, greeting elders before other adults, kissing their hands, giving them preferential
seating, and allowing them to direct the course of the conversation. Women
are expected to defer in similar ways to men of their generation or older.

Attitudes toward gender roles and the nature of gendered identity also
continue to shape matters of personal demeanor. Male qualities of strength
and social "intelligence" are seen as giving boys a charter for unrestricted
behavior.[5] Young boys have the run of the village or neighborhood, and
teenage "bachelors" (*beqarë*) are expected to do their share of adventur-
ing—an attitude that prompted many young men of the last generation to
travel overseas in search of work. Upon marriage, young men often behave
in a reserved manner in public, still very conscious of the need to defer to
their parents. Away from the older generation, however, they cultivate a certain male bravado, accompanied by such marks of masculinity as smoking
and drinking. As the years pass and they come into their own socially, men
may choose to present themselves in social situations in a particularly lively
manner, characterized by large physical movements, frequent hand gestures,
and equally frequent verbal exclamations that inject emotion and energy into
their speech. Once they become elders, however, many men retire into a state
of dignity and tranquility. It is as if, having expended their energies to the
fullest in their younger years, they no longer feel the need to do so as they
approach old age.

In contrast, a girl's behavior is carefully monitored once she approaches
puberty, in order to safeguard her virginity. Some families have restricted a
daughter's activities as much as possible to the immediate environs of her
home, and have not allowed her to venture anywhere alone. In the company
of nonrelatives, a teenage girl is expected to behave in such a way as to exhibit
her modesty, obedience, and self-control, qualities that others consider when
choosing a bride for their sons. Such behavioral expectations reach their peak
at the point that she marries. On her wedding day, a bride is expected to
adopt a stereotypic stance: almost unmoving, eyes cast to the ground. She is
said to adopt this posture out of *turp,* a word that may be translated as both
"shame" and "modesty."[6] Through this stance she projects her beauty while
masking her sexuality; she also conveys her modesty and propriety, her capacity for self-control, and her deference to both her natal family and her
new in-laws. In the past a new bride was expected to retain a slightly relaxed
version of this stance, and to behave in a particularly subdued and self-
conscious manner, upon first entering her husband's home:

> Before, a bride was very ashamed to speak: just enough to rush the
> words out of her mouth. She was embarrassed to speak and to sing.
> . . . When she sat down to eat, they would give her meat to eat and she
> wouldn't eat it . . . She would be embarrassed, so they would take the
> meat and the elders would eat it. . . . For her first week as a bride she
> kept her eyes closed. Afterwards, during her first year as a bride she
> was expected to remain . . . very quiet, not to speak much, not to move
> much, not to laugh. . . . (Interview in Chicago with a woman and her
> daughter-in-law, 1986)

Today a bride may behave in a considerably more relaxed manner in her
first years of marriage. In informal situations she no longer needs to feel
hesitant to speak out freely nor to act in a more animated fashion. But she
must still maintain an air of propriety throughout her reproductive years. It
is only when her children have married that a woman can with confidence
act in an outspoken and even boisterous fashion, although not all older
women choose to do so. In essence, her loss of fertility has freed her of the
need to be ever mindful of her demeanor.

AN OVERVIEW OF WEDDINGS AND SINGING

For those families still wishing to observe a "traditional" wedding, whether
in Prespa or abroad, intensive activities begin roughly a week before the
taking of the bride by the groom's family, with relatives and friends gathering
in the evenings at both the bride's and groom's homes. Unless the number
of persons attending is very small, all gatherings are segregated by gender.
Throughout this time, rituals addressing wedding themes are carried out,
primarily by the women of both families. Early in the week henna is sent
from the groom to be put on the bride's hair, as a first step in her transformation from girl to woman. Later, gifts of clothing and other accessories for the
bride, including her wedding attire, are packed and delivered to her home.
There they are unpacked and displayed for all to see, and the bride spends
several evenings modeling the more elaborate outfits for her female relatives.
On the wedding day the groom bathes himself and is then shaved by an older
relative as a sign of his coming of age. There is then a procession to fetch the
bride and bring her to the groom's home, where rituals incorporating her
into the household, and assuring her compliance and fertility, are performed.
In Prespa villages, an elaborate ceremony was formerly observed surrounding
the moment when the groom and bride were "closed in" to their bedroom

in order to consummate the marriage. Today, regardless of locale, it is more common for a gala dinner and dance to be held in a banquet hall.

Ritual observance, however, accounts for only a small portion of the wedding celebration. In the evenings, the men in particular assemble for gatherings that are structured so as to address larger community concerns such as the nurturing of sociability and intimacy between individuals and the expression of reciprocal obligations between families.[7] At all gatherings, regardless of whether they are structured around ritual or social concerns, singing is the major form of communication and interaction.

The songs sung during the various stages of the wedding celebration are called *këngë me të rënkuar* ("songs with droning"). All are based on pentatonic tonal formations and have a standard three-voiced structure in which two soloists sing over a choral drone. It is the first soloist who is considered to be the "singer" of the song; the second soloist, generally a more accomplished singer, is seen as providing support for the first. The soloists divide each line of text between them, so that neither sings it in full. Everyone else present of the same gender as the soloists drones on the vowel-sound *e* (see Examples 11.1–11.3 below).

The differences in the ways that Prespa women and men realize this structure must be understood within the framework of a set of commonly recognized axioms that specify the role of singing at an event such as a wedding. The first is that singing is a special type of behavior associated exclusively with social occasions. The innate gregariousness of Prespa singing is apparent in its polyphonic structure: each song requires at least three people for its performance. Presparë view singing, not as an extension of everyday behavior, but rather as a form of interaction that is meant to contrast with everyday behavior and—in that contrast—to bring to the fore communal concerns and values that are underplayed in everyday situations. Although broadly participatory, singing is also clearly regarded as a "performance," in that all individuals are aware that not only the sound of their singing, but every aspect of their behavior as they sing is subject to scrutiny and comment. Through singing, Presparë set aside the topical and individualistic concerns associated with speech in order to focus on themes of enduring importance to the group. Likewise, individualistic stylistic elements are expected to be subordinated to a manner of performance that exemplifies the ideal for one's gender and generation.

Secondly, singing is a social obligation. As a full-fledged member of the community, each adult guest is expected to "sing"—in the sense of performing the first solo line of a song—at least once during the course of any gathering as a gesture of respect and good will toward the host family. At a wedding, close relatives of the bride or groom have an additional obligation to participate in the singing associated with specific ritual moments. Above all other factors, it is this sense of singing as social duty that has sustained polyphonic singing among the current generations of Presparë. Although individuals learn to sing as children, they are only obligated to sing at social occasions once they have married and become adults. The performance styles associated with males and females may therefore be seen as embodying ideals of adult behavior.[8]

Lastly, singing is an expressly emotional form of communication. The greatest compliment that can be paid a song performance is that the singer has sung "with all his/her heart" (*me gjith zembër*). In general terms, to execute an action *me gjith zembër* means to do it sincerely, with unqualified good will. When used to describe singing it indicates, above all else, that the singer has been able to set aside feelings of self-consciousness and become so fully involved in the performance that it comes across as spontaneous and heartfelt. Presparë may explain a singer's lack of self-consciousness in two very different ways. On the one hand, they may feel that the singer was transported by the occasion into a state of heightened emotion. On the other hand, the intensity of the performance might be attributed to the experience and skill of the singer, who is able to perform confidently in any situation. In the first instance, then, Presparë view the performance as indicating the true feelings of the singer, whereas in the second, they view it as the artful embodiment of sentiment. In both cases the effect is the same: singing that conveys feeling evokes an emotional response in those listening and draws their attention to the emotional richness of the moment.

Regardless of a singer's gender, certain stylistic features are associated with performances that are deemed to be both technically accomplished and genuinely moving. These include an unhurried rendering of the text, some degree of textual and melodic embellishment, perhaps some variation in the melodic line, and a focused vocal quality that has been achieved without straining. Very basically, these are the features that transform a text as it might be recited into a song—a transformation that Presparë refer to when they say that a good singer "doesn't just say the words." Implied in this phrase is the view that a song is itself impersonal and that it only serves as a vehicle for personal expression when properly sung. A perfunctory performance neither conveys the singer's sincerity nor does it move those listening. But a performance infused with a balanced range of expressive techniques both puts across the text more powerfully and wraps it in embellishments that signal the singer's personal connection to it—and the emotional intensity that such a performance embodies is infectious.

GENDER AND SINGING
〜

Within these basic structural and stylistic parameters, the repertoires of Pre-spa women and men, and the manners in which they sing, are markedly different. Both women and men sing in their chest register, but with some-what different vocal placement. Women are commonly said to speak and sing in a "thin voice" (*zë të ollë*). Those who fit this description sing in a high tessitura, with a muted, nasal placement. Today the relatively subdued quality of women's singing contrasts strikingly with their more animated conversational style.

Within their repertoire, women distinguish between two styles of perfor-mance, both metric. Dance songs, as well as a few ritual songs, are sung in a brisk tempo with little melodic ornamentation. Such songs are often referred to as sung *lartër* ("loud/high"), meaning somewhat more loudly and at a higher pitch level. Most women's songs, however, are sung in a manner referred to as *shtruar*, meaning "calmly" or "drawn-out." For women, sing-ing *shtruar* means performing a song more softly and at a leisurely tempo that allows the melodic line to be "decorated" (*zbukuruar*) with delicate me-lismas. See Example 11.1, on the following text:

Po kjo anë e lumit	On this side of the river
ka bilbilë shumë . . .	there are many nightingales . . .
Pritmë, bandill, pritmë	(Wait for me, young man, wait for me
sa të rritem unë.	to grow up a little.)
sa të rritem unë	to grow up a little,
jam e vogël shumë . . .	for I am very young . . .
Kur s'u rrite sot	If you haven't grown up by today,
mos u rriç iç kurrë . . .	may you never ever grow up! . . .

Women also embellish the texts of songs by reiterating syllables or by adding exclamatory words such as *ajde, mori, moj,* and *aman* (all interpolated words and syllables are italicized in the transcriptions). In speech, such words imply a mild emotional reaction on the part of the speaker to what is being discussed: "*Aman mori* Fatime! Did she really tell you that?!" When inserted into a song they have no direct bearing on the meaning of the text, but rather add emphasis and signal the singer's emotional involvement in her performance. In most women's songs there are standard places in the text where such words are to be inserted, but the specific choice of words is usually up to the soloists.

EXAMPLE 11.1. "Po kyo anë e lumit." Women's song performed in *shtruar* style

For women, then, a heartfelt rendering of a song is accomplished primarily through the use of a moderate degree of melodic ornamentation and understated expressive language. In women's performances, even the most extensive use of such techniques does not prevent the song from proceeding clearly within its meter.

In contrast, male singers are particularly highly regarded if they sing in a "thick voice" (*zë të trashë*); that is, at a medium tessitura and with greater tensing of the muscles in the throat so that a tone rich in partials is produced.[9] Men who sing in this way are often said to sing "with strength" (*me fuqi*), implying that it requires the greater physical strength of a man to produce such a resonant tone. As men age, they often sing at a lower pitch level, and their voices lose much of their resonance and clarity. The contrast in timbres between women's and men's performances is therefore most applicable to younger adults.

Like women, men recognize distinct styles of songs within their repertoire. Each style is associated with a particular stage in a men's singing gathering, and some have associations with particular generations as well. At the beginning of a gathering, and especially among male elders, *shtruar* songs are sung. As with the women's repertoire, these are metric songs that are generally sung more softly and with a moderate amount of melismatic embellishment. In some performances, however, singers may choose to slow down the tempo and emphasize and prolong certain syllables to such an extent that a clear sense of meter is undermined. This is shown in Example 11.2, based on the same melodic configuration as Example 11.1, the text of which is as follows:

Në plepat Bilishtit	In the poplars of Bilisht [Albanian town near Greek border]
ranë dy martina,	two rifles went off,
u vranë dy trima,	two heroes were killed,
Maloa me Selmanë . . .	Malo and Selman . . .
Bir-o, djemt' e nën[ës]	(O son, O sons of a mother,
kë të qaj më parë?	which shall I mourn first?)
Njëri përtej lumit,	The one across the river,
tjetri më këtë anë . . .	the other on this side . . .
Që të dy që ishin	The two of them were
kushërinj të parë . . .	first cousins . . .
Nënësë së zezë	Wherever people went they said
ku vanë e i thanë	to the grieving mother:
t'u vranë dy trima,	Your two heroes were killed,
Maloa me Selmanë.	Malo and Selman.

EXAMPLE 11.2. "Në plepat Bilishtit." Men's performance of a song with a metric basis

At the very end of a gathering, in contrast, men often draw upon a group of rapid metric songs sung at full volume, in order to provide a sort of finale to the event. It appears that these songs are such a recent addition to the repertoire that there is as yet no verbal designation for them.

The epitome of the men's repertoire is a group of songs known as *këngë të lartëra,* which dominate the central portion of men's gatherings. Here, as with women's singing, *lartër* may be translated as "sung in a loud/high voice," but the style of execution of these songs has no counterpart within the women's repertoire. Many men's *këngë të lartëra* have no regularly recurring metric basis. Usually they have an exceptionally large ambitus and are sung at full volume. Extended melismas are common, and singers often elide descents of a third or fourth with a prolonged portamento. Through the use of such techniques, the rate at which the text is declaimed is slower than in other singing styles. Furthermore, any of these techniques may cause individual syllables to be sustained so much that any sense of a steady rhythmic basis is distorted, as in Example 11.3, to the following text:

Vjeshtë e tretë më të dalë	The third month of autumn was just ending
ç'u fillua Komiteti.	when the guerrilla movement began.
Komiteti mori mali	The guerrillas took to the mountains,
Panarit më luftë ranë	they fell upon Panarit [in southern Albania] in battle
u vranë dy kapetanë	and two captains were killed:
Nebi Kuçi me Rizanë.	Nebi Kuçi and Riza [Panariti].
Sali beut aber ja dhanë	The news was brought to Sali *bey*
[për Nebinë e Rizanë.]	[about Nebi and Riza.]
Sali beu tha nja dy fjalë:	Sali *bey* said a few words:
Mos, burra, qani si gratë!	Men, don't cry like women!
Mengoni nesër me natë!	By tomorrow night you must be gone!

Some singers of *këngë të lartëra* yodel or lapse into falsetto, techniques said to imitate women's lamenting and thus to infuse the rendition with a sense of melancholy. Because they are so demanding technically, *këngë të lartëra* are the special province of men in the prime of life, when their voices are still strong and supple.

In both the *shtruar* and *lartër* styles, men interpolate exclamatory words and phrases into the texts more extensively than do women, at virtually any point in the line of text. The exclamations drawn upon, such as *o-i* and *o-bo-bo*, are used in speech to express the strongest possible reaction to something, whether positive or negative:

> "*O-i! What has befallen us?*"
> "*O-bo-bo! What a beautiful girl!*"

For the bulk of their performances, then, men sing more loudly and more slowly than women, and they use various techniques of textual and melodic embellishment more extensively and freely. Any type of embellishment may be allowed to pull a song out of its rhythmic framework. A sort of rhythmic

EXAMPLE 11.3. "Vjeshtë e tretë më të dalë." Men's song in *lartër* style

elasticity is thus a prominent feature of men's singing, one that gives it an especially spontaneous and dramatic quality. In particular, *këngë të lartëra*, because of the range of evocative techniques called upon and the sheer volume at which they are sung, have a more overtly emotional character than other songs.

What emerges from a comparison of the sound of women's and men's singing is a marked contrast in the degree of emotionality that is expressed.

Women's singing implies restraint and self-control, while men's singing seems more assertive and emotionally indulgent. This contrast is reinforced by several other aspects of their singing: the characteristic demeanor that singers adopt, the subject matter of their repertoires, and the type of emotional atmosphere that they induce at their gatherings.

Women's wedding songs are concerned almost exclusively with the wedding occasion or with the future weddings of other male relatives. The feelings addressed and evoked through their song texts are very specific in their affect and grow directly out of the wedding context: joy at the groom's coming of age, sorrow at the bride's leaving her family home. A woman of the "bride" generation is expected to express the emotion that wells up inside her during a wedding through her choice of text and her rendering of the melody, but not through her demeanor. She is expected to sit very still, not exchanging glances with those listening or even with her singing partner, not gesturing with her hands (see Fig. 11.1). To behave in any other way would be considered *turp* ("shameful"). This very composed manner of performance is often referred to by the same adjective, *shtruar,* used to describe the musical style associated with women's seated (nondance) singing, as if a woman's singing style were the aural counterpart to her visual presentation of herself.[10] If a younger woman were to act out her feelings by strongly establishing eye contact with her listeners or by using dramatic gestures, she could be accused of drawing undue attention to herself in front of her elders, or even of performing in the sexually provocative manner of a professional entertainer.[11] As with the traditional bridal stance, a younger woman's subdued and self-effacing demeanor while singing expresses her deference toward those older women who are present; it is also expressly non-sensual. In every regard she presents herself as the idealized image of a modest young woman.

Although a younger woman's singing serves to highlight the emotional richness of an occasion, it may also check what might develop into an unseemly display of personal feelings. Often a woman's eyes fill with tears as she sings, and her voice becomes choked, but it would be shameful for her to let her feelings overtake her composure and interrupt her song. Likewise, she may convey her feelings by delicately ornamenting the melody and injecting subtly emotional exclamations into the text, but she must not let the expressive techniques of singing overpower the song's metric organization. In this respect women's *shtruar* singing may be seen as an aural and visual representation of feminine restraint and, more specifically, of the subordination of personal sentiment to the requirements of proper demeanor.

As women age they have considerably more social freedom as singers and need not be so attentive to their demeanor. It is women elders, rather than

Figure 11.1. Prespa women singing at an evening gathering
(Toronto, 1985). Photograph by Jane C. Sugarman; Reproduced
from Jane C. Sugarman, *Engendering Song: Singing and Subjectivity
at Prespa Albanian Weddings*. Copyright © 1997 University of
Chicago with permission of the University of Chicago Press.

younger women, whom I have seen singing boisterously and prominently
before a mixed group of men and women. They also experience greater freedom to express emotion. One of the few women whom I have heard sing in
the men's *lartër* style was an elder who, as she sang to the groom, gestured
with her hands with each phrase and reached out to stroke his cheek and
chin. Another older woman, singing to a niece about to leave the village to
live in Canada, wept in sorrow to the point that she could no longer sing.
Once women are past their reproductive years they may behave—and
sing—in a more evocative manner, closer to that characteristic of men.

In contrast, the emotional climate at men's evening gatherings is inextricably linked to the fact that they drink, generally a form of homemade brandy
known as *raki*. Among Presparë, only men drink any form of alcoholic bever-
age. The rationale seems to be that the loss of self-control that it prompts is
dangerous for women, who might be led to behave provocatively and even
promiscuously. Men might become argumentative but, if properly regulated,
their drinking is seen to have positive consequences. Men are said to drink
to become *qejfli*, or "elated." They say that, as they drink, their self-consciousness leaves them and that a state of social intimacy is generated. The

goal of a men's gathering is to nurture that quality of intimacy toward an almost ecstatic state in which the men experience a surge of affection for each other.

At their gatherings the men sing roughly in descending order of age: first elders, then adult men of the parental generation, and then, perhaps, unmarried young men and boys. Only rarely do their songs allude to the wedding taking place; more often they are concerned with historical events or romantic love. At the evening's beginning the older men sing, soberly and sedately, in *shtruar* style. By the time the younger men begin to sing, they are becoming intoxicated and the atmosphere in the room has begun to build. It is at this point that more singers take up *këngë të lartëra*. Singers explain that they embellish these songs in highly emotional ways, not as commentary upon the often tragic texts, but rather to express the sense of elation and conviviality that they are feeling, and to "lift" the emotional level of the others.

As the men feel less self-conscious, their demeanor while singing becomes more dramatic. They throw back their heads and close their eyes, or they gesture emphatically toward the men around them. Even those men droning and listening interact far more intensely than they would in any other setting: embracing and kissing each other, and hooking arms as they drink. As they experience a build-up of intense physical feelings they release them through stereotypic gestures such as pounding their fists on the table, yelling exclamations, or (where permitted) firing a loaded gun. In every way their extroverted demeanor and physical interaction contrast with the reserved and self-contained behavior of women.

It seems clear that the emotional experience associated with men's singing occasions relates directly neither to what they sing about nor to the wedding being celebrated. Unlike the definable affects evoked and then contained by women through their singing, men use singing to induce a transcendent experience, one that is beyond affect. In particular, men regard their *lartër* song style as both evoking and embodying the elation cultivated at such occasions. It is a state that is viewed as expressly male, since only men are permitted to induce it in themselves. I have already suggested that the women's manner of performance, characterized by a subdued demeanor and softer, metric singing, serves as an embodied representation of the subordination of emotion to propriety. Similarly, the men's performance style, combining dramatic behavior with resonant, overtly emotional, and rhythmically elastic singing, embodies a state in which emotion is stretched to its limits: a state that is the privilege of a man's greater social and expressive freedom within the Prespa social order.[12]

SINGING AND GENDER

~

Thus far I have outlined the stylistic features that characterize the most typical, accomplished performances by Prespa singers (see Table 11.1 for a summary), and I have suggested how contrasting clusters of musical and
behavioral features encapsulate community notions regarding gendered
identity and gendered social roles. In recent decades, ethnomusicologists
have become accustomed to search for metaphoric or homologous relationships between music and other domains of human thought and experience.
So, for example, aspects of musical practice have been analyzed as being
imaginatively linked to bird song and hence to the spirits of the deceased by
Kaluli communities in Papua New Guinea, to the shaman's journey to the
spirit world by Mapuche communities in Argentina, and to the cyclic nature
of time by communities in Indonesia.[13] Although such analyses have more
often focused upon the relationship between music and cosmological beliefs,
they have nevertheless often pinpointed gender as a major referent of musical
practice.

In our attempts to understand such relationships, however, we have often
drawn the line of causality between a society and its expressive forms in one
direction only. In other words, we have concentrated our analytical energies
on explaining musical practice with reference to other domains of belief or
experience. Many examinations of the relationship of music to gender, for
example, have focused on the ways in which the musical activities and performance styles of women and men "reflect" or are "determined" by their
community's views on gender. In the case of Presparë, singing is indeed
constrained by community notions regarding gender. But singing may also
be seen as a means both of acquiring those notions and of suggesting ways
in which they may be refined or revised.[14]

In his analysis of Kabyle Algerian concepts of social order that are not
unlike those of Presparë, sociologist Pierre Bourdieu has noted the role of all
types of symbolically structured behavior in the inculcation of what he terms
the "habitus"—the "system of dispositions" through which any individual
within a community is able to generate culturally appropriate actions. His
comments on children's perceptions are particularly astute:

> in all societies, children are particularly attentive to the gestures and
> postures which, in their eyes, express everything that goes to make
> an accomplished adult—a way of walking, a tilt of the head, facial
> expressions, ways of sitting and of using implements, always associated

TABLE 11.1

~

Comparison of the Wedding Singing of Prespa Albanian Women and Men

FEATURE	WOMEN'S SINGING	MEN'S SINGING
Singing style:		
volume	low to medium	medium to high
tempo and meter	*shtruar:* moderate, strict meter	*shtruar:* moderate to slow, meter relaxed
	lartër: rapid, metric	*lartër:* slow, nonmetric
melisma	moderate, within meter	can be extensive, out of meter
other techniques	slight portamento	prolonged portamento falsetto, yodelling (*cf.* lament)
textual interpolation	more moderate	more pervasive
	less emotional	more emotional
	within meter	pulls song out of meter
	often predetermined	more extemporized
Song texts:	courtship and marriage	historical events, romantic love
Demeanor:	little bodily motion	considerable bodily motion
	noninteractive	interactive
Emotionality:	specific affects	ineffable, beyond affect
	related to wedding theme	not related to wedding theme
	related to song texts	not related to song texts
Demeanor and emotionality:	demeanor contains emotion	emotion propels demeanor
Singing and emotionality:	emotion subordinated to propriety	emotion stretched to its limits

with a tone of voice, a style of speech, and (how could it be otherwise?) a certain subjective experience. . . .

    If all societies . . . set such store on the seemingly most insignificant details of *dress, bearing,* physical and verbal *manners,* the reason is that, treating the body as a memory, they entrust to it in abbreviated and practical . . . form the fundamental principles of the arbitrary content of culture . . . nothing seems more ineffable, more incommunicable, more inimitable, and, therefore, more precious, than the values given body, *made* body by the transubstantiation achieved by the hidden persuasion of an implicit pedagogy, capable of instilling a whole cosmology, an ethic, a metaphysic, a political philosophy, through injunctions as insignificant as "stand up straight" or "don't hold your knife in your left hand."[15]

Although Bourdieu's writings focus on everyday activities, his emphasis on aspects of behavior such as stance, gesture, and vocal manner makes his approach eminently suitable to the analysis of expressive activities such as singing, and to their role in social reproduction.

For Presparë, as for most individuals from rural areas of southeast Europe, the principal referent of music making is village society, as portrayed in an idealized manner through ritual behavior. At a wedding, individuals participate in singing according to their place within the social order, as determined by gender, generation, and kinship. In their singing style and demeanor they try to come as close as possible to an ideal performance for a person of their social category. Each wedding therefore constructs a unique visual and aural image of community views of social ordering through the way in which the singing of members of different social categories is ordered and performed.

In their youth, today's adult Presparë attended countless events at which singing was a focal activity. They were also coached not only in the texts and melodies of songs but in proper performance demeanor as well. Two of the most important attributes that they acquired in the course of becoming proficient singers were, first, confidence and composure in social situations, and second, a social demeanor that was appropriately, even quintessentially, feminine or masculine. Singing thus prepared them to behave in public as proper young women and men, and the performances of adults offered them stylized images of how they should conduct themselves as they moved through subsequent periods of life. Even today, when fewer young people learn to sing, those who do often learn the stereotypic performance stance and vocal timbre for their gender before they have mastered the musical details of the style. Adults do not merely observe the stylized image of their society that singing provides, but rather help to create that image by placing themselves within it as singers. With every performance, they are called upon to define both themselves as social beings and their place within the larger social order. The activity of singing is thus one of the principal means through which Presparë come to know, and continually reassess, the notions of social ordering that structure their community; in fact, their very sense of themselves as a coherent and ordered community is acquired through such performances.[16]

Of all the aspects of social identity that Presparë come to know through singing, gender is the most fundamental. Whenever, wherever, and however they sing, they do so as females or males. They do so because they are constrained by community-held beliefs regarding gender identity and gender relations. But through their singing they both experience those beliefs in tangible form and publicly affirm them, specifying through the act of singing what their concerns should be, what sorts of emotions they should experience, and what sorts of behavior they should adopt in response to their

innate natures and their resultant place within the social order. To paraphrase Bourdieu, singing continually "inscribes" their sense of femininity or
masculinity into their "body schema and . . . schemes of thought."[17] It is an
experience that endures through the vagaries of daily life to serve as a point
of reference, an index of Prespa femaleness and maleness. In their everyday
lives they are not held to every detail of what they experience through such
stylized behavior, since what they set forth through their singing is an imaginatively constructed ideal. But they can measure their behavior against that
ideal and decide to what degree they wish to diverge from the community
standards that they, through their performances, help to define.

At present, the image that Presparë living in North America set forth
through their singing is overwhelmingly that of the Prespa social order as
today's adults were socialized to it several decades ago. It is an image that
vies in many ways with their current lives, as well as with the image projected
by mainstream North American society, which they encounter at work and
through the media. Each wedding, however, contains countless moments
when participants might choose to structure their song performances in ways
more consistent with their present-day concepts of gender. Such innovations
are generally introduced during smaller and more informal gatherings not
connected with important ritual moments, when those assembled feel most
comfortable with each other. At one such occasion in Toronto, for example,
men and women gathered together in the guest room of the bride's home.
Although they sat in segregated groups, men and women alternated songs,
singing roughly in order of age rather than observing the traditional order in
which all men sing before all women. At that same gathering, a young wife
and husband—sitting on opposite sides of the room—performed the two
solo lines of a women's wedding song that they had learned from Albanian
radio. Through their singing, they suggested a view of social ordering different from that implied by the segregated seating formation. For as long as
today's Presparë can remember there have been a few women who successfully performed men's songs or sang in men's style. So long as they maintained a feminine demeanor and vocal timbre as they sang, their forays into
the men's repertoire were viewed as evidence of an unusual degree of intelligence and musical talent. For men, however, it can still be embarrassing to
associate oneself too much with the women's style or repertoire. Nevertheless, it is becoming more common for married couples to maintain a small
repertoire of songs that they can sing together—primarily songs in women's
style—thus suggesting a new image of the Prespa community.

In short, the relationship between gender conceptualization and musical
practice—and more broadly between a community's social ideology and its
expressive forms—is best regarded as an ongoing and reciprocal one.

Through their singing Presparë do not maintain an unchanging view of gender relations and simply "reproduce" it in subsequent generations. To the
contrary, each individual possesses the potential to contribute through his or
her singing to the incremental revision of the community's views of social
order. As a new generation of young people is marrying and takes its place
within "adult" society, its members are experimenting increasingly with ways
of conveying through song—as well as dance—new views of themselves as
women and men, and some of the more convincing experiments are gradually displacing older norms of musical practice. When one considers the very
different views of gender, and the very different musical styles, to which
young people are being exposed within the larger society, however, it is likely
that this generation or the next may revise both its views of social relations
and its musical tastes in ways far more radical than any changes experienced
in recent decades. In that process, polyphonic singing—or any singing at
all—may well cease to be regarded as a central component of an individual's
social demeanor.[18]

NOTES

~

An earlier version of this essay was published in *Ethnomusicology* 33 (1989): 191–215.
Copyright © 1989 by the Board of Trustees of the University of Illinois. I am grateful
to the Society for Ethnomusicology and the University of Illinois Press for granting
permission to reproduce it here in revised form. For this version I have altered the
wording slightly to bring it more in line with current thinking regarding gender issues, as well as with the current realities of the Prespa community. The overall argument of the article, however, remains unchanged. For an extended analysis of Prespa
weddings and singing as they relate to issues of gender, see Jane C. Sugarman, *Engendering Song: Singing and Subjectivity at Prespa Albanian Weddings* (Chicago: University of Chicago Press, 1997). Recordings of Examples 11.1 and 11.3 appear as tracks 16
and 12, respectively, on the compact disc accompanying this book.

1. *Bey* is an Ottoman honorific term by which young Prespa women have historically
   addressed men of their generation or older.
2. In parts of southern Albania, a young man is more commonly depicted in songs as a
   "falcon" (*petrit*) preying on the female game bird.
3. Here I refer to the Republic of Macedonia, which until 1991 was a republic of Yugoslavia. I conducted research there among Prespa families between 1980 and 1982, and
   have continued among immigrants in North America since 1985. Large communities
   of Presparë live in and around the cities of Toronto and London, Ontario, in Canada;
   and Detroit, Chicago, and Bridgeport, Connecticut, in the United States. There are
   also clusters of families in Florida, Texas, California, and other states. The singing
   style of Prespa families is much like that found in many parts of southern Albania;
   for more information on Albanian music, see my articles on "Albanian Music" in the
   Garland Encyclopedia of World Music, vol. 8: *Europe*, ed. Timothy Rice, James Porter,

and Chris Goertzen (New York: Garland Pub., 2000), and "Albania II: Traditional Music" in the *New Grove Dictionary of Music and Musicians,* ed. Stanley Sadie and John Tyrell, 2d ed. (2001), 1:285–89. Like other south Albanian communities in Macedonia, Presparë are Muslim, but their views on gender issues are also shared with many rural Christian Albanian communities. For an analysis of attitudes toward gender among north Albanians in Kosova, see Janet Reineck, "The Past as Refuge: Gender, Migration and Ideology among the Kosova Albanians" (Ph.D. diss., University of California, Berkeley, 1991).

4. Juliet du Boulay, "Women—Images of Their Nature and Destiny in Rural Greece," in *Gender and Power in Rural Greece,* ed. Jill Dubisch (Princeton: Princeton University Press, 1986), 163.

5. Ibid., 151.

6. The concept of female "shame" is prominent in the moral discourses of communities throughout the greater Mediterranean area. A classic collection of articles on the topic is *Honour and Shame: The Values of Mediterranean Society,* ed. John G. Peristiany (London: Weidenfeld and Nicolson, 1965); other particularly careful analyses are given for Algerian Kabyle by Pierre Bourdieu in *Outline of a Theory of Practice,* trans. Richard Nice (Cambridge: Cambridge University Press, 1977); and for Egyptian Bedouin by Lila Abu-Lughod in *Veiled Sentiments: Honor and Poetry in a Bedouin Community* (Berkeley: University of California Press, 1986).

7. For an analysis of men's singing gatherings, see my "Making *Muabet*: The Social Basis of Singing Occasions among Prespa Albanian Men," *Selected Reports in Ethnomusicology* 7 (1988): 1–42; and *Engendering Song,* chaps. 6–7.

8. For most Christian Slavic communities in Macedonia and neighboring Bulgaria, adult women are the principal singers while men are associated more with instrumental music. Within a regional context, Albanians are thus unusual in granting men such a prominent and respected role as singers. It could even be argued that Albanians have a particularly high regard for singing because of its strong association with men. On the other hand, many Muslim communities in this region, both Albanian and Slavic, do not permit females past the age of puberty to sing at large social occasions, with the result that wedding songs are performed by teenage girls. In their association of wedding singing with adult women, Presparë are therefore similar to neighboring Christian communities. Such variations in musical practice, found among communities with quite similar attitudes toward gender, point out the arbitrary and creative nature of the relationship that individual communities have fashioned between gender considerations and music.

9. Although she focuses on Javanese singing, an excellent discussion of the mechanics of this type of vocal production is provided by Gloria R. Poedjosoedarmo, "A Phonetic Description of Voice Quality in Javanese Traditional Female Soloists," *Asian Music* 19 (1998): 93–126.

10. Likewise, the word *shtruar* may be used to describe the demure dance style of young women, as in this popular song from the town of Vlorë in southern Albania:

    Dilni, shihni ju thëllëxat-o, që na marrin vallen shtruar-o.

    Come out to see the partridges/young women, leading the dance line in a *shtruar* manner.

11. I provide an account of the *çengis* or *çoçeks,* professional woman singers and/or dancers who once commonly performed in Macedonia and neighboring areas, in "'Those Other Women': Dance and Femininity among Prespa Albanians," in *Music and Gen-*

der: Perspectives from the Mediterranean, ed. Tullia Magrini (Chicago: University of Chicago Press, forthcoming). Most of these women were of Rom ethnicity rather than Albanian and, by the early twentieth century, frequently crossed gender boundaries to perform for male as well as female audiences.

At the time that the original version of this article was written, no Prespa woman had ever participated in stage performances of the community's folklore, as had several men, nor had any younger woman sung into a microphone with the band at a wedding or other such event. Since the late 1980s, however, several younger women in North America have begun singing with semiprofessional wedding bands, usually ones led by their husbands. Also in the 1980s, Eli Fara, from the town of Korçë in southern Albania, emerged as one of that country's top professional folk singers, singing a repertoire very similar to that of Prespa Albanians.

12. The association of men's singing with the drinking of alcohol, and of both with the attainment of an elated state, is widespread in the greater Mediterranean area. Some Sufi orders call upon both music and alcohol to induce an elated state within the context of religious services; see, for example, John Kingsley Birge, *The Bektashi Order of Dervishes* (London: Luzac and Co., 1937). Both have also been associated historically with the elated state (Ottoman *hal,* Arabic *tarab*) said to be induced at men's secular gatherings; see Walter Andrews, *Poetry's Voice, Society's Song: Ottoman Lyric Poetry* (Seattle: University of Washington Press, 1985); and George Dimitri Sawa, *Music Performance Practice in the Early 'Abbasid Era, 132–320 A.H./750–932 A.D.* (Toronto: Pontifical Institute of Mediaeval Studies, 1989). For an analysis of the texts of Prespa men's historical songs, see Sugarman, "Imagining the Homeland: Poetry, Songs, and the Discourses of Albanian Nationalism," *Ethnomusicology* 43 (1999): 419–58.

13. See, respectively, Steven Feld, *Sound and Sentiment: Birds, Weeping, Poetics, and Song in Kaluli Expression,* 2d ed. (Philadelphia: University of Pennsylvania Press, 1990); Carol E. Robertson, "'Pulling the Ancestors': Performance Practice and Praxis in Mapuche Ordering," *Ethnomusicology* 23 (1979): 395–416; Alton Becker and Judith Becker, "A Musical Icon: Power and Meaning in Javanese Gamelan Music," in *The Sign in Music and Literature,* ed. Wendy Steiner (Austin: University of Texas Press, 1981), 203–15.

14. For early studies arguing a reciprocal relationship between social ordering and musical practice, see Carol E. Robertson, "Process of Transmission: Music Education and Social Inclusion," in *Becoming Human through Music* (Reston, Va.: Music Educators National Conference, 1985), 95–113; and Anthony Seeger, *Why Suyá Sing: A Musical Anthropology of an Amazonian People* (Cambridge: Cambridge University Press, 1987).

15. Bourdieu, *Outline of a Theory of Practice,* 87, 94.

16. For studies of ritual that advance similar arguments, see Roy A. Rappaport, "The Obvious Aspects of Ritual," in *Ecology, Meaning, and Religion* (Richmond, Calif.: North Atlantic Books, 1979), 173–221; id., "Concluding Comments on Ritual and Reflexivity," *Semiotica* 30 (1980): 181–93; and Edward L. Schieffelin, "Performance and the Cultural Construction of Reality," *American Ethnologist* 12 (1985): 707–24.

17. Bourdieu, *Outline of a Theory of Practice,* 15.

18. For asssessments of recent changes in Prespa music and dance, see my *Engendering Song,* chap. 8; and "'Those Other Women.'"

CHAPTER TWELVE

Women Playing Men in Italian Opera, 1810–1835

Heather Hadlock

GEORGE BERNARD SHAW QUIPPED that every Italian opera is the story of a soprano and a tenor who want to go to bed together, and a baritone who wants to stop them. Many modern critics have reached a similar conclusion, albeit expressed in the soberer rhetoric of structuralism.[1] As Gilles de Van remarks, "it has often been said that these operas seem to feature the same characters, even if the names, costumes, and social standing may vary, and that they tell very similar stories in spite of historical and geographic differences."[2] Italian opera of the nineteenth century may be understood not so much as a drama of characters set to music, but as a "theater of voices" in which the primary purpose of plot is to justify appealing arrays and combinations of voices.

A similar point of view also informed Catherine Clément's *Opera, or, The Undoing of Women,* the book whose 1988 translation into English sparked what we might call the "first wave" of Anglo-American feminist opera studies.[3] Clément read opera as the bourgeois West's ritual enactment of scapegoating and sacrifice, telling and retelling a handful of myths in which soprano heroines are victimized by fate, men, and society. Clément's example, together with interpretive models borrowed from feminist analyses of literature and anthropology, inspired other models for understanding the tragic fates of heroines, as the "persecuted innocents" of melodrama, as hysterics and madwomen, and as objects of exchange in male rivalry. Almost immediately a second wave began to critique this emphasis on victimization and defeat, arguing that *plot* is ultimately a secondary concern in opera—that although the heroine may die in the plot, she triumphs through performance. Death need not be taken as the heroine's defining moment, but may equally be regarded as a last-minute detail that in no way cancels out her domination of the operatic spectacle and experience. Soprano heroines are in this view empowered and ultimately victorious through their vocal authority. This wave also wanted to take into account the power of the real people behind the performances, the prima donnas whose creative, personal, and professional lives often form an ironic counterpoint to the suffering, objectified heroines they portray. What these two approaches have in common, however, is a focus on soprano heroines and the central love triangle that Shaw described so succinctly.

Why would a feminist critic want to turn away from the standard soprano–tenor–baritone triangle and focus on other kinds of women's roles? The "master plot" of women's undoing is depressing enough. But even apart from that, Romantic opera isolates women: its most prized and characteristic sound is that of a soprano's lonely suffering, and its archetypal plots accommodate one (and only one) woman. Gabriele Baldini's summary of Verdi's *Ernani* as "a youthful, passionate female voice is besieged by three male voices, each of which establishes a specific relationship with her" might readily be adapted to fit the plots of many other Italian Romantic operas.[4] With rare exceptions such as Bellini's *Norma,* sisterhood is not powerful in this repertoire. Leading women who share the spotlight are often rivals, like the two queens of Donizetti's *Maria Stuarda* or the princesses of Verdi's *Don Carlos* and *Aida,* quarreling bitterly over men. More subtly, two female protagonists may never confront each other in the plots, but still embody opposite feminine types—ingenue and virago, virtuous girl and vixen.[5] Even if we listen without knowing the story or the words, sonority conveys the message that women are alone. Their voices are heard separately rather than in concerted affirmations of mutual support.

We must turn back to a pre-Romantic era to find a style of Italian opera that involves feminine (soprano or alto) voices in relations of love and mutual devotion as well as rivalry. If nineteenth-century Italian opera is the story of a baritone's attempts to keep tenor and soprano away from each other, serious opera of the eighteenth century might be reduced to the story of two sopranos who want to love each other nobly, and a lower voice who wants to stop them. Unlike modern listeners, eighteenth-century audiences associated a clarion soprano voice with royal, military, and amorous authority.[6] Heroic roles were sung by high-voiced performers of both sexes, either by women dressed as men or by castrati. Italian baroque opera considered voice more important for the creation and presentation of character than the sex of the body producing that voice.

In the early decades of the nineteenth century this began to change. The castrati began to disappear around 1800 (although a few, most notably Giambattista Velluti, did continue to perform and even create new roles into the mid-1820s). And at the same time, a newly strenuous and masculine tenor sound was emerging as the preferred voice for heroes. By the mid-1840s, composers and audiences had re-calibrated their ears to expect kings, warriors, lovers, and chieftains to sing with male voices.[7] The change may be measured in Verdi's reluctance in 1843 to compose the heroic role of *Ernani* for a contralto, as Bellini had been ready to do in 1830: Verdi was, as a colleague involved in the negotiations around *Ernani* reported, "a sworn foe to the idea of making a woman sing dressed up as a man."[8] Similarly, Verdi in 1848 could only use a tenor as the pirate hero of *Il corsaro,* a role that Giovanni Pacini had written for contralto in 1831.[9] By the mid-nineteenth century, the conventions of gender representation had been thoroughly "straightened out," and women had ceased to be accepted in serious or heroic male roles. The obsolescence of high-voiced heroes is one of many symptoms of Italian opera's drift toward full-blown Romanticism, with its tragic subjects, doomed tenor–soprano pair, and fascination with female suffering.

This transition did not happen all at once, though, and elements of eighteenth-century style lingered in Italian opera into the 1830s. Composers and librettists continued to write heroic roles for female contraltos and sopranos in the early decades of the nineteenth century, and several generations of female singers made their careers playing male roles in the operas of Rossini, Bellini, Donizetti, and their contemporaries. The male role played by a high voice had its own designation: rather than *primo uomo* ("first man") the singer would be listed as *primo musico*. This term, once applied to castrati, now designated a woman in a male role. Some of the parts female *musico*s played were originally written for castrati, while others, like Rossini's immensely popular *Tancredi,* were composed expressly for them. Operas with *musico* heroes present women's voices in solidarity, alliance, and mutual devotion, expressed not only in arias but also in duets, ensembles, and arias with chorus.

Many such operas were variations on a "Romeo and Juliet" archetype (albeit with happy endings): noble young lovers find themselves in conflict with the leaders and laws of a public sphere governed by fathers, politicians, rulers, and military leaders. The two leading women's voices—*prima donna* and *primo musico*—create a sonorous realm of love and private feeling besieged or constrained by a male-dominated public sphere. Two of Rossini's serious operas, very different in style, demonstrate the underlying similarity of structure. In *Tancredi* (1813), an adaptation of Voltaire's neoclassical drama *Tancrède,* the love of the exiled knight Tancredi and Amenaide is opposed by her father, who wishes to strengthen his city's military position by marrying his daughter to the general Orbazzano. *La donna del lago* (1819), set in the

Scottish highlands and based on a poem by Sir Walter Scott, has an entirely different ambience and tone but a similar structure: the love between Malcolm and Elena is forbidden by her father, who wishes to cement an alliance against the English king by marrying his daughter to the chieftain Rodrigo Dhu.[10] Examples could be multiplied of young love and personal desire suffering under paternal constraint, political conflict, and military alliances.

Although this paradigm extended into later Romantic opera, where soprano and tenor lovers suffer under the constraints of a patriarchal society represented by those interfering baritones, it did make a difference to have the heroes played by women. The two realms—a private world of love and desire opposed by fathers and governments—were more strictly (aurally) coded as female and male. A very clear example of this is Amenaide's entrance aria "Come dolce all'alma mia," in which the heroine alternates between acknowledging the formal congratulations of the male chorus for her upcoming marriage to Orbazzano, and expressing (aside) her secret longing for Tancredi to return.[11] Nor do all female characters belong to the private/feminine realm; on the contrary, secondary characters and women's choruses are usually allied with the public/patriarchal/masculine sphere, often to ironic effect. The female chorus that hails Elena as the chosen bride of "Rodrigo, the mighty" is cheerfully oblivious to her private anguish at the thought. The women do not share or affirm her emotions, but rather endorse her father's will.[12] The Act I finales of *La donna del lago* and of Bellini's *I Capuleti ed i Montecchi* (1830) are only two examples of concerted slow movements in which a pair of female lovers launch their voices in a soaring counter-melody over and against the male soloists and mixed chorus that oppose them. Although the *musico* is dressed as a man, and although the libretto rarely if ever alludes to the presence of a female singer beneath the hero's male costume, the music creates a parallel reality of pure sonority in which we cannot help perceiving her as a feminine presence. Operas with *musico* heroes thus work on two levels, as the spectacle and the "theater of voices" are mismatched.

Different works and singers managed this ambiguity differently. In this essay I will look at the very different careers and styles of three famous *musico* singers of the 1820s and 1830s as case studies in how expectations for women in male roles changed during the transition from *opera seria* to Romantic opera. In the 1820s, Giuditta Pasta (1797–1865) and Benedetta Rosmunda Pisaroni (1793–1872) were internationally famous exponents of Rossini's great trouser roles: Pasta won international fame as the title character of *Tancredi*, while Pisaroni was unsurpassed as Malcolm and Arsace, the young heroes of *La donna del lago* and *Semiramide* (1823). In these two cases we may see how variously women could be perceived in male roles, and what a range of meanings "travesty roles" could carry. A third singer, Marietta Brambilla (1807–75), established herself as the leading female *musico* of the generation after Rossini. As Maffio Orsini in Donizetti's *Lucrezia Borgia* (1833), she created a new kind of *musico* role, no longer the hero but occupying a new position vis-à-vis the soprano–tenor–baritone love triangle that would dominate emerging Romantic opera. I have chosen to focus on singers and roles in hopes of navigating between two equally important aspects of Italian opera—between a structuralist approach that would consider voice-types as the abstract essence of opera's drama, and a particular(ist) approach that would insist upon the individuality of works and the importance of specific singers as creators, shapers, and disseminators of roles. My arguments will therefore involve not only categorical terms like "the *musico*" and "the travesty hero," but also particular roles and, on a still more specific level, those roles as played by individual singers: "Pasta's Tancredi in Paris"; "Pisaroni's Arsace"; "Maffio Orsini, written for Brambilla."

GIUDITTA PASTA AS MAN AND WOMAN

In January 1821, the general director of the Parisian theaters invited the young soprano Giuditta Pasta for a season at the Théâtre Italien, insisting that only her talents could "restore the antique lustre of Italy, which in the opinion of the French *dilettanti* has begun to fall into decadence."[13] She made her debut on 5 June of that year and her success was such that, a mere three years later, a contemporary commentator remarked that "they would stare at anyone who claimed that he'd never heard Madame Pasta . . . and laugh at him."[14] During her first seasons, her performances as Desdemona, as Romeo in Zingarelli's *Giulietta e Romeo,* and as Rossini's Tancredi drew particular comment. This last role was noteworthy not only for Pasta's singing but for her thoroughly convincing embodiment of the ardent young knight (see Fig. 12.1). Although critics consistently noted the discrepancy between her female sex and the character's masculine gender, her youth and beauty did not interfere with her ability to make male heroes "real" for her audience. *La Quotidienne* remarked that "It was universally expected that the role of Tancredi would be sung by Mme Pasta in a superior manner, but nobody could have believed that a young and attractive woman could impersonate the knight of Syracuse with such imposing nobility, with a power so touching and so true . . ."[15] Far from being a liability, the mismatching of genders between Pasta and Tancredi—between performer and role—generated meaning and

Figure 12.1. Portrait of Giuditta Pasta as Tancredi. From *Oxberry's Dramatic Biography* (1827). Courtesy of Laurence Senelick.

dramatic power. What truths were revealed or constructed through her heroic disguise?

The paradox of the young girl as heroic knight was only the first of several noted in reviews of this performance. Pasta's crossing of genders became a framework for reading *Tancredi* itself, which the French audiences regarded as one of their own plays "travestied" as an Italian opera. The *Quotidienne* claimed that "When Voltaire outlined in *Tancrède* the ideal of pride and of chivalric generosity, if he had been told that one day his work, transformed by a poet from across the Alps, would return to Paris to be presented by Italian singers, the idea of such a great profanation would have made him shout with rage."[16] The national conflict was equally an aesthetic conflict, for

Tancredi straddled a number of contemporary faultlines: between the dramatic traditions of France and Italy; between spoken theater and lyric theater; between the arts of acting and of singing. The *Journal des théâtres* remarked that "It is truly singular . . . here in France, which is famous for having produced the greatest actors, to find a very young woman—daughter of that Italy whose dramatic artists were never known for anything except their buffoonery and above all their singing . . . and to see her create a new path . . . [one] worthy to serve as a model for actresses of the future."[17] Even Pasta's much-emphasized youth seemed to highlight the difference between the venerable past represented by Voltaire and the present and future represented by Rossini and Italian opera.

A few responses to Pasta's *Tancredi* did subtly register ambivalence about her effect, and suggest certain complications in so "true" a portrayal of a man by a woman. An anonymous chronicler described Mme Pasta, "in the helmet and tunic of a knight," as "ravishing," an adjective whose chivalric connotations include the violent abduction of someone against (her) will.[18] How did masculine costume confer the power to "ravish" male listeners? Stendahl, describing the experience of being overcome by Pasta-as-Tancredi, mused, "My ears and soul are still full of [Tancredi's] noble tones . . . I never anticipated that a warrior dressed in armor, covered with a helmet, could seem lovable not only to Amenaide's eyes but also to those of the sex whose clothing he wears. Who would not surrender his weapons to this adorable Tancredi? who could oppose him?"[19] It reminds him, he says, of an "old song" that warns a "handsome knight" against an unnamed person whose gaze will lure him in, then "trouble" him, then render him defenseless. There is, the song suggests, an element of danger for the man who looks, for he may simultaneously be *looked at,* a perilous position: "Handsome knight, be on your guard: / Whoever lingers too long before that gaze / feels himself troubled: / Against her charms / there are no weapons / that can defend a knight" (ibid). This warning, however, is not for Tancredi—rather, the "knight" in the song is the spectator in danger of falling under Pasta's hermaphroditic spell. Pasta, singing in her armor and helmet, is at once the knight and the charmer. The female voice emerging from Tancredi created what we might call a "double vision" of the cross-dressed performer, and that double vision seems to have produced an anxiety that Stendahl describes as fear of the singer's *gaze.* I suggest that we might, however, interpret this "gaze" not literally as "eye contact"—that is, that Pasta is actually looking at individual spectators while she sings—but rather as a metaphor for her voice that "captures" the listener and affects him in ways beyond his control. The most complex "truth" of Pasta's cross-dressing was not the reconciliation of social/cultural differences but the collapsing of fundamental distinctions between Self and Other.

Pasta gradually gave up male roles after 1830 as she became famous for playing Romantic heroines. The fame of her Tancredi was superseded by the even greater celebrity she achieved as the heroine of Rossini's *Semiramide,* and she created two other landmark title roles in Donizetti's *Anna Bolena* and Bellini's *Norma.* But the charisma and authority that she had honed in male roles carried over into her characterizations of these heroines, despite their feminine robes and heterosexual entanglements.

THE CURIOUS PUBERTY OF
ROSMUNDA PISARONI

Benedetta Rosmunda Pisaroni was recognized throughout Europe as the greatest *musico* contralto of her generation in the 1820s. In contrast with her contemporary Giuditta Pasta, she excelled in male roles because of her ugly, unfeminine appearance and her majestic low notes. In operas by Rossini and his contemporaries Pacini, Nicolini, Generali, Morlacchi, etc., she played ardent young warriors, kings, and at least one father. An exception within the beauty queen system of Italian opera, she made a piquant contrast with other female stars. And while other female *musico* performers such as Adelaide Tosi, Isabella Fabricca, and others were sometimes criticized for being too pretty, too graceful, or too charming—in a word, too feminine—to portray male heroes convincingly, Pisaroni's appearance exempted her from these complaints. Although physically slight, she inspired awe through her combination of repulsive looks and deep, majestic voice.

Ironically enough, Pisaroni did not begin her career as a contralto, much less as a specialist in male roles. She made her debut as a soprano at the age of eighteen in Mayr's *La rosa bianca e la rosa rossa* (Bergamo, 1811). Within three years, however, she had left the operatic scene and returned, after a hiatus, as a contralto. Contemporary accounts offer a variety of explanations for her new voice, often linking it to her infamous appearance. Paul Scudo explained in 1852 that, "after a grave illness suffered around 1813, she lost many notes in her high register, while the low cords acquired a potent and unforeseen resonance. So she was obliged to sing roles written for the contralto voice."[20] F.-J. Fétis's *Dictionnaire universelle des musiciens* (1866) attributed the hiatus, the voice change, and the singer's ugliness to smallpox. Marie and Léon Escudier, in another mid-century account, do not mention illness; they claim that the singer experienced an artistic epiphany that made her want to retrain her voice for Rossini's music.[21] A pamphlet written immediately after Pisaroni's death in 1872 offers yet another explanation, in which a composer's authority and a financial motive receive equal weight:

> Rossini, hearing that marvelous voice which reached from low E-flat to high D, advised her to abandon the soprano range that she had been training, rest for six months, and then begin to sing contralto. She would thus preserve her voice, make use of its more beautiful notes and those more suited to its proper quality, commanding at the same time much higher fees . . . Thus it is not true, as has been written, that she had abandoned the soprano range because illness overcame her. One can credit that such a belief had great value at the time in which she was resting before undertaking her new career.[22]

Taken together, these conflicting biographical narratives suggest that Pisaroni underwent a strange version of male puberty in 1813: an event that caused her voice to deepen, her appearance to lose all claims to feminine beauty or charm, and her demeanor to become strong and fierce. Under an influence variously figured as illness, as will, or as Rossini's personal authority, Pisaroni metamorphosed from a young woman to a quasi-man. An "Ode" by an anonymous Italian admirer (ca. 1822) praised Pisaroni's "warlike tones," speculating that if Rome's Imperial legions had heard her, they would have been inspired to defy Hannibal's elephants![23]

Pisaroni's musical and dramatic artistry were thrown into sharp relief by her lack of beauty, which might otherwise have prejudiced the audience in her favor. As the French critic Delaforest wrote, "I do not have the courage to speak of Mme Pisaroni's appearance. Advice and criticism are perfectly useless in this regard, and at least it is not her beauty that moves one."[24] It was almost *de rigueur* for reviewers of Pisaroni's performances to comment on her physical unattractiveness. Stendahl, who dedicated many pages to evoking the beauty of divas like Giuditta Pasta, could describe Pisaroni in a single sentence: "This is the ugliest singer I have ever seen." Fétis's account of Pisaroni's 1827 debut at the Théâtre Italien, as the young hero Arsace in Rossini's *Semiramide,* described her entrance and the audience's response:

> I will never forget the effect she produced on her audience when, entering and turning her back to the public to contemplate the interior of the temple, she made us hear, in a formidable and admirably produced voice, the phrase: "Eccomi al fine in Babilonia!" Unanimous transports of joy greeted these vigorous sounds and this grand manner, so rare in our times; but when the songstress turned and let us see those features, horribly disfigured by smallpox, a sort of cry of horror followed close

on our enthusiasm, and one saw spectators close their eyes so as to take
pleasure in the talent without being compelled to look at the person.[25]

It is striking that in contrast with these contemporary reports, none of the
existing portraits of Pisaroni depicts her as disfigured, fierce, or repulsive (see
Fig. 12.2). Rather she appears slight and plain: gamine at best, and homely at
worst. This admits of two possible explanations. If she were truly as ugly as
the descriptions say, it may be that artists softened her image, to flatter her
or to keep their depictions within the narrow conventions of female portrai-
ture. But if the portraits are accurate, then we may regard her reputation
for ugliness as a constructed part of her persona. Her rather nondescript
appearance, by itself, would have contributed nothing to her career. But the
mere *absence* of beauty could become an asset by being exaggerated into the
presence of a rare and scandalous ugliness. In Fétis's account we saw how it
allowed her to evoke a combination of ecstasy and horror worthy of a Romantic grotesque, a sublime figure.

The aria Fétis praised showcases the two complementary aspects of a typical *musico* hero, with its andante ("Ah quel giorno ognor rammento") devoted to sentimental reminiscence about the day he rescued his beloved
Azema from barbarian attackers, and its allegro ("O come da quel dì") ener-
getically declaring his love and resolve. The *musico* heroes of Rossini's earlier
Tancredi and *La donna del lago* had exhibited a similar mixture of fierceness
and amorous yearning. Female *musico*s had to be equally effective in vigorous
numbers, with dramatic swoops down to the bottom of the contralto range
to convey the hero's fierce energy, and in slow movements and duets with
the soprano heroine that reveal his sensitive, feeling side. Pisaroni became so
strongly identified with the role of Arsace that some journalists mistakenly
claimed it had been written for her. Malcolm, the hero of *La donna del lago*,
is the only role that Rossini composed expressly for Pisaroni, and the composer gave her fierce and vigorous style unusual prominence in the fast
movement of the entrance aria, "Mura felice" (Allegro: "O quanti lagrime").
The brusque, trumpeting melodic motive and martial dotted rhythms showcase those celebrated "warlike tones."

As Malcolm, and particularly as Arsace in *Semiramide*, Pisaroni became a
touchstone for evaluating other female *musico* singers, few if any of whom
could do equal justice to the virile aspects of these roles. While many female
*musico*s were admired for their performance of Arsace's luscious duets with
the prima donna Semiramide, Pisaroni won her greatest praise in the hero's
entrance aria and duet with the bass villain. In the Arsace–Semiramide duets,
particularly "Giorno d'orrore" (Act II, No. 15), the *musico*'s "virile" side is
temporarily subordinated to the expression of love, devotion, and pathos in

Figure 12.2. Portrait of Rosmunda Pisaroni, ca. 1830. Bibliothèque de l'Opéra. Cliché Bibliothèque Nationale de France.

melting parallel consonances between the two women's voices. The entrance aria and the duet with the bass made equally strenuous vocal and technical demands, while posing a greater acting challenge. Unlike her predecessor at the Théâtre Italien, Pisaroni held her own in these energetic masculine numbers; as one critic reported in 1827, "Her unfavourable exterior is forgotten in the warmth excited by her performance . . . now it is the little Arsace who overcomes the great Assur, Zuchelli."[26] Even twenty years later, in 1848, a review of the great contralto Marietta Alboni as Arsace reveals that the standard set by Pisaroni in the entrance aria and duet had yet to be surpassed: "One would like to see in [Alboni's] exquisite talent a little more force, more accent, and more profundity. She does not stand forth with quite enough energy in the recitative *Eccomi al fine in Babilonia* [Act I, No. 4], which Mme Pisaroni used to deliver with such majesty and breadth, and we also find her a bit weak in the duo with Assur, *È dunque vero, audace* [Act I, No. 5]. The text, a little too caressing and gentle when sung by this artist, is not articulated with enough precision."[27] More than any other *musico*, Pisaroni managed to eliminate the feminine elements of gentleness, delicacy, and charm—either of voice or of body—that might have compromised her heroic impersonations.

Yet only a few years after her splendid Paris season, other responses to Pisaroni show how easily the force and vigor that distinguished her in heroic roles could become liabilities. When she brought her signature roles of Malcolm and Arsace to London in 1829, an English critic remarked that, "Many of her notes have a hardness in them quite unfeminine, and far from agreeable."[28] The same writer described her demeanor as "positive," a word that in the nineteenth century carried strongly, even disgustingly, unfeminine connotations. Although the critic does not cite a specific example, it is easy to imagine that Pisaroni's descent to an emphatic low G at the end of Malcolm's line "Ogn'altro oggetto è a me funesto / tutto è imperfetto, tutto detesto" (Everything [but Elena] is horrible to me, all is imperfect, I detest it all) would incur displeasure for its unladylike vehemence. But if her male roles displeased these critics, she was even less successful in the part of a flirtatious comic heroine: "Of Madame Pisaroni as *Isabella* [in *L'italiana in Algeri*] we can only say, that the part is exactly suited to her voice, and as exactly unfit for her person. She ought to appear as seldom as possible out of male attire."[29] Unfortunately, appearing in male attire did not save her, for she was no more graciously received as Arsace in *Semiramide* at the King's Theatre: "her hard, masculine voice is to us so unpleasant, and her style is, upon the whole, so exactly what we cannot admire, that, with a full consciousness of her merits, which we have before confessed, we always witness her performance with pain, and quit it as a task finished."[30] Lest we be tempted to dismiss this hostility as predictable English anti-Italianism, Pisaroni was greeted with more politeness, but no greater real enthusiasm, when she returned to Italy and tried to rekindle her career there in 1830.

These negative assessments of Pisaroni are symptomatic of the way in which *musico* performers by 1830 were beginning to be squeezed between contrary demands. If a *musico* seemed "masculine" in her manly role, she betrayed her female nature. But if she acted or appeared "feminine," she fell short of the demands of drama. If she acted feminine enough for a woman, she was judged unconvincing and vain, but to act manly enough for a hero made her unnatural and repulsive. She could not be *naturally feminine* and *convincingly masculine* at the same time, and these mutually exclusive demands would shortly make the *musico* hero untenable. The realignment of voice-types and character-types in this period coincides with, and is symptomatic of, a larger shift in tastes and expectations as lingering classicism gave way to full-blown Romantic opera. This shift is marked by a new demand for realism, in that it was no longer sufficient to have a performer and voice that "stands for" the idea of masculine heroism: increasingly, Romantic opera demanded that an actual man should embody that idea. *Musico* roles written for Marietta Brambilla, the leading contralto of the 1830s and 1840s, demonstrate how the operas of the post-Rossini generation moved the cross-dressed female performer to a new function, outside of or tangential to the central love triangle.

AFTER THE *MUSICO* HERO: MARIETTA BRAMBILLA

~

When the twenty-two-year-old contralto Marietta Brambilla appeared at Milan's Teatro Carcano as Arsace in 1829, audiences and critics were quick to note her great promise: "in Brambilla one recognizes a young student of Euterpe, who through her personal and musical talents promises great success."[31] She had debuted in London two years earlier, as Arsace, and had quickly become a specialist in male roles, including Romeo in Zingarelli's *Giulietta e Romeo* and Paolo, the unfortunate Dantean lover in Generali's *Francesca da Rimini.* She spent the 1830–31 season with an Italian opera company in Barcelona. Returning to Italy, she appeared in Turin in the spring of 1832 as Romeo in Bellini's *I Capuleti ed i Montecchi* and in Stefano Pavesi's *La donna bianca.* Milan's *Il censore universale dei teatri* reported that in the latter work, "Brambilla, cross-dressed as a young officer, made a very brilliant figure and was really delightful. Her natural spontaneity in acting, her charming manner of delivering recitatives, her singing which is always correct and precise, expressive or florid when called for, and decorated with most tasteful ornaments—all these gifts, fully perceived and valued by her audience, won for her a palm, which will always be the reward for her great talent."[32] Reports of Brambilla's successes in Barcelona and Turin whetted Milan's appetite to hear her again, and in 1833 she was hired as one of the Teatro alla Scala's two *primi contralti* for the Carnival season.[33]

The description of Brambilla as Giorgio Brown, the young officer in *La donna bianca*, highlights a difference between that role and the traditional *musico* heroes she had played. For a female singer to be "deliziosa" (delightful) in a male role connotes a femininity, even a triviality, inappropriate in a Tancredi, Malcolm, or Arsace. Brilliance and delectability were traits emphasized in a new character-type for the cross-dressed contralto, designated *musichetto*. The diminutive *-etto* indicates the character's youth, light musical style, and reduced dramatic importance. Marco Beghelli contrasts the musical and dramatic place of the *musichetto* with the central part that Rossini's *musico* heroes had occupied:

If the *musico* had played the protagonist of the drama, the *musichetto* symbolized the social and geographical ambience in which the drama takes place; he is the indefatigable protagonist of games, of parties, of jokes, of the moments of *relaxation* in which the tragic action lies in wait to burst forth. Musically his presence is marginal, almost never essential: he does not sing grand arias, and is rarely heard in duets on an equal footing with the lead characters, preferring decorative numbers. His song is not courtly but rather part of everyday life; he tends to express himself in canzonettas, ballatas, and serenades.[34]

Beghelli's description offers a useful framework for discussing the part that Brambilla created at her La Scala debut on 26 December 1833: the trouser role of Maffio Orsini in the premiere of Donizetti's *Lucrezia Borgia*. The opera's Prologue establishes Orsini as an entertainer and raconteur, the natural leader of his friends, in his narrative romanza ("Nella fatal di Rimini") and in his interactions with the chorus and the tenor hero. In the final banquet scene he sings a "colorful" strophic song typical of *musichetto* parts ("Il segreto per esser felice"). Yet Orsini's part is more substantial and more complex, both musically and dramatically, than other contemporary *musichetto* roles: he leads off the Prologue's final ensemble "Maffio Orsini, signora, son io," and—most unusually—sings a duet with the tenor. This character's musical and dramatic prominence resulted not only from the opera's idiosyncracies, but also from the particular gifts of the singer for whom it was composed.

The opera, based on Victor Hugo's play *Lucrèce Borgia* (1833), partook of that work's radical theatrical qualities and thus violated a number of Italian operatic conventions. One expects operatic heroines to be sympathetic, whether noble sinners like Bellini's Norma or innocent victims like Donizetti's own Anna Bolena, but *Lucrezia Borgia* features an infamous poisoner and adulteress, popularly believed to have had liaisons with at least two of her close relatives. Illegitimacy, blasphemy, and mass murder form the fabric of a plot involving characters at once fascinating and repellent. What is more, the spies and betrayers laugh with their victims; murders are discussed, plotted, and perpetrated in a light tone. Hugo's mingling of tragic and comic tones had been radical enough in spoken theater, and was even more so in opera. Indeed, Felice Romani declared in his preface to the libretto that he had never had such difficulty honoring the style and tone of a play while adapting it to the sensibilities of an Italian opera. Another distinctive feature of the play was its large roster of secondary characters: while most operas would have a generic male chorus, *Lucrezia Borgia* features eight named roles, each with solo material. Brambilla's character Maffio Orsini, a prominent secondary role in the play, became even more important in the opera.

The part of Orsini offered a unique opportunity to an ambitious young contralto, for this was a radically new type of *musico* role, both in musical style and in relation to the opera's structure of vocal-dramatic types. Where Rossinian serious operas had typically featured a *musico* hero vying with a male rival for the love of a soprano heroine, the "love triangle" in *Lucrezia Borgia* involves Lucrezia (soprano), her secret illegitimate son Gennaro (tenor), and her husband Duke Alfonso (bass). Alfonso, mistaking Lucrezia's interest in Gennaro for romantic intrigue, vows to kill the young man. Lucrezia saves her son from this misguided revenge in Act I, but unintentionally kills him herself in Act II while in the process of poisoning his rowdy friends, who have offended her in various ways. As the leader of the friends, Gennaro's companion Maffio Orsini represents a kind of "fourth leg" of the central love triangle: although connected intimately to one member of the triangle (Gennaro), he is not caught up in the sexual jealousies and misunderstandings that entangle the three main characters. His insouciance contrasts with the dark and conflicted psychologies of Gennaro and Lucrezia, and his numbers are as different from theirs as from the elaborate arias assigned to earlier *musico* heroes.

Part of the reason Brambilla succeeded so brilliantly in this part is that Romani and Donizetti had developed the character with her in mind. In Hugo's *Lucrèce Borgia,* Maffio Orsini had of course been played by a male actor, but because the impresario Visconti wanted to feature Brambilla in a leading part, it was decided that she would play Orsini as a trouser role and that the character should be expanded to accommodate several solo pieces. Romani invented three new numbers for the character: the narrative song "Nella fatal di Rimini" and the duet with the tenor were interpolated in scenes where Hugo had given Orsini only a passing importance, while the drinking song "Il segreto per esser felice" replaced the blasphemous ditty sung by another character, Gubetta, in Hugo's banquet scene.[35] Thus the role was conceived from the beginning to showcase Brambilla's talents. The ominous "Nella fatal di Rimini" demonstrated her dramatic panache, and the drinking song gave full rein to her brilliant coloratura. Both numbers stand out as innovative even within *Lucrezia Borgia*'s remarkably progressive score.[36]

Romani, Donizetti, and Brambilla created a new type of *musico* role in Maffio Orsini. No longer a paragon of noble devotion, virtue, or honor, the cross-dressed contralto is now an elegantly irresponsible hedonist, even something of a rogue. In his song at the fatal banquet in Act II he explains his philosophy that "The secret of being happy" is to live for today, to laugh and jest in the face of death itself. This strophic song, with its jaunty triple meter, instantly memorable melody, and exhilarating coloratura refrain, epitomizes the "picturesque" musical style typical of Donizetti's *musichetto* roles. Yet the number is more than a catchy showpiece, for it contains the opera's most celebrated stroke of Romantic contrast: tolling bells and chanting monks interrupt Orsini's merry refrain, foreshadowing Lucrezia's revenge. In this *coup de théâtre,* Orsini's song epitomizes the whole opera's mixture of light and darkness, mirth and murder.

While "Il segreto" is radical in style, Orsini's Act II duet with Gennaro is perhaps the most regressive number in the opera. It comes rather late in the plot, when the action is well under way: Gennaro has already been poisoned by Alfonso and saved by Lucrezia, and is preparing to flee Ferrara. Orsini persuades him to stay and attend one more party, promising that at dawn they will leave together. The duet is unusual in several ways. First, this is our only glimpse of Orsini "off-stage," in a private conversation rather than a rhetorical performance. In all his other scenes we see him as a raconteur or performer, whether telling a highly stylized story in "Nella fatal di Rimini," leveling melodramatic accusations at Lucrezia in the ensemble "Maffio Orsini, signora, son io," or entertaining his friends with a drinking song. Second, the form of this duet adheres more closely to the Rossinian model than do the opera's other duets. A *scena,* or opening dialogue, establishes the situation (Gennaro's planned departure: "Sei tu? son io."). The two characters express their feelings about it in a slow lyric movement (Orsini encourages him to stay, and Gennaro resists: "Onde a lei ti mostri grato"). A transitional dialogue passage, or *tempo di mezzo,* brings about a reversal of affect (Gennaro decides to stay another night, and Orsini promises to accompany him tomorrow: "Va, se vuoi: tentar m'è caro"). The concluding fast movement, or cabaletta ("Sia qual vuolsi il tuo destino"), expresses their joy at this solution. The Rossinian jauntiness of this cabaletta is particularly dissonant with the darkness of the opera's other numbers; nowhere else in *Lucrezia Borgia* do we hear these bumpy phrases, galloping rhythm, and vaudevillian full repeat. How might we interpret the tenor and *musico*'s affirming their friendship with such an old-fashioned piece?[37] I believe this duet covertly acknowledges the *musico*'s old-fashioned status, but to argue that point I must first argue another: namely, that the piece creates a new set of sexual connotations for the cross-dressed woman. For if the form of the duet is old, the relationship it establishes between the *musico* and the tenor hero is new.

While trouser roles in bel canto opera have traditionally been regarded as devoid of any sexual charge (Julian Budden's reference to Arsace's "sexless *musico* heroics" is typical), several critics in the 1990s attributed a covert lesbian eros to plots and scenes in which a woman dressed as a man sings love duets with another woman.[38] Traditionally, a *musico* was paired with the heroine: at least one duet for the soprano lovers was standard in Rossinian operas, while duets between the *musico* and other male characters were optional. Donizetti's *musichetto* characters are also usually young men attached to the heroine, even if they now sing characteristic songs to her rather than duets with her: Smeton is devoted to Anna in *Anna Bolena,* Pierotto to Linda in *Linda di Chamounix,* etc. But in *Lucrezia Borgia* the *musico* has almost no contact with the prima donna, and the implicit eros in this opera is the bond between Gennaro and Orsini. Hugo's play had endowed the young men's friendship with a barely covert homoeroticism, and the playwright achieved some comic and titillating moments by shadowing the "natural" relation of masculine companionship with the taboo relation of homosexual love. In Hugo's banquet scene, for example, Orsini flirts with the Princess Negroni, who parries his gallantry with teasing remarks about his devotion to his best friend. Introducing Gennaro to her, Orsini says, "We are never apart. We live together. A Gypsy predicted that we shall die the same day."

> The Princess: Did he say whether at night or in the morning? [a coy allusion, perhaps, to the Renaissance use of "dying together" as a metaphor for orgasm] . . . So, you love this young man?
> Orsini: As much as a man can love a man.
> The Princess: Well then! You are enough for each other. Lucky you.[39]

But if Hugo could toy with allusions to male homosexuality for comic effect, Italian serious opera had no place for it, and Romani's libretto omits such banter.

Even in the opera, however, the two men's rhetoric of boon companionship is virtually indistinguishable from that of love. Their cabaletta, with its vow of eternal devotion, acceptance of a shared fate, and exchange of endearments, is the nearest thing the opera offers to a conventional love duet:

> [BOTH:]   Sia qual vuolsi il tuo destino!
> Esso è mio: lo giuro ancora.
> [ORSINI:]   Mio Gennaro!
> [GENNARO:] Caro Orsino!
> [ORSINI:]   Teco sempre . . .
> [GENNARO:] O viva, o mora.
> Qual due fiori a un solo stelo,
> qual due frondi a un ramo sol,
> noi vedrem sereno il cielo,
> o sarem curvati al suol.

Whatever your destiny requires, so let it be! It is mine as well, I swear it again. My Gennaro! Dear Orsini! With you forever . . . in life or in death. Like two flowers on a single stem, like two leaves on a single bough, we shall behold the clear sky, or we shall be bowed down to the ground.

Orsini and Gennaro's relationship becomes ambiguous in this duet: according to the plot they are two male comrades, but the music makes them a male–female couple. Music reveals the otherwise unacknowledged difference between characters of putatively the same gender. This is the inverse of the image of feminine narcissism in earlier duets for prima donna and *musico,* which had seemed to suggest an otherwise hidden similarity between characters of different genders.

Indeed, this duet makes it possible to interpret the *musico* casting of Orsini as a prudish strategy for diffusing the male homoeroticism that shadows Orsini's and Gennaro's friendship. By casting a woman as Orsini, and making her vocally subordinate to Gennaro, Donizetti "naturalized" their relationship, for the androgynous figure of Brambilla/Orsini could simultaneously embody two functions—that of (male) comrade and of (female) lover/ beloved. While the libretto celebrates egalitarian comradeship, the music encodes a modern structure of male dominance within proper male–female relationships (as opposed to the perverted, improper relationship of Lucrezia and Gennaro) by making the alto musically and dramatically subordinated to the tenor throughout the piece. The Larghetto ("Onde a lei ti mostri grato") highlights the tenor's more strenuous, "effective" singing through contrast with the *musico*'s less impressive opening statement: his stanza is a high-lying, highly chromatic, minor-mode variation on her comfortably low and diatonic melody; her barcarolle rhythm and steady arpeggiated accompaniment give way to a declamatory response supported by agitated orchestral figures. At the end of this movement, where the characters sing together, Donizetti gives the melody to the tenor, while the alto—though technically "above" him—sings an accompanying line. While the two singers present the melody and accompaniment "upside down," the orchestra plays it correctly, with the tenor's melody sounding in the highest instruments and the alto's accompanying line a third below. The tenor's dominance becomes still more pronounced in the cabaletta (Allegro vivace: "Sia qual vuolsi il tuo destino"), where Gennaro sings the trumpeting theme while Orsini chants an accompaniment in the middle of her range. Even when the alto reaches her highest note, F, the effect is overshadowed by the tenor simultaneously singing his more penetrating high A.[40] If Orsini as a male companion represents an alternative to and shelter from the perils of heterosexual entanglement, his feminine voice evokes a "good woman" supporting Gennaro against Lucrezia's dangerous allure. The ambiguity attendant on the travesty role—that doubleness of function, the male exterior shadowed by a woman within—was on the brink of obsolescence in 1833. As a manifestation of love between characters who are at once different and the same, Gennaro's and Orsini's duet belongs to the musical past.

Their relationship is in turn essential to the larger structure of the opera, and it is within that larger structure that the old-fashioned musical idiom of the duet achieves its full significance. The structure could be described as two interlocking "love triangles," both involving Gennaro, of which one is overt and one hidden. While the overt triangle involves Gennaro, Lucrezia, and the jealous Duke Alfonso, Gennaro himself is the object of covert competition between Lucrezia and Orsini. The casting of Orsini as a trouser role betrays the symmetry between these two, for Orsini's female voice places him opposite Lucrezia in the structure: this male character is also a rival to the femme fatale. The boon companion and the alluring woman represent two poles of attraction for Gennaro: Orsini's world of fighting, roaming, carousing, of life lived in and for the moment, is opposed by Lucrezia's world of erotic attraction, kinship, and memory. Their rivalry is established in the Prologue, which introduces Gennaro as part of Orsini's carefree, all-male world. When Gennaro falls asleep on stage during the first scene, his slumber symbolizes his life with Orsini as the oblivion of a perpetual present, in ignorance of his parents, his origins, even his last name. He lives in a state of innocence, not yet ensnared in or by sexuality and family. Gennaro, an abandoned child who has idealized his lost mother, cannot resist the mixture of sensuality and maternal affection that the disguised Lucrezia offers in their first encounter. In a duet filled with hints about his lost mother and the secret of his origins, the veiled woman seems not only to love him but also to promise him a history and a future. It takes the concerted efforts of Orsini and the male chorus (who recognize the *femme fatale* despite her mask and veil) to drive her away and persuade Gennaro of her evil nature in the Prologue's final ensemble. But despite their temporary victory, the next two acts will draw him out of his male homosocial sphere into an Oedipal nightmare dominated by a vindictive father/rival and a mother/love object who proves seductive, life-giving, and ultimately fatal.

The friendship affirmed in Gennaro's Act II duet with Orsini, then, has already become part of his past. Orsini can still position himself as Lucrezia's rival for Gennaro, but events will soon confirm the hopeless asymmetry of this rivalry. Indeed it is an illusion, for the rest of Act II reveals that behind the apparent structure of two realms competing for Gennaro's allegiance lies a more fundamental structure in which Lucrezia dominates everything.

Lucrezia has cast a baleful shadow over Gennaro's and Orsini's friendship from the very beginning, and it is their adherence to Orsini's creed of pleasure and obliviousness that finally places them in Lucrezia's power. The banquet scene reveals, too late, that the young men's world is already subordinated to Lucrezia's sphere, fulfilling the prophecy that Orsini had recounted in "Nella fatal di Rimini." As the spectral voice had predicted, no one can escape la Borgia: "dov'è Lucrezia, è morte" (where Lucrezia is, there's death), and libertine frivolity offers only an illusion of escape from the deadly seriousness she embodies.

Within this new Romantic world, dominated by the fatal woman's poisonous maternity/heterosexuality, Orsini's and Gennaro's oaths to each other assume a poignancy commensurate with their futility. No longer the hero, the *musico* now represents a failed refuge from perilous heterosexual entanglement. The old-fashioned musical form in which Orsini and Gennaro affirm their friendship aligns their homosocial realm with the past: not only the characters' past, but also the past of Italian opera. The Rossinian duet is overshadowed by the modern musical style that surrounds it. The character and the duet are analogous in that each is about to be overtaken and made obsolete: Orsini by Lucrezia, and the Rossinian style by *Lucrezia Borgia*.

While *Lucrezia Borgia* is not the last opera to feature a female *musico*, it represents a turning point in the use of that character-type, a new conception of where the trouser role fits into the plot. It might seem mere coincidence that Brambilla happened to create this first exemplar of the new type, were it not for the fact that future roles written for her would be similar. Over the next decade she would create many variations on this character-type, including the trouser roles in two late Donizetti operas: the heroine's naive friend Pierotto in *Linda di Chamounix* (1842) and the bon vivant Armando di Gondì whose light-hearted joking sets in motion a fatal heterosexual love triangle in *Maria di Rohan* (1843). In Auber's *Gustave III* and later in Verdi's *Un ballo in maschera*, the page Oscar incarnates the sunny, playful side of the tenor hero's personality, a complement to the dark side that gets caught up in erotic obsession and fatal jealousy. Where Giuditta Pasta and Rosmunda Pisaroni had played heroic male roles, Brambilla created the "post-heroic" ones. The *musico* of the 1830s and 1840s was no longer the noble protagonist of his own love story, but rather an auxiliary figure, singing and jesting on the margins of the tragic love plot. He shadows the central romance between tenor and soprano, representing an alternative (but ultimately powerless) love for the hero or heroine. This repositioning of the cross-dressed woman is both symptom and demonstration of the changes in tastes and expectations in *bel canto* opera of the first half of the nineteenth century, the emergence of Romantic opera with its resolute heterosexism and tragic sensibility.

NOTES

1. For discussions of the relationships between voice- and character-types, see Gilles de Van, *Verdi's Theater: Creating Drama through Music,* trans. Gilda Roberts (Chicago: University of Chicago Press, 1998), 93–110; Catherine Clément, "Through Voices, History," in *Siren Songs: Representations of Gender and Sexuality in Opera,* ed. Mary Ann Smart (Princeton: Princeton University Press, 2000), 21–25; Mario Lavagetto, *Quei più modesti romanzi: tecniche costruttive, funzioni, poetica di un genere letterario minore* (Milan: Garzanti, 1979); Philip Gossett, "History and Works that Have no History: Reviving Rossini's Neapolitan Operas," in *Disciplining Music: Musicology and its Canons,* ed. Katherine Bergeron and Philip V. Bohlman (Chicago: University of Chicago Press, 1992), 103–7.
2. de Van, *Verdi's Theater,* 93.
3. Catherine Clément, *Opera, or, The Undoing of Women,* trans. Betsy Wing (Minneapolis: University of Minnesota Press, 1988).
4. Gabriele Baldini, *The Story of Giuseppe Verdi: From Oberto to Un ballo in maschera,* trans. Roger Parker (Cambridge: Cambridge University Press, 1980), 74.
5. Piero Mioli, "Dalla prima sfera all'ultimo cartello: prime, seconde, terze parti nel melodramma italiano all'epoca di Donizetti," in *Il teatro di Donizetti,* vol. 1: *La vocalità e i cantanti,* ed. Francesco Bellotto and Paolo Fabbri (Bergamo: Fondazione Donizetti, 2001), 241–43.
6. See Roger Covell, "Voice Register as an Index of Age and Status in Opera seria," in *Opera and Vivaldi,* ed. Michael Collins and Elise K. Kirk (Austin: University of Texas Press, 1984), 193–210; and the discussion of Margherita Durastante in Stephen LaRue, *Handel and his Singers: The Creation of the Royal Academy Operas, 1720–1728* (Oxford and New York: Oxford University Press, 1995). See also Ellen Harris's essay in this book, chap. 10.
7. This process is surveyed by John Rosselli in *Singers of Italian Opera: The History of a Profession* (Cambridge: Cambridge University Press, 1992). For an examination of changing tenor roles in the works of one bel canto composer, see William Ashbrook, "The Evolution of the Donizettian Tenor-Persona," in *Opera Quarterly* 14 (1998): 24–32.
8. Letter from Antonio de Val to Brenna, 24 August 1843. Quoted in Julian Budden, *The Operas of Verdi* (London: Cassel, 1973), 1:143.
9. Markus Engelhardt examines earlier operas based on subjects eventually set by Verdi in *Verdi und Andere: Un giorno di regno, Ernani, Attila, Il corsaro in Mehrfachvertonungen* (Parma: Istituto Nazionale di Studi Verdiani, 1992). On the heroines of Pacini's and Verdi's *Il corsaro,* see Heather Hadlock, "'The firmness of a female hand' in *The Corsair* and *Il corsaro,*" *Cambridge Opera Journal* 14 (2002), 47–57.
10. Stefano Castelvecchi explains how Scott's narrative poem was adapted to fit the conventions of Italian opera in "Walter Scott, Rossini e la couleur ossianique: Il contesto culturale della *Donna del lago,*" *Bollettino del centro rossiniano di studi* (1993): 57–71.
11. Gioacchino Rossini, *Tancredi,* Act I, No. 2.
12. Rossini, *La donna del lago,* Act I, Introduzione.
13. Victor de Chabrand to Giuditta Pasta, 24 January 1821, in *Giuditta Pasta e i suoi tempi* (Milan: Cromotipia E. Sormani, 1935), 35–36.

14. Maurice Alhoy, *Grande Biographie dramatique . . . par l'Hermite du Luxembourg*, 1824, quoted in *Rossini à Paris* (Paris: Société des Amis du Musée Carnavalet, 1992), 13.

15. *La Quotidienne* 23 April 1822.

16. Ibid.

17. *Journal des Théâtres*, 18 June 1822.

18. Anon. [Stendahl?], in *Annales de la Littérature et des Arts*, Paris, 31 December 1825.

19. Stendahl, letter to Pierre Rapenouille, 28 February 1823, in *Giuditta Pasta e i suoi tempi*, 51.

20. Paul Scudo, "L'Art du Chant en Italie: Les Contralti—Mme Alboni," in *Critique et litterature musicale* (Paris, 1852), 92–115, at 108.

21. Marie and Paul Escudier, "Mme Pisaroni," in *Vie et aventures des cantatrices célèbres* (Paris: E. Dentu, 1856).

22. C. Pavesi, *Benedetta Rosmunda Pisaroni* (Piacenza: Marchesetti e C., 1872), 5–6.

23. Anon., "Oda Saffica" (Brescia, ca. 1822).

24. M. A. Delaforest, "Théâtre Royal Italien, 27 Mai 1827," repr. in *Théâtre moderne: Cours de littérature dramatique* (Paris: Allardin Libraire, 1836), 370.

25. F.-J. Fétis, cited in Arthur Pougin, *Marietta Alboni* (Paris: Librairie Plon, 1912), 84.

26. *Harmonicon* 5 (July 1827): 143.

27. *Revue des deux mondes*, quoted in Pougin, *Marietta Alboni*, 94–95.

28. "The Drama: King's Theater," *Harmonicon* 7 (March 1829): 69. Review of *La donna del lago* (January–February 1829).

29. "The Drama: King's Theater," *Harmonicon* 7 (March 1829): 69. Review of *L'italiana in Algieri* (17 March 1829).

30. *Harmonicon* 7/6 (July 1829): 150.

31. "nella Brambilla [riconobbe] una giovine alunna d'Euterpe, che per le sue doti personali e musicali promette una felicissima riuscita . . ." *Il censore universale dei teatri*, 33 (25 April 1829): 120.

32. "la Brambilla poi, travestita da uffizialetto, fece la più brillante figura e fu propriamente deliziosa. La sua naturale disinvoltura nell'agire, la sua bella maniera di porgere i recitativi, il suo cantare sempre giusto ed esatto, espressivo quando occorre, quando occorre fiorito, e sparso di vezzi di ottimo gusto, tutti questi pregi dal suo uditorio pienamente distinti e valutati le guadagnarono una palma, che sarà sempre il premio del suo bel talento." *Il censore universale dei teatri* 55 (11 July 1832): 220.

33. *Il censore universale dei teatri* 102 (21 December 1833): 406.

34. Marco Beghelli, "Il ruolo del musico," in *Donizetti, Napoli, L'Europa*, ed. Franco Carmelo Greco and Renato di Benedetto (Naples: Edizioni Scientifiche Italiane, 2000), 334.

35. Alessandro Roccatagliati has analyzed Romani's adaptation and versification of Hugo's play in detail in "Felice Romani rifà Hugo: dentro la fucina poetica di *Lucrezia Borgia*," in *Lucrezia Borgia* (Milan: Edizioni del Teatro alla Scala, 1998), 81.

36. For discussions of *Lucrezia Borgia*'s progressive features, particularly the ways in which it resembles and anticipates Verdi's *Rigoletto*, see Gary Tomlinson, "Italian Romanticism and Italian Opera: An Essay in Their Affinities," *Nineteenth Century Music* 10 (1986–87): 43–60; and Will Crutchfield, "Dark Shadows," *Opera News* 63 (July 1998): 32–35.

37. The libretto published for the Milan revival of 1840 suggests that this duet was perceived as old-fashioned even in its own time, for it was cut from that performance and replaced with a tenor aria at the beginning of the act. See the critical edition of

the libretto, *Gaetano Donizetti: Lucrezia Borgia: Libretto di Felice Romani,* ed. Eduardo Rescigno (Milan: Ricordi, 1998), 90.

38. For readings of bel canto heroes as women-loving women in disguise, see Margaret Reynolds, "Ruggiero's Deceptions, Cherubino's Distractions," and Hélène Cixous, "Tancredi Continues," in *En Travesti: Women, Gender Subversion, Opera,* ed. Corinne Blackmer and Patricia Juliane Smith (New York: Columbia University Press, 1995), 132–51; 152–68.

39. Victor Hugo, *Lucrèce Borgia,* Act III, Scene 1. [Ed. Henry Bonnier, p. 711].

40. This might seem an inevitable effect of pairing tenor and alto, but note by contrast how Rossini let the *musico*'s Tancredi dominate her duet with the tenor Argirio: accompanimental figures and orchestral doublings support the *musico* and make clear that the tenor is the subordinate voice. See the duet "Ah se de mali miei . . . Il vivo lampo," is Act II, No. 11 in Rossini, *Tancredi,* ed. Philip Gossett (Milan: Ricordi, 1984).

CHAPTER THIRTEEN

Shifting Selves

EMBODIED METAPHORS IN *NIHON BUYO*

Tomie Hahn

IEMOTO (HEADMASTER) TACHIBANA YOSHIE related to me, "Without experiencing life, without personality, you have no dance, no *kokoro* [heart, spirit, or soul], and you are invisible . . . but if you have a sense of self, then you can become any character on stage—a woman, a young boy, an old man."[1] Her statement conceptually linked performance and the formation of a dancer's identity. Iemoto emphasized the notion that the ability to be flexible within the self is a sign of strength and character—a particularly poignant statement for me, posed at the close of my dance lesson. In this essay I examine how the structures of shifting or codeswitching in dance metaphorically provide women who study *nihon buyo* (Japanese dance) with a flexible sense of self through the transmission of embodied cultural knowledge.

Today *nihon buyo* is a genre dominated by women, while kabuki remains an all-male genre. These gender-specific genres stem from the historic banning of women from theatrical stages in the early seventeenth century. The growing popularity of female performing troupes at this time alarmed government officials. Fearing rampant prostitution as a threat to the government's control, an edict was issued in 1629, banning women from the kabuki stage. Women's performance became marginalized from a very visible and economically lucrative position to a private, hidden domain. This edict, however, did not stop women from performing. The following section provides a general overview of the position of women in the history of Japanese dance.

PLACING WOMEN
～

In Japanese mythology and history, the theatrical ability to enact a variety of characters on stage convincingly wielded great power over audiences. The *Kojiki* (A.D. 714) and *Nihon Shoki* (A.D. 720), Japan's earliest known written documents, tell the mythological tale of the Sun Goddess Amaterasu-no-omikami. Insulted by the mischievous pranks of her brother Susanoo-no-omikoto (guardian of the underworld), Amaterasu hid herself within a cave. Darkness immediately fell upon the heavens. This greatly troubled the gods. They summoned Ama-no-uzume-no-mikoto (a lesser goddess). She fashioned a headdress of *sasaki* branches and performed a comical, erotic dance for the gods on an overturned tub near the cave opening. Reacting to her dance, the gods were overcome with uproarious laughter, which soon aroused the Sun Goddess's curiosity. Amaterasu wondered what the commotion could be and peeked out. Instantly her brilliant rays spread out to the world.

While introducing Japanese dance during a lecture in New York City, Iemoto Tachibana Yoshie humorously explained "Kabuki gave birth to *nihon buyo*"—she grasped her abdomen and gracefully swept her hands downward in pantomime of giving birth. In this swift gesture, she told the tale of history. The "birth" of *nihon buyo* from kabuki lies in the history of their common origin—the famous story of the renowned seventeenth-century priestess of the Izumo Shrine named Okuni. After the *Sengoku jidai* (the "one hundred years war" in the late sixteenth century) the Japanese people, tired of fighting, needed entertainment to express their joys. In the bustling city of Kyoto, street performers set up makeshift shops and small stages along the Kamo River between Shijo and Gionsha avenues. Here a *miko* (temple priestess) from Izumo named Okuni created a stir with her style of *nembutsu odori* (Buddhist dances). Apparently these performances were far from religious and bordered on erotic themes. Okuni donned unusual costumes, carried a sword, and danced in a style foreign to the district. This drew crowds of onlookers and her dance became widely known as *kabuki odori*. The word *kabuki* at that time meant "wild," "avant garde," or "unusual" dance.[2] Despite the lack of specific accounts of Okuni's life, she continues to be hailed as the originator of kabuki dance.

The early years of kabuki are referred to as *onna kabuki* (women's kabuki). Apparently the line between performer and prostitute was quite narrow. There are numerous accounts of the questionable character of performers, who were treated as outcasts.[3] The popularity of kabuki dance grew rapidly, and performances soon spread to other metropolitan centers, such as Edo (Tokyo). The government was concerned with the developing trend, especially its associations with prostitution, and banned women from the kabuki stage in 1629. This closed the era of *onna kabuki*. In light of the attribution of the "birth" of Japanese dance and the origin of kabuki to female figures, it is ironic that women were forbidden from performing kabuki.

MOVING WOMEN

Yet despite the Tokugawa edict banning women from the stage, women had plenty of opportunities to continue practicing dance. The professional tradition of geisha performing dance and music never ceased. Geisha were not the only female performers, however, for women from the middle class also continued to study dance as part of basic etiquette training. The various arts, from tea ceremony and flower arrangement to dance, were considered a means of developing a woman's social graces. In a society that places great value on deportment, women's manners signaled rank and upbringing. In the mid-eighteenth century, small neighborhood schools (*terakoya*) not only taught reading and writing, but also dance and music for etiquette. If a woman's manners were proper, then her family could arrange for her to marry into an affluent family. Her chances of gaining employment, moreover, would be far greater with suitable etiquette training.

It was during the Edo period that the merchant class became powerful. Wealthy merchants, wanting to elevate their social status, enrolled their daughters in dance and music lessons. Since private dance and music performances were often presented at the homes of *samurai*, these merchants hoped that a powerful official would employ their daughters.

According to Nishikata Setsuko, dance schools for women were particularly popular during the mid-nineteenth century. She cites one publication, "Kamikuzu kago" ("The Waste Paper Basket"), which mentions the popularity of women dancers in the Nakamura and Iwada schools.[4] Nishikata also reveals that while the legitimate (all-male) kabuki performances continued on the "surface" (*omote*) to be publicly quite visible, lesser publicized performances by women were also to be found within a "hidden side" (*ura*) of society. Furthermore, she states, by the Meiji period, women performers greatly influenced the kabuki world from this seemingly weak position.[5]

In modern Japan, the varieties of leisure activities enjoyed by women have increased dramatically, ranging from tea ceremony, flower arrangement, golf, knitting, aerobics, and ballroom dancing to the traditional performing arts such as *nihon buyo*. Although women or men do not exclusively practice Japanese dance, women currently dominate the *nihon buyo* dance world and performances are not as widely publicized as kabuki.

The difficulty of defining and categorizing *nihon buyo* generally gives way to extraordinary lists of genres and techniques. The various performing arts in Japan are not as segregated from one another as in the West. Distinctions between theater, dance, and music are often blurred. Practitioners frequently have strong backgrounds in several disciplines. In addition, specific performance genres have become intertwined; they have influenced one another so greatly over time that it is difficult to unravel and differentiate one from the other. These genres, such as *noh, kyogen* (comic theater), kabuki, bunraku (puppet theater), *minzoku geino* (folk or popular arts), and *nihon buyo,* have a complex historical relationship, in which they have borrowed stylistic features, movement vocabulary, musical styles, and story plots from one another. References can be as subtle as a gesture within a phrase or as overt as the appropriation of full story narratives. Quoting or referencing another genre reinforces stylistic borrowing between these genres, but further complicates the distinctions between them. For audience members and performers, however, this eclecticism is an exciting aspect of the performing arts.[6]

The history of constant stylistic borrowing between *nihon buyo* and other genres does not end in the Tokugawa period. The influence of Western dance styles from ballroom dancing to ballet, modern dance, and folk dance, for example, has been significant in their historical development. The strict hierarchical (*iemoto*) social structure governing the arts provided for a highly selective transmission process for inclusion or exclusion of specific influences on dance within a particular school. This created myriad dance style nuances or an individual school taste with varying degrees of Western influences (Western is often synonymous with modern). A number of schools have become well known for their spectacular modern styles. Some have continued to perform the traditional repertories in addition to creating new works that reflect contemporary society.

The three movement elements of *nihon buyo* are considered to be *mai* (a refined, reserved, expressive style of dance with few jumps or quick, folk-like, movements), *odori* (a lively style, displaying some leaps and quick, energetic movements), and *furi* (the pantomime movements from kabuki dance). Combinations of each of these stylistic ingredients are what flavor particular sub-genres and dances. Each sub-genre may emphasize one of the three styles, but, in general, these are the basic elements that characterize Japanese dance. An important point is that, through *furi,* "the body can reveal its true inner self" (*katachi ni arawasu*).[7] Interweaving the qualities of pantomime (*furi*), *mai,* and *odori, nihon buyo* has inherited a wide palette of physical vocabularies with which to express the narrative. The subtleties are endless.

LEARNING TO SHIFT

~

Transmission of dance is a particularly rich setting for observing contemporary culture in action as well as the shaping and orienting of the body/self for artistic expression. In general, systems of transmission structure experience so that, within a particular social group, the world appears similarly constructed and members know how to interact within it. I believe performance provides a special metaphoric space that often reveals how people make sense of their lives and community.[8] Through fieldwork, we are offered a glimpse at a sub-culture's performance practice and "techniques of the body" as shared cultural knowledge.[9] Susan Leigh Foster underscores what observations of such techniques can uncover: "Any standardized regimen of bodily training, for example, embodies, in the very organization of its exercises, the metaphors used to instruct the body, and in the criteria specified for physical competence, a coherent (or not so coherent) set of principles that govern the action of that regimen. These principles, reticulated with aesthetic, political, and gendered connotations, cast the body who enacts them into larger arenas of meaning where it moves alongside bodies bearing related signage."[10] As a window to embodied expression, fieldwork in music and dance can reveal how a community attends to the world and constructs its identity and art from shared sensibilities.

I began studying *nihon buyo* at the age of four in Japan. However, only through a close analysis of the transmission process twenty years later did I come to comprehend aspects of the tradition that I already "knew" in an embodied, intuitive way. My research lens enabled me to view and embody the duality of insider and outsider simultaneously—the analytic (body) informing the intuitive body, the intuitive body informing the analytic, until there did not appear to be a difference. A reflexive resynthesis process between these modes of knowing revealed layers of embodied cultural knowledge both within the dance and my own research process.

I observed that *nihon buyo* training transmits concepts of a shifting or flexible sense of self within the choreographic structures of the dance genre. *Nihon buyo* is primarily based on a narrative. Dancers tell the story with their bodies, while a vocalist narrates the plot in song, including the voices of all the various characters. In some dance pieces (especially those drawn from kabuki), performers assume a single character role for the duration of the performance. In other styles, a performer takes on multiple roles within one piece, requiring her to shift smoothly between characters in order to convey the narrative. Within a minute of dance in such pieces, a performer can move between as many as ten contrasting characters. The embodiment of multiple roles by one performer is a structural device choreographed into a dance to convey the narrative. Through training a performer must learn to articulate physically each persona with expressive clarity so that the individual characters appear distinct.

SHIFTING CHARACTERS

The opening of the dance "Ame no shiki" reveals how vital character shifting is within the performance practice. "Ame no shiki," or "Rain in the Four Seasons" (choreographed by Tachibana Hoshu), provides a clear example of character-shifting techniques. The dance poetically depicts a male traveler encountering seasonal rains in picturesque Edo, and the performer must shift between numerous contrasting roles throughout the dance to illustrate his journey. Armed with only a simple paper fan, a dancer must convincingly animate and transform the prop into a variety of objects to narrate the story, or essence of the dance.

There are no costume changes to match each passing character (in dances where codeswitching serves as a structural element). Since both men and women traditionally wear kimono, the costume itself does not distract, but rather supports, the flexibility of character switching. In comparison with women's kimono, the men's differ in color and pattern design; the inner seam of the sleeves is not open (the seam below the shoulder), and the obi (sash) is narrower and slung lower, below the abdomen. The traditional costuming for "Ame no shiki" is a dark men's kimono and obi. Although women dancers are "cross-dressed" for the entire performance, the basic construction of the kimono allows for subtle transformations of these characters. In *nihon buyo,* the kimono becomes a prop, in a sense—the dancer must use her skills to transform the kimono subtly in the mind's eye of the on-looker. For example, as the following passage reveals, the use of the sleeves enables the dancer to become a bird. Also, when the transformation from male traveler to female character occurs, the dancer's treatment of the kimono hem supports a stereotypic female characterization conveying her modesty and attention to appearance.

First emerges the male traveler, the main character who leads the audience through the dance narrative. A single *shamisen* (three-stringed lute) plays a very slow lyrical melody, soon joined by a male vocalist narrating the scene in a low register. The dancer holds a male carriage: feet shoulder-width apart; toes pointed slightly out; legs in an open (vs. turned inward) position; elbows away from the body; and a broad, erect torso. The traveler shields his face from the rain with a straw hat, mimed with an upturned fan. Facing away from the audience, he peeks out from under his hat to see rain still falling. In Figure 13.1 the traveler can be seen holding his straw hat, sidestepping puddles as he meanders along the path. Notice the dancer's male carriage, elbows turned outward and away from the body, broad shoulders, and his feet lifting up off the ground. Facing the audience, he peers out and sees the rain has stopped. Removing his hat with a shake (that closes the fan), the traveler continues along his way. Japanese music often reveals atmospheric changes and the mood of a dramatic scene—a change of weather in this case. When the rain ceases the musical pulse doubles and we enter into a festival interlude, with bells, flutes, and drums added to the ensemble. This uplifting passage continues yet gradually slows as a chorus of singers is included. The festival music signals the traveler's arrival at a bustling temple festival (*matsuri*) scene. Several sights along the road amuse him, such as birds soaring in the sky. The traveler's kimono sleeves are transformed into wings as he flutters his arms like a bird. Here the character shifting is complex, as the (female) dancer portrays a male traveler who mimes a bird within the dance. Next the traveler points his fan to folk musicians in the distance, and sits for a moment to tap along to the festive beat, a soundworld setting created by the music ensemble for the dancer. The traveler stands and continues on his journey, pointing out various amusements along his path.

Several minutes into the passage, the dancer transforms into a contrasting character—a mother with her child in tow. Now the dancer's quality of movements becomes clearly feminine: elbows close to the body, knees bent, legs together, and toes pointed slightly inward (which keeps the line of the kimono trim and composed when walking). The open fan, held by the paper tip in her right hand, represents the woman's child at her side. At the moment of the codeswitch from traveler to mother, we hear the ensemble support the shift with a contrasting passage—it is a return to a solo male vocalist in a much slower tempo. However, this time the vocalist's (male) voice is in a higher range with a "feminine," lilting, melodic line. She stands for a moment, holding the child's hand, and looks off in the distance. With gentle movements, the mother adjusts her hair and then gestures to attract her child's attention. The mother points ahead, showing the child where they will visit. This pose is captured in Figure 13.2. Note the fan assuming the role of the child holding mother's hand. The dancer's right foot is pointed inward

Figure 13.1. Portrayal of the male traveler in "Ame
no shiki." Photograph by Curtis Bahn.

and just barely visible below her kimono hem. Unlike the male traveler, her
feet and ankles are not displayed, but instead the bent knees and inwardly
pointed feet maintain a discreetly narrow and composed kimono line. After
walking forward the mother notices that the moon has appeared and points
it out to the child. Festivals are often held on Buddhist and Shinto temple
grounds, and within this mother–child passage, sound effects from the music
ensemble, such as a bell for prayer, provide a soundscape of temple activities.
The moon and bell are classic Buddhist metaphors for spiritual realization
or awakening. Paired here in sound and gesture, a context of emotional
warmth and devotion permeates this mother–child scene. The child tugs at
the mother's kimono sleeve, begging to be carried. She obliges. Walking
ahead they come to a series of vendors along the avenue. Here the musical

Figure 13.2. Portrayal of a mother with her child, in "Ame no shiki." Photograph by Curtis Bahn.

ensemble picks up the tempo, setting the stage with a folk-style melodic figure. The child sees *miso dango* (a sweet dumpling served on a stick, dipped in a fermented bean paste) being sold by a peddler and wants one. The mother purchases the *dango,* dips it in *miso,* and feeds it to her child. Immediately following this vignette, the dancer turns and shifts to the character of a candy peddler.

At the point of the character switch, the music changes dramatically to usher us into the new setting. A number of street vendors appear in the following scene and the music links them together as a soundscape to maintain the character of the bustling street. A repetitive *shamisen* figure in a lively folk style continues throughout, as the solo vocalist sings in a syllabic, rhyming pattern of phrases. This passage is somewhat comical in its portrayal in both sounds and gesture, revealing a running social commentary on the rustic street folk. The relationship between the dancer's movements and sounds (stamps and claps) are more coordinated with individual instrumental articulations than in the previous passages. In other words, the dancer's steps, claps, head and arm movements coordinate with drumbeats, fully integrating the dancer's (vendor's) body within the folk soundscape.

The candy peddler appears balancing his wares on his head. He makes his presence known by hitting a small gong, which the dancer mimes with her left hand held above her head. The candy man finds a customer, takes the money with his right hand, and puts it into his left kimono sleeve. He plucks a stick of candy from his display and passes it to the eager customer. Smoothly, the dancer now shifts to a series of four fruit peddlers in rapid succession. First she mimes the peach seller with her gestures—holding the luscious large peach cupped in the left palm while her right hand polishes it with a circular movement. The vendor demonstrates to customers how juicy the fruit is by wiping his mouth with one swift sweep followed by a second shake of the hand to fling the peach juice off his fingers. The dancer then sways her hands inside her sleeves, a movement that abstractly represents mandarin orange and apple vendors. Finally, the dancer tosses the fan from her head to her hand, and by closing it transforms the fan to a banana, which the vendor holds high in the air while circling the area in a lively step to peddle his fruit.

The closed fan transforms from banana to a pestle as a sesame seed peddler appears. The dancer kneels facing the audience and rapidly grinds the sesame seeds in a mortar. The dancer points at more vendors in the distance. Out comes the watermelon hawker. The fan becomes a watermelon slice as the dancer swings the fan open. She mimes holding a knife and cuts the melon in two, then picks up half (the fan) and takes a bite, roughly spitting the seeds off to the ground.

Standing, the dancer transforms into the berry peddler. Then, sitting again, she mimes tying a *tenugui* (a cloth used as a bandanna) to her head and claps loudly to attract customers. The clap occurs at a precise moment in the music—again, an instance of integrating the dancer/vendor within the instrumental texture. She then takes up the open fan, which now becomes a paper cone (an old-style bag) and blows on it to open it up. With her left hand, she holds up a berry to display it to the passersby and pops it into the cone. The dancer stands, balancing the fan on her head, and walks to the back of the room. This opening scene provides ample examples of code-switching techniques embodied in this style of dance.

CODESWITCHING

~

I propose that the learned ability to "shift" between characters in dance metaphorically mirrors a social coordination of self present in daily life in Japan, where clear delineations between men and women, various social circles, and the young and old are reflected in enculturated behavior and speech. In the past two decades, research of "self" in Japanese culture has received a considerable amount of attention.[11] Social anthropologists have proposed that the flexibility of self permits Japanese to interact in a wide variety of social circles in which each social context carries strong cultural markers of morals and obligations. Identity is considered to be relational, or contextually based. As Jane Bachnik explains, "Japanese choose appropriate behavior situationally, from among a range of possibilities, resulting in depictions of the Japanese self as 'shifting' or 'relational.'"[12] This developed sensitivity to social interactions and the ability to coordinate one's path in social situations is acquired through enculturation.

While conducting fieldwork in Japan, Matthews Hamabata, a Japanese American, experienced what is referred to as *tatemae* (surface reality) behavior, and reflected: "Japanese, unlike Americans, can easily accept duality in their lives; in other words, what appears on the surface may not necessarily correspond to the inner reality. Americans would tend to think that the inner reality is in some way 'more real' and would, therefore, try to bring the inner to the surface. They would consider that to be honesty. Elite Japanese would see that as a sign of being ill-bred and ignorant, for the surface reality is just as real as the inner, private reality."[13]

Since the 1970s, binary models have served as strong structural foundations of theoretical discourses on selfhood both in and outside of Japan. Bachnik offers examples of the dualities often related to the Japanese shifting process: "contrasts between discipline/distance and spontaneity/intimacy . . . are commonly expressed in the Japanese language as paired sets of terms, which include *omote* 'in front; surface appearance' versus *ura* 'in-back, what is kept hidden from others.'"[14] Though the positing of dualities was an important developmental stage in the history of social research, I believe that a binary analytical frame reduces the complexity of multi-faceted identities and the social roles they reflect within Japanese society. Codeswitching is not comparable to a light switch—an on/off binary toggle. Instead, I find that the subtleties of embodying such a switching process and the depth of its multiplicity reflect a profoundly complex, contextually based way of life in Japan. At the core of Hamabata's, T. Lebra's, and Bachnik's work is a focus on the process-oriented nature of shifting abilities, revealing the cultural significance of honing and coordinating social sensitivities. Bachnik points out that shifting "refers, not to the content of *omote* and *ura,* but rather to a participant's ability to differentiate between them, and is therefore meta-level knowledge—knowledge about knowledge."[15] Therefore, the honing of skills and disciplines for future use, rather than a gathering of material for a specific content, are emphasized as an important aspect of the shifting process. The acquisition of flexible social skills enables a person to navigate easily within a variety of contexts.

In daily life in Japan, the reality of "codeswitching" is clearly evident. Several women (dancers and non-dancers) have expressed to me that they draw upon a wide palette of personal identities in order to interact in different social contexts in their everyday lives. In fact, some say that shifting is something that they constantly engage in throughout their day—going to the grocery store, riding the subway, talking to the boss, at the playground, or at home.

Codeswitching is embodied in a variety of communication modes. For example, conversational style and linguistic levels of speech from the familiar to honorific are chosen situationally, as is the vocal pitch and voice quality, manner of dress, body language (such as bowing and other social coordinations within a space), and, for performers and artists, the various names individuals acquire in their artistic practices. For codeswitching to be functional in a social context, it must rely on shared modes of communication within a subculture. In fact, codeswitching can be a mode that strengthens bonds within a given community; as Kathryn Woolard points out, codeswitching is "an ingroup phenomenon restricted to those which share the same expectations and rules of interpretation for the use of the two languages."[16]

Research on codeswitching in linguistics and social anthropology has revealed that codeswitching patterns enable individuals access to a variety of social identities. In cultures where codeswitching is prevalent, individuals negotiate multiple frames of reference, with multiple roles and role relationships within the society.[17] Carol Myers Scotton, in her analysis of verbal codeswitching in East Africa, notes aspects of self-definition through codeswitching: "It is as if the switch is made to remind other participants that the speaker is a multi-faceted personality, as if the speaker were saying 'not only am I X, but I am also Y.' This ploy, in and of itself, is a powerful strategy because the speaker 'enlarges' himself/herself through marked choices in a mainly unmarked discourse, asserting a range of identities."[18]

IMAGING WOMEN

~

Feminist theory offers contrasting perspectives on issues of the multiplicity of self. Some view multiplicity as a fragmentation or distortion of women's sense of self (and self-image), while others see multiplicity as a vibrant marker of women's plural identity.[19] As Catriona MacKenzie and Natalie Stoljar write: "Diversity critiques parallel postmodern critiques in challenging the assumption that agents are cohesive and unified. Such critiques claim that each individual has a 'multiple identity,' which reflects the multiple groups to which the individual belongs."[20] In the case of codeswitching in Japanese dance, it may be argued that the highly stylized portrayal of characters in many Japanese dances restricts the repertoire of identity representations to a narrow vocabulary of stereotypes that reinforce male-dominated hierarchical social systems. I find, however, that dance lessons, where women are encouraged to enact roles physically beyond their daily repertory of identities (demons, animals, young, old, male, female), provide a rare setting to "imagine oneself otherwise," to borrow Catriona Mackenzie's phrase. Mackenzie writes, "I contend that our ability to imagine ourselves otherwise— that is, our ability to imaginatively distance ourselves from our habitual modes of self-understanding and to envisage, in imaginative representations, alternative possibilities for ourselves—plays an important role in practical reflection and deliberation about the self, and hence in self-definition."[21] Building on her idea, I propose that physical activity through role playing significantly reinforces an expanded image of self through the vocabulary of embodied memories in dance. I propose that the *process* of embodiment, the enactment of a wide variety of characters has a powerful effect on dancers' identities. Extreme role playing such as a witch, a demon, or a rude, spoiled child, can provide an emotional outlet as well as an expanded vocabulary of identity. Further, dance lesson contexts are a socially acceptable and a "safe" haven to playact expressive modes not deemed appropriate outside the dance studio in Japanese public life.

I find that the continuous codeswitching exemplified in the dance "Ame no shiki" is conceptually similar to the codeswitching one may experience outside of the dance studio. Like codeswitching in everyday life, the codeswitching in dance is founded upon a common vocabulary of communication. Shared physical expressive vocabulary is vital in any narrative artistry in order for the audience to comprehend the story line and the development of a plot. It can be argued that the codeswitching experienced in daily life is founded on social, ethical, and moral situations an individual must spontaneously interact within, whereas dance is a fixed artistic practice. What I find fascinating is that in both settings codeswitching reveals social structures through metaphor. I believe that the very complex sensitivities needed in contrasting social relationships in everyday life form the foundation of choreographic structures in many *nihon buyo* dances. Dance serves as a valuable model of embodied metaphors, which inform how techniques of the body in motion are culturally and historically situated.

EXPERIENCING MULTIPLICITY

In my experience of learning "Ame no shiki" and observing other students learning the dance, I find that focused attention to the subtleties of character portrayal and shifting is crucial. In the dance studio, the process of dance transmission is sensually rich, where teachers pass down dances through oral/aural, kinesthetic, visual, and tactile methods of transmission.[22] Iemoto draws our attention to the subtle details of each character, from carriage, gesture, gaze, facial expression, costume, to prop use. She often takes a moment during lessons to describe the character clearly and the context of his/her (or the animal's) appearance. When I learned the sesame seed vendor passage Iemoto commented—"Do you know what you're doing? Have you ever ground sesame seeds?" While the portrayal of grinding the seeds is performed in a stylized manner, the mimetic act must convey the process of grinding to the audience, otherwise "How will they know what you are doing?"

Iemoto pays particular attention to the moment of transformation between characters. Clarity in the role shift supports the narrative. She teased me and made her point clear: "You can't be the (male) vendor but still have feminine feet (from the last character)!" This type of verbal instruction is often coupled with a visual and tactile cue—Iemoto, acting as a kind of puppeteer, guides my body through the proper movement and pose for that character and narrative. In Figure 13.3, for example, Iemoto can be seen clearly adjusting my character portrayal through such visual and tactile cues. Notice her embrace and the particular points of contact. With her right hand, she grasps my wrist and, hidden from view, her left hand gently encircles my waist, and she leans into my body space. Experiencing this kind of transmission can be exhilarating, as I can actually feel Iemoto's embodiment of specific characters directly—in a way, she dances a character *into* my body.

I am often asked if learning to embody stylized stereotypes in dance constricts dancers' sense of individual identity. From personal experience as a dancer and researcher, I actually find the opposite to be true—that it is the

Figure 13.3. Iemoto Tachibana Yoshie with the author.
Tachibana School, Tokyo, Japan. Photograph by Walter
Hahn.

relationship of physical expression in everyday life and dance that provides
an abundant palette of selves to express one's inner sense of self. I believe
Iemoto's illustration, "without experiencing life, without personality, you
have no dance, no *kokoro* [heart, spirit, or soul], and you are invisible . . .
but if you have a sense of self, then you can become any character on
stage—a woman, a young boy, an old man," resonates the profound relationship between a dancer's sense of self (and character) both inside and outside
of dance. As the headmaster of the Tachibana school, it is Iemoto's obligation
to transmit the way of dance to her students. It is, however, clear to me in
our lessons that her guidance reaches far beyond dance to a deeper level of
comprehending one's self relative to others and the world.

The direct physical transmission of multiple characters in the dance studio
teaches stylized roles, yet it also imparts a way of knowing self and character

through the body, which passes beyond superficial mimicking. *Nihon buyo* offers women powerful expressive means to transcend the boundaries, which might be confining in daily life in Japan. Strict social rules, expectations, and obligations restraining women's behavior can create a high level of pressure. I believe dance provides a liberating opportunity for women to act out (roles)—consider transforming into a monkey, a lower-class character, a princess, a ghost, a drunkard, or a bold demonic witch. There is, however, a complex set of traditional social obligations attached to *nihon buyo* life. The strict *iemoto* (headmaster) system, which enforces the continuity of the oral tradition and dance family heritage, for example, overlays yet another complex web of multiplicity. I am sure this idea of added obligation and perceived confinement of behavior must dissuade many women from entering into the *nihon buyo* world. I acknowledge these pressures exist, though I personally find them outweighed by the deep bonds I experience in the Tachibana dance family. The commitment of these women to the art inspires me to move and write.

Performance provides a vehicle to express complex identities and even to broaden personal expressive vocabularies. Richard Bauman sees performance as a means "for the encoding and presentation of information about oneself in order to construct a personal and social image."[23] I see performance as a process where boundaries of identity (gender, ethnicity, age, social class, etc.) are negotiated metaphorically. Through performance within a community, a shared sense of meaning and self can be conveyed and acquired. Self is shaped via performance. In Japan, performance is considered to embody mystical powers. Might it be possible to transgress the boundaries of our everyday identities through the structures of choreographed codeswitching?

In the practice of *nihon buyo*, women learn from a very early age how to express a diversity of character portrayals. Teachers transmit a wide vocabulary of embodied gender ideologies via the teaching process. The tradition of metaphoric shifting provides students with a variety of abilities to negotiate and comprehend multiple identities on the dance floor and in their lives. I believe the metaphoric shifting present in *nihon buyo* choreography offers women an embodied understanding of multiple identities as well as flexible notions of self within a society that has historically restricted their expression.

NOTES

~

I would like to acknowledge the American Association of University Women for granting me an Educational Foundation American Fellowship and Tufts University for academic research leave. These grants enabled me to finalize the research and writing of this article during the fellowship year.

1. Fieldnotes, 9 October 1993. I refer to Tachibana Yoshie as "Iemoto" (headmaster) throughout this essay because this is how she is referred to within the school. The East Asian convention of placing the family name before an individual's given name has been followed for Japanese names except in the endnotes, where the family name appears second.

2. In the late sixteenth century, *kabuki* was an everyday word for things that were uncommon or departed from the norm. Later in time the word *kabuki* was written with different *kanji* characters breaking down to: *ka*—song; *bu*—dance; and *ki*—skill.

3. Masakatsu Gunji, *Kabuki to Yoshiwara* (Tokyo: Asaji Shobo, 1956), and id., *Kabuki* (Tokyo: Kodansha International, 1985).

4. Setsuko Nishikata, *Nihon buyo no kenkyu* [The World of Japanese Dance] (Tokyo: Kodansha, 1988), 52.

5. Ibid.

6. See Yoshihiko Tokumaru, "Intertextuality in Japanese Traditional Music," in *The Empire of Signs: Semiotic Essays on Japanese Culture*, ed. Yoshihiko Ikegami (Amsterdam and Philadelphia: John Benjamins Publishing, 1991) for background on the complexities and nuances of intertextuality in Japanese *shamisen* music.

7. Nishikata, *Nihon buyo no kenkyu*, 80.

8. *Performance, Culture, and Identity*, ed. Elizabeth Fine and Jean Haskell Speer (Westport, Conn.: Praeger Publishers, 1992).

9. Marcel Mauss, "The Notion of Body Techniques," in *Sociology and Psychology: Essays* (London and Boston: Routledge and Kegan Paul, 1979). Susan Leigh Foster, "Dancing Bodies," in *Meaning in Motion: New Cultural Studies of Dance*, ed. Jane Desmond (Durham, N.C.: Duke University Press, 1997).

10. Susan Leigh Foster, "An Introduction to Moving Bodies: Choreographing History," in *Choreographing History, Unnatural Acts, Theorizing the Performative*, ed. Susan Leigh Foster (Bloomington: University of Indiana Press, 1995), 8.

11. To list a few: Jane Bachnik, "*Kejime*: Defining a Shifting Self in Multiple Organizational Modes," in *Japanese Sense of Self*, ed. Nancy R. Rosenberger (Cambridge: Cambridge University Press, 1992); John Clammer, *Difference and Modernity: Social Theory and Contemporary Japanese Society* (London: Kegan Paul International, 1995), 59–97; George DeVos, "Dimensions of Self in Japanese Culture," in *Culture and Self: Asian and Western Perspectives*, ed. Anthony Marsella, George DeVos, and Francis Hsu (New York: Tavistock Publications, 1985); Takeo Doi, *Omote to ura/The Anatomy of Self* (New York: Kodansha International, 1988); Takeo Doi, *Amae no kozo/The Anatomy of Dependence* (New York: Kodansha International, 1981); Matthews Hamabata, *Crested Kimono: Power and Love in the Japanese Business Family* (Cambridge: Cambridge University Press, 1990); Thomas P. Kasulis, "The Body—Japanese Style," in *Self as Body in Asian Theory and Practice*, ed. Thomas P. Kasulis, Roger T. Ames, and Wimal Dissanayake (Albany: State University of New York Press, 1993), 321–46; Dorinne Kondo, "Multiple Selves: The Aesthetics and Politics of Artisanal Identities," in *Japanese Sense of Self*, ed. Rosenberger, 40–66; T. Lebra, *Japanese Patterns of Behavior* (Honolulu: University of Hawaii Press, 1976); *Japanese Sense of Self*, ed. Nancy R. Rosenberger (Cambridge: Cambridge University Press, 1992); Yasuo Yuasa, *The Body: Toward an Eastern Mind-Body Theory* (Albany: State University of New York, 1987); Yasuo Yuasa, *The Body, Self-Cultivation, and Ki-Energy* (Albany: State University of New York, 1993).

12. Bachnik, "Kejime," 152.

13. Hamabata, *Crested Kimono,* 10.

14. Bachnik, "Kejime," 153.

15. Ibid., 156.

16. "Codeswitching and Comedy in Catalonia," in *Codeswitching: Anthropological and Sociolinguistic Perspectives,* ed. Monica Heller (Berlin and New York: Mouton de Gruyter, 1988), 69.

17. See Monica Heller, *Codeswitching: Anthropological and Sociolinguistic Perspectives,* 8.

18. Carol Myers Scotton, "Codeswitching as Indexical of Social Negotiations," in *Codeswitching,* ed. Heller, 170. For codeswitching in music and performance see Mark Slobin, "Code Switching and Code Superimposition in Music," in *Working Papers in Sociolinguistics,* no. 63 (1979); id., *Subcultural Sounds: Micromusics of the West* (Hanover, N.H.: Wesleyan University Press, 1993); and Amelia Maciszewski, "Multiple Voices, Multiple Selves: Song Style and North Indian Women's Identity," *Asian Music* 32 (2001): 1–40 for issues of multiple selves in music performance.

19. See Morwenna Griffiths, *Feminisms and the Self: The Web of Identity* (London and New York: Routledge, 1995); *Feminists Rethink the Self,* ed. Diana Tietjens Meyers (Boulder, Colo.: Westview Press, 1997); Maria Lugones, "On the Logic of Feminist Pluralism," in *Feminist Ethics,* ed. Claudia Card (Lawrence: University Press of Kansas, 1991); Deborah K. King, "Multiple Jeopardy, Multiple Consciousness: The Context of a Black Feminist Ideology," *Signs* 14 (1988): 42–72.

20. Catriona MacKenzie and Natalie Stoljar, "Autonomy Refigured," in *Relational Autonomy: Feminist Perspectives on Autonomy, Agency, and the Social Self,* ed. Catriona MacKenzie and Natalie Stoljar (New York: Oxford University Press, 2000), 11.

21. Catriona MacKenzie, "Imagining Oneself Otherwise," ibid., 139.

22. See Tomie Hahn, *Sensational Knowledge: Teaching Japanese Dance* (Middletown, Conn.: Wesleyan University Press, forthcoming); "Sensational Knowledge: Transmitting Japanese Dance and Music" (Ph.D. diss., Wesleyan University, Middletown, Conn., 1997); and "Singing a Dance: Navigating the Musical Soundscape in Nihon Buyo," in *Asian Music* 33 (2001): 1–40 for more detailed information on *nihon buyo* transmission at the Tachibana school, including visual, oral/aural, tactile, and kinesthetic modes of transmission.

23. Richard Bauman, *Story, Performance and Event: Contextual Studies of Oral Narrative* (Cambridge: Cambridge University Press, 1984), 21.

GENERAL READINGS

Ammer, Christine. *Unsung: A History of Women in American Music.* Westport, Conn: Greenwood Press, 1980.

Barkin, Elaine, and Lydia Hamessley, eds. *Audible Traces: Gender, Identity, and Music.* Zurich and Los Angeles: Carciofoli Verlagshaus, 1999.

Battersby, Christine. *Gender and Genius: Towards a Feminist Aesthetics.* Bloomington: Indiana University Press, 1989.

Blackmer, Corinne E., and Patricia Juliana Smith, eds. *En Travesti: Women, Gender Subversion, Opera.* New York: Columbia University Press, 1995.

Bowers, Jane, and Judith Tick, eds. *Women Making Music: The Western Art Tradition, 1150–1950.* Urbana: University of Illinois Press, 1986.

Brett, Philip, Elizabeth Wood, and Gary C. Thomas, eds. *Queering the Pitch: The New Gay and Lesbian Musicology.* New York: Routledge, 1994.

Citron, Marcia J. *Gender and the Musical Canon.* Cambridge and New York: Cambridge University Press, 1993.

Clément, Catherine. *Opera, or, The Undoing of Women.* Translated by Betsy Wing. Minneapolis: University of Minnesota Press, 1988.

Cook, Susan C. "'R-E-S-P-E-C-T. Find Out What It Means to Me': Feminist Musicology and the Abject Popular." *Women & Music* 5 (2001): 140–45.

——— and Judy S. Tsou, eds. *Cecilia Reclaimed: Feminist Perspectives on Gender and Music.* Urbana: University of Illinois Press, 1994.

Cusick, Suzanne G. "'Eve . . . Blowing in Our Ears?' Toward a History of Music Scholarship on Women in the Twentieth Century." *Women & Music* 5 (2001): 125–39.

———. "Gender, Musicology and Feminism." In *Rethinking Music*, ed. by Nicholas Cook and Mark Everist, 471–98. Oxford: Oxford University Press, 1999.

Dellamora, Richard, and Daniel Fischlin, eds. *The Work of Opera: Genre, Nationhood, and Sexual Difference.* New York: Columbia University Press, 1997.

Drinker, Sophie. *Music and Women: The Story of Women in their Relation to Music.* New York: Coward-McCann, 1948. Repr. Washington, D.C.: Zenger Publishing, 1977. Repr. with preface by Elizabeth Wood and afterword by Ruth A. Solie, New York: Feminist Press at the City University of New York, 1995.

Dunn, Leslie, and Nancy Jones, eds. *Embodied Voices: Representing Female Vocality in Western Culture.* Cambridge: Cambridge University Press, 1994.

Fuller, Sophie, and Lloyd Whitesell, eds. *Queer Episodes in Music and Modern Identity.* Urbana: University of Illinois Press, 2002.

Herndon, Marcia, and Susanne Ziegler, eds. *Music, Gender, and Culture.* International Council for Traditional Music Study Group on Music and Gender. Intercultural Music Studies, no. 1. Wilhelmshaven: Florian Noetzel, 1990.

Koskoff, Ellen. "Gender, Power, and Music." *The Musical Woman: An International Perspective* 3 (1986–90): 769–88.

————, ed. *Women and Music in Cross-Cultural Perspective.* Urbana: University of Illinois Press, 1989.

Marshall, Kimberly, ed. *Rediscovering the Muses: Women's Musical Traditions.* Boston: Northeastern University Press, 1993.

McClary, Susan. *Feminine Endings: Music, Gender, and Sexuality.* Minneapolis: University of Minnesota Press, 1991.

Moisala, Pirkko, and Beverley Diamond, eds. *Music and Gender.* Urbana: University of Illinois Press, 2000.

Monson, Ingrid. "Music and the Anthropology of Gender and Cultural Identity." *Women & Music* 1 (1997): 24–32.

Neuls-Bates, Carol. *Women in Music: An Anthology of Source Readings from the Middle Ages to the Present.* Boston: Northeastern University Press, 1996.

Pendle, Karin, ed. *Women and Music: A History.* 2d rev. ed. Bloomington: Indiana University Press, 1991.

Placksin, Sally. *American Women in Jazz: 1900 to the Present: Their Words, Lives, and Music.* New York: Wideview Books, 1982.

Robertson, Carol E. "Power and Gender in the Music Experiences of Women." In *Women and Music in Cross-Cultural Perspective,* ed. Ellen Koskoff, 225–44. Urbana: University of Illinois Press, 1989.

Sarkissian, Margaret. "Gender and Music." In *Ethnomusicology. I: An Introduction.* The New Grove Handbooks in Music, ed. Helen Myers, 337–48. New York and London: W. W. Norton, 1992.

————. "Thoughts on the Study of Gender in Ethnomusicology: A Pedagogical Perspective." *Women & Music* 3 (1999): 17–27.

Smart, Mary Ann, ed. *Siren Songs: Representations of Gender and Sexuality in Opera.* Princeton: Princeton University Press, 2000.

Solie, Ruth A. "Defining Feminism: Conundrums, Contexts, Communities." *Women & Music* 1 (1997), 1–11.

————. "Feminism." *The New Grove Dictionary of Music and Musicians.* Edited by Stanley Sadie and John Tyrrell, 2d ed. London: MacMillan, 2001, 8:664.

————. "Sophie Drinker's History." In *Disciplining Music: Musicology and Its Canons,* ed. Katherine Bergeron and Philip V. Bohlman, 23–43. Chicago: University of Chicago Press, 1992.

————, ed. *Musicology and Difference: Gender and Sexuality in Music Scholarship.* Berkeley and Los Angeles: University of California Press, 1993.

Tick, Judith, and Ellen Koskoff. "Women in Music." *The New Grove Dictionary of Music and Musicians.* Edited by Stanley Sadie and John Tyrrell, 2d ed. London: MacMillan, 2001, 27:519–42.

FOR FURTHER STUDY

⁓

PART ONE:
PUBLIC VOICES, PRIVATE VOICES

Books and Articles

Abu-Lughod, Lila. *Veiled Sentiments: Honor and Poetry in a Bedouin Society.* Berkeley and Los Angeles: University of California Press, 1986.

Ahmed, Leila. *Women and Gender in Islam*. New Haven: Yale University Press, 1992.

Babiracki, Carol M. "What's the Difference? Reflections on Gender and Research in Village India." In *Shadows in the Field: New Perspectives for Fieldwork in Ethnomusicology*, ed. Gregory F. Barz and Timothy J. Cooley, 121–38. Oxford and New York: Oxford University Press, 1997.

Bernstein, Jane A. "'Shout, Shout, Up with Your Song!' Dame Ethel Smyth and the Changing Role of the British Woman Composer." In *Women Making Music*, ed. Bowers and Tick, 304–24.

Brooks, Jeanice. "*Noble et grande servante de la musique*: Telling the Story of Nadia Boulanger's Conducting Career." *Journal of Musicology* 14 (1996): 92–116.

Brown, C. Mackenzie. "The Theology of Radha in the Puranas." In *The Divine Consort: Radha and the Goddesses of India*, ed. John Stratton Hawley and Donna Marie Wulff, 57–71. Boston: Beacon, 1982.

Cai, Camilla. "Fanny Mendelssohn Hensel." In *Women Composers: Music through the Ages*, vol. 6: *Composers Born 1800–1899. Keyboard Music*, ed. Sylvia Glickman and Martha Furman Schleifer, 21–43. New York: G. K. Hall, 1999.

———. "Texture and Gender: New Prisms for Understanding Hensel's and Mendelssohn's Piano Pieces." In *Nineteenth-Century Piano Music: Essays in Performance and Analysis*, ed. David Witten, 53–93. New York: Garland Publishing Co., 1997.

Citron, Marcia J. "The Lieder of Fanny Mendelssohn Hensel." *Musical Quarterly* 69 (1983): 570–93.

———. "Mendelssohn (-Bartholdy) [Hensel], Fanny Cäcilie." *The New Grove Dictionary of Music and Musicians*. Edited by Stanley Sadie and John Tyrrell. 2d ed. London: Macmillan, 2001, 16:388–89.

Cobb, Jodi. *Geisha: The Life, the Voices, the Art*. New York: Alfred A. Knopf, 2000.

Cooper, John Michael, and Julie D. Prandi, eds. *The Mendelssohns: Their Music in History*. Oxford: Oxford University Press, 2002.

Dalby, Liza. *Geisha*. Berkeley and Los Angeles: University of California Press, 1983.

Danielson, Virginia. "Moving toward Public Space: Women and Musical Performance in Twentieth-Century Egypt." In *Hermeneutics and Honor: Negotiating Female "Public" Space in Islamic/ate Societies*, ed. Asma Afsaruddin, 116–39. Cambridge, Mass: Center for Middle Eastern Studies, Harvard University, 1999.

Doubleday, Veronica. "Courtesan." *New Grove Dictionary of Music and Musicians*. Edited by Stanley Sadie and John Tyrrell. 2d ed. London: Macmillan, 2001, 6:609–11.

Ellis, Katharine. "Female Pianists and Their Male Critics in Nineteenth-Century Paris." *Journal of the American Musicological Society*, 50 (1997): 353–85.

Fauser, Annegret. "Lili Boulanger's *La Princesse Maleine*: A Composer and Her Heroine as Literary Icons." *Journal of the Royal Musical Association* 122 (1997): 68–108.

Forney, Kristine. "'Nymphes gayes en abry du laurier': Music Instruction for the Bourgeois Woman." *Musica Disciplina* 49 (1995): 151–87.

Fruzzetti, Lina. *The Gift of a Virgin: Women, Marriage, and Ritual in a Bengali Society*. Delhi: Oxford University Press, 1990.

Gold, Ann Grodzins. "Purdah is as Purdah's Kept: A Storyteller's Story." In *Listen to the Heron's Words: Reimagining Gender and Kinship in North India*, ed. Gloria Goodwin Raheja and Ann Grodzins Gold. Berkeley: University of California Press, 1994.

Hensel, Fanny. *The Letters of Fanny Hensel to Felix Mendelssohn*. Collected, edited, and translated with introductory essays and notes by Marcia J. Citron. Stuyvesant, N.Y.: Pendragon Press, 1987.

———. *Tagebücher.* Edited by Hans-Günter Klein and Rudolf Elvers. Wiesbaden: Breitkopf & Härtel, 2002.

Hensel, Sebastian. *Die Familie Mendelssohn 1729–1847: Nach Briefen und Tagebüchern,* 2d rev. ed. Berlin: B. Behr's Buchhandlung, 1880. 2 vols. In English translation, *The Mendelssohn Family (1729–1847): From Letters and Journals.* Translated by Carl Klingemann and an American Collaborator. New York: Harper & Brothers, 1881.

Jones, L. JaFran. "A Sociohistorical Perspective on Tunisian Women as Professional Musicians." In *Women and Music in Cross-Cultural Perspective,* ed. Koskoff, 69–83.

Kallberg, Jeffrey. "Harmony of the Tea Table: Gender and Ideology in the Piano Nocturne." In *Chopin at the Boundaries: Sex, History, and Musical Genre.* Cambridge, Mass: Harvard University Press, 1996.

Kersenboom-Story, Saskia C. *Nityasumangali: Devadasi Tradition in South India.* Delhi: Motilal Banarsidass, 1987.

Kimber, Marian Wilson. "The 'Suppression' of Fanny Mendelssohn: Rethinking Feminist Biography." *19th-Century Music* 26 (2002): 113–29.

Lee, Byong Won. "Evolution of the Role and Status of Korean Professional Female Entertainers (Kisaeng)." *World of Music* 21 (1979): 75–83.

Leppert, Richard. "Sexual Identity, Death, and the Family Piano." *19th-Century Music* 16 (1992): 105–27.

Marglin, Frederique Apffel. *Wives of the God-King: The Rituals of the Devadasis of Puri.* Delhi: Oxford University Press, 1985.

Mendelssohn, Fanny. *Italienisches Tagebuch.* Edited by Eva Weissweiler, 2d ed. Darmstadt: Luchterhand Verlag, 1988.

Mernissi, Fatima. *Beyond the Veil: Male-Female Dynamics in Modern Muslim Society.* Rev. ed. Bloomington: Indiana University Press, 1987.

Newcomb, Anthony. "Courtesans, Muses, or Musicians? Professional Women Musicians in Sixteenth-Century Italy." In *Women Making Music,* ed. Bowers and Tick, 90–115.

Oldenburg, Veena Talwar. "Lifestyle as Resistance: The Case of the Courtesans of Lucknow, India." *Feminist Studies* 16 (1990): 259–87.

Post, Jennifer C. "Erasing the Boundaries between Public and Private in Women's Performance Traditions." In *Cecilia Reclaimed,* ed. Cook and Tsou, 35–51.

———. "Professional Women in Indian Music: The Death of the Courtesan Tradition." In *Women and Music in Cross-Cultural Perspective,* ed. Koskoff, 97–109.

Qureshi, Regula Burckhardt. "In Search of Begum Akhtar: Patriarchy, Poetry, and Twentieth-Century Indian Music." *The World of Music* 43 (2001): 97–137.

Ramanujan, A. K. "On Women Saints." In *The Divine Consort: Radha and the Goddesses of India,* ed. by John Stratton Hawley and Donna Marie Wulff, 316–24. Boston: Beacon, 1982.

Reich, Nancy. "Clara Schumann." In *Women Making Music,* ed. Bowers and Tick, 249–81.

———. *Clara Schumann: The Artist and the Woman.* Ithaca: Cornell University Press, 1985.

———. "Women as Musicians: A Question of Class." In *Musicology and Difference,* ed. Solie, 125–46.

Rosand, Ellen. "The Voice of Barbara Strozzi." In *Women Making Music,* ed. Bowers and Tick, 168–90.

Rosenstiel, Léonie. *The Life and Works of Lili Boulanger.* Rutherford, N.J., and London: Fairleigh Dickinson University Press, 1978.

———. *Nadia Boulanger: A Life in Music.* New York and London: W. W. Norton, 1982.

Rothenberg, Sarah. "Fanny Mendelssohn's Musical Diary." *Keyboard Classics* (July/August 1991): 6–7, 43.

————. "Thus Far, but no Farther: Fanny Mendelssohn-Hensel's Unfinished Journey." *Musical Quarterly* 77 (1993): 689–708.

Rutherford, Susan. "The Voice of Freedom: Images of the Prima Donna." In *The New Woman and Her Sisters: Feminism And Theatre, 1850–1914,* ed. Vivien Gardner and Susan Rutherford, 95–113. Ann Arbor: University of Michigan Press, 1992.

Silverman, Debora. "The 'New Woman,' Feminism, and the Decorative Arts in Fin-de-Siècle France." In *Eroticism and the Body Politic,* ed. Lynn Hunt, 144–63. Baltimore and London: The Johns Hopkins University Press, 1991.

Sirota, Victoria. "The Life and Works of Fanny Mendelssohn Hensel." Mus. A.D. diss., Boston University, 1981.

Tick, Judith. "Passed Away is the Piano Girl: Changes in American Musical Life, 1870–1900." In *Women Making Music,* ed. Bowers and Tick, 325–48.

Tillard, Françoise. *Fanny Mendelssohn.* Translated by Camille Naish. Portland, Ore.: Amadeus Press, 1996.

Torjesen, Karen Jo. "Martyrs, Ascetics, and Gnostics." In *Gender Reversals and Gender Cultures: Anthropological and Historical Perspectives,* ed. Sabrina Petra Ramet, 79–91. London: Routledge, 1996.

Wallace, Sean Michael Hamilton. "Fanny Mendelssohn Hensel: A Comprehensive Bibliography. Part I: Books, Dissertations, and Choral Music." *Research Memorandum Series* 177 (summer 2000); "Part II: Articles, Essays and Recordings." *Research Memorandum Series* 178 (summer 2001).

Wollny, Peter. "Sara Levy and the Making of Musical Taste in Berlin." *Musical Quarterly* 77 (1993): 651–88.

Recordings

Boulanger, Lili. *Du fond de l'abîme, Psaume 24, Psaume 129, Vielle prière, Pie Jesu.* Orchestre Lamoureux. Igor Markevitch. Everest EVC 9034 (1995).

————. *Faust et Hélène, D'un matin de printemps, D'un soir triste, Psaume 130 "Du fond de l'abîme," Psaume 24.* BBC Philharmonic. Yan Pascal Tortelier. Chandos 9745 (1999).

Mendelssohn Hensel, Fanny. *Das Jahr.* Sarah Rothenberg, piano. Arabesque Z6666 (1996).

————. *Das Jahr.* Ulrich Urban, piano. Koch International 367192 (1998).

————. *Klavierwerke.* 2 vols. Liana Serbescu, piano. CPO 999013–2 (1986); CPO 999015–2 (1987).

————. *Lieder.* Susan Gritton, soprano; Eugene Asti, Piano. Hyperion CDA67110 (2000).

————. *Lieder für Sopran und Klavier, opp. 1, 7, 9, 10.* Isabel Lippitz, soprano; Barbara Heller, piano. CPO 999011–2 (1986).

————. *Overture* (ca. 1830). The Women's Philharmonic, JoAnn Falletta, cond. Koch International 3–7169–2H1 (1992).

————. *Selected Music for Piano.* Sontraud Speidel, piano. Brioso 107, n.d.

Schumann, Clara, and Fanny Mendelssohn. *Piano Trios.* Dartington Piano Trio. Hyperion CD66331 (1988).

PART TWO:
CLOISTERED VOICES

Books and Articles

Baldauf-Berdes, Jane L. "Anna Maria della Pietà: The Woman Musician of Venice Personified." In *Cecilia Reclaimed,* ed. Cook and Tsou, 134–55.

————. *Women Musicians of Venice: Musical Foundations, 1524–1855.* Oxford: Oxford University Press, 1993.

Davidson, Audrey Ekdahl, ed. *The Ordo Virtutum of Hildegard of Bingen: Critical Studies.* Kalamazoo: Western Michigan University Press, 1992.

Doubleday, Veronica. *Three Women of Herat.* Austin: University of Texas Press, 1990.

Dronke, Peter. *Women Writers of the Middle Ages.* Oxford: Oxford University Press, 1981.

————, trans. and ed. *Nine Medieval Latin Plays.* Cambridge and New York: Cambridge University Press, 1994.

Fassler, Margot. "Composer and Dramatist: 'Melodious Singing and the Freshness of Remorse.'" In *Voice of the Living Light,* ed. Barbara Newman, 149–75. Berkeley: University of California Press, 1998.

Flanigan, Sabina. *Hildegard of Bingen, 1098–1179: A Visionary Life.* Rev. ed., London and New York: Routledge, 1998.

Handy, D. Antoinette. *The International Sweethearts of Rhythm: The Ladies Jazz Band from Piney Woods Country Life School.* Rev. ed. Lanham, Md.: Scarecrow Press, 1998.

Hildegard of Bingen. *The Letters of Hildegard of Bingen.* Translated by Joseph L. Baird and Radd K. Ehrman. 2 vols. to date. New York: Oxford University Press, 1994–.

————. *Scivias.* Translated by Columba Hart and Jane Bishop; introduced by Barbara J. Newman; preface by Caroline Walker Bynum. New York: Paulist Press, 1990.

————. *Symphonia: A Critical Edition of the Symphonia armonie celestium revelationum (Symphony of the harmony of celestial revelations).* Introduction, translations, and commentary by Barbara Newman. 2d ed. Ithaca: Cornell University Press, 1998.

Holsinger, Bruce. *Music, Body, and Desire in Medieval Culture: Hildegard of Bingen to Chaucer.* Stanford: Stanford University Press, 2001.

Iversen, Gunilla. "Réaliser une vision. La dernière vision de *Scivias* et le drame *Ordo virtutum* de Hildegarde de Bingen." *Revue de musicologie* 86 (2000): 37–63.

Kendrick, Robert L. *Celestial Sirens: Nuns and their Music in Early Modern Milan.* Oxford and New York: Oxford University Press, 1996.

————. "Feminized Devotion, Musical Nuns, and the 'New Style' Lombard Motet of the 1640s." In *Rediscovering the Muses,* ed. Marshall, 124–39.

Koskoff, Ellen. "Both In and Between: Women's Musical Roles in Ritual Life." In *Music and the Experience of God,* ed. David Power, Mary Collins, and Mellonee Burnim, 82–93. Edinburgh: T. & T. Clark Ltd., 1989.

————. "Miriam Sings Her Song: The Self and the Other in Anthropological Discourse." In *Music and Difference,* ed. Solie, 149–63.

————. "The Sound of a Woman's Voice: Gender and Music in a New York Hasidic Community." In *Women and Music in Cross-Cultural Perspective,* ed. Koskoff, 213–23.

Monson, Craig A. *Disembodied Voices: Music and Culture in an Early Modern Italian Convent.* Berkeley: University of California Press, 1995.

————, ed. *The Crannied Wall: Women, Religion, and the Arts in Early Modern Europe.* Ann Arbor: University of Michigan Press, 1992.

Montford, Kimberlyn. "L'Anno santo and Female Monastic Churches: The Politics, Business and Music of the Holy Year in Rome (1675)." *Journal of Seventeenth-Century Music* 6 (2000) (online) http://www.sscm-jscm/v6/no1/Montford.html.

————. "Music in the Convents of Counter-Reformation Rome." Ph.D. diss., Rutgers University, 1999.

Myers, Margaret. "Searching for Data about European Ladies' Orchestras, 1870–1950." In *Music and Gender,* ed. Moisala and Diamond, 189–213.

Neuls-Bates, Carol. "Women's Orchestras in the United States, 1925–45." In *Women Making Music*, ed. Bowers and Tick, 349–69.

Newman, Barbara, ed. *Voice of the Living Light: Hildegard of Bingen and Her World*. Berkeley: University of California Press, 1998.

Nolan, Edward Peter. *Cry Out and Write: A Feminine Poetics of Revelation*. New York: Continuum, 1994.

Reardon, Colleen. *Holy Concord within Sacred Walls: Nuns and Music in Siena, 1575–1700*. Oxford and New York: Oxford University Press, 2002.

Reinhard, Ursula. "The Veils are Lifted: Music of Turkish Women." In *Music, Gender, and Culture*, ed. Herndon and Ziegler, 101–13.

Tucker, Sherrie. *Swing Shift: "All-Girl" Bands of the 1940s*. Durham, N.C.: Duke University Press, 2000.

Yardley, Anne Bagnall. "'Ful weel she soong the service dyvyne': The Cloistered Musician in the Middle Ages." In *Women Making Music*, ed. Bowers and Tick, 15–38.

Recordings

Canti nel chiostro: Musiche nei monasteri femminili del '600 a Bologna. Cappella Artemisia. Tactus TC 600001 (1994).

Chiara Margarita Cozzolani: I Vespri Natalizi (1650). Cappella Artemisia. Tactus TC600301 (1997).

Donne Barocche: Women Composers from the Baroque Period. Bizzarrie armoniche. Opus 111 OP30341 (2001).

Hildegard of Bingen. *Canticles of Ecstasy*. Sequentia. Deutsche Harmonia Mundi (1994).

———. *A Feather on the Breath of God: Sequences and Hymns*. Gothic Voices, Christopher Page, director. London: Hyperion CDA 66039 (1982).

———. *Ordo virtutem*. Sequentia. Deutsche Harmonia Mundi (1998).

———. *Saints*. Sequentia. Deutsche Harmonia Mundi (1998).

Rosa Mistica: Musiche delle monache lombarde del '600. Cappella Artemisia. Tactus TC 600003 (1999).

Songs of Ecstasy and Devotion from a 17th Century Italian Convent: Lucrezia Vizzana Componimenti Musicali (1623). Musica Secreta. Linn CKD 071 (1998).

Videos

Hildegard of Bingen. *Ordo virtutem*. Vox Animae, films for the Humanities and Sciences, 10815. 70 min. Petri/Visser Production. 1997.

PART THREE:
EMPOWERED VOICES

Books and Articles

Anderson, Marian. *My Lord, What a Morning: An Autobiography*. Urbana: University of Illinois Press, 2002.

Baez, Joan. *And a Voice to Sing With: A Memoir*. New York: Summit Books, 1987.

———. Interview by Charles Fuss. In brochure notes to *Rare, Live, and Classic*, Vanguard VCD3–125–27 (1993).

Blum, Stephen. "Hearing the Music of the Middle East." In *The Garland Encyclopedia of*

World Music, vol. 6: *The Middle East*, ed. Virginia Danielson, Scott Marcus, and Dwight Reynolds, 3–13. New York: Routledge, 2002.

Burns, Laurie, and Mélisse Lafrance. *Disruptive Divas: Feminism, Identity and Popular Music*. New York: Routledge, 2002.

Cooper, Sarah. *Girls! Girls! Girls! Essays on Women and Music*. New York: New York University Press, 1996.

Cormier, Rebecca. "The Relationship between Music, Text, and Performer in the Latin American *Nueva canción* as seen the Repertory of Mercedes Sosa." Master's thesis, Tufts University, 1999.

Danielson, Virginia. "Artists and Entrepreneurs: Female Singers in Cairo during the 1920s." In *Women in Middle Eastern History: Shifting Boundaries in Sex and Gender*, ed. Nikki R. Keddi and Beth Baron, 292–309. New Haven and London: Yale University Press, 1991.

———. *"The Voice of Egypt": Umm Kulthum, Arabic Song and Egyptian Society in the 20th Century*. Chicago: University of Chicago Press, 1997.

Denisoff, R. Serge. *Great Day Coming: Folk Music and the American Left*. Urbana: University of Illinois Press, [1971].

Fuss, Charles J. *Joan Baez: A Bio-Bibliography*. Westport, Conn: Greenwood Press, 1996.

Hajdu, David. *Positively 4th Street: The Lives and Times of Joan Baez, Bob Dylan, Mimi Baez Fariña, and Richard Fariña*. New York: Farrar, Straus and Giroux, 2001.

Keiler, Allan. *Marian Anderson: A Singer's Journey*. New York: Scribner, 2000.

Makeba, Miriam, with James Hall. *Makeba: My Story*. New York: New American Library, 1987.

McDonnell, Evelyn, and Ann Powers. *Rock She Wrote*. New York: Delta, 1995.

Moreno, Albrecht. "Violeta Parra and 'La Nueva Canción Chilena.'" *Studies in Latin American Popular Culture* 5 (1986): 108–26.

O'Brian, Lucy. *She Bop: The Definitive History of Women in Rock, Pop and Soul*. New York: Penguin, 1995.

Pope, Rebecca A., and Susan J. Leonardi. "Divas and Disease, Mourning and Militancy: Diamanda Galás's Operatic Plague Mass." In *The Work of Opera*, ed. Dellamora and Fischlin, 315–33.

Pring-Mill, Robert. *"Gracias a la vida": The Power and Poetry of Song*, The Kate Elder Lecture 1. London: University of London, Department of Hispanic Studies, 1990.

Reuss, Richard A., with JoAnne C. Reuss. *American Folk Music and Left-Wing Politics, 1927–1957*. Lanham, Md.: Scarecrow Press, 2000.

Reynolds, Simon, and Joy Press. *The Sex Revolts: Gender, Rebellion and Rock 'n' Roll*. Cambridge, Mass.: Harvard University Press, 1995.

Rodnitzky, Jerome L. *Minstrels of the Dawn: The Folk-Protest Singer as a Cultural Hero*. Chicago: Nelson-Hall, 1976.

Rogers, Kalen. *Tori Amos All These Years: The Authorized Illustrated Biography*. New York: Omnibus, 1994.

Rohter, Larry. "Mercedes Sosa: A Voice of Hope." *New York Times*, Sunday, 9 October 1988, sec. 2, 21.

Rosenberg, Neil V. *Transforming Tradition: Folk Music Revivals Examined*. Urbana and Chicago: University of Illinois Press, 1993.

Sawa, Suzanne Meyers. "Historical Issues of Gender and Music." In *The Garland Encyclopedia of World Music*, vol. 6: *The Middle East*, ed. Virginia Danielson, Scott Marcus, and Dwight Reynolds, 293–307. New York: Routledge, 2002.

"Sibyl with Guitar." *Time,* 23 November 1962, 54–60.

Sultan, Nancy. "Private Speech, Public Pain: The Power of Women's Laments in Ancient Greek Poetry and Tragedy." In *Rediscovering the Muses,* ed. Marshall, 92–110.

Van Nieuwkerk, Karin. *A Trade like any Other: Female Singers and Dancers in Egypt.* Austin: University of Texas Press, 1995.

Wald, Gayle J. "Just a Girl? Rock Music, Feminism, and the Cultural Construction of Female Youth." *SIGNS* 23 (1998): 585–611.

Whiteley, Sheila. *Women and Popular Music: Sexuality, Identity, and Subjectivity.* London and New York: Routledge, 2000.

————, ed. *Sexing the Groove: Popular Music and Gender.* London and New York: Routledge, 1997.

Recordings

Amos, Tori. *Little Earthquakes.* Atlantic 82358–2 (1991).

Baez, Joan. *Farewell Angelina.* Vanguard VMD-79200 (1982).

————. *The First 10 Years.* Vanguard VCD-6560/1 (1987, 1986).

————. *Rare, Live, and Classic.* Vanguard VCD3–125–27 (1993).

Odetta. *Best of the Vanguard Years.* Vanguard 79522–2 (1999).

Sainte-Marie, Buffy. *The Best of Buffy Sainte-Marie.* Vanguard 3/2–2 (1987).

Sosa, Mercedes. *30 años.* Philips 314 518 789–2 (1993).

————. *Gracias a la vida.* Philips 832314–2 (1987).

————. *Live in Argentinien.* Tropical Music 680.916 (1986).

Videos

Amos, Tori. *Little Earthquakes.* 55 min. New York: A*Vision Entertainment, 1992. Video-cassette.

Argentinísima (in Spanish). Los Angeles: Media Home Entertainment, 1982. Videocassette.

Don't Look Back. Prod. Albert Grossman and John Cort; dir. D. A. Pennebaker. 96 min. New York: New Video, 1967; 1999. Videocassette and DVD.

Joan Baez. Dir. Hedda Garza, 30 min. Bala Cynwyd, Pa.: Schlessinger Video Productions, 1995.

Umm Kulthūm: A Voice Like Egypt. Prod. and dir. Michal Goldman. 68 min. Waltham, Mass.: Filmmakers Collaborative, 1996. Videocassette.

We Shall Overcome. Prod. Ginger Group Productions. 58 min. Beverly Hills: PBS Home Video, 1990. Videocassette.

Woodstock: Three Days of Peace and Music. Dir. Michael Wadleigh. 225 min. Burbank: Warner Home Video, 1969; 1997. DVD.

PART FOUR:
LAMENTING VOICES

Books and Articles

Agawu, V. Kofi. "Music in the Funeral Traditions of the Akpafu." *Ethnomusicology* 32 (1988): 75–105.

Alexiou, Margaret. *The Ritual Lament in Greek Tradition.* Cambridge: Cambridge University Press, 1974.

Auerbach, Susan. "From Singing to Lamenting: Women's Musical Role in a Greek Village." In *Women and Music in Cross-Cultural Perspective,* ed. Koskoff, 25–44.

Baker, Houston. *Blues, Ideology and the Harlem Renaissance.* Chicago and London: University of Chicago Press, 1987.

Bourgeois, Anna Strong. *Blues Women: Profiles and Lyrics, 1920–1945.* Jefferson, N.C.: McFarland and Company, Inc., 1996.

Brooks, Jeanice. "Catherine de Médicis, *nouvelle Artémise:* Women's Laments and the Virtue of Grief." *Early Music* 27 (1999): 419–35.

Caraveli, Anna. "The Bitter Wounding: The Greek Lament as Social Protest in Rural Greece." In *Gender and Power in Rural Greece,* ed. Jill Dubisch, 169–94. Princeton: Princeton University Press, 1986.

Carby, Hazel. "It Just Be's Dat Way Sometimes: The Sexual Politics of Women's Blues." In *Feminisms: An Anthology of Literary Theory and Criticism,* ed. Robyn R. Warhol and Diane Price Herndl, 746–58. New Brunswick, N.J.: Rutgers University Press, 1991.

Cusick, Suzanne. "'There was not one lady who failed to shed a tear': Arianna's Lament and the Construction of Modern Womanhood." *Early Music* 22 (1994): 21–41.

Davis, Angela Y. *Blues Legacies and Black Feminism: Gertrude "Ma" Rainey, Bessie Smith, and Billie Holiday.* New York: Pantheon Books, 1998.

Feld, Steven. *Sound and Sentiment: Birds, Weeping, Poetics and Song in Kaluli Expression.* 2d ed. Philadelphia: University of Pennsylvania Press, 1990.

Garon, Paul and Beth. *Woman with Guitar: Memphis Minnie's Blues.* New York: Da Capo Press, 1992.

Hampton, Barbara L. "Music and Ritual Symbolism in the Ga Funeral." *Yearbook for Traditional Music* 14 (1982): 75–105.

Harris, Ellen T. *Handel as Orpheus: Voice and Desire in the Chamber Cantatas.* Cambridge, Mass: Harvard University Press, 2001.

Harrison, Duval. *Black Pearls: Blues Queens of the 1920s.* Rutgers, N.J.: Rutgers University Press, 1998.

Holford-Strevens, Leofranc. "'Her eyes became two spouts': Classical Antecedents of Renaissance Laments." *Early Music* 27 (1999): 379–93.

Kerns, Virginia. *Black Carib Kinship and Ritual: Women and Ancestors.* Urbana and Chicago: University of Illinois Press, 1983.

Lipking, Lawrence. *Abandoned Women and Poetic Tradition.* Chicago: University of Chicago Press, 1988.

Lomax, Alan. *The Land Where the Blues Began.* London: Minerva, 1997.

MacNeil, Anne. "Weeping at the Water's Edge." *Early Music* 27 (1999): 407–17.

Mazo, Margaret. "Wedding Laments in North-Russian Villages." In *Music-Cultures in Contact: Convergences and Collisions,* ed. Margaret J. Kartomi and Stephen Blum, 21–39. Basle: Gordon and Breach, 1994.

Nketia, J. H. *Funeral Dirges of the Akan People.* New York: Negro Universities Press, 1969.

Oakley, Giles. *The Devil's Music: A History of the Blues.* New York and London: Harcourt Brace Jovanovich, 1976.

Racy, Ali Jihad. "Lebanese Laments: Grief, Music, and Cultural Values." *World of Music* 28 (1986): 27–40.

Rosand, Ellen. *Opera in Seventeenth-Century Venice: The Creation of a Genre.* Berkeley and Los Angeles, 1991.

Segal, Charles. "The Gorgon and the Nightingale: The Voice of Female Lament and Pindar's Twelfth *Pythian Ode.*" In *Embodied Voices,* ed. Dunn and Jones, 17–34.

Stewart-Baxter, Derrick. *Ma Rainey and the Classic Blues Singers.* New York: Stein and Day Publishers, 1970.

Sultan, Nancy. "Private Speech, Public Pain: The Power of Women's Laments in Ancient Greek Poetry and Tragedy." In *Rediscovering the Muses,* ed. Marshall, 92–110.

Tolbert, Elizabeth. "Magico-Religious Power and Gender in the Karelian Lament." In *Music Gender, and Culture,* ed. Herndon and Ziegler, 41–56.

———. "The Voice of Lament: Vocality and Performative Efficacy in the Finnish-Karelian Itkuvirsi." In *Embodied Voices,* ed. Dunn and Jones, 179–94.

Urban, Greg. "Discourse, Affect and Social Order Ritual Wailing in Amerindian Brazil." *American Anthropologist* 90 (1988): 385–400.

van Orden, Kate. "Female *Complaintes:* Laments of Venus, Queens, and City Women in Late Sixteenth-Century France." *Renaissance Quarterly* 54 (2001): 801–45.

Yurchenko, Henrietta. "Mean Mama Blues: Bessie Smith and the Vaudeville Era." In *Music, Gender and Culture,* ed. Herndon and Ziegler, 241–57.

Recordings

Four Women Blues: The Victor/Bluebird Recordings of Memphis Minnie, Mississippi Matilda, Kansas City Kitty and Miss Rosie Mae Moore. RCA 07863667192 (1997).

Handel, George Frideric. *Cantates, La Lucrezia; Armida abbandonata; Agrippina condotta a morire. Les Basses Réunies.* Véronique Gens, voice. London: Virgin Classics, 724354528323 (1999).

———. *Delirio amoroso; Alla caccia (Diana); Ah! crudel, nel pianto mio.* Patrick Peire, cond. Deborah York, voice. Eufoda (Bel) 1297 (2000).

———. *Trois Cantates pour Soprano et Instruments, Ero e leandro (Hero), Nó se emenderà jamás, Clori, mia bella Clori.* August Wenzinger, cond. Lina Maria Akerlund, voice. Accord (Fra) 201102 (1995).

I Can't Be Satisfied: Early American Women Blues Singers: vol. 1: *Country;* vol. 2: *Town.* Yazoo B000000G92, B000000G93 (1997).

Memphis, Minnie. *Fly Right.* LP 108.

———. *Hustlin' Woman's Blues.* Bluebird B-6202, Stash LP 117.

———. *Memphis Minnie-Jitis Blues.* Vocalion 1588 (1930).

Rainey, Ma. "Prove it on me Blues." *Ma Rainey: The Complete 1928 Sessions in Chronological Order.* Document Records, DOCD-5156 (1996).

Videos

Wild Women Don't Have the Blues. Directed by Christine Dall; produced by Carole Doyle van Valkenburg and Christine Dall. Calliope Films Resources. San Francisco: California Newsreel, 1989.

PART FIVE:
GENDERED VOICES AND PERFORMANCE

Books and Articles

Bashant, Wendy. "Singing in Greek Drag: Gluck, Berlioz, George Eliot." In *En Travesti,* ed. Blackmer and Smith, 216–41.

Cixous, Hélène. "Tancredi Continues." In *En Travesti,* ed. Blackmer and Smith, 152–68.

Clément, Catherine. "Through Voices, History." In *Siren Songs,* ed. Smart, 21–25.

Covell, Roger. "Voice Register as an Index of Age and Status in Opera Seria." In *Opera and Vivaldi*, ed. Michael Collins and Elise K. Kirk, 193–210. Austin: University of Texas Press, 1984.

Cowan, Jane K. *Dance and the Body Politic in Northern Greece*. Princeton: Princeton University Press, 1990.

Cowgill, Rachel. "Re-gendering the Libertine; or, the Taming of the Rake: Lucy Vestris as Don Giovanni on the Early Nineteenth-Century London Stage." *Cambridge Opera Journal* 10 (1998): 45–66.

Cusick, Suzanne G. "On Musical Performances of Gender and Sex." In *Audible Traces*, ed. Barkin and Hamessley, 25–48.

Czekanowska, Anna. "Towards a Concept of Slavonic Women's Repertoire." In *Music, Gender, and Culture*, ed. Herndon and Ziegler, 57–70.

Emigh, J., and J. Hunt. "Gender Bending in Balinese Performance." In *Gender in Performance: The Presentation of Difference in the Performing Arts*, ed. Laurence Senelick. Hanover, N.H.: University Press of New England, 1992.

Fine, Elizabeth, and Jean Haskell Speer, eds. *Performance, Culture, and Identity*. Westport, Conn.: Praeger Publishers, 1992.

Garber, Marjorie. *Vested Interests: Cross-Dressing and Cultural Anxiety*. New York and London: Routledge, 1992.

Griffiths, Morwenna. *Feminisms and the Self: The Web of Identity*. London and New York: Routledge, 1995.

Hadlock, Heather. "The Career of Cherubino, or the Trouser Role Grows Up." In *Siren Songs*, ed. Smart, 67–92.

———. "'The firmness of a female hand' in *The Corsair* and *Il corsaro*." *Cambridge Opera Journal* 14 (2002), 47–57.

Hahn, Tomie. *Sensational Knowledge: Teaching Japanese Dance*. Middletown, Conn.: Wesleyan University Press, (forthcoming).

———. "Sensational Knowledge: Transmitting Japanese Dance and Music." Ph.D. diss., Wesleyan University, 1997.

———. "Singing a Dance: Navigating the Musical Soundscape in Nihon Buyo." *Asian Music* 33 (2001): 1–40.

Heller, Monica. *Codeswitching: Anthropological Sociolinguistic Perspectives*. Berlin: Mouton de Gruyter, 1988.

Heriot, Angus. *The Castrati in Opera*. London: Calder and Boyars, 1975.

Kasulis, Thomas P., Roger T. Ames, and Wimal Dissanayake, eds. *Self as Body in Asian Theory and Practice*. Albany: State University of New York Press, 1993.

Keeling, Richard. "Contrast of Song Performance Style as a Function of Sex Role Polarity in the Hupa Brush Dance." *Ethnomusicology* (1985): 185–212.

Kligman, Gail. *The Wedding of the Dead: Ritual, Poetics, and Popular Culture in Transylvania*. Berkeley and Los Angeles: University of California Press, 1988.

Kondo, Dorinne. "Multiple Selves: The Aesthetics and Politics of Artisanal Identities." In *Japanese Sense of Self*, ed. Nancy R. Rosenberger, 40–66. Cambridge: Cambridge University Press, 1992.

Mackenzie, Catriona, and Natalie Stoljar, eds. *Relational Autonomy: Feminist Perspectives on Autonomy, Agency, and the Social Self*. New York: Oxford University Press, 2000.

McClary, Susan. "Gender Ambiguities and Erotic Excess in Seventeenth-Century Venetian Opera." In *Acting on the Past: Historical Performance across the Disciplines*, ed. Mark Franko and Annette Richards, 177–200. Hanover, N.H.: Wesleyan University Press, 2000.

Meyers, Diana Tietjens, ed. *Feminists Rethink the Self.* Boulder, Colo.: Westview Press, 1997.

Miller, Felicia. "Farinelli's Electronic Hermaphrodite and the Contralto Tradition." In *The Work of Opera,* ed. Dellamora and Fischlin, 73–92.

Petrovic, Ankica. "Women in the Music Creation Process in the Dinaric Cultural Zone of Yugoslavia." In *Music, Gender, and Culture,* ed. Herndon and Ziegler, 71–84.

Reynolds, Margaret. "Ruggiero's Deceptions, Cherubino's Distractions." In *En Travesti,* ed. Blackmer and Smith, 132–51.

Rice, Timothy. *May It Fill Your Soul: Experiencing Bulgarian Music.* Chicago: University of Chicago Press, 1994.

Rosselli, John. *Singers of Italian Opera: The History of a Profession.* Cambridge: Cambridge University Press, 1992.

Senelick, Laurence. *The Changing Room: Sex, Drag and Theatre.* London and New York: Routledge, 2000.

Slobin, Mark. *Subcultural Sounds: Micromusics of the West.* Hanover, N.H.: Wesleyan University Press, 1993.

Sugarman, Jane C. *Engendering Song: Singing and Subjectivity at Prespa Albanian Weddings.* Chicago: University of Chicago Press, 1997.

———. "'Those Other Women': Dance and Femininity among Prespa Albanians." In *Music and Gender in Mediterranean Cultures,* ed. Tullia Magrini. Chicago: University of Chicago Press, (forthcoming).

Treadwell, Nina. "Female Operatic Cross-Dressing: Bernardo Saddumene's Libretto for Leonardo Vinci's *Li zite 'n galera* (1722)." *Cambridge Opera Journal* 10 (1998): 131–56.

Yano, Christine. *Tears of Longing: Nostalgia and the Nation in Japanese Popular Song.* Cambridge, Mass.: Harvard University Asia Center (distributed by Harvard University Press), 2002.

Yuasa, Yasuo. *The Body: Toward an Eastern Mind-Body Theory.* Albany: State University of New York, 1987.

Recordings

Albania: Central Balkans: 1920–1940. Music of the Balkans. Vol. 1. Comp. Petros Tabouris. FM Records [Greece] FM 706 (n.d.).

Albania: Vocal and Instrumental Polyphony. Comp. Bernard Lortat-Jacob and Beniamin Kruta. Chant du Monde LDX 274897 (1988).

Cry You Mountains, Cry You Fields: Traditional Songs and Instrumental Music from S. E. Albania. Prod. Gef Lucena and Chris Johnston. Saydisc CD-SDL 431 (1999).

Donizetti, Gaetano. *Lucrezia Borgia.* RCA Italiana Opera Orchestra and Chorus. Cond. Jonel Perlea; with Shirley Verrett as Maffio Orsini. RCA 6642 (1989).

Famille Lela de Përmet: Polyphonies vocales et instrumentales d'Albanie. Remzi Lela and Ensemble. Label Bleu LBLC 2503/Harmonia Mundi HM 83 (1992).

Folk Music of Albania. Comp. A. L. Lloyd. Topic TSCD 904 (1994).

Music from Albania. Comp. Bruno B. Reuer. Rounder CD 5151 (1999).

Rossini, Gioacchino. *Semiramide.* London Symphony Orchestra. Cond. Ion Marin; with Jennifer Larmore as Arsace. Polygram Records 437797 (1994).

———. *Tancredi.* Münchner Rundfunkorchester. Cond. Roberto Abbado; with Vessalina Kasarova as Tancredi RCA 68349 (1996).

Songs from the City of Roses. Laver Bariu and Ensemble. GlobeStyle CDORBD 091 (1995).

There Where the Avalanche Stops: Music from the Gjirokastra Folk Festival, Albania 1988. Vol. 1. Comp. M. Harding, L. McDowell, J. Wozencraft, and S. Shituni. Touch T33.11 (1990).

Vocal Traditions of Albania. Rec. Radio Tirana. Saydisc CD-SDL 421 (1997).

Yougoslavie 2 (Macédoine: Polyphonies tosques): Sous les Peupliers de Bilisht. Comp. Herman C. Vuylsteke. Ocora (LP) 558572 (1981).

Videos

Donizetti, Gaetano. *Lucrezia Borgia.* Covent Garden. Cond. Richard Bonynge; with Anne Howells as Maffio Orsini. Prod. John Copley. Videocassette 157 min. West Long Beach, N.J.: Kultur, 1980.

Rossini, Gioacchino. *Semiramide.* Metropolitan Opera. Cond. James Conlon; with Marilyn Horne as Arsace. Prod. Metropolitan Opera and NHK Enterprises. Videocassette and Videodisc. 222 min. West Long Beach, N.J.: Kultur, 1991.

———. *Tancredi.* Süddeutscher Rundfunk Stuttgart. Cond. Gianluigi Gelmetti; with Bernadette Manca di Nissa as Tancredi. Prod. Teatro all Scala and Brilliant Media. Videocassette 166 min. New York: BMG Classics Video, 1994.

Contributors

Carol M. Babiracki, Associate Professor of Ethnomusicology in the Fine Arts Department at Syracuse University, is known for her research on South Asian music and dance, ethnic and immigrant music and dance in the United States, and music of the Middle East. She has recently completed a book on tribal music and dance in India.

Jane A. Bernstein is the Austin Fletcher Professor and former Chair of the Department of Music at Tufts University. She is well known for her research in Renaissance music, in particular the French chanson and Italian music print culture, as well as women's studies. Her 1998 book *Music Printing in Renaissance Venice: The Scotto Press (1539–1572)* received the Otto Kinkeldey Award, a prize given by the American Musicological Society for the most distinguished musicological work of the year.

Virginia Danielson is the Richard F. French Librarian of the Eda Kuhn Loeb Music Library at Harvard University. She is a noted ethnomusicologist with expertise in Arabic and Middle Eastern music. In 1998, her biography *The Voice of Egypt: Umm Kulthūm, Arabic Song and Modern Egyptian Society* received the Alan Merriam Prize by the Society of Ethnomusicology for the most distinguished monograph in ethnomusicology.

Margot Fassler is Professor of Music and Director of the Institute of Sacred Music at Yale University. She is a renowned musicologist specializing in medieval studies. Her book *Gothic Song: Victorine Sequences and Augustinian Reform in Twelfth-Century Paris* won the Otto Kinkeldey Award in 1994 from the American Musicological Society. Currently, she is working on a monograph on Hildegard of Bingen and is supervising a video series on musical and liturgical practices, including one on the Benedictine nuns from the Abbey of Regina Laudis in Bethlehem, Connecticut.

Annegret Fauser has recently joined the faculty at the University of North Carolina, Chapel Hill, as Associate Professor of Music. She is an expert on late nineteenth-century French music. She is currently working on a book on women as composers, performers, and patrons in fin-de-siècle France.

Bonnie Gordon is Assistant Professor of Music History at the State University of New York at Stony Brook. Her book *Monteverdi's Unruly Women* will be published by University of California Press. She is currently co-editing a volume of essays about courtesans.

Heather Hadlock is Assistant Professor of Music at Stanford University. She is the author of *Mad Loves: Women and Music in Offenbach's Les Contes d'Hoffmann,* published by Princeton University Press, and is now working on a book on female travesty in nineteenth-century opera.

Tomie Hahn, Assistant Professor of Performance Ethnology in the Arts Department at the Rensselaer Polytechnic Institute, is an ethnomusicologist with scholarly interests in Japanese traditional performing arts. She is also a performer of shakuhachi (Japanese bamboo flute) and of *nihon buyo* (Japanese traditional dance), holding the professional stage name Samie Tachibana. Her book *Sensational Knowledge: Teaching Japanese Dance* is forthcoming from Wesleyan University Press.

Ellen T. Harris, Class of 1949 Endowed Professor of Music, former Associate Provost for the Arts, and former Head of the Music Division at MIT, is a distinguished scholar of Baroque opera, specializing in the music of Handel and Purcell. Her books include *Handel and the Pastoral Tradition* and *Henry Purcell's Dido and Aeneas.* In 2001, her book *Handel as Orpheus: Voice and Desire in the Chamber Cantatas* received the prestigious Otto Kinkeldey Award from the American Musicological Society.

Tammy L. Kernodle, Associate Professor of Music at Miami University in Ohio, is a musicologist with expertise in African-American music. Her article on the American composer William Grant Still appeared in the *Musical Quarterly.* She is currently completing a book on the jazz composer and pianist Mary Lou Williams, to be published by Northeastern University Press.

Craig A. Monson is Professor and former Chair of the Department of Music at Washington University, St. Louis. His wide-ranging musical interests include Elizabethan and Jacobean music, Baroque keyboard music and opera, and Native American music. He has published widely on music in Italian nunneries, including two books: *Disembodied Voices: Music and Culture in an Early Modern Italian Convent* and *The Crannied Wall: Women, Religion, and the Arts in Early Modern Europe.*

Nancy B. Reich, noted scholar, teacher, and lecturer, was awarded the Robert Schumann Prize by the city of Zwickau in 1996. Her book *Clara Schumann, the Artist and the Woman,* first published in 1985 by Cornell University Press, received the Deems Taylor award from ASCAP; it has been translated into several languages, including German, Japanese, and Chinese. A revised edition of the book was published in 2001. She is currently working on an annotated translation of Clara Schumann's early diaries (*Jugendtagebücher*).

Jane C. Sugarman, Associate Professor of Music at the State University of New York at Stony Brook, is an ethnomusicologist who specializes in the music of southeastern Europe and the Middle East. She has conducted field research in Albania and the former Yugoslavia, as well as among immigrants in Western Europe and North America. Her publications include the book *Engendering Song: Singing and Subjectivity at Prespa Albanian Weddings.*

Index

a cappella groups, 89
Abbate, Carolyn, 12n. 14
ʿAbd al-Nāṣir, Jamāl, 145, 155, 163
Abū 'l-Faraj al-Isbahānī: *Kitāb al-Aghānī*, 161
Abū al-ʿIla Muḥammad, 148
Abu-Lughod, Ibrahim, 158
Académie des Beaux-Arts, 61–65, 71, 73, 75, 77–79
Adam of St. Victor, 102
Afghanistan, 88; Herat, 88
African American culture, 214, 223
African American music, 177, 211, 216; field hollers, 215; spirituals, 144, 215; work songs, 215. *See also* blues
Aḥmad, Zakariyā, 152, 153
al-Aṭlāl, 153–54
Alboni, Marietta, 295
Alfonsín, Raúl, 173
Allende, Salvador, 170, 175
Almanac Singers, 177
Amateur choral societies, 89
"Ame no shiki," 313–17, 320–21
Amos, Tori, 4, 146; cofounder of RAINN, 194; and confessional music, 193; "Crucify," 194; "Icicle," 189; *Little Earthquakes*, 187, 192, 193; "Me and a Gun," 9, 146, 187–88, 192, 194, 195, 198–200, 203–5; musical training, 190; performance style, 190; position in popular culture, 189; "Precious Things," 190; as rape survivor, 194; "Silent all these Years," 188, 199–200, 204–5; stage persona, 189
Anderson, Marian, 143
Andrews Sisters, 89
androgyny, 291; in Christ, 97; in Italian opera, 302; and Lili Boulanger, 80; in singing style, 52, 168
Annunciation, 96,
Arab music: introduction to, 148; modes in, 148, 152, 154, 159
Aragona, Tullia d', 15
Arcadian Academy, 243
Argentina, 145, 167–68, 171–72, 174–76; Buenos Aires, 173; Mapuche of, 278
Ariadne, 210–11, 240–43, 247
Armstrong, Louis, 227
Arnim, Bettina von, 26
Arnstein, Fanny von, 22–23
Ariosto, Ludovico: *Orlando furioso*, 210
aṣīl, 147–48
Attridge, Harold, 117

Auber, Daniel-François-Esprit: *Gustave III*, 304
Audan, Marguerite, 73
Australia, 263
Austria: Vienna, 23
auto-harp, 168

Bach family, 24
Bach, Carl Phillip Emanuel, 23
Bach, Johann Sebastian, 29; *St. Matthew Passion*, 23
Bach, Wilhelm Friedemann, 23
Bachnik, Jane, 318
Badawi, M. M., 155
Baez, Joan, 4, 9, 145, 168, 175–76; early song repertory, 179; involvement in peace movement, 180; life of, 178 n. 36, 185; physical appearance, 167; as song writer, 182; persona as virginal figure, 167, 178, 180, 182
bahānā, 41, 43, 56
Baker, Janet, 259
Baldini, Gabriele, 286
bands, all-girl, 89
banjo, 168, 215
Baraka, Amiri, 223
Barilli, Antonio, 125
Barzun, Jacques, 3
Bauman, Richard, 323
Beethoven, Ludwig von, 23; *Fidelio*, 24
Beghelli, Mario, 297
Beijing Opera, 89, 258
Belafonte, Harry, 180
Bell, Susan Groag, 25
Bellini, Vincenzo, 287; *I Capuleti ed i Montecchi*, 288, 297; *Norma*, 286, 292, 298
Benedict, Saint, 88, 110
Berenson, Edward, 61
Berger, Ludwig, 19
Bertolini, Anna Maria, 135
Bigot, Marie, 19, 26
Biondi, Giovanni Battista (pseud. Cesena), 124–25
Björk, 193
black feminism, 214
blues, 7, 177, 180, 193; AAB verse form, 218, 224, 228; and African lament, 214; antecedents of, 215; and black women's experiences, 225–26; classic, 222–25; documenting life events, 221, 226–29; female classic singers, 4, 218; female rural singers, 4, 216–18; as male genre, 214, 216,

blues *(cont.)*
218; melodic "blue notes," 219; relationship
with New Orleans jazz style, 227; rural tradition, 215–16; sexual content of texts, 225;
Texas, 215, 217–19
Blum, Stephen, 156–57, 162
Boccaccio, Giovanni, 240
body, 7, 9, 96, 189, 198–99, 279, 312, 321, 323; and
performance, 6, 9; in opera, 6. *See also* voice
Bolivia, 168
bombo leguero (drum), 168
Book of Revelation, 125; high altar of the Lamb,
95–97, 124
Boswell Sisters, 89
Boulanger, Lili, 60–61, 79–81; as femme fragile,
79–80; *Faust et Hélène*, 79
Boulanger, Nadia, 60–61, 70, 74–79, 80–81
Bourdieu, Pierre, 278–80
bourgeoise, 8, 64, 67–68
Bousquet, Georges, 29
Bradford, Perry, 217
Bradon, Anne, 179
Brambilla, Marietta, 289, 297–99, 302, 304
Brazil, 173
Brel, Jacques, 177
Bromberg, Sarah, 110
Brooks, Peter, 6
Budden, Julian, 300
bunraku, 311
burqa, 42
Bush, Josie, 217
Butler, Judith, 6, 258

Calderón, Natalio, 161
Canada, 263; Toronto, 281
canciones de lucha y esperanza, 169
canon: musicological construction of, 5, 133, 160
Caribbean, 214–15
caste, 8, 15, 40
castrato, 233, 258–59, 286–87
Catholic Church: and convent reform at Council
of Trent, 118–19, 131; in Latin America, 169, 171;
liturgy of, 93–96; restrictions on women's
participation in, 87
Caviness, Madeline, 110
çengi, 14, 283
chant, 92
charango, 168
Chaumié, Joseph, 62–63
Child, Francis: *English and Scottish Popular
Ballads*, 179
Chile, 168–70, 173
China, 89, 258; ancient, 14
Chopin, Frederic, 31
Chorley, Henry, 18, 25
Chung, Connie, 199
Ciccone, Madonna 189, 193
class, 14, 19, 170, 200, 217, 223–24; and gender

theory, 6; and sexual politics, 8, 18, 25, 32, 67,
70, 310
Clément, Catherine, 285
codeswitching, 9, 259, 308, 313, 317–20, 323
Cohen, Leonard, 177
Collins, Judy, 168, 177
commedia dell'arte, 258
complainte, 145
concerti delle donne, 15, 122–23, 125
confessional songs, 193
Conservatoire, Paris, 60, 62–67, 73
convents, 8, 88, 93, 98, 100, 110; in Milan, 118,
120; music and myth of Echo, 122; musical education in, 137; musicians and music making
in, 8, 131, 133; reform by Catholic church, 119;
in Rome, 118–19; in Siena, 118–19. *See also* Rupertsberg; Santa Cristina della Fondazza, Bologna
convertite, 125
cortigiane oneste, 14
costumes, 15, 155, 167, 190, 258, 264, 321; used as
prop, 313
courtesans 14, 16, 39, 42–43, 51, 57, 189. *See also*
nacnī
cross-dressed roles, 9, 233; female, 258–59, 288,
291, 297, 299–300, 304, 313; male, 89, 258
"Cuando tenga la tierra," 173
Cuba, 171, 173
Cusick, Suzanne, 6, 9

da capo aria form, 236
"Dames d'honneur," 145
dan singers, 89, 258
dance, 258; African American, 224; barn, 217; binary form, 236; and the blues, 215; in the Car-
ribean, 214; classical Indian, 44; and courtesans, 14–15; female, in Egypt, 156; in northeast India, 8, 16, 36–43, 45, 47–49, 51, 52, 54–56;
and the *nueva canción*, 170, 174, 176; at Prespa
Albanian weddings, 267, 269, 282; orchestras,
89, 222; and Tori Amos, 190; traditional Japanese, 4, 89, 259, 308 (*see also nihon buyo*)
davul (drum): as male instrument, 258
De Lauretis, Teresa, 258
Debussy, Claude, 63
Delacroix, Eugène: *Liberty Guiding the People*,
166
delbek (frame drum): as feminine instrument,
258
Denisoff, R. Serge, 168
devadāsī, 39, 46, 59
Devi, Chaiti, 55–56
Devi, Janki, 40, 44, 49, 53–54
Devi, Mangala, 44, 54
dholak (drum), 48, 55
Dido, 210–11, 240–41, 248
diva, 9, 143–46; "convent," 120, 127; cross-
dressed, 259, 288–89, 293; "scream," 145

Divine Office, 93–94, 97, 99, 113
domestic music making, 13, 25, 39, 62
Domingo, Placido, 175
Donizetti, Gaetano, 287; *Anna Bolena*, 292, 298, 301; *Linda di Chamounix*, 301, 304; *Lucrezia Borgia*, 289, 298–304; *Maria di Rohan*, 304; *Maria Stuarda*, 286
Douglas, Lizzie (pseud. Memphis Minnie), 217, 220, 223; as guitarist, 218–19, 221–22; "Hustlin' Woman Blues," 221; "Memphis Minnie-Jitis Blues," 226–27; "Outdoor Blues," 228–29; themes of her songs, 221
dowries, 15; convent, 8, 131, 133–38
Drinker, Sophie, 3, 10
Dronke, Peter, 110, 111
drums, 47, 132–33, 314; as feminine instrument, 258; as masculine instrument, 40–41, 258; played by men, 39–40, 48, 55–56, 258; played by women, 38
Du Boulay, Juliet, 263
Dube, Ganesh Ram, 37, 40, 54
Dubois, Théodore, 65, 71, 74
Dugasseau, Charles, 29
dulcimer, 168
Dunn, Leslie, 4
Durastante, Margherita, 233, 305
Dylan, Bob, 180; "A Hard Rain's a Gonna Fall," 181–82; influence on Joan Baez, 182; "With God on Our Side," 181

Ecclesia, 95, 109, 113
eclectic multiplicity, 6
Egypt, 9, 15, 39, 145, 147, 149–51, 155, 157–59, 162–63; Cairo, 15, 88, 147
Elizabeth of Schönau, 99, 115
England: London, 232, 296
Escudier, Léon, 292
Escudier, Marie, 292
Eskeles, Caecilie von, 22, 23
Este, Alfonso II, d', 123
estribillo, 174, 176
etiquette, social, 14, 62, 310
Eucharist, 96–97, 109, 111

Fabricca, Isabella, 292
Fārūq, King, 147
Fauré, Gabriel, 60, 65, 68, 73–74, 77–78
feminine accomplishment, 14, 18, 25
feminine attributes and behavior, 68, 81, 263, 265, 292, 295, 310, 314
feminist literary criticism, 4, 6, 285–86
feminist musicology, 6, 10n. 6, 285–86
feminist theory, 188, 193, 202, 258, 320
feminization of music, 105
femme fatale, 303
femme fragile, 9, 79–81
femme nouvelle, 8–9, 63, 68, 70, 77–78, 80, 82
Ferlinghetti, Lawrence, 177
Fétis, François-Joseph, 292–94

fiddle, 215; as masculine instrument, 258
firāqiyya, 210
Fleury, Hélène, 60–61, 65, 70, 71, 73, 76–81
folk music revival, 176–78
folklorista, 168–70, 172
Foster, Susan Leigh, 312
France, 8, 16, 61–63, 144, 166; Paris, 170, 289–90, 296 (*see also* Paris Conservatoire; Prix de Rome)
Franco, Veronica, 14
Frigeri, Antonio, 132
Frith, Simon, 160
furi, 311
Fuss, Charles, 179

Galás, Diamanda, 145
Ganguli, Ram Krishna, 45, 46
Gautier, Théophile, 257
gaze, 321; fear of singer's, 291; manipulation of, 203; object of, 146, 167, 203, 291; power of, 42
geisha, 14, 43, 310
gender: and age, 266, 276, 283n. 8; bias against women, 5–6, 25, 73, 78–79, 85n. 55; binary construction of, 6, 9, 13, 51, 257; and body, 312; and class, 5, 7, 25; encoding in music, 6; and feminist theory, 258; ideologies, 6, 87, 323; and power, 5–6, 188; and race, 6, 12n. 13, 143; representation of, 6, 258; and sexuality, 6; and singing, 269, 275, 278
gender identity, 7, 9, 48, 53, 56, 61, 257–59, 265, 278, 280, 320, 323
gender roles, 9, 20, 257–59, 265, 278, 302; reversal of, 15, 42, 52, 188, 233, 258–59, 286–90
gendered musical repertories, 48, 179–80, 257–58, 269, 271–75
gendered performance, 6, 9, 48, 51–52, 257, 259
gender-specific genres, 14, 89, 258, 308
Generali, Pietro, 292; *Francesca da Rimini*, 297
genius: as a cultural construct, 5, 160; as persona of Lili Boulanger, 80–82
Germany, 8, 61; Berlin, 19, 20, 22–25, 31; Bingen, 88, 92, 93, 110, 118; Cologne, 99; Hamburg, 254; Hanover, 232; Leipzig, 31
Ghana: Akpafu, 210
Giddens, Anthony, 161
Gilbert, Ronnie, 168
Ginsberg, Allen, 177
girl groups, 90
Giunta, Francesca, 136
Gluck, Christoph Willibald Ritter von, 24; *Orfeo ed Euridice*, 259
Goethe, Johann Wolfgang von, 26, 28, 156
Gold, Ann Grodzins, 42
Gounod, Charles, 29, 35
Greece: ancient, 14, 144, 210, 258; modern, 39, 210
Greenpeace, 182
Grout, Donald J., 118
Grumbach, Marthe, 73, 74
Guardian Angels, 182

guitar, 14, 216, 218; association with folk culture, 168; as instrument suitable for women, 14; as a political force, 168
Guthrie, Woody, 168, 179
Gypsy. *See* Rom

Hamabata, Matthews, 318
Handel, George Frideric, 8, 211, 232; *Abdolony-mus*, 234, 236–37, 240; *Agrippina condotta a morire*, 234–36, 248, 250; *Armida abbandonata*, 234–35, 248, 250; cantatas, men depicted in, 234, 239–40, 246; cantatas, texts of, 233, 240; cantatas, women depicted in, 234–38, 240, 242, 246; *Diana cacciatrice*, 234–36; *E partirai, mia vita?*, 243, 246; *Ero e Leandro*, 234, 236, 252; *Lucrezia*, 234, 236–40, 243, 248, 250; *Nel dolce dell'oblio*, 234–35; *Notte placida*, 234, 236; operas, 249–50; oratorios, 8, 24, 249–50; *Tra le fiamme*, 234, 246; and woman's voice as self-expression, 8, 248
Hanna, Kathleen, 190
harp: as instrument suitable for women, 14
Harris, David, 180
Haydn, Franz Joseph, 23
Hays, Lee, 177
Heilbrun, Carolyn, 81
Hellerman, Fred, 177
Hensel, Fanny Mendelssohn, 8, 16; as housewife, 20, 23; as pianist, 29, 31, 32; *Das Jahr*, 30–31; death of, 24, 32; education of, 19; Italian trip, 29; *Lobgesang* cantata, 26; musical works, 27; Piano Trio, 32; publishes her music, 31; relationship with brother Felix, 26, 28; songs, 25–26; *Sonntagsmusik*, 23–24, 27
Hensel, Sebastian, 19
Hensel, Wilhelm, 20, 24, 29, 30, 33
Heredia, Victor, 173
hermaphroditic: contralto voice, 257; Pasta as Tancredi, 291
Herz, Henriette, 24
Heuvelmans, Lucienne, 73, 79
Hildegard of Bingen, 8, 88, 92, 118; chants for St. Disibod, 93; chants for St. Ursula, 8, 93, 95, 98–100, 111; dating of works, 94; Marian chants, 96; musical collections, 93; "O Ecclesia," 100–102, 104–5, 110, 116n. 23; *Ordo virtutem*, 8, 95, 105, 110–15; religious writings 92–94; *Scivias*, 8, 93, 95–96, 98, 100, 110–11, 113, 115; sequences, 98, 101–2, 109
Hugo, Victor: *Lucrèce Borgia*, 298–99, 301
Hunter, Alberta, 225
"Huwwa Ṣaḥīḥ il-Hawá Ghallāb," 152–53

Iemoto, 308, 311, 323
Illapu, 168
India, 15, 42, 46; Delhi, 14; Lucknow, 14, 42; north, 42–43; northeast, 8, 16; south, 39. *See also* Jharkland
Indonesia, 278

instruments, musical: gender associations of, 14, 39, 56, 206n. 5, 257–58, 283n. 8
interiority, 187, 198
Inti-Illimani, 168
iqāʿāt, 159
Ireland, 210
Isambert, Maria, 63
Isella, César, 173
Islam: segregation of sexes in, 87, 148
Italy, 9, 254, 289–91; Bologna, 8, 88, 118–19, 122, 124–25, 127, 131–38; Brescia, 134; Cagli, 136; Carpi, 138; Cento, 138; Correggio, 138; Fabbriano, 134; Faenza, 138; Fano, 136; Ferrara, 15, 123, 127, 136; Florence, 127, 232; Genoa, 138; Imola, 138; Jesi, 136; Milan, 135, 297; Modena, 138; Pesaro, 136; Ravenna, 138; Rimini, 138; Rome, 29, 63, 119, 122, 125, 136, 232, 243, 258; Siena, 119; Venice, 14, 88, 258
Itzig family, 20
Itzig, Isaac Daniel, 22
Iversen, Gunilla, 110

Jackson, Mahalia, 180
Japan, 9, 14, 43, 89, 258–59, 308–12, 318–19
Jara, Victor, 170
Jharkhand, 36, 39–40, 42, 44, 47, 56
jhumar, 45; *janānī* (women's), 47, 50–53; *mardānā* (men's), 41, 47–49, 51–53
jitia, 50
Joan of Arc, 81
Johnson, K. D., 219
Johnson, Lonnie, 220
Johnson, "Signifyin" Mary, 220
Jones, Leroy. *See* Baraka, Amiri
Jones, Nancy, 4
Joplin, Scott, 219
Judaism: role of women in, 20, 39; segregation of sexes in, 87. *See also* Mendelssohn family, as Jews

kabuki, 14, 89, 258, 308–9, 311, 324
Kabyle Algerians, 278
kalākār, 44
Kalkbrenner, Frederic, 26
Kaluli, 278
kathakkathak, 42
Keiler, Allan, 144
kena (end-blown flute), 168
Kendrick, Robert, 118, 135
Kerouac, Jack, 177
Keudell, Robert von, 29, 31
Kimbrough, Lottie, 217
kimono, 259, 313–15, 317
King, Martin Luther, Jr., 180, 182
Kistomani, 16, 36–40, 43, 45, 49, 52–56
Kojiki, 309
kokoro, 308, 322
koto: as instrument suitable for women, 14
Krishna, 36–37, 39–40, 43–44, 46–47, 54–55

Kulthūm, Umm, 4, 9, 15, 88; dress and demeanor, 155–56; musical repertoire, 149–50, 152–55, 159; as national icon, 145; persona of, 147; singing style, 151
kyogen, 311

La Liberté, 166
Labille, Adelaide, 62
lament, 7, 193, 209, 243, 248; in African-American communities, 215; in ancient Greece, 144, 210; as expression of empowerment, 144, 211; in Lebanon, 210; in life-cycle events, 209; in Mapuche community of Andean Argentina, 278; in modern Greece, 210; in Papua, New Guinea, 210, 278; as political force, 145; in Scotland and Ireland, 210; in sixteenth-century France, 144; in South Africa, 210; as a topos, 7, 209–10; in West Africa, 210, 213–14
Lanier, Nicholas: *Hero and Leander*, 248
lartër (singing style), 269, 272–73, 276–77
Latin America, 9, 167, 169; and Catholicism, 169, 171, 178
Lazarus, Emma, 166
launda (female impersonator), 37, 39, 53, 58n. 23
Leadbelly. *See* Ledbetter, Huddie
Lebra, T., 318
Lebrun, Elisabeth Vigée, 62
Ledbetter, Huddie (pseud. Leadbelly), 177
Lee, Bertha, 217
Lenepveu, Charles, 73, 77–79
Levine, Lawrence, 215
Levy, Sara, 22, 24
life-cycle rituals, 4, 7, 40, 47, 50, 88, 94, 209–10, 213–15, 257–58. *See also* lament; wedding rituals
Lind, Jenny, 15
Lipking, Lawrence, 247, 254
List, Emilie, 24
Liszt, Franz, 31, 33, 206n. 5
Locatelli, Sebastiano, 120
Lomax family, 179
"Lord Randal," 181
los desaparecidos, 171
lurs (long trumpet): instrument played by women, 258
Lury, Celia, 193
lute: as suitable instrument for women, 14

McClary, Susan, 11n. 11, 255n. 19
McCoy, Kansas Joe, 220–21, 228
McCurdy, Ed, 181
Macedonia, 261–63
machismo, 171
McGuire Sisters, 89
Mack, Ida May, 217
MacKenzie, Catriona, 320
Madonna. *See* Ciccone, Madonna
Madres de Plaza de Mayo, 171
mahfil, 37, 38, 41

Maḥmūd, Muṣṭafá, 147
Mahto, Lakhicharan, 55
mai, 311
Makeba, Miriam, 144
Mancini, Francesco, 244
māndar (drum), 48
Manns, Patricio, 170
Mapuche, 278
maqāmāt, 150, 159
March on Washington, 180
Marchesini, Chiara, 136
marianismo, 171
Marianne. *See* La Liberté
Marshall, Jeanne, 118
Martin, Gregory, 119
masculine attributes and behavior, 265, 314
Mass, 96–97, 112–13, 120
Massenet, Jules, 67–68, 74, 78
mater dolorosa, 180
matsuri, 314
Matus, Manuel Oscar, 172
Mayr, Simon: *La rosa bianca e la rosa rossa*, 292
Mazellier, Jules, 77–78
Medico, Barbara Gioconda dal, 132
Melville, Sir James, 13
Memphis Minnie. *See* Douglas, Lizzie
Men: as blues singers, 214, 216, 218, 223; in choruses, 89, 288, 303; as instrumentalists, 39, 206n. 5, 258; as public performers, 39; as singers, 262, 271–73, 277, 314; in song/dance performance, 36, 47–49, 51, 53, 257. *See also* voice, male
Mendelssohn family, 19; as Jews, 20, 22–23, 25
Mendelssohn, Felix, 19, 26, 31; *St. Paul*, 26; *Walpurgisnacht*, 32
Mendelssohn, Henriette, 20
Mendelssohn, Lea Salomon, 22–23, 31
Mendelssohn, Moses, 19–20, 25
Merson, Luc Olivier, 61
mestizo, 168, 170–71, 176
Metastasio, Pietro, 243
Middleton, Richard, 159–60
milonga, 174
minzoku geino, 311
Mitchell, Joni, 189; "Blue," 193
Monteverdi, Claudio: "Lamento d'Arianna," 211, 242–43, 247; operas, 242, 247
Montford, Kimberlyn, 118–19
Moore, Undine Smith, 213, 215
Morganfield, McKinley (pseud. Muddy Waters), 220
Morlacchi, Francesco, 292
Morton, Jelly Roll, 227
Moscheles, Ignaz, 26
Mozart, Wolfgang Amadeus: *Le Nozze di Figaro*, 259
Muddy Waters. *See* Morganfield, McKinley
musica segreta, 123

musichetto, 297–98, 301
musico, 9, 259, 287–88, 292, 294, 296–98, 304

nacnī, 15, 37–38, 44, 46, 54, 59; interconnection between men and women, 40, 47, 52; life of, 42–43; as outcaste, 40–41, 56; and power, 8, 15–16, 36; as "public woman," 39; shifts to professional stage singer, 53; singing style of, 52
naddāba, 210
nagāṛā (drum), 48
Nagpuri: musico-linguistic region, 36, 47–49; dance style, 52
Nājī, Ibrāhīm, 154
al-Najmī, Kamāl, 148
Narogin, Mudrooroo, 161
Nascimento, Milton, 173
Nati, Catarina, 134
Nayak, Mukund, 40, 56
Negri, Anna, 125
New Guinea: Papua, 210, 278; West Irian, 210
Newport Folk Festival, 178
Nicolini, Giuseppe, 292
nihon buyo, 9, 14, 89, 259, 308–9, 311–12, 321, 323. *See also* dance, traditional Japanese
Nihon Shoki, 309
Nishikata Setsuko, 310
Nketia, J. H., 215
Nobili, Maria Geltrude, 134
noh, 89, 311
Notker, 102
nueva canción, 175–76; in Argentina, 171–73; in Chile, 169–70; in Cuba, 171; as expression of resistance, 171; history of, 169
nueva trova, 171
Numhauser, Julio, 173

Odah, Muḥammad, 150
Odetta, 168, 177, 185n. 36
odori, 311
Odum, Howard, 215
Offen, Karen, 25
Okuni, 309
Oldenburg, Veena, 42
Oliver, Joe "King," 227
onnagata, 89, 258
orchestras, ladies', 89
Orlandi, Maria Gesualda, 135
orphanages, 88, 135
Orpheus, 167, 247–48, 255n. 19, 259
Ottoman Empire, 14, 148
Our Lady of Guadalupe, 178
Ovid, 248; *Heroides,* 240

Pachamama, 167
Pacini, Giovanni, 292; *Il corsaro,* 287
Páez, Fito, 173
Palacios, Margarita, 172
Paleotti, Gabriele, 119–20, 125, 127, 131

Palisca, Claude V., 118
Pancpargania: dance style, 52, 55; musico-linguistic region, 45, 47
panpipes (zamponas, sikus, rondeador), 168
pardah, 42
Paris Conservatoire, 64–68, 70–71, 73–74, 77; and women, 60, 62–63, 79
Parra, Violeta, 169, 173–74; "La carta," 170; "Gracias a la vida," 173, 175–76; "Me gustan los estudiantes," 170; "Yo canto la diferencia," 170
Pasta, Giuditta, 288–89, 292–93, 304; as Tancredi, 289–91
Patton, Charley, 218, 220
Pavesi, Stefano: *La donna bianca,* 297
People's Songs Inc, 177
Pereira-Arnstein, Henrietta, 23
performance: audience response to, 147–49; critics' reviews of, 182, 191, 289–91, 293–94, 295–96, 297; and feminist musicology, 6; multiple-role, 9, 89, 258–59, 313; segregated by gender, 13, 39–40, 47; talking about, 156. *See also* women performers and musicians
performance theory, 6, 258
Peru, 168
Peter, Paul, and Mary, 180
Phair, Liz, 190
pianists, female: 15, 16, 18, 23, 24–25, 29, 31–32, 34n. 27, 67–68, 70, 77, 83n. 15, 177, 190
piano: as instrument suitable for women, 14, 26, 62
Pindar, 209
Pisaroni, Benedetta Rosmunda, 288–89, 292–93, 304
Pleyel, Marie Moke, 18, 25, 34
popular music: and the female voice, 188
Pougin, Arthur, 74
Predieri, Giacomo, 137
Prespa Albanians, 9, 259, 261–63
Press, Joy, 193
Pring-Mill, Robert, 169, 176
Prix de Rome, 8, 16, 29, 60, 70; description of competition, 65; description of prizes, 82; prestige of, 63
prostitutes, 39–40, 43, 125, 180, 221, 309
protest song, 9, 176–77; and civil rights and anti-war movements, 167; use of term in Latin America, 169
public vs. private spheres, 4, 39–40, 87–88, 122, 192; ambiguities of, 7–8; as a binary construct, 13–16, 318; and blues women singers, 7, 223, 229; in fin-de-siècle Paris 61–63, 67–68; in Italian opera, 287–88; in Japanese performing arts, 308, 310; and lamenting, 209–10
pueblo, 167–68, 174, 182
Purcell, Henry: *Dido and Aeneas,* 211, 248; *The Fairy Queen,* 248; *King Arthur,* 248

al-Qabbānī, Nizār, 162

qaṣīda, 149–51, 153–54
qiyān, 14
Quechua, 171, 174
quena. *See* kena
Qur'ān: recitation of, 147, 151, 159

race: injustices concerning, 143–44, 146, 180, 183, 222–23, 226; issues of, 6, 12n. 13, 211, 213
Radha, 36–37, 39, 41, 44, 46, 55
Rainey, Gertrude ("Ma"), 216, 224–25
Rainey, William ("Pa"), 224
rape, 9, 57, 146, 187–88, 193–95, 198, 234, 248, 250
ras, 36–39, 44, 46–47, 52–53
rasikā, 36–37, 43–46, 54
Ravel, Maurice, 73
Reardon, Colleen, 118, 119
Republican motherhood, 62–63
Reynolds, Malvina, 181
Reynolds, Simon, 193
Richardis of Stade, 94, 110, 115n. 11
Ritchie, Jean, 168, 177
Riviera, Dorothea, 137
Robeson, Paul, 185n. 36
Rodríguez, Silvio, 173
Rom, 284; bands, 263; musicians, 258
Romano, Felice, 298
Ros, Antonio Tarrago, 173
Rosand, Ellen, 243
Rosenstiel, Léonie, 75, 78
Rossini, Gioachino, 287, 292–93, 297; *La donna del lago*, 287–88, 294; *Semiramide*, 288, 292–94; *Tancredi*, 259, 287–91, 294
Roujon, Henri, 63–64
Rousseau, Jean-Jacques, 87
Rupertsberg, 93, 110

sa-yalab, 210
Sainte-Marie, Buffy, 168, 177, 185n. 36
Saint-Saëns, Camille, 68, 75–76
Salomon, Bella, 22
salons, 8, 14, 23–24, 33n. 18, 67–68
"Salū Qalbī," 149, 151, 153
Santa Cristina della Fondazza convent, Bologna, 118; architecture of, 120–22; dedication of music publication to, 124; dowry reductions at, 133; hidden choir rooms at, 121, 125; and motet by Lucrezia Orsina Vizzana, 125–31; music education at, 137, 141n. 38; organ rooms at, 120; outside musicians at, 137
Scarlatti, Alessandro, 244
Scary, Elaine, 198
Schlegel, Dorothea Veit, 20, 34
Schlegel, Friedrich, 21
Schleiermacher, Friedrich, 22
Schumann, Clara Wieck, 15, 18, 24, 27, 31; Piano Trio, Op. 17, 24
Schumann, Robert, 15, 31; *Das Paradies und die Peri*, 24
Scott, Sir Walter, 288

Scotton, Carol Myers, 319
Scudo, Paul, 292
Seeger, Pete, 177, 181
Senelick, Laurence, 258
sex: as biological category, 257; segregation by, 87, 262–63
sexual behavior, 15, 39–40, 42, 46, 96, 101, 190
sexual imagery, 101, 109, 112
sexuality, female, 39–40, 46, 52, 167, 187, 189, 191–94, 205, 224
shakuhachi (end-blown flute): instrument played by men, 14
shamisen (three-stringed lute), 313, 316; as instrument suitable for women, 14
Sharp, Cecil, 179
Shaw, George Bernard, 285, 286
Shawqī, Aḥmad, 149–51
Sheingorn, Pamela, 110
Shirelles, 90
shtruar (singing style), 269, 271, 273, 275, 277, 283
Shūsha, Muḥammad, 151
Singakademie, Berlin, 19, 23
Singh, Jaimangal, 38, 55
singing style: of American folk singers, 168; of Arabic song, 150, 151; of Baroque operatic laments, 211; of Bolognese nuns, 125, 127; in Brush Dance ceremony, 257; of female musicos in Italian opera, 294, 297; in Handel cantatas, 233; of Prespa Albanians, 9, 259, 262, 273, 275, 280; of women blues singers, 216, 218–19, 224–25, 228. *See also* lartër; shtruar
Smith, Bessie, 225
Smith, Clara: "Strugglin' Woman's Blues," 225
Smith, Mamie, 216
Soavi, Maria Angela, 134
Solomon, Maynard, 185n. 36
Solomon, Seymour, 185n. 36
Somerville, Margaret, 161
Sondheim, Stephen, 177
Song of Songs, 8, 95–98, 100–102, 110–11
Sosa, Mercedes, 4, 9, 145, 168, 175; called "La Negra," 173; life of, 172–73; as maternal figure, 167, 171, 182; physical appearance, 167; song repertory, 173
South Africa, 144, 210
Spain, 168, 173
Spivey, Victoria: "Dirty T.B. Blues," 227
Statue of Liberty, 166; as maternal icon, 183
Stendahl, 291, 293
Stoljar, Natalie, 320
strategic expression, 193
Strauss, Richard: *Der Rosenkavalier*, 259
Strozzi, Barbara, 15
al-Sunbāṭī, Riyāḍ, 150, 153–54
Supremes, 90
Sweden, 258

Tachibana dance family, 323
Tachibana Hoshu, 313

Tachibana Yoshie, 308–9, 321, 324
Tasso, Torquato: *Gerusalemme liberata*, 210
tawā'ifs, 14–15, 42–43, 52
Tejada Gómez, Armando, 173
Thalberg, Sigismund, 31
theater of voices, 285
Thomas, Elvie, 218
Tienamen Square, 182
Tinelli, Don Ercole, 125
TOBA, 223, 230
Tosi, Adelaide, 292
Toutain, Juliette, 60, 63–65, 68, 77, 81
trouser roles, 9, 233, 259, 298, 300. *See also* cross-dressed roles
Tucker, Bessie, 217, 219–20; "Penitentiary Blues," 219
al-Tūnisī, Bayram, 152
Tunisia, 88
Turino, Thomas, 161

United States, 9, 14, 89–90, 161, 166, 168, 263; Boston, 178; California, 178, 257; Chicago, 220, 222, 227; Cincinnati, 222; civil rights and anti-war movements, 146, 167, 176–77, 180–81; Cleveland, 223; Dallas, 223; Galveston, 223; and the Great Migration, 222; Jacksonville, 223; Kansas City, 223; Kentucky, 177, 216; Memphis, 221, 223, 226–27; Mississippi Delta, 215–18; New York City, 144, 166, 177, 222, 226; Pittsburgh, 222; protest music, 169; racial segregation, 143; and the slave trade, 214; Washington, D.C., 144, 180
Ursula, Saint, 8, 93, 95, 98–102, 104–5, 109
Uruguay, 174

Van, Gilles de, 285
Vanguard Records, 177, 185n. 36
Vargas, Elizabeth, 199
Varnhagen von Ense, Rahel Levin, 24, 26
Vechten, Carl Van, 225
Velluti, Giambattista, 286
Venturoli, Angela, 133
Verdi, Giuseppe: *Aida*, 286; *Don Carlos*, 286; *Ernani*, 286–87; *Il corsaro*, 287; *Un ballo in maschera*, 304
Vernizzi, Ottavio, 137
Viardot, Pauline, 259
video performance, 5, 7, 9, 37–38, 54, 164n. 12, 185n. 44, 187, 190, 192, 200, 202–4
Viglietti, Daniel, 169
Vigri, Saint Catherine, 132–33
Virgin of Lujan, 171
Virgin Mary, 95–96, 98; in Latin America, 171, 178
virginals: as feminine instrument, 14
Vitali, Carlo, 135
Vivaldi, Antonio, 88
Vizzana, Lucrezia Orsina, 118, 125, 127, 133; *Com-*

ponimenti musicali de motetti a una e più voci, 125
vocal ranges, 52, 105, 168, 190, 202, 233
voice: angelic, 87–88, 104, 122, 125; authorial, 6, 12n. 14, 144, 190, 286; and body, 6, 9, 188–89, 194–95, 203; cloistered, 4, 7–8, 87, 90, 119, 123; defined, 4; disembodied, 88, 119, 122, 203, 224; embodied, 145, 188–89; empowered, 4, 7, 9, 143–46, 167, 171, 188, 213, 286; female, 4, 8–9, 51, 87–88, 92–93, 105, 122, 125, 188–89, 233, 286, 291, 303; in feminist theory, 4, 4l; and interiority, 146, 187–88, 198–200, 202; literary, feminine, 41, 94, 144–45, 180, 182, 233–35, 240–42, 247–48, 254; male, 47, 51, 93, 105, 109, 211, 216, 220, 233–34, 236, 246, 271, 286–87; as political expression, 4, 7, 143–46, 151, 155, 167–69, 177, 181–82, 210, 248, 250
Voice of Egypt, 145
voice of the people, 143, 148, 153, 154, 161, 167; concept of, 9
voice types: baritone, 285–86; bass, 233; castrato, 233, 259, 286; contralto, 168, 177, 224, 259, 286, 287, 292; in Italian Baroque opera, 233, 286; soprano, 168, 233, 259, 285–86, 292; tenor, 285–86, 287
Voltaire: *Tancrède*, 287, 290, 291
Vuillermoz, Emile, 60, 81

Walsh, María Elena, 173
Waters, Ethel, 225
Watt, James, 220
"We Shall Overcome," 180
Weavers, 177; 185n. 36
wedding rituals, 4, 87–88, 147, 209, 258; as metaphor for union with Christ, 95–98, 100, 102, 105, 110–11, 252; and *nacnīs*, 40, 46–47, Prespa Albanian, 259, 261, 263, 265, 266–68, 275–77, 280–81
Weill, Kurt, 177
Widor, Charles-Marie, 65, 70, 73, 74, 77, 78
Wilder, Billy: *Some Like It Hot*, 89
Wiley, Geeshie, 217, 218
Williams, Clarence, 217
Williams, J. Mayo, 217
Williams, Raymond, 159, 161, 162
women as composers, 8, 14–16, 18, 20, 24–25, 27, 61, 92, 95, 118, 124–25, 133, 170, 213; persona of, 71, 78, 82; and the *Prix de Rome*, 63–64, 71–72, 75–76, 79–81. *See also* Amos, Tori; Douglas, Lizzie; Hensel, Fanny Mendelssohn; Hildegard of Bingen; Vizzana, Lucrezia Orsina
women as conductors, 24, 65, 81, 83n. 24
women in music: methodologies on the study of, 5; research on, 3, 5
women musicians and performers, 5, 24, 37, 87–88; costumes of, 15, 155, 190, 313; education of, 14, 19, 89, 137, 155, 310, 321–22; as mediators, 7, 176, 209; persona of, 15, 143, 155–56, 162, 167, 189–90, 224, 261, 275, 277, 280, 296; as a politi-

women musicians and performers *(cont.)*
cal force, 4, 9, 143–46, 151, 167, 173, 181; public attitudes toward, 125, 135; restrictions on, 14, 18, 67, 87–89, 119, 131, 137–38, 308, 323

women, representation of: as abandoned, 8, 211, 232, 248; as dangerous to men, 87, 189, 235, 248–50, 286; as insane, 211, 242, 285; as maternal figure, 9, 38–39, 167; as political metaphor for the oppressed, 250; as victim, 285; as virginal figure, 9, 167

women as singers, 4, 9, 14–15, 89–90, 143–46; in Arab society, 155; blues, 7, 217–18, 224–25; of folk music, 168, 177, 193, 210; in Italian convents, 122, 125, 127, 131; in northeast India, 50–51, 55–56; in opera, 258–59, 288–89, 292–93, 297; Prespa Albanian, 269–71, 275–76. *See also* Amos, Tori; Baez, Joan; Brambilla, Marietta; Kulthūm, Umm; Pasta, Giuditta; Pisaroni, Benedetta Rosmunda; Sosa, Mercedes

Woolard, Kathryn, 319

Woolf, Virginia, 5

Yupanqui, Atahualpa, 173; "Los hermanos," 173–74, 176

Zavatieri, Angela Mariana, 135

Zelter, Carl Friedrich, 19

Zeno, Apostolo, 243

Zingarelli, Niccolò: *Giulietta e Romeo*, 289, 297

zurna (shawm): as male instrument, 258